Cultural Heritage and Contemporary Change
Series IV, Western Philosophical Studies, Volume 8
Series VIII, Christian Philosophical Studies, Volume 8
General Editor
George F. McLean

Towards a Kenotic Vision of Authority in the Catholic Church

Western Philosophical Studies, VIII
Christian Philosophical Studies, VIII

Edited by
Anthony J. Carroll
Marthe Kerkwijk
Michael Kirwan
James Sweeney

The Council for Research in Values and Philosophy

Copyright © 2015 by
The Council for Research in Values and Philosophy

Box 261
Cardinal Station
Washington, D.C. 20064

All rights reserved

Printed in the United States of America

Library of Congress Cataloging-in-Publication

Towards a kenotic vision of authority in the Catholic Church / edited by Anthony J. Carroll, Marthe Kerkwijk, Michael Kirwan, James Sweeney. -- first edition.

pages cm. -- (Cultural heritage and contemporary change. Christian philosophical studies; Volume VIII)

Includes bibliographical references and index.

1. Authority--Religious aspects--Catholic Church. I. Carroll, Anthony J., 1965- editor of compilation.

BX1753.T6725 2014   2014012706
262'.'088282--dc23   CIP

ISBN 978-1-56518-293-6 (pbk.)

TABLE OF CONTENTS

Introduction: The Exercise of Magisterial Authority   1
in the Roman Catholic Church
    Anthony J. Carroll

Part I: Authority in Biblical Sources

Chapter I: "It Shall Not Be so among You": Authority and   15
Service in the Synoptic Gospels
    Sean Michael Ryan
Chapter II: Authority without Sovereignty: Towards   41
a Reassessment of Divine Power
    Roger Mitchell

Part II: Sociological and Philosophical Perspectives

Chapter III: The Magisterium: Conjunctions and Disjunctions   55
in Modernity: A Historical-Sociological Analysis
    Staf Hellemans
Chapter IV: Post-metaphysical Authority   73
    Anthony J. Carroll
Chapter V: Disagreement and Authority: Comparing Ecclesial   91
and Scientific Practices
    Louis Caruana, SJ

Part III: Theological perspectives

Chapter VI: Authority in the Church: Authentic and Effective?   105
    James Sweeney, CP
Chapter VII: Authority and Magisterium: A Lesson from   119
the Seventh Century
    Richard Price
Chapter VIII: Be Subject to Every Human Creature for God's Sake: 131
St Francis of Assisi and the Experience of Authority
    Paul Rout, OFM
Chapter IX: Imagining Authority in a Kenotic Church: 147
Magisterium in the Contemporary Church
    Gemma Simmonds, CJ
Chapter X: The "Ugly Broad Ditch": Authority in a Kenotic Church   165
    Michael Kirwan, SJ
Chapter XI: Responsible, Critical Assent   183
    Karen Kilby

Appendix I: Obedience and the Church's Teaching Authority: 195
The Burden of the Past
   Francis Oakley
Appendix II: Subsidiarity: Does It Apply also to the Life of 213
the Church?
   Daniel Deckers

Bibliography 247
Index 265

INTRODUCTION

THE EXERCISE OF MAGISTERIAL AUTHORITY IN THE ROMAN CATHOLIC CHURCH

ANTHONY J. CARROLL

AUTHORITY AS A BLESSING

Few would doubt that our age is one of conflicting interpretations. Whether over questions of the human person, the purpose of society, or the natural environment radically different interpretations vie for dominance in a way that seems to characterise this period of history. In such a pluralistic age the appropriate understanding of the nature and extent of authority takes on a particularly important role. Understood as neither authoritarianism nor merely the aggregate of individual preferences an authority can provide guidance as to the better option, the choice which leads to flourishing rather than to diminishment.

Perhaps somewhat paradoxically, the exercise of authority understood in this sense is oriented towards the freedom of the other; enabling the freedom of the other to choose what is really in their interests and not simply opting for a short-term solution which appears to be. Facilitating this choice is the role of authority, which helps to provide confidence and reassurance that we are not simply alone in making our choices. There is a community of wisdom that is expressed in the exercise of magisterial authority and which accompanies us on the way of freedom. It is the exercise of this form of magisterial authority which is truly a blessing for the church. As such, it enables the resources of tradition and experience to shed light on contemporary challenges and also provides support and encouragement as we face a myriad of decisions which can bewilder even the most decisive amongst us.

The specific area of competence within which the magisterial authority of the church operates is that of faith and morals. In ensuring fidelity to the legitimate tradition of the church, the Magisterium guards what is sometimes called the "deposit of the faith". That is, the core teachings which constitute the heart of belief in the gospel and in the loving God revealed in Jesus Christ. Gradually built up over centuries, the tradition of the church regulates the faith by defining orthodox belief. It removes the burden of having to work out what previous generations have already struggled to do. The heritage of the doctrinal beliefs developed during the councils of the church defines the parameters of legitimate belief. This does not foreclose new interpretations of doctrine but rather is meant to regulate it within parameters of legitimate possibility. These parameters are the results of former debate and discussion concerning the fundamental beliefs of the Christian community. To ignore them would be both irresponsible and disrespectful of a tradition which has developed over two thousand years of history. Understood in this way tradition is neither a straitjacket constraining individual freedom nor a definitive interpretation of God's revelation but rather an ongoing reception of the self-communication of God in Jesus Christ to humanity. Each age must receive these events anew in the light of the Holy Spirit and with attention to the signs of the times. Since, whilst God has been revealed in Jesus Christ the working out of the historical implications of this Revelation will be ongoing until the end of time (John 16: 13).

The role of the Magisterium is to regulate interpretations of the deposit of faith in such a way that they are both faithful to the traditional teachings of the church and expressed in a manner which speaks to our times. The dynamic nature of the reception of Revelation is due to the continual workings of the Holy Spirit in the hearts of all women and men of goodwill growing like a mustard seed in the often hidden soil of history (Matthew 13: 31-32; Mark 4: 30-32; Luke 13: 18-19). The Kingdom of God which grows in this way is intermingled with elements which diminish humanity and whilst inseparable from these elements in time, nevertheless, vigilance is required to guard against correctable corruption (Matthew 13: 24-43). The guarding of the integrity of the tradition by the Magisterium cannot thus be otherwise than also dynamic lest the unfolding of the Kingdom of God be ignored in favour of closing off one's attention to the voice of the Holy Spirit speaking today. Conservation and innovation are in this way in a continual force field of dynamic relations as the deposit of faith is legitimately regulated by the Magisterium of the church. Avoiding both an idolatrous fixing of the faith in an idealised past and seduction by the current passing fashions of the day the continual reform of the church accompanies her pilgrim journey in history. The gradual historical purification of ideological elements in the church is a consequence of recognising faults and failings which have compromised fidelity to the gospel. Such a humble attitude of the Magisterium, expressed in several recent papal pronouncements and most especially in *Evangelii Gaudium*, is characteristic of a true encounter with the Risen Lord and is an evangelical sign of God's presence in the church (Luke 18: 10-14). It demonstrates that the origin of the authority of the Magisterium is to be found not in itself but in the One from whom it is sent (Matthew 28: 19).

Such conviction arises out of being confirmed in the mission of the Lord which liberates the church from following its own agendas or of justifying itself. In a characteristically evangelical attitude the Magisterium, when it is true to itself, is not interested in itself, it is self-forgetful because its heart lies outside of itself in the One who has sent it. Such a blessing of generosity and charity is made possible only by a gift which no manner of effort can generate. It confers the blessing of humility and gratitude on the one who receives it as they realise the liberation from self which this inaugurates. As a consequence, the charismatic attraction of the Magisterium transcends the celebrity culture of film stars and politicians who have achieved their fame and status by their own efforts and the efforts of others. The evangelical witness of the Magisterium lies precisely in the realisation that it has been chosen, although unworthy, to serve in this way. As such a natural humility is associated with it when it is exercised authoritatively. So, beyond being an institution within the church which guards the deposit of the faith the Magisterium is also an evangelical sign of the presence of the Kingdom of God.

The love of the faithful for the hierarchy originates in the recognition of the vocation of the Magisterium to lead and to guide as much by example as by formal teaching (Philippians 2: 6). Such a kenotic style of leadership should characterise the church as it patterns the mind of the Lord in the institution and makes visible the face of the Lord in the Magisterium. Immediately recognisable as reflecting the presence of the Lord, the enthusiastic greeting of leaders of the church, such as the pope, echoes that of the encounter of Peter with the Risen Lord on the Sea of Tiberias (John 21: 1-19). In this way, the Magisterium brings people to the Risen Lord by making Him visible in the kenotic witness of His living presence animating the church. This is why images of the pope kissing babies, or visiting prisoners, even forgiving those who have tried to kill him, are such a powerful sign of the gospel. They manifest the infinite love of God of which each human heart has its own experience, however wounded and darkened by life's struggles. In Christ, love has overcome even death and it is this joy which is echoed in simple but profound gestures of the Magisterium. The media interest in Pope Francis and images of his riding on the subway in Buenos Aires as Cardinal Bergoglio provoke this identification with the humble Christ who emptied himself in Jesus. Simple, ordinary, even banal images such as these carry significance far beyond their immediate reality. They point towards the self-emptying God in whom paradoxically divine transcendence and omnipotence are manifested in human immanence and powerlessness (2 Corinthians 12: 7-10).

Such authenticity conveys divine authority rather than the pseudo-authority of the scribes and doctors of the law who merely quoted from the scriptures and tradition rather than lived by them (Matthew 7: 29). The teaching authority of the Magisterium is truly a blessing for the church when it follows this divine pattern exemplified in Jesus as he taught the nature of true discipleship to the crowds (Matthew 7: 21-27). Moreover, only through such virtuous living can one have any real sense of the Kingdom of God (Matthew 5: 20). When theory and practice are so disunited that the truth spoken of is not lived then intellectual knowledge about God is substituted for knowledge of God. The union of both in the Magisterium makes statements of the church both credible and authoritative and of interest to people far beyond the official church. Understandably, the degree to which this authenticity is manifest by the Magisterium determines, for many people, the level of impact that statements from the church have and the seriousness with which the teachings of the church are taken. No matter how eloquent someone is and no matter how important a person is in an institution if there is a suspicion of hypocrisy severe damage can be done to the credibility of the message being communicated. In fact, amongst what one might call the credibility conditions for a message to be successfully heard in an 'age of authenticity' such as ours, where former conventions of deference and automatic acceptance of authority no longer hold, authenticity holds a privileged place as a necessary condition of communicative competence.

The current leadership of the Roman Catholic Church by Pope Francis is moving encouragingly in the direction of humility, simplicity and authenticity. Whilst some have found little substantive change in his communications clearly the tone is different. And matters of tone are significant. They announce by their style of delivery a certain attitude of openness and dialogue which the Second Vatican Council inaugurated. By all accounts there is much to do to spread this humble tone into the structures of the Vatican. But Pope Francis has made significant first steps in this renewal by his gestures and by his addresses. The rejection of the papal red cape trimmed with ermine during his papal inauguration spoke of the end to a 'sacral kingship' model of the papacy that Francis Oakley's paper has described. His remarks, such as those made on the return journey from Brazil to Rome, in which he emphasised the importance of not judging gay people and for the need for a more simple style of church life indicate that he desires to carry forward a reform agenda for the church. The translation of these gestures and sayings into policy and structure will clearly take time. Yet, there is a widespread yearning in the church for reform so that the true blessing which the Magisterium represents may really foster the positive development of the church and society at large. This dynamic moment in the church's history may well be a time of special grace as the Holy Spirit renews the structures of the church.

The selection of the first ever pontiff from Latin America is in itself a sign that in order for the church to be truly catholic the whole planet needs to be represented. The former European dominance of the church is with all likelihood a thing of the past and the future will be increasingly characterised by greater representation and participation in the magisterial structures of the church by members of the church from the southern hemisphere. Viewed in this way, the church should be seen more as an unfinished project rather than an old institution creaking at the seams. It may well be that we are on the dawn of a truly catholic church as the universality which was initially envisioned begins to be translated into reality in the third millennium. The shift from a predominantly European Magisterium to a global one will take the church into new waters as the different experiences of the world begin to be translated into the governance of the church. The hope which this inspires is grounded in a faith that knows that however great the challenges which lie ahead we are not alone in striving for a church which mirrors ever more closely the Kingdom of God which it preaches.

THE NEED FOR REFORM OF THE MAGISTERIUM

Whilst it is clear that properly understood the Magisterium of the church is a real blessing, as Pope Francis clearly acknowledges, it would be dishonest to see this as the current state of affairs. *Evangelii Gaudium* (EG) courageously speaks of this in terms of the need for reforming the church in line with mission. It is only through an internal reform of the structures of the church, and even of the papacy itself (EG 32), that the church can fulfil its mission of *going forth* in the joyful service of the gospel.

Since the sexual abuse crisis became known it is evident that there is a systematic dysfunction in the operations of the church. Concerned more with the preservation of its own image and power, the Magisterium has behaved in a way which negates its purpose. The characteristics of this failure are by now well-known. Less clear, however, are the reasons for just how it was that the church could have slipped so deeply into disrepair. Clearly a culture of clericalism has dogged the church for a long while. The use of clerical power in this context has been part and parcel of a fundamental asymmetry between the magisterial structures of the church and the model of servant leadership about which the gospels speak (Matthew 20: 26; 23:11; Luke 22: 26). The 'sacral-kingship' model of the papacy to which Francis Oakley refers has coloured the way in which priesthood in the Roman Catholic Church has been perceived for generations. This focus on the importance of the ordained priesthood has often been counterbalanced by the stress on the vocation of the laity. But, whilst the rhetoric has been present since the Second Vatican Council the translation of this into representative structures in the church has been absent. Governance within the church is still carried out by clergy and appeals to the importance of lay people and the value of women in the church seem increasingly hollow in this context. This attitude of the church looks increasingly out of step in the modern democratic world which values equality between the sexes and the inclusion of female voices at all levels of governance. This is not to presume that all is well in secular society. Systematic abuse of power and a lack of incorporation of women in civil institutions are by no means simply a problem of former times but are alive and well in an often patriarchal society. Nevertheless, the declaration by Pope John Paul II that discussion on women's ordination is closed has left many with a sense that magisterial authority has slipped into 'magisterial authoritarianism' on this issue. There is clearly divided opinion on this matter and the decision to foreclose debate has short circuited the necessary consultation of the *sensus fidelium* that is required for these decisions to carry legitimacy.

Magisterial behaviour, such as in the debate over the ordination of women, reveals a wider issue concerning magisterial authority. It raises the issue of how the Magisterium comes to its declarations of what is and what is not consonant with the deposit of the faith. Given that certain issues have really not arisen before this is not simply a matter of checking whether examples of this have occurred in the past. New situations are arising for the church and whilst *Ressourcement* and *Aggiornamento* theologies are important tools to renew the church they may well be insufficient as theological frameworks of church renewal today. The problem of the extent of the deposit of the faith is clearly at issue here. Is it part of the deposit of the faith that only men can be priests and that the structure of the church must remain a certain way? Or rather, is the deposit of the faith concerned with doctrines such as the Incarnation, the Trinity, and the Resurrection? Raising matters of church governance, though of importance, to the status of axiomatic beliefs seems to force issues such as debates over the ordination of women in a direction of unnecessary confrontation. Once a pope, in this case John Paul II, has made a declaration on this it is very difficult for a successor to overturn it. As recent statements by Pope Francis have indicated it was Pope John Paul II who has closed the door on the issue of the ordination of women and attempting to open it again would be tantamount to heresy.

As a case study in the exercise of magisterial authority the ordination of women issue is instructive. It reveals a number of matters that go to the heart of the difficulties with the contemporary exercise of magisterial authority. This is, of course, not to pronounce on the substance of the issue which may well indicate that there could be legitimate differences that individuals and indeed whole cultures will wish to raise. Rather, it highlights a number of issues which, when not sufficiently taken into account, seem to significantly diminish the credibility of the exercise of magisterial authority.

First, it shows an understanding of the papacy as somehow in a position to decide this without sufficient general consultation. The view that the pope has a "hotline to God" is, though clearly a caricature, nevertheless functionally operative in the decision to "end discussion" on the matter. It represents a legacy of absolutism that has roots in the later medieval era of the eleventh century and has continued into the modern church. The theological problem with this is that it runs in the face of the new form of authority spoken of in the New Testament and which is meant to mirror the way Christ exercises authority. This humble and servant model of authority breaks with the tradition of the Greco-Roman world within which Christianity as a religion was born. It scandalised the "authorities" of the time and represented a revolution in thinking about structures of power and authority. The turn towards an absolutist model of authority in the church is a move away from this New Testament model and towards the Greco-Roman traditions which preceded it. It mirrors the absolutist conception of God that became popular during the rise of Nominalism at the origins of Western modernity. Fundamentally, the problem with this understanding of authority is that it portrays an authoritarian image of God that is patterned in the structures of the Magisterium as authoritarianism.

Second, the position of the Magisterium with respect to the ordination of women results from the claim that the church does not have the authority to change this as God has made His will clear on the matter. As to why God only wants men to be priests this is less clear. None of the arguments presented stand the test of open critical scrutiny and one is left with the impression that the Magisterium has utilised a version of the "God of the gaps" argument in declaring its position as against women priests. The fundamental problem with this approach is that the Catholic Church claims to hold a mutual correlation between faith and reason, and yet on such matters leaps of faith or submissive obedience seem to be required. As a consequence, the result is a contradiction between on the one hand the claim that faith and reason are correlated and on the other hand saying, in a nominalistic way which finds echoes in the notion of the arbitrary will of God clearly rejected by Pope Benedict XVI in the published version of his Regensburg speech, that this is God's will and we simple have to obey it. This is not to deny that there are mysteries of the faith such as the suffering of the innocent and so on which defy clear and full rational explanation. But to align the ban on the ordination of women with such mysteries of the faith is at best exaggerated and at worst ideological. It undermines a traditional Catholic understanding of the correlation of faith and reason and veers towards a more Protestant *fides aut ratio* (faith or reason) conception.

Third, it indicates a culture of unhealthy silence by which much of the purported unanimity of the Catholic Church is actually held in place. Speaking openly and honestly becomes a drama in such a situation because it is neither allowed nor encouraged. A cognitive dissonance develops in those caught in this dilemma as silence becomes heroically sublimated into obedience of superiors and mortification of the will. But this creates an unhealthy culture in the church of people being afraid to speak out because it will threaten their own and perhaps other people's positions. Disagreement in this context is understood as disobedience and perhaps even heresy with possible personal and professional consequences. Such policing of opinion in the Catholic Church is more akin to the techniques of political regimes rather than a gospel centred community oriented towards freedom. This encourages an immature culture on both sides of this divide. On the side of the individuals who disagree with the church's teaching such silence can undermine all trust and confidence in the institution and encourage a culture of cynicism and irony which destroys the trust required for healthy relations between the hierarchy and priests and people. Much like a politician defending a party line in which they do not believe, the results can be the undermining of one's own integrity. On the side of the hierarchy a focus on such issues can become obsessive and result in a frosting out of those who are seen to be dissenters, a making sure that such people do not take on positions of responsibility. In such a context neuralgic issues, such as the position taken on the ordination of women, become defining features of orthodoxy. Rather than the pastoral qualities and leadership potential of an individual it is their orthodoxy which is seen as central to who is chosen for positions of authority and who is not. Moreover, such focus on orthodoxy in the hierarchy can result in bullying behaviour as people known to hold opposing views become marginalised. The power differential between the hierarchy and the priests and people is abused in this situation and rather than encouraging open and frank discussion it closes it down.

Perhaps even more insidious in this culture of silence is the lack of courage which it fosters. It schools people in not speaking out against injustice and of rather fitting in and enjoying the comfort of institutional protection. Whilst the church may rightly foster this courage when it comes to speaking out against injustices in secular society it is often reticent to see its own compromises on these issues. This abuse of loyalty undermines the church's credibility as people understand it to be no different than the compromises they are forced into in their own ordinary work situations and social contexts. But the claim for the church to be more than this highlights the disjunction even more acutely. Moreover, defending this position by saying that the church is not perfect is no justification for it. Rather, it reveals a deep cynicism and a lack of faith which is really oriented towards preserving one's own position and perhaps those of others in the institution. Such behaviour is clearly understandable but nevertheless it lacks credibility. It undermines the authority of the church as grounded in the freedom of the followers of Christ. Viewed in this way, the church becomes just like any other organisation with a particular agenda, for which it is prepared to sacrifice its integrity. But as has become clear in the sexual abuse crisis when the importance of the power and status of an institution replaces the service of the people, the praise and worship of God which should be at the core of the church is replaced by the idolatry of self- and institutional-worship.

CONCLUSION

At a time of conflicting interpretations having an authority that one can trust is an unequivocal good. This is why rightly understood and properly practiced the exercise of magisterial authority should be a blessing for the church and for the wider society. Yet, what should be a blessing has sadly fallen well short of this. The need for reform has been known for some time now and the reform of the papacy is something that Pope John Paul II spoke of in his 1995 encyclical *Ut Unum Sint*. However, it is really only in the election of Pope Francis that reform of the Magisterium has taken on such urgency. The importance of this for Pope Francis is determined by the necessity of renewal in order to be able to better fulfil the mission of the church. It is not reform for reform's sake, but rather reform in the service of the mission of the gospel which often goes unheard today because of the crisis of credibility. Attempts to downplay the urgency and importance of this task merely compound the problem. Following the sexual abuse crisis confidence in the hierarchical church has been deeply and perhaps mortally damaged and some even ask whether it is too late to save the church. Whether the Catholic Church is able to reform may well determine the answer to that question. The hope of this collection of essays is that it still can.

Whilst many of the participants in this volume share a kenotic understanding of the exercise of magisterial authority, this should not be seen as if kenosis is an end in itself. This emptying out is a prerequisite for the missionary *going forth* in the power of the Spirit. Such kenotic exercise of authority is thus not drawn out of its own resources but rather participates in the Trinitarian *going forth* which is the missionary life of the church. As such the process of searching for new structures, forms, and patterns of authority in the church is very much one of discernment. It is through looking for the movement of the Spirit in the church and the world in the joys and sorrows of our time that a way forward is to be found. Confident in the presence of the Spirit in this labour of discernment it is with renewed effort that we should humbly go forth in the joyful service of the gospel. But lest we forget in whose authority we do this, we need to be reminded that this authority is a gift which we always receive anew. Our incompleteness and our own sinfulness is healed by this grace but not eliminated. Remaining inadequate to the task we go forth knowing that, like those to whom we are sent, we are never worthy disciples. In the light of this self-knowledge, our desires to foster reform of the exercise of magisterial authority in the church are nurtured by an understanding and acceptance that reform will remain incomplete in history. Rather than moving us to a spirit of desolation, this experience empowers us to a greater search for an authentic way that is neither beholden to an illusionary perfectionism nor satisfied with a comfortable status quo. In this journey of reform all are pilgrims on the way searching together for a path ahead.

In drawing on both the tradition of renewal that emerged out of the *Ressourcement* and *Aggiornamento* movements which led to the Second Vatican Council and also in proposing new strategies for reform that go beyond those traditions, the collection of essays presented here provide resources for rethinking the exercise of magisterial authority in the church in our era.

In the essay by Sean Michael Ryan, he offers an analysis of the disjunction between the political authority structures and the ecclesial organisation in the Synoptic Gospels. Developing both an engagement with the interpretation of the historical context of the gospels and a close exegetical study of the rhetorical force of a selection of relevant synoptic sayings, Ryan argues that whilst the ambiguities remain in the Markan and Matthean descriptions of authority the Lukan narrative could serve as a catalyst for contemporary models of authority in a variety of spheres. Roger Mitchell also draws upon an analysis of biblical material, especially Lukan and Johannine, to argue that there has been a colonisation of the understanding of transcendence by sovereignty. Inspired by the theology of Hans Urs von Balthasar and the work of Michel de Certeau, Mitchell argues that recovery of a kenotic understanding of authority, conceptualised by Mitchell as "kenarchy", substantiates an understanding of authority without sovereignty that serves to promote the authority of love.

In the following three essays the focus shifts from the biblical to the sociological and philosophical dimensions of authority. Staf Hellemans offers an historical-sociological investigation into the conjunctions and disjunctions of the magisterium of the Catholic Church and modernity. Arguing that both liberal and reactionary approaches face problems and that only by developing a form of magisterium and church which is conducive for people to live a fulfilled life can the exercise of authority regain legitimacy. Anthony J. Carroll in his essay proposes a rethinking of the question of change in the context of a postmetaphysical account of authority and of the development of doctrine. Favouring a kenotic exercise of this authority, Carroll sees the resulting participative consensus building approach as itself a constitutive dimension of mission properly understood in the contemporary global age. Louis Caruana draws on the insights of both John Henry Newman and Charles Sanders Peirce to argue that approaches to structures of authority and decision-making in both the church and the scientific community are not as different as sometimes thought. Furthermore, Caruana concludes that the correspondence model of truth often employed in scientific work has important insights which may complement the coherence model stressed more in the church's system of doctrinal authority.

The theological contributions to the volume are wide-ranging covering pastoral theology (James Sweeney), church history (Richard Price), spiritual theology (Paul Rout), ecclesiology (Gemma Simmonds), and issues of systematic theology (Michael Kirwan and Karen Kilby). James Sweeney tackles the principal question of pastoral theology, namely, how can ecclesial authority be exercised in such a way as to have a positive impact on the lives of women and men in the church and more broadly in society at large? Sweeney argues that the church needs to find its way of negotiating through the social processes by which social and cultural values are both generated and accepted, and so find an authoritative voice in pluralistic and differentiated contexts. Richard Price draws on the example of the monoenergist-monothelete controversy of the seventh century to indicate that unconditional consent is due only to that which is explicit in the tradition, as contained in the Scriptures and the Fathers, and which guided and has been codified in the early ecumenical councils. He concludes that declarations of incompatibility with Catholic doctrine should be limited to those areas which contradict this unbroken tradition. Paul Rout also draws on a lesson from church history in his reflection upon the life and witness of St. Francis of Assisi as a model of authority. He explores the understanding of the nature and purpose of authority that arose in the Franciscan tradition as developed in the theological and spiritual writings of

St. Bonaventure. Rout concludes that the witness of the example of both St. Francis and the Franciscan tradition has found echoes in the current papacy of Pope Francis in his words and his deeds. Gemma Simmonds draws particularly on the writings of John Henry Newman to argue for a kenotic exercise of magisterial authority which requires bringing into dialogue the concerns and preoccupations of the receiving community and the content of the faith as mediated by the tradition of the church. Such means of open and respectful dialogue needs to be fostered in the church as this is a privileged place in which to listen to the voice of the Holy Spirit speaking through the signs of the times. Michael Kirwan offers a theological reading of José Casanova's description of the crisis in the church due to the disjunction between societal morality and church morality on issues of gender and sexuality. Drawing on a range of perspectives and disciplines, he concludes that an eschatological imagination as manifested in St. Paul is one way in which the gap between the persecutor and the victim can be envisioned to be healed in God's own messianic time. Karen Kilby's contribution finishes the volume by outlining how obedience to the faith often requires a wrestling with challenges and difficulties that can sometimes lead to criticism and even dissent. However, under normal circumstances she reminds us that assent and dissent should combine in more organic ways which flow out of the even more fundamental assent that we give to the authority of the gospel.

Included as an appendix to this volume are two contributions previously published in *Church and People: Disjunctions in a Secular Age*[1]. Both of these contributions preceded the work on the question of authority that was taken up by the Heythrop team and collaborators, and they often informed the work of the present project. As a consequence, it seems appropriate to include them as an appendix to this current volume.

The first article by Francis Oakley provides a concise historical overview of just how it was that what he terms an "obedience model of authority", came to dominate in the Roman Catholic Church. Outlining the various factors that he considers to have been responsible for this state of affairs, he argues that the result has been an aversion to historicity in church teaching and a fostering of a tendency to abstraction that displays little concern for the concrete pastoral reality of the faithful. Oakley sees in this development an inability of the church to carry out Vatican II's teaching on

---

[1] Charles Taylor, Jose Casanova, and George F. McLean, eds., *Church and People: Disjunctions in a Secular Age* (Washington: The Council for Research in Values and Philosophy, 2012), 51–101 This volume brought together scholars to consider the four disjunctions outlined by Charles Taylor, José Casanova, and George McLean at a conference in Vienna in June 2011. Written during the papacy of Pope Benedict XVI, and following the revelations of various scandals in the church, the atmosphere at the time was undoubtedly more pessimistic than it is now.

episcopal collegiality and a spreading of this general tendency to the exercise of magisterial authority over the ordinary faithful.

The second article by Daniel Deckers tackles the question of whether the principle of subsidiarity, which has been commonly associated with Catholic Social Teaching, applies equally to the life of the church. Deckers probes the possibility that the disjunction between the exercise of magisterial authority and the manner of functioning in the modern world may be overcome by adopting the principle of subsidiarity to the life of the church itself. Faithful to the traditional teaching of the church and also attuned to the practices of modern democracies, Deckers argues that the principle of subsidiarity still has much to teach the church in the modern world.

Clearly in a volume such as this with a diversity of approaches, intellectual traditions, and central concerns the question of the unity and overall vision of the project is raised. Is there a common approach to the exercise of magisterial authority towards which the various contributions point? The reader will no doubt make up their own minds about this, but it may not be unhelpful to proffer a suggestion. Attempting to be faithful to the gospel and conscious of the continual need for purification, the vision of authority which shines forth from these pages is one which is both deeply human and divine. Such a vision is inspired by the belief that authority is ultimately a God given gift and a service that is humanly exercised. This dialectical approach to the understanding of magisterial authority situates it as part of a kenotic mission of the church, which is both a project in history and also an eschatological horizon which orients the direction of the church in the world. Being both at the same time, the exercise of magisterial authority manifests this dual nature of the Kingdom of God as already amongst us and as still yet to come. At this moment in the history of the church, and in a context of conflicting interpretations, the need to recover a credible manner of exercising authority that is attuned to the movement of the Holy Spirit in our times is paramount for an effective witness to the gospel.

The intention of this volume has been neither to shy away from confronting a crisis in the church today concerning the credible exercise of magisterial authority, nor to presume that the church is unable to find ways beyond the current situation in which it finds itself. Grounded in the conviction that a serious and critical engagement with this issue requires a spirit of creative fidelity, the contributors have attempted both to develop strands within the tradition which need to be unearthed, recovered, and developed, and also to think anew using resources outside the traditional teaching of the church. Not representing a single school of thought or theological, philosophical, or sociological orientation, the contributors to this volume have attempted to offer reflections in their particular areas of expertise to aid in thinking through just how such a crisis might be overcome. If we have offered some resources that serve this end then the effort which lies behind them will not have been in vain.

PART I

AUTHORITY IN BIBLICAL SOURCES

CHAPTER I

"IT SHALL NOT BE SO AMONG YOU": AUTHORITY AND SERVICE IN THE SYNOPTIC GOSPELS
(MARK 10:35-45 // MATTHEW 20:20-28 //LUKE 22:24-27)

SEAN MICHAEL RYAN

INTRODUCTION

This paper considers the ostensibly sharp disjunction that is drawn between political authority structures and ecclesial organization in the Synoptic Gospels. In Mark 10:35-45 and parallels (Matthew 20:20-28 // Luke 22:24-27) civil hierarchies function as a negative foil to the ideals recommended for the Twelve: the rulers of the Gentiles "exercise lordship over" (κατακυριεύω) or "have power over" (κατεξουσιάζω) (Mk 10:42) their subjects, "but it is not to be so among you" (οὐχ οὕτως δέ ἐστιν ἐν ὑμῖν) (Mk 10:43). Instead, greatness and pre-eminence are intimately linked to the function of servant (διάκονος) or slave (δοῦλος), echoing the self-offering service (διακονέω) of the Son of Man (Mk 10:45).

This paper will scrutinize two interrelated interpretative issues. The first issue concerns the *historical context* of these texts, notably the linkage between ruler and servant or slave in the Graeco-Roman era. How countercultural would it be to depict an ideal ruler as a servant or slave of his subjects? The first section will sketch the backdrop of competing models of ideal kingship in the philosophical literature of the Hellenistic and Roman eras (νοταβλψ περὶ βασιλείας 'On Kingship' treatises).

The second issue concerns the rhetorical force of the injunctions in the respective *literary contexts* of each Synoptic text. What is the extent of the critique of hierarchical systems of governance in Mk 10:35-45 and parallels? Is the target the *misuse* of power by tyrants, or are all hierarchical systems caricatured and critiqued by this negative example, irrespective of the virtues of the leader? Is the alternative model of service that is delineated a concrete countercultural blueprint or a transitory utopian ideal? This section will offer a close exegetical study of Mk 10:42-45 // Mt 20:25-28 // Lk 22:25-27 in their respective literary contexts, considering the differing emphases of each narrative, particularly attentive to the vocabulary of 'benefaction' (εὐεργεσία) contained in the Lukan version.

Given the subtleties and ambiguities inherent in this Synoptic parallel, evidenced in the differing nuances of each version in their distinctive literary and historical context, the precise contours of a 'servant model' of leadership continues to pose searching questions for contemporary interpreters as to how, precisely, such a paradoxical Gospel ideal may be delineated and realised.

CULTURAL CONTEXT: RULER AS SERVANT OR SLAVE IN GRAECO-ROMAN POLITICAL THOUGHT?

Critical reflection on the characteristics of an 'ideal king' was a source of endless fascination to Greek and Roman intellectuals, philosophers, rhetoricians, and panegyrists, from the classical era through to the Hellenistic and Roman eras.[1] Seminal works on this subject in the classical era emphasize how the virtues of the ideal (philosopher-)king (cf. Plato's *Republic* and *Politicus,* Arisotle's *Politics,* and Xenophon's *The Education of Cyrus* (*Cyropaedia*) and *Memorabilia*) should foster the virtues of the citizens, as the king functions as an ideal model to *imitate*:

> [Cyrus] believed that he could in no more effectively way inspire a desire for the beautiful and the good than by endeavouring, as their sovereign, to set before his subjects a perfect model of virtue in his own person. (Xenophon, *Cyropaedia,* 8.1.21) (c. 430-354 BCE)[2]

As the virtues of the sovereign determined the justice and harmony of the state over which he presided, it was imperative that he be advised and taught by philosophers, who functioned as 'special advisors' to the monarch at the royal court.[3] Accordingly, treatises 'On Kingship' (περὶ βασιλείας) proliferated in the Hellenistic era (c. 4th-1st century BCE), as evidenced by the plethora of titles that are known from this period, although only

---

[1] E. R. Goodenough, "The Political Philosophy of Hellenistic Kingship," *YCS* 1 (1928): 55-102; Francis Dvomik, *Early Christian and Byzantine Political Philosophy: Origins and Background,* 2 vols. (Washington DC: Dumbarton Oaks Center for Byzantine Studies, 1966); Oswyn Murray, "Philosophy and Monarchy in the Hellenistic World," in *Jewish Perspectives on Hellenistic Rulers,* ed. Tessa Rajak et al. (Berkeley: University of California Press, 2007), 13-28; Julien Smith, *Christ the Ideal King: Cultural Context Rhetorical Strategy and the Power of Divine Monarchy in Ephesians,* WUNT 313 (T: Mohr Siebeck, 2011), 19-89.

[2] Walter Miller, ed., *Xenophon, Cyropaedia, Vol II. Books 5-8,* Loeb Classical Library (Cambridge MA: Harvard University Press, 1914).

[3] Murray, "Philosophy and Monarchy in the Hellenistic World," 16-17, 27: "…the philosopher…held the same position as the…economic expert today. Like them, he was welcomed at court, was paid huge sums, and was listened to attentively; his advice formed the basis of policy and of action; his jargon dominated the civil service."

fragmentary extracts and summaries survive embedded in later writings.[4] Nonetheless, the broad contours of variant models of the ideal king are recoverable from the extant sources:[5]

> The king as the perfect man must have all the virtues that the particular philosophical sect considered important; these varied slightly, some being thought more essential than others by different philosophers. But it was more often a question of emphasis than one of substance. The king must of course have all the normal virtues, such as courage, self-control, wisdom…justice, honesty, friendliness, truthfulness, kindness and so on; most treatises *On Kingship* will have been in the form of lists of virtues that the king ought to possess, and reasons why they are especially important for a king; in general, the king stands on a pedestal visible to all and has the duty of leading his subjects to virtue; he therefore has especial need of virtue himself. One virtue was central for the king: *philanthropia*, love of his subjects. From this all the others would flow. He would seek to be just, to bring his people to virtue, and above all to benefit them: *euergesia* [benefaction] was a direct consequence of *philanthropia*.[6]

In the main, Roman literature in the Republican and Imperial eras adopted and modified the central ideals of Hellenistic kingship, reshaping it to form an ideology of imperial rule characterized as the legitimate heir to the Ptolemaic/Seleucid dynasties.[7]

---

[4] On the fragmentary nature of the evidence see Murray, "Philosophy and Monarchy in the Hellenistic World"; and Goodenough, "The Political Philosophy of Hellenistic Kingship."

[5] Smith, *Christ the Ideal King: Cultural Context Rhetorical Strategy and the Power of Divine Monarchy in Ephesians*, 34-47 offers a comparable summary of the ideal king in Hellenistic kingship treatises, laying particular emphasis on the king as benefactor and model to imitate: "[Hellenistic literature] portray[s] the ideal king as a divine and beneficent being, the source of divine benefits for his people. Such a king is able to transform his subjects by the radiance of his divine presence. He rules justly through the animate law within him, by which he also effects harmony within his realm and between his people and God." p. 46.

[6] Murray, "Philosophy and Monarchy in the Hellenistic World," 24.

[7] Cf. Elizabeth Rawson, "Caesar's Heritage: Hellenistic Kings and Their Roman Equals," *JRS* 65 (1975): 148-59; Smith, *Christ the Ideal King: Cultural Context Rhetorical Strategy and the Power of Divine Monarchy in Ephesians*, 47-89 One striking counter-example is the scathing critique of the military dictatorship of Julius Caesar by Cicero, De Officiis (44 BCE), immediately following Caesar's assassination. Cicero equates kingship (*rex*) with tyranny

Stoic treatises 'on kingship' tended to emphasize the high standards that a king must strive to attain as a wise man (cf. Chrysippus),[8] notably the absence of emotion in making decisions (ἀπάθεια), which jarred with other virtues ordinarily ascribed to the ideal ruler (notably gentleness, forgiveness, and above all φιλανθροπία). The Roman Stoic, Seneca, addresses this incongruity in his treatise *De Clementia* (c. 55/56 CE), in which he urges Nero to rule his people with *clementia* [mercy/forbearance], in order to foster the moral character of his subjects rather than dealing with their failings through punitive justice.[9]

Dio Chrysostom (c. 40-120 CE) in his fourth oration *On Kingship*, imagines a scene in which the young Alexander the Great is engaged in dialogue with Diogenes the Cynic. The role of the Cynic philosopher is here foregrounded, as one who will speak out openly (παρρησία), and so has a crucial role in speaking out against the vices of a tyrannical monarch, implicitly here against the militarism of Trajan. The young Alexander is advised to demonstrate his divine descent as king, not by empty display (diadem, tiara or sceptre), but through his virtue, by seeking wisdom (*Oration* 4.70).[10]

According to Plutarch (c. 50-120 CE), the strongest counter-cultural voice may be ascribed to the Epicureans, who urged philosophers to stop pandering for positions of influence at royal courts (cf. Plutarch, *Moralia* 1095c).[11] The polemical nature of Plutarch's extract, however, jars with more positive relationships between Epicurean philosophers and Hellenistic monarchs.[12]

(tyrannus) and the enslavement of a free people; cf. E. M. Atkins, "Cicero," in *The Cambridge History of Greek and Roman Political Thought* (Cambridge: Cambridge University Press, 2000), 477-516; and Peter Stacey, *Roman Monarchy and the Renaissance Prince* (Cambridge: Cambridge University Press, 2007), 23-30.

[8] As cited by Diogenes Laertius, cf. Tiziano Dorandi, ed., *Diogenes Laertius/Lives of Eminent Philosophers* (Cambridge: Cambridge University Press, 2013).

[9] Cf. Susanna Braund, ed., *Seneca: De Clementia* (Oxford: Oxford University Press, 2009).

[10] Cf. J. W. Cohoon, ed., *Dio Chrysostom/Discourses 1-11*, Loeb Classical Library (Cambridge MA: Harvard University Press, 1932).

[11] Cited by Murray, "Philosophy and Monarchy in the Hellenistic World," 18-19.

[12] For a critique of Plutarch's reliability on this issue see Jeffrey Fish, "Not All Politicians Are Sisyphus: What Roman Epicureans Were Taught about Politics," in *Epicurus and the Epicurean Tradition*, ed. Jeffrey Fish and Kirk R. Sanders (Cambridge: Cambridge University Press, 2011), 102-4. According to the Epicurean Philodemus, a virtuous man can rule well, and Epicurean philosophy can help such a ruler distinguish and mitigate against avoidable disturbances.

Urbane Jewish authors of the Hellenistic and Roman eras engaged creatively with this literary tradition. Perhaps the most striking example is the 2nd century BCE treatise, the *Letter of Aristeas*, which principally recounts an elaborate narration of the production of the Septuagint translation, aimed at validating its authoritative status.[13] This work includes an extended digression (Aristeas 187-300) in which the Ptolemaic king who is sponsoring the production of the translation hosts a series of seven banquets/symposia at which 72 philosophical questions are discussed, notably the virtues required of an ideal king, a Jewish spin on the *peri basileias* tradition.[14]

> ...a noble character (ἦθος) which has had its share of (suitable) education is capable of ruling. Just as you rule, O mighty King, and are distinguished not so much by the outstanding glory and wealth of your kingdom but because you excel all men in your moderation (ἐπιείκεια) and humanity (lit. philanthropy (φιλανθρωπία) – God having endowed you with these gifts. (*Letter of Aristeas*, 290)[15]

The Jewish translators who respond to the king's questions emphasize that the king is the model for the virtuous behaviour of his subjects, and the king's character is in turn patterned on the model of God (YHWH = Zeus, cf. Aristeas 15-16)[16] who rules the universe with moderation (ἐπιείκεια) (cf. Aristeas 188).

To what extent did philosophical reflection on the virtues required of an 'ideal king' include any suggestion that the king should be servant or slave of his subjects, or that kingship was a form of 'servitude'?

---

[13] For the scholarly debate as to the principal purpose of the Letter of Aristeas see Sylvie Honigman, *The Septuagint and Homeric Scholarship in Alexandria: A Study in the Narrative of the "Letter of Aristeas"* (London: Routledge, 2003) ch. 4; Sylvie Honigman, "The Narrative Function of the King and the Library in the 'Letter of Aristeas,'" in *Jewish Perspectives on Hellenistic Rulers*, ed. Tessa Rajak et al. (Berkeley: University of California Press, 2007), 128-46; and Jennifer Dines, *Septuagint* (London and New York: T & T Clark/Continuum, 2004), 28-33.

[14] Cf. Oswyn Murray, "Aristeas and Ptolemaic Kingship," *JTS* 18 (1967): 337-71; Smith, *Christ the Ideal King: Cultural Context Rhetorical Strategy and the Power of Divine Monarchy in Ephesians*, 133-41.

[15] R.J.H. Shutt, "Letter of Aristeas," in *The Old Testament Pseudepigrapha*, ed. James H. Charlesworth, vol. 2 (London, Darton: Longman & Todd, 1985), 32; Greek text http://ocp.tyndale.ca/letter-of-aristeas.

[16] Ibid., 13"These people worship God the overseer and creator of all, whom all men worship including ourselves, O King, except that we have a different name. Their name for him is Zeus and Jove."

Seeley has sought to identify traces of such language in Hellenistic and Roman περὶ βασιλείας literature, notably the orations of Dio Chrysostom, but the parallels he cites do not apply the language of 'slave' or 'service' directly to a king, but rather use more positive characteristics, notably φιλανθρωπία or benefactor (εὐεργέτης).[17] The closest analogy in Greek is the fragmentary saying attributed to the Macedonian philosopher-king, Antigonos Gonatas (c. 320-239 BCE): 'Do you not understand, my son, that our kingdom is held to be a noble servitude (ἔνδοξος δουλεία)'.[18] But even here, the harsh image of slavery is tempered by the high status adjective ἔνδοξος 'honoured, distinguished' that is juxtaposed with it.

This same conception of imperial rule as 'noble servitude' is picked up by Seneca in his fictive dialogue with the young emperor Nero, in a context that exemplifies the distance that separates this metaphorical designation, as applied to a ruler, from the degrading social reality of a slave:[19]

> You think it is severe for kings to be deprived of that freedom of speech which the lowest enjoy. 'That amounts to slavery (*servitus*) not sovereignty (*non imperium*)', you say. What! Are you not aware that sovereignty is a noble slavery for you? (*nobilem esse tibi servitum*) Your situation is quite different from that of people who are invisible in the crowd they never emerge from and whose virtues have a long struggle to be seen and whose faults keep to the shadows. The actions and words of you and those like you are seized by rumour. For that reason, no group should take more care over their reputation than people who, whatever they actually deserve, are going to have an important reputation....You cannot escape your position. It besieges and follows you wherever you descend with enormous pomp. This is the slavery experienced by the highest importance – to be unable to become less important. But that constraint you share with the gods. The fact is that they too are fettered by heaven. It is no more possible for them to come down than it is

---

[17] David Seeley, "Rulership and Service in Mark 10:41-45," *NovT* 35 (1993): 234-9 The remainder of Seeley's essays draws parallels with the notion of the Cynic philosopher as "slave", who is also termed king.

[18] H. Collins and R. Evans, *Rethinking Expertise* (Chicago: Chicago University Press, 2007), 499 and; Hans Volkmann, "Die Basileia Als ENDOXOS DOULEIA," in *ENDOXOS DOULEIA: Kleine Schriften Zur Alten Geschichte*, by Hans Volkmann (Berlin and New York: De Gruyter, 1975), 74-81.

[19] Cf. also Dio Chrysostom, Orations 3.75 who draws an analogy between the sun's slavery to duty and that of a ruler. Cohoon, *Dio Chrysostom/Discourses 1-11*.

safe for you to do so: you are nailed to your pinnacle. (Seneca, *De Clementia*, 8.1-3)[20] (c. 55/56 CE)

The paradoxical concept 'noble slavery' is assimilated to the aristocratic pretensions of Graeco-Roman kingship ideology, a servitude analogous to that of the gods, deriving from the high status of the role.[21] Marcus' assessment of the cultural context of Mk 10:35-45 offers a succinct summation of the extant sources:

> Outside the Christian sphere, there are few approximations to the idea that a leader ought to be his people's slave. The idea of the meek and magnanimous king is common in Hellenistic literature....This is not the same thing, however, as associating kingship with the degradation of slavery, and when the "servant king" idea appears in Graeco-Roman sources, it is customarily used in a negative sense to denounce demagogues who pander to the crowd and thus act as "slaves" to the lower classes. (cf. Cicero, *On the Paradoxes of the Stoics*, 51; Philo, *On Joseph*, 35).[22]

How, then, might the language of Mk 10:35-45 and parallels with its valorizing of a slave's status and role[23] for potential leaders be understood against the pervasive backdrop of Graeco-Roman ideology of an 'ideal king' as the leading figure in society, pre-eminent in virtue, who functions as a benefactor for his subjects and a model to imitate?

---

[20] Braund, *Seneca: De Clementia*, 107-9.

[21] Ibid., 244 "[Seneca] elaborate[s] upon the contrast in freedom and responsibilities between the situation of insignificant members of society and that of the emperor" which includes an encomium that draws an analogy with the role of the gods (1.8.3).

[22] Joel Marcus, *Mark 8-16: A New Translation with Introduction and Commentary* (New Haven and London: Yale University Press, 2009), 748.

[23] The legal and social status of a Roman slave was the very antithesis of a free Roman citizen: "Legally, the slave was res, a thing, property, an object. Roman law acknowledges slave as people and distinguishes human property from other kinds of property...[Nonetheless] The slave, like a piece of land, an animal, or an inanimate object could be sold, lent, mortgaged, given away, or bequeathed in a will. As property slaves lacked all that defined freeborn Roman citizens: legitimate kinship relations acknowledged in law and by society, physical integrity, the ability to set law in motion on their own behalf, and ownership of property" Sandra R. Joshel, *Slavery in the Roman World* (Cambridge: Cambridge University Press, 2010), 38.

SERVANT MODELS OF LEADERSHIP: MK 10:35-45 // MT 20:20-28 // LK 22:24-27 IN NARRATIVE CONTEXT

Mk 10:35-45

A decisive turning-point (περιπέτεια) occurs at Mk 8:27ff,[24] on the first occasion in the Markan narrative at which a human character perceives Jesus' true identity as Messiah (σὺ εἶ ὁ χριστός) (Mk 8:29).[25] Nonetheless, despite this positive acclamation, the character of Peter almost immediately rejects the explication of this messiahship as one involving suffering and death leading to vindication (Mk 8:31-33). This recurrent motif of the incomprehension/opacity of the disciples escalates in the second half of the Markan narrative, setting in motion a threefold pattern of passion prediction, followed by incomprehension/non-acceptance by the disciples, resulting in further explication, in the transitional section on the 'way' from Galilee to Jerusalem (Mk 8:27-11:1).[26]

Passion Prediction	Incomprehension/Rejection by the disciples/Twelve	Further Teaching about discipleship
Mk 8:31 Son of Man to suffer, be rejected, killed, and rise.	**Mk 8:32-33** Peter rejects this and is reprimanded	**Mk 8:34-9:1** (crowd + disciples) Followers are required to deny themselves, take up their own cross and follow Jesus.
Mk 9:30-31 Son of Man to suffer, be rejected, killed, and rise.	**Mk 9:32** Disciples do not understand	**Mk 9:33-37** (disciples/Twelve) Disciples reprimanded for arguing about 'who (is) the greatest' (τίς

---

[24] Mary Ann Tolbert, *Sowing the Gospel: Mark's World in Literary-Historical Perspective* (Minneapolis: Fortress Press, 1989), 74-75.

[25] Jesus' identity as Messiah/Son of God is otherwise disclosed by the narrator to the narratee in the introductory sentence (Mk 1:1), by the character of God to Jesus (and four privileged disciples, Peter, James and John, cf. Mk 5:35-43, 13:3-37, 14:32-42) at the baptism and transfiguration Mk 1:9-11, 9:2-13, and by characters from the subterranean realm (unclean spirits/demons) (cf. Mk 3:11, 5:7) to Jesus.

[26] On the incomprehension of the disciples as a stock character group in Mk see Elizabeth Struthers Malbon, *In the Company of Jesus: Characters in Mark's Gospel* (Louisville KY: Westminster John Knox Press, 2000), 41-99; and Paul L. Danove, *The Rhetoric of the Characterization of God, Jesus and Jesus' Disciples in the Gospel of Mark*, JSNT Sup 290 (London and New York: T & T Clark/Continuum, 2005), 90-126.

		μείζων). Using the example of a child, they are instructed that whoever wishes to be first (πρῶτος) must be last of all (πάντων ἔσχατος) and servant of all (πάντων διάκονος).
Mk 10:32-34 In Jerusalem, the Son of Man is to suffer, be rejected, killed, and rise.	Mk 10:35-40 James and John request places of honour 'in your glory' (ἐν τῇ δόξῃ σου).	Mk 10:41-45 (Twelve) The Twelve are instructed not to imitate the model of Gentile rulers, but rather whoever wishes to be great (μέγας) is to be your (pl.) servant, (ὑμῶν διάκονος) and whoever wishes to be first (πρῶτος) is to be slave of all (πάντων δοῦλος), analogous to the actions of the Son of Man.

Accordingly, Mk 10:35-45 is the culmination of a recurring pattern of teaching in Mk 8-10, which further explicates the role of a disciple in the light of the suffering/death/resurrection of the Son of Man (Mk 8:31, 9:31, 10:33-4). Each scene focuses in more narrowly on the in-group: the teaching is directed first to the disciples and the wider crowd (Mk 8), then to the disciples alone (Mk 9), and finally to the Twelve (Mk 10). The in-group, specifically the inner core of the Twelve (or the Three: Peter, James, and John), receive privileged teaching that teases out the 'mystery of the kingdom of God', which remains inexplicable and intentionally opaque for outsiders (cf. Mk 4:10-12, alluding to Isaiah 6:9).

What, precisely, is the privileged position that James and John (two of the inner-core of disciples in Mark) are requesting from the Markan Jesus in Mk 10:35-37?[27]

> The saying probably presupposes that Jesus will be enthroned as the king and judge of the new age as God's agent. The Similitudes of Enoch portray God's "Chosen One", the messiah, as sitting on "the throne of glory" on "that day" (1 Enoch 45:3). The Matthean Jesus prophesies that the Son of Man will sit on

---

[27] Note that all three of the "inner-core" of disciples are reprimanded in these scenes: Peter in Mk 8:32-33 and James and John in Mk 10:35-45.

the throne of his glory and that the Twelve will sit on thrones as well judging the twelve tribes of Israel (Matt 19:28; cf. 25:31).[28]

The conceptual background to this passage is the Markan image of the eschatological *parousia* of the Son of Man (cf. Mk 8:38, 13:26, 14:62), that is, the return of the *glorified* Son of Man as eschatological ruler.[29] It is possible, although difficult to verify given the brief and allusive references, that the Markan narrative envisages an interim messianic kingdom on earth (cf. Mk 13:27), which will precede the general resurrection and final judgement (cf. 1 Thessalonians 4:13-18, Rev 20:4, IV Ezra 7:26-28).[30] Unlike the Matthean parallel referred to by Collins, in Mk the emphasis is predominantly upon the Son of Man returning as *glorified king* to gather the elect (who survive the eschatological tribulation, Mk 13:26-27, 14:62) such that the function of judge is somewhat effaced (cf. Mk 8:38).

It is nonetheless apparent that James and John are depicted as requesting places of honour, next in rank to Jesus, in the hierarchy of the new eschatological kingdom, enthroned alongside him (right and left hand) in his royal court. This corresponds to the obsession with graded hierarchies of holiness in the broadly contemporary Qumran community, for example in

---

[28] Collins and Evans, *Rethinking Expertise*, 495; For the potential influence of the Similitudes of Enoch on the Markan portrayal of the Son of Man see James D.G. Dunn, "The Son of Man in Mark," in *Parables of Enoch: A Paradigm Shift*, ed. Darrell L. Bock and James H. Charlesworth (London: Bloomsbury, 2013), 18-34 and; George W.E. Nickelsburg and James C. VanderKam, *1 Enoch 2*, Hermeneia (Minneapolis: Fortress Press, 2012), 70-74.

[29] Edward Adams, "The Coming of the Son of Man in Mark's Gospel," *Tyndale Bulletin* 56 (2005): 39-61; Edward Adams, *The Stars Will Fall from Heaven: Cosmic Catastrophe in the New Testament and Its World [LNTS 347]* (London and New York: T & T Clark/Continuum, 2007), 133-181 who defends the majority view (that Mk 13:24-27 describes the parousia of the Son of Man) against the revisionary readings of; N.T. Wright, *Jesus and the Victory of God* (London: SPCK, 1996), 320-268 and; R.T. France, *The Gospel of Mark: A Commentary on the Greek Text*, NIGTC (Grand Rapids MI: Eerdmans, 2002), 530-7 (who relate it to heavenly ascent/glorification as in Dan 7). On the political backdrop to παρουσία imagery, namely state visits of the Emperor to subject cities in the Roman empire era see; James R. Harrison, *Paul and the Imperial Authorities at Thessalonica and Rome*, WUNT 273 (Tübingen: Mohr Siebeck, 2011), 56-59.

[30] Seth Turner, "The Interim, Earthly Messianic Kingdom in Paul," *Journal for the Study of the New Testament* 25 (2003): 323-42; For the dominant image of the kingdom of God/messianic kingdom as located on the earthly plane in Second Temple Jewish literature see George W.E. Nickelsburg, "Where Is the Place of Eschatological Blessing?," in *Things Revealed: Studies in Early Jewish and Christian Literature in Honor of Michael E. Stone*, ed. Esther G. Chazon, David Satran, and Ruth A. Clements, JSJSup 89 (Leiden: Brill, 2004), 53-71.

1QSa (*The Rule of the Congregation*), which outlines the membership of the 'congregation of Israel' at the end of days, in which members are seated, each according to 'his dignity (*kabod* = Greek δόξα)'.

> At [a ses]sion of the men of renown, [those summoned to] the gathering of the community council, when [God] begets the Messiah with them: [the] chief [priest] of all the congregation of Israel shall enter and all [his] br[others, the sons] of Aaron, the priests [summoned] to the assembly, the men of renown, and they shall sit be[fore him, each one] according to his dignity. After, [the Mess]iah of Israel shall [enter] and before him shall sit the heads of the th[ousands of Israel, each] one according to his dignity, according to [his] po[sition] in their camps and according to their marches. ((1Q28a) 1QSa II.11-15)[31]

The brothers are disappointed to learn that whilst their suffering and death (alluded to using the resonant symbols of cup and baptism) are assured,[32] the places of honour which they sought are not in the Markan Jesus' gift to distribute (Mk 10:38-40). Nonetheless, the request itself stirs up hostility among other members of the Twelve (Mk 10:41), and it is the Markan Jesus' more detailed response to this issue that is our central object of concern (Mk 10:42-45).

Mk 10:42-44
⁴²καὶ προσκαλεσάμενος αὐτοὺς ὁ Ἰησοῦς λέγει αὐτοῖς·
οἴδατε ὅτι οἱ δοκοῦντες ἄρχειν τῶν ἐθνῶν κατακυριεύουσιν αὐτῶν
καὶ οἱ μεγάλοι αὐτῶν κατεξουσιάζουσιν αὐτῶν.
⁴³ οὐχ οὕτως δέ ἐστιν ἐν ὑμῖν,
ἀλλ' ὃς ἂν θέλῃ μέγας γενέσθαι ἐν ὑμῖν ἔσται ὑμῶν διάκονος,
⁴⁴ καὶ ὃς ἂν θέλῃ ἐν ὑμῖν εἶναι πρῶτος ἔσται πάντων δοῦλος·

⁴²So Jesus called them and said to them,
"You know that among the Gentiles those whom they recognize as their rulers lord it over them,

---

[31] Florentino Garcia Martinez and Eibert J.C. Tigchelaar, eds., *The Dead Sea Scrolls Study Edition*, vol. 1 & 2 (Grand Rapids MI and Leiden: Eerdmans/Brill, 1997), 102-3.

[32] Acts 12:1-2 refers to the execution of James by "King Herod" [= Julius Agrippa I, a grandson of Herod the Great] (c. 37-44 CE) "by the sword" – the standard Roman death penalty. A person of higher social rank found guilty of a capital offence is more likely to have his/her property and status removed by exile). On patristic testimony of traditions relating to James and especially John see R. Alan Culpepper, *John: The Son of Zebedee. The Life of a Legend* (Edinburgh: T & T Clark, 2000), 107-250.

> and their great ones are tyrants over them.
> ⁴³ But it is³³ not so among you;
> but whoever wishes to become great among you must be your servant,
> ⁴⁴ and woever wishes to be first among you must be slave of all. (NRSV)

Before delineating the recommended course of action (vv 43-44), the Markan Jesus first sketches a political model to avoid, one presumed to be familiar to his listeners (you (pl.) know (οἴδατε)). Whilst it is apparent that the focus is directed at non-Judean (i.e. 'Gentile') political hierarchies, it is less clear whether the target is the misuse of authority by *tyrants* (as suggested by the NRSV translation above, 'lord it over', 'tyrants') who fall short of the virtues required for just rule, or whether all hierarchical authority is set aside regardless of the character of the leader. Much depends upon the force of the two compound verbs, prefixed by κατα- (κατακυριεύω and κατεξουσιάζω). It is often held that the κατα- prefix has an intensive force, highlighting the oppressive wielding of power. Cranfield comments: 'The κατα- gives it the sense of using lordship over people to their disadvantage and to one's own advantage', whilst Marcus highlights a range of occurrences in the Septuagint which indicate violent conquest or oppression (e.g. Num 21:24, Ps 109:2 LXX, 1 Macc 15:30).³⁴ The detailed study of Clark, however, scouring the uses of (κατα-)κυριεύω in the Septuagint, Oxyrhynchus papyri and patristic authors, finds no distinction between the root verb and the compound form, and concludes: 'we find the meaning of [κατα]κυριεύω to be consistent, "to rule over, lord over", with shades of meaning influenced by the context. There is no suggestion anywhere of the meaning "to lord it over".³⁵

If Clark's analysis is accepted, the focus lies not on a pejorative barb against Gentile *misrule*, but rather Gentile rule *per se*. The model that is to be avoided is the 'Gentile' model of hierarchical rule *in toto* in which 'those

---

³³ The present tense of the verb "it is" (ἐστιν) is the most strongly attested reading in the manuscript tradition (א B C* D L W), whilst the alternative reading of the future tense "it will be" (ἔσται) (A C³ f¹ ¹³) appears to represent an assimilation to vv 43b, 44 and the Matthean parallel (Mt 20:26), and an attempt to account for the incongruity with the present actions of the Twelve; cf. Colin Adela Yarbro, *Mark* (Minneapolis: Fortress Press, 2007), 494.

³⁴ C.E.B. Cranfield, *The Gospel According to St Mark*, Cambridge Greek Testament Commentary (Cambridge: Cambridge University Press, 1966), 341; Marcus, *Mark 8-16: A New Translation with Introduction and Commentary*, 748; France, *The Gospel of Mark: A Commentary on the Greek Text*, 419.

³⁵ Kenneth Willis Clark, "The Meaning of [KATA]KYPIEYEIN," in *The Gentile Bias and Other Essays*, by Kenneth Willis Clark, NovTSup 54 (Leiden: Brill, 1980), 210. He traces the English expression back to 18th century idiom "to overrule", "to overmaster", which simply denoted "to rule over", "to have mastery over", with no pejorative force.

acknowledged to rule (οἱ δοκοῦντες ἄρχειν)³⁶ the Gentiles, exercise lordship over them' and 'their great men (οἱ μεγάλοι) exercise authority over them' (i.e. Gentiles). It is the exercise of lordship or authority over others that is rejected, not merely the misuse of such authority.

Within the Markan narrative itself, a set of character-types may be identified that map neatly onto the pair of ruling figures depicted. Mk 6:14-29 contains a lengthy digression that recounts the execution of John the Baptist, the only extended scene in the Markan narrative in which the protagonist, Jesus, is absent.³⁷ In Mk 6:17 the 'back-story' of John the Baptist's decapitation on a capital charge is recounted for critiquing the monarch's less than virtuous appropriation of his brother's wife.³⁸

Herod is stereotyped in the Markan narrative as a stock character-type, namely a non-virtuous ruler (cf. Mk 6:14, 22, 25, 26, 27 (βασιλεὺς)).³⁹ Darr and Smith highlight the recurring literary cliché of the charismatic/philosopher (notably Cynic-Stoic philosopher) as outspoken opponent of a 'tyrant' in Graeco-Roman literature (cf. philosophical treatises on the topic by Epictetus, 'How ought we to bear ourselves toward tyrants?', and Dio Chrysostom, 'Sixth Discourse: Diogenes, or: On Tyranny'). This conventional literary trope underlies Mk 6:14-29, and its characterization of Herod and his court, emphasizing the virtues of the charismatic/philosopher, retaining self-control and speaking out against the

---

³⁶ It is possible that οἱ δοκοῦντες ἄρχειν discloses an "apocalyptic" worldview that unveils the true order of the cosmos: the Gentile rulers only "appear" (δοκέω) to rule over their subjects (cf. Marcus 2009: 755, cf. Daniel 7-12). It is more plausible, however, that the designation does not carry such a subtle undertone, as "οἱ δοκοῦντες" = "men of repute" is a characteristic way of referring to people of standing or influence in society (cf. Colin Adela Yarbro, *Mark* (Minneapolis: Fortress Press, 2007), 499; France, *The Gospel of Mark: A Commentary on the Greek Text*, 418).

³⁷ Cf. Abraham Smith, "Tyranny Exposed: Mark's Typological Characterization of Herod Antipas," *Biblical Interpretation* 14, no. 2006 (n.d.): 259-93; Caroline van der Stichele, "Herodias Goes Headhunting," in *From the Margins. Vol 2. Women of the New Testament and Their Afterlives*, ed. Christine E. Joynes and Christopher Rowland (Sheffield: Sheffield Phoenix Press, 2009), 164-75, and compare John Darr, *Herod the Fox: Audience Criticism and Lukan Characterization*, JSNT Sup 163 (Sheffield: Sheffield Academic Press, 1998), 92-136. on Lk 9:9, 13:31-33, 23:6-12 (on Jesus' opposition to Herod according to the pattern of a philosopher opposing a tyrant).

³⁸ Contrast the motivation for John the Baptist's execution in Josephus, *Antiquities* 18.118-119 (to pre-empt a popular revolt).

³⁹ On Herod as a stock character in Mark see Smith, "Tyranny Exposed: Mark's Typological Characterization of Herod Antipas," 269-281. Note that Herod is repeatedly referred to as a "king" (βασιλεὺς) despite his lower rank of tetrarch.

more powerful ruler (cf. Mk 6:17-18), who, by contrast, loses self-control. Herod utters a rash oath to give his daughter any gift she wishes, leading to him act against his own previously disclosed intention to protect John the Baptist from Herodias (Mk 6:20)).

Accordingly, Herod and his courtiers function as stock-characters exemplifying flawed rulers/authorities in the Markan narrative. That these characters serve as the literary model for the rulers/great men of Mk 10:42-44 is highlighted by *verbal parallels* between the two passages:

Mk 6:21

...Herod, on his birthday, gave a banquet for his 'great men' (μεγιστάνοι) [cf. μεγάλοι, Mk 10:42]
and officers and for the 'preeminent men' (πρῶτοι) of Galilee.[cf. πρῶτος, Mk 10:44]

Herod and his courtiers function as stock character-types,[40] exemplifying an unrighteous king (cf. Mk 6:17-18) and his court, whose exercise of authority functions as a negative foil to the model of authority recommended as its alternative (Mk 10:42-44).

Paradoxically, the way to achieve pre-eminence in the kingdom of God, to be 'great' (μέγας) or 'first' (πρῶτος) (contrast Mk 6:21) is not to exercise lordship (as ruler) or to exercise authority (as a courtier), but rather to become servant (dia,konoj) or slave (δοῦλος) of all (Mk 10:43-44; cf. Mk 9:35). Whilst Herod and his courtiers (Mk 6:14-29) function as negative foils, a positive model to imitate is provided by the Markan Jesus, in the Christological rationale ('for', 'because' (γὰρ)) that concludes this passage:[41]

Mk 10:45
καὶ γὰρ ὁ υἱὸς τοῦ ἀνθρώπου οὐκ ἦλθεν διακονηθῆναι ἀλλὰ διακονῆσαι καὶ δοῦναι τὴν ψυχὴν αὐτοῦ λύτρον ἀντὶ πολλῶν.

For the Son of Man came not to be served but to serve,
and to give his life a ransom for many. (NRSV)

---

[40] Cf. Tolbert, *Sowing the Gospel: Mark's World in Literary-Historical Perspective*, 157-8, who considers that Herod and the rich young man of Mk 10:17-22 exemplify the character type of seed sown among thorns in the Parable of the Sower, interpreted as those for whom riches and worldly care take precedence over responsiveness to the Word (Mk 4:18-19).

[41] Adela Yarbro, *Mark*, 499. "This saying [Mk 10:45] provides both a warrant and a model for the teaching expressed in vv 43-44."

What does it mean for the Twelve to be 'slave of all' (πάντων δοῦλος) (Mk 10:44) or 'servant of all' (πάντων διάκονος) (Mk 9:35)? They are advised to eschew the 'Gentile' model of lordship exemplified by Herod and his courtiers (Mk 6:14-29) and imitate instead the pattern exemplified by the Son of Man, who combined divinely mandated authority (Mk 1:22, 1:27, 2:10) with service (Mk 10:45), culminating in his offering of his life as a 'ransom' (λύτρον) for many.[42] The broader pattern of the Markan passion predictions is recalled: disciples are required to deny themselves and follow Jesus on the path to suffering and, potentially, death (Mk 8:34-5). Authority and greatness are no longer to be attained through striving for places of honour, but rather divinely bestowed on those who choose the path of service. Marcus summarises the apocalyptic reversal succinctly in his comment on Mk 9:35:[43]

> Jesus does not condemn the disciples' desire to be preeminent, but takes it for granted; the issue is not so much whether one should want to be great as the manner in which true greatness is to be achieved. The answer Jesus proffers is that, in the upside-down logic of the dominion of God, the person who wants to

---

[42] It is much debated whether Mk 10:45 echoes the "suffering servant" passage of Deutero-Isaiah (Is 52:13-53:12), specifically whether the verbal imagery of "ransom" (λύτρον), a slave-market metaphor, equates with the cultic metaphor of giving his life as a guilt/reparation offering (*asham*) (cf. Lev 15:14-16:7) in Isa 53:10 LXX (περι ἁμαρτιας). Contrast the positive evaluation of Marcus, *Mark 8-16: A New Translation with Introduction and Commentary*, 755-7 and; France, *The Gospel of Mark: A Commentary on the Greek Text*, 42001. on the basis of broad thematic connections throughout the Markan Passion narrative, with the negative appraisal of Moma D. Hooker, "Isaiah in Mark's Gospel," in *Isaiah in the New Testament*, ed. Steve Moyise and Maarten J.J. Menken (London and New York: T & T Clark/Continuum, 2005), 48-9; and Kelli S. O'Brien, *The Use of Scripture in the Markan Passion Narrative*, LNTS 384 (London and New York: T & T Clark/Continuum, 2010), 76-87.ho considers the verbal parallels to be too slight for an ancient audience to detect. I concur with Hooker and O'Brien as the key term λύτρον in Mk 10:45 has no verbal connection with Isa 53:10 LXX.

Watson compares and contrasts Mk 10:45 with Plato's contention that the best way to gain honour is by serving (δουλεύω) honourably, rather than ruling honourably (Laws, IV.762E): "Yet even here Jesus' words are clearly different, in that being "last", a slave, and a servant are themselves to be "first" and "great" (David F. Watson, "The Life of Aesop and the Gospel of Mark: Two Ancient Approaches to Elite Values," *JBL* 129 (2010): 708.)".

[43] Narry F. Santos, *Slave of All: The Paradox of Authority and Servanthood in the Gospel of Mark* (Sheffield: Sheffield Academic Press, 2003), 208.

become first must make him- or herself last of all and servant of all.[44]

The characteristic eschatological reversal is evident, but leaves an array of loose ends. Is the pattern of authority and lordship simply *deferred*, postponed until the imminent establishment of the (messianic) kingdom, when the Son of Man will be enthroned as king surrounded by the Twelve as enthroned co-rulers/courtiers (cf. Mt 19:28, implicit in Mk 10:40)? Are Graeco-Roman hierarchical structures deconstructed in the present only to be re-inscribed in the future, modelling the eternal polity on the irreplaceable pattern of Roman imperialism?[45] What of the interim period, are the Twelve to eschew all claims to authority and hierarchical structures of self-organization in the present, wholly centred on self-offering service (to the point of death), or are leadership roles retained but re-defined by self-giving service? What balance is envisaged in the Markan narrative between authority and service in this interim period?[46]

The apocalyptic backdrop of the Markan narrative appears to indicate an eschatological inversion of status roles with the advent of the in-breaking (messianic) kingdom, whilst retaining the élite value-system of Roman imperialism. Authority roles remain in force (first/greatest/king), but the incumbents of the positions are selected on altered terms – the lowest are promoted to the seats of honour, those who 'serve all' will reign.[47]

> The Gospel of Mark…reverses the system of values that define the qualities of the power elite, primarily through the actions and teachings of Jesus…in Mark being "great" and "first" among the people of God means being like the people who conventionally enjoy the least prestige and power. Being "great" and "first" now has no legitimate meaning apart from identification with the people conventionally regarded as the lowest members of society. Moreover, they are honorable not in

---

[44] Marcus, *Mark 8-16: A New Translation with Introduction and Commentary*, 681.

[45] Stephen D. Moore, *Empire and Apocalypse: Postcolonialism and the New Testament* (Sheffield: Sheffield Phoenix Press, 2006).

[46] Santos opts for a balancing act, "…the paradox of authority and servanthood in the Markan narrative is meant to persuade them [implied readers] to balance the two motifs, in relation to their own discipleship role within the community of believers", but the text is ambiguous on this point and so remains open to alternative interpretations (Santos, *Slave of All: The Paradox of Authority and Servanthood in the Gospel of Mark*, 271).

[47] As D.H. Lawrence memorably commented on the ideology of the Apocalypse, the "bottom dogs" were going to become the "top dogs" D.H. Lawrence, *Apocalypse and the Writings on Revelation* (Cambridge: Cambridge University Press, 1980), 63.

spite of the fact that many of them are slaves who serve and follow a crucified criminal, but *because* of this. By connecting the divine perspective with aspects of culture that were despised, and especially with low markers of status and power, Mark's Jesus undercuts the very values that make the socially privileged privileged. This is not, however, an egalitarian vision. Rather than abolishing hierarchies, Mark offers a new, inverted hierarchy of honor. These Christians now have a new, divinely warranted identity. Likewise, the great and powerful members of society also have a new identity – they simply are not aware of it.[48]

Mt 20:20-28

The Matthean version of the passage occurs in a broadly comparable narrative context to its Markan source, similarly situated in a dialogue between Jesus and the Twelve on the way to Jerusalem following the third passion prediction (Mt 16:21, 17:22-23, 20:17-19). Mt 20:25-28 is a very lightly redacted version of its Markan source with only three noteworthy alterations (οἱ ἄρχοντες ('the rulers', Mt 20:25) in place of the potentially pejorative Markan (οἱ δοκοῦντες ἄρχειν) 'those reputed (or: acknowledged) to rule' (Mk 10:42), the shift of tense, from present ('is') to future ('shall'), functioning as an *imperative* directed to the Twelve ('it *shall* not be so among you') (Mt 20:26, cf. Mk 10:43), and a heightening of the parallelism between the two clauses in Mt 20:26-27 (*your* (ὑμῶν) servant/*your* (ὑμῶν) slave), lessening the potential escalation of the Markan injunction beyond the boundaries of the community (*your* servant/slave *of all* (πάντων) (Mk 10:44).[49]

---

[48] Watson, "The Life of Aesop and the Gospel of Mark: Two Ancient Approaches to Elite Values," 714.

[49] Cf. W.D. Davies and Dale C. Allison, *A Critical and Exegetical Commentary on the Gospel According to St Matthew*, ICC (Edinburgh: T & T Clark, 1997), 84-86, 92-101; Ulrich Luz, *Matthew 1-7, 8-20, 21-28*, Hermeneia (Minneapolis: Fortress Press, 2001), 541-8; John Nolland, *The Gospel of Matthew: A Commentary on the Greek Text*, NIGTC (Grand Rapids MI: Eerdmans, 2005), 816-826, and the underlined words in the table, below. The most striking redactional alteration occurs in the first half of the passage, Mt 20:20-23, in which it is the *mother* of the two sons of Zebedee who makes the request for honoured status on her sons" behalf. Whilst this redactional change is often interpreted merely as a plot-device to lessen the volition of the sons in making a direct request, that would be to overlook the more developed role of this female character in Matthew, who reappears as a witness to the crucifixion alongside Mary Magdalene and Mary the mother of James and Joseph (Mt 27:56) – in place of Salome (Mk 15:40) – yet is absent from the resurrection

> **Mt 20:25-28**
> ²⁵οἴδατε ὅτι <u>οἱ ἄρχοντες</u> τῶν ἐθνῶν κατακυριεύουσιν αὐτῶν
> καὶ οἱ μεγάλοι κατεξουσιάζουσιν αὐτῶν.
> ²⁶ οὐχ οὕτως <u>ἔσται</u> ἐν ὑμῖν,
> ἀλλ' ὃς ἐὰν θέλῃ ἐν ὑμῖν μέγας γενέσθαι ἔσται ὑμῶν διάκονος,
> ²⁷ καὶ ὃς ἂν θέλῃ ἐν ὑμῖν εἶναι πρῶτος ἔσται <u>ὑμῶν</u> δοῦλος·
> ²⁸ ὥσπερ ὁ υἱὸς τοῦ ἀνθρώπου οὐκ ἦλθεν διακονηθῆναι ἀλλὰ διακονῆσαι
> καὶ δοῦναι τὴν ψυχὴν αὐτοῦ λύτρον ἀντὶ πολλῶν.
>
> ²⁵ "You know that <u>the rulers</u> of the Gentiles lord it over them,
> and their great ones are tyrants over them.
> ²⁶ It <u>will</u> not <u>be</u> so among you;
> but whoever wishes to be great among you must be your servant,
> ²⁷ and whoever wishes to be first among you must be <u>your</u> slave;
> ²⁸ just as the Son of Man came not to be served but to serve,
> and to give his life a ransom for many." (NRSV)

Despite the near identical wording of the Matthean version, the force of the passage is subtly distinct from its Markan source owing to its recontextualization in the altered contours of the Matthean narrative. Two points are particularly worthy of further elaboration.

First, in line with a prominent emphasis in the Matthean narrative on scribal study and teaching,[50] especially of the Torah (cf. Mt 5:17-20), there are some striking verbal parallels with Mt 23:1-12, suggesting that the Pharisees and scribes function as additional negative foils to the Gentile models of leadership critiqued in the present passage.[51] The disciples are to avoid the designations 'rabbi' (23:7-8) or 'instructor' (καθηγητὴς)[52] (23:10), and the desire for respect and acknowledgement from the local populace sought by the scribes and Pharisees. Instead, the Matthean disciples are to consider themselves students of the Messiah (23:8, 11) and servants of one another ('The greatest among you will be your servant' (ὁ δὲ μείζων ὑμῶν ἔσται ὑμῶν διάκονος) (cf. Mt 20:26b)). Such close verbal parallels are

---

appearance to the two Marys (Mt 28:1-10) (cf. Emily Cheney, "The Mother of the Sons of Zebedee (Matthew 27:56)," *JSNT* 68 (1997): 13-21.).

[50] Cf. Dennis C. Duling, "The Matthean Brotherhood and Marginal Scribal Leadership," in *Modelling Early Christianity: Social-Scientific Studies of the New Testament in Its Context*, ed. Philip F. Esler (London and New York: Routledge, 1995), 174. "...the author of the Gospel is most likely a scribe (13:52). He is educated, literate, and sees the secrets of scripture in a sophisticated fashion"; cf. O. Lamar Cope, *Matthew, a Scribe Trained for the Kingdom of Heaven* (Washington DC: Catholic Biblical Association of America, 1976).

[51] Cf. Davies and Allison, *A Critical and Exegetical Commentary on the Gospel According to St Matthew*, 94, 264-281.

[52] καθηγητὴς "...means "leader" or "guide", most often academic leader or guide, that is "teacher", "tutor", "professor"." (Ibid., 278).

suggestive of a concrete illustration of the behaviour recommended for the target audience of Matthew: recognition and respect is not to be sought from the local populace, but rather from God alone, by an attitude of dedicated study of scripture, as interpreted by the Messiah, a community of students serving one another.

> Unlike the scribes and Pharisees (v 7), authorities in the church are to shun titles. Such titles are inconsistent with the demand for humility and mutuality and the need to restrict certain appellations to God and Christ. Brothers are equals, and none should be exalted by unnecessary adulation.[53]

Second, the positive model that is to be imitated, namely Jesus' offering his life as a ransom for many (Mt 20:28) has a greater potential to echo the figure of the "suffering servant" (cf. Isa 52:13-53:12) than its Markan counterpart (Mk 10:45), despite the absence of verbal parallels in this identically worded saying. This is because the broader Matthean narrative contains explicit allusions to the 'servant of YHWH' in two of the "fulfilment formulae" (cf. Mt 8:17 // Isa 53:4; Mt 12:17-21 // Isa 42:1-4).[54] Nonetheless, the extent to which the Christology of the Gospel of Matthew is shaped and informed by the '(suffering) servant' figure of Second Isaiah, is a complex question. Part of the complexity arises from the reception of the '*ebed* YHWH' in Second Temple Judaism more broadly. Whilst there is some evidence that this figure was picked up and reinterpreted messianically in certain Jewish circles (notably *the Similitudes of Enoch* (1 Enoch 37-71) (c. 1st century BCE/CE)), nonetheless, there is no suggestion that this exalted messianic figure was understood to suffer vicariously for others.[55] The pattern of the humiliation, death and vindication of God's

---

[53] Ibid., 275.

[54] Cf. Richard Beaton, "Messiah and Justice: A Key to Matthew's Use of Isaiah 42:1-4?," *JSNT* 75 (1999): 5-23; Richard Beaton, *Isaiah's Christ in Matthew's Gospel [SNTSMS 123]* (Cambridge: Cambridge University Press, 2002); Richard Beaton, "Isaiah in Matthew's Gospel," in *Isaiah in the New Testament*, ed. Steve Moyise and Maarten J.J. Menken (London and New York: T & T Clark/Continuum, 2005), 63-78; A.M. Leske, "Isaiah and Matthew: The Prophetic Influence in the First Gospel: A Report on Current Research," in *Jesus and the Suffering Servant: Isaiah 53 and Christian Origins*, ed. William H. Bellinger and William R. Farmer (Eugene OR: Wipf & Stock, 2009), 152-69; Maarten J.J. Menken, *Matthew's Bible: The Old Testament Text of the Evangelist* (Leuven: Peeters, 2004). chs. 2-4.

[55] On the reception of the "servant songs" of Second Isaiah in Second Temple Jewish literature, notably *1 Enoch* 37-71, see Martin Hengel and Daniel P. Bailey, "The Effective History of Isaiah 53 in the Pre-Christian Period," in *The Suffering Servant: Isaiah 53 in Jewish and Christian Sources*, ed. Bernd Janowski and Peter Stuhlmacher (Grand Rapids MI: Eerdmans, 2004); Darrell

'son' certainly fits the contours of the Matthean narrative, but the extent to which this has been shaped by the 'servant songs' of Second Isaiah remains a much debated issue.

Overall, the models to imitate and avoid are more sharply delineated in the Matthean version. The target audience are to avoid the caricatured self-aggrandisement of Gentile rulers (Mt 20:25-28) and Judean Torah experts (Mt 23:1-12) in favour of a model of discipleship imagined as a community of students taught by the Messiah, serving one another.[56] Furthermore, the positive role model of the self-giving service of the Son of Man may be traced, more evocatively, in the image of the servant of YHWH of Deutero-Isaiah that flows beneath the surface of the Matthean narrative, occasionally breaking the surface.[57]

Lk 22:24-27

The Lukan revision of the scene is re-contextualized in a more appropriate setting – the after-dinner discussion of a symposium (= Last Supper) (Lk 22:14-38),[58] corresponding more closely to περὶ βασιλείας conventions (cf. *Letter of Aristeas* 187-300).

Lk 22:24-27
Ἐγένετο δὲ καὶ φιλονεικία ἐν αὐτοῖς, τὸ τίς αὐτῶν δοκεῖ εἶναι μείζων.
²⁵ ὁ δὲ εἶπεν αὐτοῖς· οἱ βασιλεῖς τῶν ἐθνῶν κυριεύουσιν αὐτῶν
καὶ οἱ ἐξουσιάζοντες αὐτῶν εὐεργέται καλοῦνται.

D. Hannah, "Isaiah within Judaism of the Second Temple Period," in *Isaiah in the New Testament*, ed. Steve Moyise and Maarten J.J. Menken (London and New York: T & T Clark/Continuum, 2005); Joseph Blenkinsopp, "Reading Isaiah in Early Christianity with Special Reference to Matthew's Gospel," in *Opening the Sealed Book. Interpretations of the Book of Isaiah in Late Antiquity*, by Joseph Blenkinsopp (Grand Rapids MI: Eerdmans, 2006), 129-68.

[56] Cf. Warren Carter, *Matthew and the Margins: A Socio-Political and Religious Reading*, JSNT Sup 204 (Sheffield: Sheffield Academic Press, 2000), 46. "[The Gospel of Matthew] offers the audience a vision of life as voluntary marginal...."

[57] Cf. David Hill, "Son and Servant: An Essay on Matthean Christology," *JSNT* 6 (1980): 2-16.

[58] Cf. Dennis E. Smith, *From Symposium to Eucharist: The Banquet in the Early Christian World* (Minneapolis: Fortress Press, 2003), 262-, "...the entire Last Supper pericope shows signs of extensive editing by the author. This is evident not only in his unusual version of the meal itself (22:14-19a) but also in the extended 'table talk' of Jesus during the meal (22:21-38)" (262). Luke brings together a series of previously independent sayings, spoken in other contexts, to present Jesus instructing the disciples, in his last speech prior to death, on their continuing responsibilities and destinies (cf. C.F. Evans, *Saint Luke* (Philadelphia and London: Trinity Press International/SCM Press, 1990), 791-2).

> ²⁶ ὑμεῖς δὲ οὐχ οὕτως,
> ἀλλ' ὁ μείζων ἐν ὑμῖν γινέσθω ὡς ὁ νεώτερος καὶ ὁ ἡγούμενος ὡς ὁ διακονῶν.
> ²⁷ τίς γὰρ μείζων, ὁ ἀνακείμενος ἢ ὁ διακονῶν; οὐχὶ ὁ ἀνακείμενος;
> ἐγὼ δὲ ἐν μέσῳ ὑμῶν εἰμι ὡς ὁ διακονῶν.
>
> A dispute also arose among them as to which one of them was to be regarded as the greatest.
> ²⁵ But he said to them, "The kings of the Gentiles lord it over them; and those in authority over them are called benefactors.
> ²⁶ But not so with you;
> rather the greatest among you must become like the youngest, and the leader like one who serves.
> ²⁷ For who is greater, the one who is at the table or the one who serves? Is it not the one at the table?
> But I am among you as one who serves. (NRSV)

The tertiary-educated author of Luke's gospel clarifies the issue for his literate patron:[59] the focus of the debate is the Hellenistic conception of an 'ideal ruler', the model of a virtuous monarch who is perceived to be a 'benefactor' (εὐεργέτης) to his subjects. As noted earlier, one of the recurrent motifs of an 'ideal king' in Hellenistic περὶ βασιλείας literature is his role as 'benefactor' of his subjects, through gifts of grain, funding civic building projects, patronizing temples, and endowing cultic celebrations.[60] '...a benefactor maintained his reputation by repeated benefactions such that "euergetism was a long-term reciprocal relationship between a benefactor and his/her community"'.[61]

> A good king must extend assistance to those in need of it and be beneficent, and this assistance should be given not in one way only but in every possible manner....Good kings, indeed, have dispositions similar to the Gods, especially resembling Zeus, the universal ruler who is venerable and honourable through the

---

[59] On the compositional skills of the author of Luke-Acts that cohere with a writer who received at least a minimal tertiary education in prose composition (προγυμνασματα exercises) see Mikeal C. Parsons, "Luke and the Progymnasmata: A Preliminary Investigation into the Preliminary Exercises," in *Contextualizing Acts: Lukan Narrative and Greco-Roman Discourse*, ed. Todd Penner and Caroline van der Stichele (Atlanta GA: SBL, 2003), 43-63.

[60] Cf. Jonathan Marshall, *Jesus, Patrons and Benefactors: Roman Palestine and the Gospel of Luke*, WUNT 259 (Tübingen: Mohr Siebeck, 2009), 25-53; Stephan Joubert, *Paul as Benefactor: Reciprocity, Strategy and Theological Reflection in Paul's Collection*, WUNT 124 (Tübingen: Mohr Siebeck, 2000), 17-70.

[61] Marshall, *Jesus, Patrons and Benefactors: Roman Palestine and the Gospel of Luke*; Joubert, *Paul as Benefactor: Reciprocity, Strategy and Theological Reflection in Paul's Collection*, 57-8.

magnanimous pre-eminence of virtue. He is benign because he is beneficent and the giver of good. (Diotogenes, Pythagorean philosopher (c. 3rd/2nd century BCE?)[62]

It is this concept of the 'ideal king', so prevalent in Hellenistic and Graeco-Roman literature, that Luke first summarizes in v 25: 'The kings of the Gentiles exercise lordship (κυριεύουσιν) over them and those in authority over them are called benefactors (εὐεργέται)'.[63]

The precise force of the Lukan critique of rulers as authority figures and benefactors (vv 26-27) is more difficult to tease out, not least the opening critique ὑμεῖς δὲ οὐχ οὕτως (v 26a), literally 'but not so you (pl)'. What is being disavowed for disciples: the role of benefactor *per se*, or the manner in which the benefaction system currently operates in the Roman Empire?[64] The latter alternative is more plausible not least because the author of Luke-Acts uses the language of 'benefaction' elsewhere to encapsulate Jesus' role. Peter's speech to the centurion, Cornelius, is couched in vocabulary tailored for a civic functionary:

Acts 10:36, 38

> You know the message he [God] sent to the people of Israel, preaching peace by Jesus Christ – he is lord of all (πάντων κύριος)...how God anointed Jesus of Nazareth with the Holy Spirit and with power; how he went about doing good

---

[62] As cited in Johannes Stobaeus 4.7.62 (5th century CE), Smith, *Christ the Ideal King: Cultural Context Rhetorical Strategy and the Power of Divine Monarchy in Ephesians*, 41.

[63] The initial reference to kings as benefactors carries no pejorative overtones. Marshall, *Jesus, Patrons and Benefactors: Roman Palestine and the Gospel of Luke*, 306. "Luke seems to use εὐεργέτης without an inherent critique of those who have the title within the term itself". This is further corroborated by the positive use of related nominal and verbal forms in Acts to refer to the good deeds/benefactions of apostles (Acts 4:9) and Jesus (Acts 10:38).

[64] A minority third option is that Lk 22:24-27 advocates the Roman benefaction system *as it stands* for disciples to imitate (David J. Lull, "The Servant-Benefactor as a Model of Greatness (Luke 22:24-30)," *NovT* 28 (1986): 289-305.), the critique of v 26a directed against their present failure to do so: "But you are not so [called]" (ie. benefactors), supplying an indicative form of the verb καλέω as the implied verb in the clause. For a critique of this reading see Peter K Nelson, "The Flow of Thought in Luke 22.24-27," *JSOT* 43 (1991): 113-23; Halvor Moxnes, "Patron-Client Relations and the New Community in Luke-Acts," in *The Social World of Luke-Acts: Models for Interpretation*, ed. Jerome H. Neyrey (Peabody MA: Hendrickson, 1991), 241-68; Yong-Sung Ahn, *The Reign of God and Rome in Luke's Passion Narrative: An East Asian Global Perspective* (Leiden: Brill, 2006).

(εὐεργετῶν) [lit. 'being a benefactor'] and healing all who were oppressed by the devil, for God was with him.[65]

The language of 'benefaction' is similarly applied to the healing ministry of the apostles (Peter and John) in another of Peter's speeches in Acts, before the Judean ruling class:

Acts 4:8-10

> Then Peter, filled with the Holy Spirit, said to them, "Rulers of the people (ἄρχοντες τοῦ λαοῦ) and elders,[9] if we are questioned today because of a good deed (εὐεργεσίᾳ) [benefaction] done to someone who was sick and are asked how this man has been healed, [10] let it be known to all of you, and to all the people of Israel, that this man is standing before you in good health by the name of Jesus Christ of Nazareth, whom you crucified, whom God raised from the dead.[66]

Luke-Acts *appropriates* the model of the Roman patron-client system as a template for depicting the divine benefits that are mediated through Jesus and the apostles as *benefactors*, in such a way that an alternative hierarchy is sketched:

> Rather than adopting the hierarchy of his day with the emperor on top and Herodian or Roman leaders on the second tier, Jesus presents a new hierarchy with God on top, Jesus as a mediator, and the apostles on the third rung.[67]

This alternative template is not limited, however, to a superficial alteration of the names on the 'organizational chart' of the Roman patron-client system (i.e. the Roman Emperor's name is erased and replaced by 'Jesus'). Central to the Lukan model is the contrast between the *manner* in which rulers in the Roman imperial system function as leaders (exercise

---

[65] Mikeal C. Parsons, *Acts*, Paideia (Grand Rapids MI: Eerdmans, 2008), 153.: "...Peter's speech characterizes Jesus' ministry as one of benefaction....Benefaction is a particularly appropriate image for a Gentile audience familiar with patronage...[Luke] argues...that Jesus' healing ministry was itself the act of a generous benefactor engaged in a struggle against demonic forces...."

[66] Ibid., 63. "Peter...identifies the healing as a "good deed" (4:9) or "benefaction" (*euergesia*). This is the technical word associated with the benefaction system so prominent in the social structures of the ancient Graeco-Roman world...."

[67] Marshall, *Jesus, Patrons and Benefactors: Roman Palestine and the Gospel of Luke*, 321.

lordship over others) (v 25) and the *manner* in which disciples are advised to function as leaders (adopting the status of servant/lowest rank (= youngest)) (v 26). Accordingly, the Lukan narrative has potentially revolutionary force: "The 'servant benefactor' model Luke imagines cannot be established without destroying the Roman patron-client system."[68] The unequal, reciprocal, relationship between patron and client is detonated in the Lukan reconfiguration of the benefaction model, eschewing the controlling power of the benefactor over his clients (cf. Lk 6:34-35 'If you lend to those from whom you hope to receive, what credit is that to you? ...lend, expecting nothing in return').

How, precisely, are the apostles to exercise leadership (ὁ ἡγούμενος) (Lk 22:26) as those who are of lowest rank (slave/youngest)? As in the Markan passage, Jesus is pointed to as the model to imitate: despite his evident leadership role over the group, reclining at table as the host of this symposium (Lk 22:14), he nonetheless characterizes his role not as 'one who reclines' (ὁ ἀνακείμενος) but as 'one who serves' (ὁ διακονῶν) (Lk 22:27). Unlike the comparable Johannine scene in which the role of servant is enacted by Jesus in undertaking the menial task of footwashing (Jn 13:1-20), in the Lukan narrative the antithesis between saying and action are simply juxtaposed, as the Lukan Jesus remains at his place at table. Jesus' role as one who serves must therefore be sketched from the broader contours of the Lukan plot, and the manner of Jesus' service of others throughout the narrative culminating in his death/resurrection.[69]

As a consequence of this alternative system of divine benefactions, the eschatological authority of the Twelve, as enthroned kings and judges in the kingdom of God (Lk 22:28-30), is not to be striven for in the present, but rather conferred as a gift by Jesus, the benefactor *par excellence* in the Lukan narrative, as a reward for remaining (διαμένω) with him in his trials (v 29). An inherent tension is once again evident: is the Roman imperial model of sovereignty and authority merely deferred, reinscribed once more in the eschatological kingdom, when the Twelve will once again recline at the top table, rather than waiting upon others in service?[70]

CONCLUSION

The Synoptic Gospels' paradoxical image of a ruler as "slave of all" (Mk 10:35-45 and parallels) struck a powerful counter-cultural note in its

---

[68] Ahn, *The Reign of God and Rome in Luke's Passion Narrative: An East Asian Global Perspective*, 166.

[69] Cf. Joel B. Green, "The Death of Jesus, God's Servant," in *Reimaging the Death of the Lukan Jesus*, ed. Dennis D. Sylva (Frankfurt: Anton Hain, 1990), 18-28, 170-73. Green considers that the central Christological image in Luke-Acts is the presentation of Jesus as the humble and exalted Servant of YHWH (Deutero-Isaiah).

[70] Cf. Don Garlington, "Who Is the Greatest?" *JETS* 53 (2010): 287-316.

original historical setting. Hellenistic and Roman models of an 'ideal king' in περὶ βασιλείας literature emphasize the pre-eminent role of the virtuous monarch as a pattern for his subjects to *imitate*. This motif rarely depicts the philanthropic ruler as a servant/slave of his subjects, and even on sporadic occasions when it does so the notion of 'noble servitude' that occurs (e.g. Seneca, *De clementia*) retains an emphasis upon royal privilege.

In the Markan and Matthean versions the injunction – "it shall not be so with you" – serves as a sharp critique and rejection of all contemporary authority models, ranging from the stock-character type of the unrighteous Gentile ruler/tyrant Herod (cf. Mk 6:14-29) to the caricatured foil of Judean scriptural authorities (scribes and Pharisees, Mt 23:1-12). Greater nuance is evidenced in the Lukan version, in which the patron-client system is dislodged and reappropriated, such that Jesus and the apostles now function as the divinely mandated *benefactors* of all (cf. Acts 4:8-10, 10:36-8).

Nonetheless, tensions and ambiguities remain in the idealistic descriptions and temporary duration of the alternative models sketched. In the Markan and Matthean versions titles (king, teacher, rabbi) and authority roles are rejected as part of the old order that is passing away in the eschatological ferment, categorically dismissed in favour of a life of self-giving service – to the point of death – in imitation of the Son of Man (Mk 10:45 pars). Yet, those same hierarchies of Roman imperial oppression which were so summarily dismissed are re-inscribed, post eschaton, when Jesus, and the Twelve, are envisioned as enthroned in the roles of ruler and courtiers in the (messianic) kingdom (cf. Mt 19:27-30, Mk 10:40). The template is only temporarily effaced, returning once again in the eschatological kingdom, altered only by the identities of those who occupy the places of honour (last becoming first) (Mk 10:31, Mt 20:16).

The Lukan narrative offers greater potential for a constructive model of servant-leadership in the interim period between cross and eschaton (cf. Lk 22:28-30), [71] in its re-imagining of the patron-client system, divested of the coercive power of the benefactor. The Lukan insight to express and reimagine the idealistic injunction of his source-text (Mk 10:35-35) by means of a critical engagement with the concrete social/political/economic model of patron-client relations, serves as a catalyst for a postmodern reimagining of twenty-first century social/political/economic models of authority in critical dialogue with the counter-cultural force of these Synoptic texts.

Heythrop College, London, Great Britain

---

[71] Cf. P. De Mey, "Authority in the Church: The Appeal to Lk 22:21-34 in Roman Catholic Magisterial Teaching and in the Ecumenical Dialogue," in *Luke and His Readers: Festschrift A. Denaux*, ed. R. Bieringer, G. van Belle, and J. Verheyden (Leuven: Leuven University Press, 2005), 307-23.

CHAPTER II

AUTHORITY WITHOUT SOVEREIGNTY: TOWARDS A REASSESSMENT OF DIVINE POWER

ROGER MITCHELL

Two key components of the work of Hans Urs von Balthasar provide convenient signposts for the direction this chapter takes. I refer to his reaffirmation of the transcendental of beauty,[1] and his emphasis on *diastasis*.[2] For I suggest that his recognition of the need to proceed beyond truth and goodness marks his insight into the consequence of a historical distortion of these first two transcendentals. A distortion brought about by what we might call the subsumption, or colonization of transcendence by sovereignty, the effects of which have rendered the difference between the divine and human, the creation and God, distinctly problematic in a way that would not necessarily have been the case without it. To put it another way, there is no essential reason why truth and virtue should become the source of oppression, nor the difference between the divine and human be used to justify hierarchy and inequality. However, once the exercise of sovereign, hierarchical power is perceived to be the means to the eschatological peace proclaimed by the gospel, then the possession of true knowledge and the codification of the common good become the weapons of social subjugation and control, and the ontological differences between the divine and the human provide the legitimation for the supposedly undeniable status of ruler over ruled. The word 'sovereignty' derives from 'sovereign,' which, in its original use according to the Oxford Dictionary, denotes "a supreme ruler, especially a monarch." 'Sovereignty' refers to the expression of the rule of such a sovereign and is associated with the terminology of power, dominion, and authority and is closely linked in its etymology with the word 'empire.' 'Sovereignty' emphasizes the character of rule as supreme while the word 'empire' identifies the nature of rule as ordered. Together they carry the idea of hierarchy under a supreme rulership. This chapter proposes that sovereignty and empire are secular political forms that have deeply penetrated the Western perception of power but are incompatible with the divine nature as revealed in the testimony of Jesus.

---

[1] Fergus Kerr, *After Aquinas: Versions of Thomism* (London: Blackwell, 2002). 1.

[2] Lucy Gardner and David Moss, "Something Like Time; Something like the Sexes - an Essay in Reception," in *Balthasar at the End of Modernity* (Edinburgh: T & T Clark, 1999). 70.

Given that a misconception of the nature of the divine and its relation to the human race has befallen us, then an investigation into the affective apprehension of God and the characteristics of the divine and human natures indicates the way forward for a contemporary rediscovery of the nature of authority. This aspect of Balthasar's renewed emphasis on the affective impact of the beautiful, and the use of analogy that the perceived *diastasis* between the divine and human opens up, provides a welcome response to modernity's suspicion of transcendence *per se* as the cause of oppression and inequality. It also resonates with a similar earlier response to the perceived ecclesial monopoly of truth, morality and the mediation of ultimate knowledge about the human and divine that took place at the end of the medieval era. I allude here to the questions raised over the nature of knowledge of the divine by the univocalists and nominalists associated with the thought of Duns Scotus and William of Ockham, whose work challenged the accepted hierarchies of knowledge of both church and empire. It has been suggested that these theologians were the precursors of the subsequent rejection of transcendence and embrace of secularization that developed from the enlightenment onwards and has characterized modernity and its aftermath.[3]

A Long, Deep, Trajectory of Suspicion

The prefiguring by the nominalists of Balthasar's emphases suggests a far longer, deeper, trajectory for the suspicion of doctrinaire configurations of truth and goodness and differences between the divine and human that hierarchical mediations by ecclesiastical and sacerdotal authorities are supposedly necessary to bridge. All of which suggests that a sense of oppression and loss has pervaded the history of Western Christianity for a very long time. The work of Michel Certeau on the fifteenth century mystics characterizes this as the loss of a body,[4] and Henri de Lubac traces this loss back to an inversion between the *corpus verum* and *corpus mysticum* that took place in the twelfth century.[5] Recognizing an underlying genealogy of sovereign power to be responsible for the defamation of truth and goodness by their association with juridical configurations of authority, Paul Fletcher has called for the excavation of the process whereby faith became beholden to the force of law. He considers that the historical development of what he

---

[3] See John Milbank, *The Word Made Strange* (Oxford: Blackwell Publishers, 1997); John Milbank, "Postmodern Critical Augustinianism," in *The Radical Orthodoxy Reader*, ed. John Milbank and Simon Oliver (London and New York: Routledge, 2009).

[4] Michel De Certeau, *The Mystic Fable* (Chicago: University of Chicago Press, 1992). 79-80.

[5] Henri De Lubac, *Corpus Mysticum: The Eucharist and the Church in the Middle Ages*, ed. Laurence Paul Hemming and Susan Frank Parsons (London: SCM Press, 2006). 80.

calls "juridico-politics" has brought theology itself to a point beyond which it survives only as a parasite.[6]

If the subsumption of transcendence by sovereignty is a historical reality responsible for obscuring the true referent for faith, and is as serious as Fletcher suggests, then a thorough historical-theological investigation is clearly called for. My own response to this clarion call has resulted in the extensive research presented in my books *Church, Gospel and Empire: How the Politics of Sovereignty Impregnated the West*, and *The Fall of the Church* and indicates a point of penetration or fall at the time of the 4th century partnership between church and empire choreographed by Eusebius of Caesarea and the Roman Emperor Constantine. It suggests that since then the correlation of transcendence and sovereign power has been so prevalent as to impregnate the perception of the gospel testimony itself. As a result the incarnation is assumed to reveal a divine kingship able to be equated with an earthly Caesar and to justify, if not actually cause, the imperial authority of the papal monarchs and their earthly partners throughout the history of Western Christendom. The effect of this has been so pervasive that it has consistently circumvented attempts to return to the *corpus verum* of the lowly Jesus of Nazareth such as the lives of Francis of Assisi, Mother Teresa and other radical reformers exemplify.

A Completely Different Configuration of Power

It appears to be necessary to initiate a recovery of the kenotic understanding of authority, not as a nuance or qualification to sovereignty but as a completely different alternative configuration of divine power. Such a configuration, in accord with Balthasar's emphasis on the beautiful, needs to engage the affections, along the lines of the economy of response developed by Graham Ward,[7] which encourages attention to those aspects of the text that locate the reader firstly within the emotive and relational aspects of the narrative. Rather than depending any longer on the primacy of the mind or conscience, a process of giving ourselves to and receiving back from the text provides the means to bypass the distorted image and recover the incarnate God of love. Walter Brueggermann, drawing on Paul Ricoeur's work on the hermeneutic of suspicion, indicates a process whereby it is possible to return to the previously negatively received components of the narrative.[8] Hopefully it will then prove possible to recover an expression of truth and virtue uncontaminated by a mistaken perception of the divine nature. But we have to get there first.

---

[6] Paul Fletcher, *Disciplining the Divine* (Farnham and Burlington: Ashgate, 2009). 178.

[7] Graham Ward, *Christ and Culture* (Oxford: Blackwell, 2005), 59.

[8] Walter Brueggemann, *Deep Memory, Exuberant Hope: Contested Truth in a Post-Christian World* (Minneapolis: Augsburg Fortress, 2000), 44-45.

Contemporary work on kenotic theology illustrates the importance of taking time to recover a thorough reconfiguration of authority through a kenotic lens. Kenotic theology, of course, is no recent or marginal innovation. In the estimation of David Brown "by the latter half of the twentieth century most major theologians had come to speak of kenosis as lying at the very heart of the life of God as Trinity."[9] Yet such is the longevity and deep structural character of the subsumption of the divine by sovereign power, there remains a tendency for kenotic theology itself to default to sovereign power rather than engender a different kind of power altogether. David Brown, despite his exhaustive and insightful overview of kenotic theology, himself offers an analogy of incarnation that falls short of escaping the thralls of sovereign power. Brown suggests that the role of God in the incarnation is like that of Stanislavsky's Method actor.[10] The difficulty here is not with the analogy itself, which works well to illustrate Brown's point. Rather the problem is that it puts God in a position in which he may not be essentially kenotic in his use of power, but just pretending, or putting on an act, which he later relinquishes when once he has made his point. Brown goes on to say "the attempt to follow Christ in this world should not always take the kenotic path. Sometimes power is the right instrument to use."[11] In fact Brown goes so far as to suggest that the resurrection may be an example of this non-kenotic use of power.

The Nature of the Difference between Divine and Human

This differentiation between kenosis and power takes us to the heart of the primary concerns of this chapter. Here the deepest issues of *diastasis* come to the forefront. They may even present a problem for Balthasar's panoramic analogy of Theo-drama itself. What is the nature of the difference between the divine and human? How can the creature comprehend the creator? What is the nature of the power that created us and could save and resurrect us? Above all, can we move to a standpoint that breaks completely with sovereign power? These are questions that the incarnation might be expected to resolve. But if, as has already been suggested, our understanding of the incarnation has been deformed by the subsumption of transcendence by sovereignty, to the degree that Jesus' claims to truth and goodness raise suspicion of religious oppression and subjugation, a new approach to the incarnation is needed. A further problem is that if the extent of the perceived *diastasis* between the human and the divine renders the incarnation at best only an analogy, a picture, a dramatic act, and not the full revelation of the character of the divine and its image in

---

[9] David Brown, *Divine Humanity: Kenosis Defended and Explored* (London: SCM Press, 2011), 3.
[10] Ibid., 251-3.
[11] Ibid., 264.

humanity, then room for oppressions based on inequalities of difference remains.

These are profound and potentially controversial matters. But they are of vital importance. Graham Ward, for example, in his discussion of the otherness of God, understands the incarnation itself to be an analogy, and lest we should be in any doubt about what he implies, refers to the "ineliminable aporia, an eradicable secondariness, a following after, which is the hallmark of human figuration ultimately understood as discipleship."[12] In a similar way, in an exciting attempt to reimagine politics through the lens of the eucharist, William Cavanaugh still falls short of dealing with the implications of priestly mediation for a genuinely egalitarian configuration of human relations. Does the testimony of Jesus point to a hierarchical priesthood or not? If it does not, the task of configuring leadership without hierarchy is a challenge we must face, as Leonardo Boff attempted when he positioned the eucharist at the heart of base communities without "rigid rules; hierarchies; prescribed relationships in a framework of a distinction of functions, qualities, and titles."[13]

If in our desire to honour God's greatness and the wisdom of past thinkers, we apportion qualities to God that justify domination, then we are on dangerous ground. As Richard Rohr has expressed it "We end up worshipping Jesus as a quasi-substitute for following him, which is of course what he actually proposed."[14] If, however, the sense of otherness or wonder is a response to the depth of divine love, not its difference in kind to its image in humanity, then we are able to speak of a different kind of power to sovereignty. Instead of applying the commonly accepted human forms of power to God, we ask whether it is possible to find a way to apply the divine power seen in the incarnation to humanity. Can we discover a power that is given to humanity and not exercised over humanity? This is the nub of the matter. It is the proposal of this chapter that just such a power, the power of love, is revealed in the gospel testimony of Jesus, who according to the Johannine account, famously said to Philip, "He who has seen Me has seen the Father."[15] If we argue from Jesus to God, and not the other way round, we will end up with a divine and human template that is wholly characterized by kenotic love.

Arguing from Jesus to God

Just as there is nothing essentially new about kenotic theology, there

---

[12] Graham Ward, "Kenosis: Death, Discourse and Resurrection," in *Balthasar at the End of Modernity* (Edinburgh: T & T Clark, 1999), 44.

[13] Leonardo Boff, *Ecclesiogenesis* (New York: Orbis Books, 1996), 4.

[14] Richard Rohr, "The Franciscan Opinion," in *Stricken By God?*, ed. Brad Jersak and Michael Hardin (Grand Rapids MI and Cambridge: Eerdmans, 2007), 208 note 4.

[15] John 14: 9.

is nothing unique in this endeavour to argue from Jesus to God. Barth states unequivocally of our understanding of deity that "it cannot be gathered from any notion of supreme, absolute, non-worldly being. It can only be learned from what took place in Christ" and asserts that we must "learn to correct our notions of the being of God" in the light of the incarnation.[16] John Milbank makes a similar point when he suggests that to point to the narrative of the life of Jesus is the only certain way we can say anything definite about God.[17] N.T. Wright explains that it is "not that we know what the word God means and can discover the extent to which this God was present in, or revealed through, Jesus; rather that, by close attention to Jesus himself, we are invited to discover, perhaps for the first time, just who the creator and covenant God was and is all along."[18] Bruce McCormack's work affirms the direction even more strongly when he suggests "reversing the *genus maiestaticum* ('the genus of majesty') of classical Lutheranism and its *genus tapeinoticum* ('the genus of humility'), now to be applied directly to God the Son: instead of divine attributes given to the human, the communication of human attributes to the divine."[19]

The particular burden of the argument being laboured here is the need to achieve an incarnational understanding of the authority of love untrammelled by the vestiges of sovereign power. The concern is to substantiate an authority without sovereignty. In order to distinguish between kenotic theology in general, with its possible corruption by sovereignty, and a kenosis argued directly from Jesus to God defined by self-giving love unadulterated by sovereignty, some of us have concocted the word *kenarchy*. Derived from *keno* to empty and *archē* to rule, kenarchy refers to the authority of love without sovereignty. While kenosis, in its traditional understanding, is defined in the Oxford dictionary as "the renunciation of the divine nature in the incarnation," kenarchy understands the incarnation as the full revelation of the divine nature. It signals that to empty out power as a love gift to the other is the very essence of both divine authority and its human image.

So what does love without sovereignty look like? There are several key gospel texts that portray this clearly, such as the descent from the high place of the mountain down to the level place among the people in Luke 6, with the ensuing call to love one's enemies. In particular there are the events of the last supper surrounding the discussions of who is the greatest. Luke's account of Jesus' question to his disciples configures leadership without sovereignty, "For who is greater, the one who reclines at the table

---

[16] Karl Barth, *Church Dogmatics*, ed. G. W. Bromley and T. E. Torrance (Edinburgh: T & T Clark, 1956), 177 and 186.

[17] Milbank, "Postmodern Critical Augustinianism," 55.

[18] Wright, *Jesus and the Victory of God*, 214.

[19] Bruce McCormack, "The Humility of the Eternal Son: A Reformed Version of Kenotic Christology," *International Journal of Systematic Theology* 8 (2006): 243-251.

or the one who serves? Is it not the one who reclines at the table? But I am among you as the one who serves."[20] The Johannine story of the footwashing clearly casts the divine authority in contrast to Satanic rebellion and human betrayal in a way that prefigures the cross and poignantly points forward to the Philippian hymn to Jesus' kenotic love. Here "love to the end" that comes from God and goes back to God is manifest in human terms when Jesus "got up from supper, and laid aside His garments; and taking a towel, He girded Himself. Then He poured water into the basin, and began to wash the disciples' feet and to wipe them with the towel with which He was girded."[21]

The Full Theopolitical Impact of the Gospel

In preference to proof texts, however, it is more faithful to the testimony of Jesus to view the whole chronology of the incarnation as the manifestation of the authority of love. By this means the full theopolitical impact of the gospel can be exposed and the resurrection seen as the political act that substantiates a new humanity, as the apostle Paul saw so clearly. To this end the final part of the chapter begins with the initial sequence of the introductory events of Jesus' ministry and indicates their progress to culmination at the cross. In so doing crucial aspects of the authority of love without sovereignty are explicated. The sequence of the Jesus story leads to the proposal that there are five key components of the authority of love, all of which result from the first and culminate in the last. The first is a relational encounter with love, which as the narrative goes on to show, undoes sovereignty, disarms the powers, empowers the powerless and substantiates a new humanity. Luke places the relational encounter with love in an emphatically trinitarian context that forms the climax to his account of Jesus' baptism, where "the Holy Spirit descended upon Him in bodily form like a dove, and a voice came out of heaven, 'You are My beloved Son, in You I am well-pleased.'"[22] The self-emptying kenotic act of baptism is affirmed by the descent of the Spirit and the loving affirmation of the Father. In this way the whole of Jesus' ministry is rooted in the loving interrelationship of the Father and the Spirit. The context of the association of the Godhead together in the sin of the human race represented by Jesus' own participation in John's baptism of repentance is proof of a love that extends beyond the exclusive love of one's own kind and includes the other, specifically one's enemies. It is impossible to overestimate the impact and importance of a deep relational encounter with a love that loves through and beyond us and includes our enemies. This is the kind of love that completes me but is not only about me. Without this, love has no authority. As Luke later describes, Jesus was very clear about this, for "even sinners love those

---

[20] Luke 22: 27.
[21] John 13: 4-5.
[22] Luke 3:22.

who love them."[23] The original loving authority that undoes empire, disarms the powers, empowers the powerless and substantiates a new humanity is not a self-centered love but flows out from the love between the Father, Son and Holy Spirit. It is a love that so affirms the identity and value of a human being that the whole of humanity is thereby affirmed. The story of Jesus affirms the existence of this kind of love.

An Authority That Undoes Empire

Contemporary theological, archaeological and historical research puts beyond reasonable doubt the claim that Jesus' ministry confronted the Roman Empire. King Herod in the north of Israel and the high priestly family of Annas and Caiaphas in the south were the puppet representatives of Roman rule.[24] The stones that cried out ascribed divine titles to Augustus and Tiberias Caesar, titles like Son of God and Saviour that Jesus applied to himself.[25] In this way the kingdom of love he proclaimed was positioned as a qualitatively different authority to empire from the very start. The authority of this kingdom of love undoes empire in three ways. Firstly, the government of love is measured by love for one's enemies. But, as Carl Schmitt shows, sovereignty is defined by the distinction between friend and enemy.[26] So the authority of love quite literally undoes the very foundations of empire by making my enemy my friend, even at the cost of my death. Quite literally the authority of love provides for a government of peace that makes wars to cease. The domination of the other, with their territory and resources, for the benefit of a particular tribe, city, people group, religion, culture or civilization is rendered inoperative by the government of love. Secondly, the authority of love replaces the fear of lack that is basic to empire with faith in a divine generosity based on an economy of gift and so removes the need for dependence on an economics of domination. Luke's account of Jesus' words underlines this clearly. "Do not seek what you will eat and what you will drink, and do not keep worrying. For all these things the nations of the world eagerly seek; but your Father knows that you need these things. But seek His kingdom, and these things will be added to you."[27]

Thirdly, love embraces the penalty for resistance that undergirds the sovereignty system. Jesus introduced the cross from the start of his public teaching as the essential symbol of what it meant to follow him, long before

---

[23] Luke 6:32.

[24] Richard Horsley, *Jesus and Empire* (Minneapolis: Fortress Press, 2003), 34.

[25] John D. Crossan and Jonathan L. Reed, *In Search of Paul* (New York: Harper San Francisco, 2004), 11.

[26] Carl Schmitt, *Theory of the Partisan: Intermediate Commentary on the Concept of the Political* (New York: Telos Press, 2007), 85.

[27] Luke 12: 29-31.

he began to point towards it as the literal and inevitable culmination of his life. In this way Jesus' death and resurrection measure the heart of the praxis and the consequence of the government of love. It is the heart of kenarchy from which all the further characteristics of the authority of love flow. It measures an unquenchable authority that ultimately carries all before it, not because it insists on its own way, but because it willingly embraces the worst that any alternative force can do. The work of contemporary Italian philosopher Giorgio Agamben can help us here. Drawing on Carl Schmitt's configuration of sovereignty, Agamben exposes what he calls the state of exception that lies behind all sovereign power.[28] It signals the point at which the military, legal and economic norms are suspended when an alternative, other, behaviour threatens the continuation of the existing order. Agamben suggests that the imprisonment and torture without trial in the no-man's land of Guantanamo is the sign of the state of exception in contemporary America. In the Roman Empire of Jesus' day, it was crucifixion. This is part of the significance of the cross, and the reason why it featured so soon and centrally long before the culmination of Jesus' love for his enemies at Calvary. The cross is the willing embrace of the worst deterrent or punishment that can, will or might be put in place to stop someone from acting in such a way as to ultimately damage or contradict the perceived self-interest of a given sovereign society. It is the decision to love one's enemies in a way that willingly embraces death at the hands of the existing political system if that is the outcome of loving others.

An Authority That Disarms the Powers

The sequence of the Jesus story takes us directly from his own trinitarian relational encounter with love to a major confrontation with Satan. Straight after his baptism the Spirit led him to confront the devil in the wilderness.[29] I suggest that the three temptations that make up that confrontation expose deep structures of evil that undergird the foundations of sovereign power.[30] All three configure a self-centered use of power, and the social and political structures that emanate from them and the evil spirit behind them constitute the powers. By this measure the essential powers of empire are the economics that preserve one's personal and tribal survival at the expense of other human beings; the politics that dominate one's fellow humans and their socio-cultural lives; and the competitive drive to risk all to gain the high ground of religion, fame and popularity. It is important to recollect how the story depicts the way an encounter with altruistic love accentuates an awareness of the powers. The authority of love then deliberately confronts them head on, but not with the violence, law and

---

[28] Giorgio Agamben, *State of Exception*, trans. Kevin Attell (Chicago and London: University of Chicago Press, 2005), 32.

[29] Luke 4: 1.

[30] Matthew 4: 1-13; Luke 4: 1-11.

appeasement that are the tools of sovereign power, but with the word of love from the mouth of God that the baptism incident narrates, with its resultant worship, service and humility. Even in relations with the devil, seen here as representing ultimate evil, dialogue replaces violence, and the use of the written word is conversational not judicial. The devil remains free to leave. The final "be gone" is until "an opportune time," until another opportunity to oppose Jesus presents itself, and there is certainly no attempt here to appease the devil. When the culmination of the confrontation of Jesus and the powers takes place at the cross it is this same loving authority that is manifest. The authority of love at the cross is seen in Jesus' willing suffering at the hand of the powers in order to prove the enduring victory of a life given in love for the other, not in violent retribution against the powers.

An Authority That Empowers the Powerless

In the Magnificat, Mary spells out her insight into the divine nature as the authority that empowers the powerless: "He has brought down rulers from their thrones, and has exalted those who were humble."[31] In so doing she exemplifies the first gospel category for the empowerment of the powerless, for her own attraction of the divine favour marks the instatement of women that the testimony of Jesus achieves. Her focus on the hungry marks the second category, the poor. Altogether there are some six main foci of empowerment in the gospel narrative, instating women, prioritizing children, advocating for the poor, caring for the creation, freeing prisoners and caring for the sick. A great deal of work to meet the physical needs of the powerless among people and the rest of the creation has already been attempted in the history of the Church and the Western world as a result of the gospel, and continues. But it is frequently vitiated by the overarching context of sovereign power. The church, instead of being a prophetic servant community able to challenge or support the prevailing political power, becomes a legitimating tool for the contemporary government or its resistance, or subsides into an ineffective and irresponsible sub-culture. William Cavanaugh unpacks the twentieth century implications of this in his analysis of the church in General Pinochet's Chile.[32] But the authority of love squares the circle of need and powerlessness. As the apostle Paul saw so clearly, reconciliation and empowerment together make up the fullness of divine authority. God shares his throne with us and that changes everything.[33] Power sharing makes government and empowerment a single, synonymous initiative, not mere associates, let alone competitors. The practice of empowering the powerless soon clarifies who are friends and

---

[31] Luke 1: 52.

[32] cf. William Cavanaugh, *Torture and Eucharist* (Oxford and Malden MA: Blackwell Publishers, 1998), 110.

[33] Ephesians 2: 6.

who are enemies, for if these six categories identify the primary targets of kenotic love, those individuals and institutions that deliberately or unconsciously oppress them are identified as enemies. These in turn provide a measure for the chasm of difference that needs to be crossed and the extent of love that is required for peace to be realised. Jesus' encounter with the powers choreographs the way.

An Authority That Substantiates a New Humanity

By manifesting the authority of love as a human being, the incarnation of Jesus not only reveals the divine nature, it recovers the image of God in human nature. Kenotic love is the essence of the authority of God and is given back to the world in the incarnation as the basis for a new humanity. Thomas Torrance helpfully describes this as the vicarious humanity of Christ.[34] In order to substantiate this new humanity or what Michael Hardt and Antonio Negri term "construct the multitude,"[35] it was necessary for Jesus to take on all that stood in the way of the authority of love. Undoing empire, disarming the powers, empowering the powerless, all brought him inexorably to the cross where he confronted them all with a love measured by loving his enemies, even to the point of laying down his life for them in death. It is clear from the synoptic writers' insistence on Jesus' repeated statements of his need to go to Jerusalem and be crucified and slain, and rise again on the third day, that without laying down his life the authority of love would remain unsubstantiated. The disciples, with their sovereignty understanding of power, simply did not understand this. This is also the clear point of the Johannine note in qualification of Jesus' description of the coming of the Spirit: "But this He spoke of the Spirit, whom those who believed in Him were to receive; for the Spirit was not yet given, because Jesus was not yet glorified." The authority of love is the life laid down in love to the point of death itself, and its first fruit is resurrection. Until Jesus had established this, the authority was only potential, and a new humanity was a hope not a certainty. Once the whole genealogy had been completed then the resurrection became, as N. T. Wright has put it, "*the* political act" that substantiates the new humanity.[36] The resurrection is the proof not only of the authority of divine power, but the authority of human power. This is why without it we would be of all people the "most to be pitied."[37] Given that Christ *is* raised, there is much work to do! For it will be clear by now that the theological implications of a reassessment of the nature of divine

---

[34] Thomas F. Torrance, *Incarnation: The Person and Life of Christ*, ed. Robert T. Walker (Downers Grove, IL: IVP Academic, 2008), 205.

[35] Michael Hardt and Antonio Negri, *Multitude* (New York: Penguin Books, 2004), 352.

[36] Matthew, 1.

[37] 1 Corinthians 15: 19.

power that this chapter, and indeed this whole book, ventures towards, are huge. This work is, I believe, the prophetic task of the moment.

Lancaster University, Lancaster, Great Britain

PART II

SOCIOLOGICAL AND PHILOSOPHICAL PERSPECTIVES

CHAPTER III

THE MAGISTERIUM: CONJUNCTIONS AND DISJUNCTIONS IN MODERNITY: A HISTORICAL-SOCIOLOGICAL ANALYSIS

STAF HELLEMANS

The Catholic Church today is in several ways out of phase with the world it wants to speak to. This is particularly the case in the West....The disjunction is very evident in the model of authority which the official Church seems to hold to. – Charles Taylor

As we understand it today, the *magisterium* – the wide range of authoritative teaching activities of bishops and, especially, popes – is largely a 19th century invention, a product of a determined papal policy. Strikingly, particularly for outsiders, the faithful generally heeded the call to obey this authority until the 1950s. An historically singular conjunction of Church hierarchy and the faithful was thus realised. In the second and third parts of this contribution, the emergence of the modern *magisterium* and the reasons why it was established with so much authority in the 19th century will be analysed. Yet, as is well known, after 1960, a deep disjunction became particularly visible when the great majority of the faithful was non-receptive to the encyclical letter *Humanae Vitae* of 1968. In sections 4 to 6, we will look at the emergence of the disjunction between the Church and the faithful after 1960, at the reasons explaining it, and at a possible way forward. Since the popes are the leading players, this contribution will focus on the papal *magisterium*.

PRELIMINARY ASSUMPTIONS

The authority of the *magisterium* is not a one-way-issue. Since the popes and Rome play the leading roles, it is understandable that they receive most attention. Nevertheless, there are two sides involved: the *magisterium* on the one hand, and the faithful and the public on the other hand. It is thus crucial to study the connections and the interactions between these two sides, namely, how the connections are forged or undone and why. Authority relations change over time and sometimes they change quite drastically. These drastic changes are themselves the result of the processing of the major societal changes to which one is responding. This is also the case for the Catholic Church. After the French Revolution of 1789, society was, notwithstanding the efforts at restoration, geared in new tracks – and so was the Church. After 1960, society was once more reconfigured in ways that differed so much from the time before that this period is to be considered a new stage in the history of modernity – resulting in a new Catholic Church.[1] I will call the era between the French Revolution and 1960 'the first modernity', and the time after 1960 'the second' or 'advanced modernity'. The invention of the *magisterium* and the tight conjunction between the Church hierarchy and the faithful took place in the first modernity. The disjunction between them occurs in the second modernity.

The teaching authority is linked to other aspects of the Church: to the frame of mind of its leaders, to its internal organisation, to the insertion of the Church in society and in people's daily lives. To understand the issue of the *magisterium*, we thus need to look at the Church in its many dimensions. Let us take the years after 1960. The Catholic Church is getting smaller. It no longer encompasses its faithful 'from cradle to grave'. Dissent and threat of exit by the faithful have become a structural characteristic of church life. Consequently, the connections between the *magisterium* and the public also change. For example, the faithful undergo a change from a deferent to a critical attitude, which precludes the old, mythologised Roman ideal "*Roma locuta, causa finita*" – an ideal that really only applied (with restrictions, of course) to the 19th and early 20th centuries. However, the erosion of the closed Catholic subcultures opens up, at the same time, new opportunities, foremost of which is a possible direct appeal to a worldwide public.

CONJUNCTION: THE RISE AND HEIGHT OF THE MAGISTERIUM (1789-1960)

The *magisterium* as we know it today is mainly a 19th century invention.[2] Of course, teaching and preaching were always central to Christianity. The pope and his chancellery – Rome – were key players in Western Christianity from early Christian times, and even more so in later times[3]. However, individual bishops and theologians were also equally active in an independent way until the French Revolution. Pronouncements by popes, often embroiled in political power games, were, at times, heavily criticised. As late as the 18th century, more than half of the German bishops

---

[1] S. Hellemans and J. Wissink, eds., *A Catholic Program for Advanced Modernity* (Vienna and Berlin: LIT Verlag, 2012).

[2] Yves Congar, "A Semantic History of the Term 'Magisterium,'" in *The Magisterium on Morality*, ed. Charles Curran and R. A. McCormick, vol. 3, Readings in Moral Theology (New York and Ramsey: Paulist Press, 1982a), 297-313; Yves Congar, "A Brief History of the Forms of the Magisterium and Its Relations with Scholars," in *The Magisterium on Morality*, ed. Charles Curran and R. A. McCormick, vol. 3, Readings in Moral Theology (New York and Ramsey: Paulist Press, 1982b), 314-31.

[3] See the Gregorian Reform of the 11th to 13th centuries and the Counterreformation in the 16th and early 17th centuries.

refused to support in their dioceses the papal condemnation of Febronianism in 1764[4]. In the Middle Ages, the theologians of the major universities, in their capacity as experts in doctrine, considered it their duty to judge the orthodoxy of theological teachings. The *magisters* of the University of Paris, the major theological centre of the time, were, until the beginning of the 17th century, pre-eminent.[5] In sum, before modernity, the teaching authority of the Church was scattered over a great many instances, which mirrored the scattered institutional organisation of the Church.

It was only after 1830 that the popes advanced to become the all-important instructors and directors of faith, thereby pushing the other instances into a subservient position. In this respect, and drawing on a long tradition of claims to papal supremacy and on the more recent resurgence of papal power and authority since the Congress of Vienna in 1815 (the restoration of the Papal States and the conclusion of many concordats), the pontificate of Gregory XVI (1831-1846) was decisive. Confronted with the end of the Restoration era (1815-1830) and the rise to power of liberalism in several countries, signalling in his eyes a potential return of the revolutionary period, Gregory XVI pursued a vigorous policy of papal empowerment and unity in the Church. To this end, he multiplied his interventions and concomitant claims to obedience in both theology[6] and in politics.[7] It is in this context that Gregory XVI, according to most scholars[8], introduced into papal declarations the term *magisterium* in the sense we still use it today. The encyclical letter *Commissum divinitus* of 17 May 1835, which again condemned liberalism, states:

> He (=God) who made everything and who governs by a prudent arrangement, wanted order to flourish in His Church. He wanted some people to be in charge and govern and others to be subject and obey. Therefore, the Church has, by its divine institution, the power of the *magisterium* to teach and define matters of

---

[4] L.J. Rogier, *De Kerk in Het Tijdperk van Verlichting En Revolutie*, vol. 7, Geschiedenis van de Kerk (Hilversum and Antwerp: Paul Brand, 1974), 103.

[5] J. Gres-Gayer, "The Magisterium of the Faculty of Theology of Paris in the Seventeenth Century," *Theological Studies*, no. 53 (1992): 424-0.

[6] Cf. the condemnations of Lamennais and Hermes.

[7] Cf. the condemnations of liberalism, most famously in the encyclical letter *Mirari Vos* of 1832.

[8] Congar, "A Semantic History of the Term 'Magisterium,'" 307; L. Orsi, "Magisterium: Assent and Dissent," *Theological Studies* 48 (1987): 477; Anthony J. Figueiredo, *The Magisterium-Theology Relationship: Contemporary Theological Conceptions in the Light of Universal Church Teaching Since 1835 and the Pronouncements of the Bishops of the United States* (Rome: Pontificia Universita Gregoriana, 2001), 168-171.

faith and morals and to interpret the Holy Scriptures without danger of error (par. 4).[9]

Note that, for Gregory, the notion of *magisterium* was indissolubly linked to the right to govern on the part of the Church hierarchy and the duty of obeisance on the part of the faithful. Teaching was regarded as an integral part of governance. Following a long tradition, he defined, at the same time, that only the Church, and not worldly powers, can legitimately wield the *magisterium*:

> This power of teaching and governing in matters of religion, given by Christ to His Spouse, belongs to the priests and bishops. Christ established this system not only so that the Church would in no way belong to the civil government of the state, but also so that it could be totally free and not subject in the least to any earthly domination. Jesus Christ did not commit the sacred trust of the revealed doctrine to the worldly leaders, but to the apostles and their successors (par. 5).

Though attributing the *magisterium* in these two articles rather generally to "the Church" or "the priests and bishops," he makes clear towards the end of *Commissum Divinitus* that the pope should have the leading role:

> It is Church dogma that the pope, the successor of St. Peter, possesses not only primacy of honour but also primacy of authority and jurisdiction over the whole Church. Accordingly the bishops are subject to him (par. 10).

In short, the basics of the ultramontane thinking with regard to the *magisterium* are here already presented. In the decades afterwards, it will be expanded intellectually and institutionally.

Indeed, starting with Gregory XVI and increasing much more after him, papal pronouncements were made on almost any subject. They were made frequently and the faithful paid great attention to them. As a result of this, and in secondary fashion so to speak, the bishops' teaching authority in their own dioceses was equally and through similar means enhanced: episcopal letters abounded on festive occasions (e.g. Lent or Easter) or as comments on papal pronouncements (e.g. in the wake of *Rerum Novarum* of 1891). A whole 'machinery' was put in place, both theologically and practically, for ensuring that the papal *magisterium* could be exercised on a continuous basis.

---

[9] Gregorius XVI, "Commissum Divinitus," 1835, http://www.papalencyclicals.net/Greg16/g16commi.htm.

The authority of the pope to make pronouncements with the right to be obeyed was, first of all, strengthened theologically. Gregory XVI and his successor Pius IX were themselves the great promoters. They consciously took up selected theological ideas, concepts, and distinctions that were rumouring among theologians: the concept of the *magisterium* (see above), the distinction between *ecclesia docens* ('teaching church') and *ecclesia discens* ('learning church'), the distinction between ordinary and extra-ordinary *magisterium* and, most famously, the notion of papal infallibility. The dogma of papal infallibility, which was promulgated at the First Vatican Council in 1870, was very restrictive with regard to its use and was thus considered as constituting a form of the extra-ordinary *magisterium*. Yet, it legitimised the far more important, and far more amply used, ordinary *magisterium*. The encyclicals and other statements by the pope or approved by the pope addressing all the faithful, enjoy the status of the ordinary *magisterium*. Though their theological status ranks lower, they were supposed to be no less obeyed.

Alongside the scope and modalities of the *ecclesia docens*, the question of the reception of the teachings by the faithful also gained more attention in the 19th century. Pope Gregory was content to stress the duty to obey. But as soon as papal pronouncements began to inflate, more precision was needed. In the letter "Tuas Libenter" of 21 December 1863, Pope Pius IX thus demanded the subjection of the theologians – and by extension, of all the faithful – not only to the dogmas of the Church, but also to "decisions pertaining to doctrine which are issued by the Pontifical Congregations".[10] However, Church tradition also acknowledges a more active role of the faithful, expressed in the theological notions *sensus fidei* ('sense of faith') and *sensus fidelium* ('sense of the faithful'). Both notions refer to a sort of spiritual instinct of the faithful in perceiving the religious truths of Christianity. Lacking unequivocal adherence in the past, the sense of the faithful was, among other things, invoked by Pius IX as a ground for the solemn definition and proclamation in 1854 of the dogma of the Immaculate Conception of Mary.[11] On the other hand – and this was regarded with distrust by many in the hierarchy – John Henry Newman, referring to the passing dominance of Arianism among Roman emperors and bishops in the 4th century, called attention to the *consensus fidelium* ('the agreement of the faithful') as bearer of the true faith in times of "a temporary suspense of the functions of the *Ecclesia docens*".[12]

The publication of encyclical letters, expositions in which the papal views on particular issues were extensively presented, became the prime

---

[10] Pius IX, "Tuas Libenter, D 1684," 1863, http://denzinger.patristica.net/.
[11] Ibid., par. 19-22.
[12] John Henry Newman, "On Consulting the Faithful in Matters of Doctrine (excerpts)," in *Readings in Church Authority: Gifts and Challenges for Contemporary Catholicism*, ed. G. Mannion et al. (Aldershot: Ashgate, 2003), 294.

medium to instruct the faithful on matters of faith and beyond. Gregory XVI (1831-1846) issued 9 of them, Pius IX (1846-1878) 38, Leo XIII (1878-1903), the most prolific writer of encyclical letters, 86, Pius X (1903-1914) 17, Benedict XV (1914-1922) 12, Pius XI (1922-1939) 31, and Pius XII (1939-1958) 41. Yet, not only encyclicals, but all utterances of the popes were now watched attentively throughout the Catholic world.

In conclusion, we can say that both the practice of the papal teaching authority and the doctrine of the *magisterium* were only fully elaborated in the 19th century. The constellation would remain in place with minor alterations until the death of Pius XII in 1958.

REASONS EXPLAINING THE CONJUNCTION IN THE FIRST MODERNITY

Among scholars, the story just told is, in broad terms, well known – although I did not find much in the way of detailed historical treatments of the rise of the *magisterium*.[13] But how is the rise in the teaching authority of the Church, and in particular of the pope, to be explained? And why did the height of the *magisterium* fall so late in the first modernity? There are, as mentioned in the first section, two sides to the question: first, the rise of the capabilities of and demand for papal interventions and, second, the readiness with which the faithful received papal instructions.

With regard to the first side of the question, the rise in papal teaching authority was part of the much broader rise of the modern papacy as the daily leader of the World Church. At the First Vatican Council, next to papal infallibility, the supreme jurisdictional authority of the pope to govern and discipline the Church was explicitly confirmed. Canon law was further elaborated, trimmed, and restyled towards decision making in Rome, culminating in the promulgation of the Code of Canon Law in 1917.[14] Helped by campaigns in the Catholic press and by mass pilgrimages to Rome, papal devotion by Catholics highly increased. Above all, Rome and the local churches became more tightly linked. At the beginning of the 19th century, the pope only appointed the bishops of the Papal States directly. A century later, almost half of the world episcopate was appointed by the pope.[15] Episcopates founded national colleges in Rome in which talented young priests could internalise the Roman spirit (and build up connections!). The system of nuncios, part papal legates to states and part supervisors of the local churches, was extended. The episcopal chancelleries

---

[13] The two short but rich contributions by Congar, written in the 1970s, remain the best historical accounts to date.

[14] R. Metz, "Pouvoir, Centralisation et Droit. La Codification Du Droit de l'Eglise Catholique Au Début Du XXe Siècle," *Archives Des Sciences Sociales Des Religions* 26, no. 1 (1978): 49-64.

[15] W. F. Akveld, *De Romeinse Curie. De Geschiedenis van Het Bestuur van de Wereldkerk* (Nijmegen: Valkhof Pers, 1997), 78-79.

and Roman congregations became more closely connected. The organisation of the Church was thus greatly strengthened. It became a centralised organisation, with a pope at the apex who could reach down via the episcopate and the priests and religious to every Catholic on the ground. Only in the 19th century were the institutional conditions created that allowed the Church, and the pope in particular, to make authoritative pronouncements in an effective way.

At the same time, the demand and drive for doctrinal statements was heightened as a corollary of the transition to a modern society. There are two aspects here. A general reason is that modern society is more complex and that it changes fast. Hence, the necessity or, at least, the urge to make statements on new issues or to specify earlier statements increased greatly. This drive will become all the more urgent after 1960. A more specific facet is that Rome felt that the Church was fatally threatened by a derailing modern society. The statements of the popes exhibit a pervasive sense that they are surrounded by evil forces and grave errors. Let me cite as an example – others could be given – from the key encyclical *Mirari Vos* by Gregory XVI of 15 August 1832:

> Depravity exults; science is impudent; liberty, dissolute. The holiness of the sacred is despised; the majesty of divine worship is not only disapproved by evil men, but defiled and held up to ridicule. Hence sound doctrine is perverted and errors of all kinds spread boldly. The laws of the sacred, the rights, institutions, and discipline – none are safe from the audacity of those speaking evil (par. 5)[16].

The alliance between church and state was indeed broken up. The Papal States would soon disappear as a political entity. Not only politics threatened to move towards independence or even antagonism. Threats were also growing, again in the eyes of the Church, in the realm of science (e.g. Darwinism, historical research of the Bible and of Christianity's history), in the social realm (e.g. the estrangement of parts of the bourgeoisie and of the working classes), in the realm of culture (here, above all, in Romanesque literature and theatre). The Church was thus mobilising its intellectual resources to warn the faithful and to counter what were perceived as lethal threats.

We now turn to the other and more astonishing side of the question: why were the faithful so faithful? What made them agree with and take up the surge in doctrinal papal pronouncements?

The most important explanation, it seems to me, has to do with the rising relevance of the Church for the faithful in the 19th and early 20th centuries: the Church took up, directly and indirectly, more societal

---

[16] Gregorius XVI, "Mirari Vos," 1832, http://www.papalencyclicals.-net/Greg16/g16mirar.htm.

functions than ever before in history. This increasing relevance was ideology-driven. Pius X's device of *Instaurare omnia in Christo* ('To restore all things in Christ'), can also be taken to characterize the Church during this whole era. The Church and, in particular, the pope felt they had the duty to direct the faithful in all matters of life, not only in doctrinal and moral matters, but also in cultural and leisure activities, in state and electoral matters, in social and economic issues – hence, the development of the so-called 'social doctrine of the Church'. The result: a never-ending flux of pronouncements. To ensure that these would be more than mere words and to prepare for the eventual re-conquest of modernity, multitudes of associations and organisations were, at the same time, founded in all sectors of life. Most of them, in particular, the more secular ones like political parties or socio-economic organisations, were founded and directed by lay Catholics, but the Church and the clerics were always heavily involved. In fact, they were the true leaders of this Catholic world of organisations and movements. With so many central items of life in modern society shaped directly or indirectly by the Catholic Church, the faithful were inclined to lend a favourable ear to the leaders of their world. After all, the Catholic Church acted as the intermediary through which the legitimate fruits of modernity came within reach of the population at large.

Moreover, the Church still was, as in the past, an institution at the centre of society. Its 'work force' – priests and religious – was far better educated than most of the faithful. They self-assuredly frequented the circles of the political, social, and cultural elite, from the parish to the national level. Church and clerics thus enjoyed a high prestige, which was conducive for a deferent attitude towards their authoritative statements.

Ultramontane mass Catholicism between 1850 and 1960 was thus a time of intense and tight connections between the Church and its faithful. The reasons can be summarised in one sentence: the Church was the leader of a whole world ("l'Eglise, c'est un monde"[17]). And although the tensions were many – between liberal and ultramontane Catholics, between the classes – never before and never after was the conjunction between the Church and the faithful so strong as in the first modernity.

DISJUNCTION IN ADVANCED MODERNITY

This historically extraordinary tight and authoritative conjunction between the papal *magisterium* and the faithful did not last after 1960, although this was not due to a lack of effort on the part of the teaching authorities.

First, the popes and bishops continue to issue statements of all sorts. The popes, in particular, are omnipresent and have become even more visible than they were already. Traditional means of magisterial

---

[17] Emile Poulat, *L'Eglise, c'est un monde: l'ecclésiosphère* (Paris: Editions du Cerf, 1984).

pronouncements in the form of written declarations (motu proprio, apostolic constitution, encyclical, apostolic letter, apostolic exhortation) remain in use. Let us take again encyclical letters as an example. John XXIII (1958-1963) issued 8 encyclicals, Paul VI (1963-1978) 7, John Paul II (1978-2005) 14, Benedict XVI (2005-2013) 3. Encyclicals still constitute favourite papal teaching instruments, though it is clear that the number of encyclicals issued since John XXIII has declined. In addition to the older forms of written declarations, new forms of papal public utterances have made headway, which more than compensate for the decline of older forms. The popes now appear frequently on television. They travel abroad for pastoral visits and use these occasions to give speeches. They give discourses at weekly general audiences in Rome. They give interviews and publish books. In short, they have become public figures. Every word they utter is screened.

Second, after some hesitation, the teaching authorities demand obedience on the part of the faithful to no less of a degree than in the first modernity. Initially, with the stiffening control in the 1950s in mind, the Second Vatican Council gave more leeway to the faithful and theologians. As well, Paul VI wanted to refrain from excessive centralisation and from all-too-frequent imperative doctrinal declarations. A good example is his *Octogesimo Adveniens* of 14 May 1971, which he deliberately called an apostolic letter and not an encyclical.[18] It is modest in tone. It acknowledges the diversity of situations and leaves the particularities of decision making to the local Christian communities and the conscience of the believer (par. 3-4 and 49-50). At the end, it presents the ideas set forth as "reflections" rather than as authoritative teachings (par. 52). Nevertheless, Paul VI, confronted with growing polarisation and the spiral of radical progressive ideas, did not find a way forward for the *magisterium*. While many major documents saw the light in the 1960s, this almost came to a standstill in the 1970s.[19] More tellingly, Paul VI and the leadership of the Church went on the defensive. A typical example of the new mood is the 'Declaration in defense of Catholic doctrine on the Church against certain errors of the present day', *Mysterium ecclesiae* of June 24, 1973 from the Congregation for the Doctrine of Faith, which was ratified by Paul VI. It condemned radical ecumenist ideas and the questioning of the infallibility of the Church and the *magisterium*.[20] The same Congregation started investigating the work of several leading theologians, among them Hans Küng and Edward

---

[18] Paul VI, "Octogesimo Adveniens," 1971, http://www.vatican.va/-holy_father/paul_vi/apost_letters/documents/hf_p-i_apl_19710514_octogesima-adveniens_en.html.

[19] To be fair, two major documents appeared which were not called encyclicals: the Apostolic Letter *Octogesimo Adveniens* of 1971 and the Apostolic Exhortation *Evangelii Nuntiandi* of 1975.

[20] Congregation for the Doctrine of the Faith, "Mysterium Ecclesiae," 1973.

Schillebeeckx. Under John Paul II, the hesitations gave way to a much more active and firm approach. John Paul II resumed the tradition of promulgating encyclicals and he did not hide that they were meant as authoritative teachings.[21] Nor did his other major declarations leave room for ambiguity. The Apostolic Letter *Ordinatio Sacerdotalis* of 22 May 1994, which affirmed the reservation of priestly ordination for men alone, closed by stating, "in order that all doubt may be removed...that this judgment is to be definitively held by all the Church's faithful".[22] Under his prefect Joseph Ratzinger, the Congregation for the Doctrine of Faith became all the more active: liberation theology was ruled out as a legitimate approach, 'relativistic' theories on religious pluralism were condemned, and a number of individual theologians were notified and/or sanctioned.[23] In sum, the *magisterium* endeavoured, after allowing for a short time greater theological freedom and experiments during and after the Second Vatican Council, to tighten again its grip.

Nevertheless, we are far from a full return to the situation prior to 1960. If one wants to call this period a restoration, it is certainly only a partial restoration for which I can only give some tentative indications – the subject needs more thorough research. It seems to me that the rate and the scope of the major doctrinal statements have declined. Before 1960, the popes issued more encyclicals, with Leo XIII and Pius XII contributing the most (cf. supra), and did so on a greater variety of subjects. The documents entailed more prescriptions and condemnations. The popes treated the subjects with more self-assurance and with more precision than is generally the case nowadays. Prescribing a specific philosophical school (neo-Thomism) or a particular political strategy (the *ralliement* of Catholics to the French Republic in 1892), as Leo XIII did, is indeed past history. By the way, the protests against and the failure of the *ralliement* policy show that there were limits to the *magisterium* too, prior to 1960. To come back to the time after 1960, the tone of the magisterial documents has changed as well. The phrasing is less harsh [24] and the style is, by and large, less imperative. The encyclicals strive especially to come across as spiritual documents.[25]

---

[21] See, for example John Paul II, "Veritatis Splendor," 1993, par. 26-27 and 114-116, http: www.vatican.va/holy_father/john_paul_ii/encyclicals/documents/hf_jp-ii_enc_06081993_veritatis-splendor_en.html.

[22] John Paul II, "Ordinatio Sacerdotalis," 1984, http://www.vatican.va/-/holy-father/john_paul_ii/apost_letters/documents/hf_jp-_ii_apl_22051994_ordinatio-sacerdotalis_en.html.

[23] On the tense relations between Rome and prominent theologians, see a.o. Michael J. Lacey and Francis Oakley, *The Crisis of Authority in Catholic Modernity* (Oxford: Oxford University Press, 2011); Richard R. Gaillardetz, *When the Magisterium Intervenes: The Magisterium and Theologians in Today's Church* (Collegeville: Liturgical Press, 2012).

[24] Compare with Gregorius XVI, "Mirari Vos."

[25] The three encyclicals of Benedict XVI are fine examples.

Moreover, though supervision has again increased, this in no way amounts to the hunt scenes provoked by the condemnation of 'modernism' by Pius X at the beginning of the 20th century, or to the systematic disciplining of theologians under Pius XII. Decisive for the fundamental change, however, is a third factor: the reception of the *magisterium* by the faithful. Let us now turn to this side of the coin.

Before 1960, papal pronouncements were often hailed by the Catholic faithful as major landmarks on the way towards a Catholic society. After the publication of Leo XIII's encyclical *Aeterni Patris* of 4 August 1879, universities such as Louvain (Belgium) and Laval (Québec, Canada) hastened themselves to offer the Pope their support in fostering neo-Thomism (while the tensions were kept secret!). In Louvain, a centre of international renown headed by the future Cardinal Mercier was set up in the following years.[26] In time, the seminary education all over the world became neo-Thomist. The encyclicals *Rerum Novarum* of 1891 and the sequel *Quadragesimo Anno* of 1931 had a similar lasting impact: the sprawling Catholic social movements, foremost the Catholic labour movements, referred to these encyclicals as their 'Magna Charta'. The contrast with our time is striking. The recent social encyclicals, for example, the 2009 *Caritas in Veritate* of Benedict XVI, received some press reactions, but all-in-all reaction is limited. What is more, they faded away in a murmur without any visible impact. The last enthusiast reception of an encyclical is, I think, Paul VI's *Populorum Progressio* of 1967. The publication of *Humanae Vitae* a year later garnered few approvals and loads of disapprovals. When, thereafter, a lively discussion over a magisterial document erupts, it usually means that it is strongly criticised. A good example is the flood of negative press over the Apostolic Letter *Ordinatio Sacerdotalis* of 1994[27] or over the Declaration from the Congregation for the Doctrine of Faith, *Dominus Iesus* of 2000.[28]

This leads us to the question: why this fundamental change? Why did the faithful react so eagerly or, at least, so respectfully before 1960 and why does this change in 1968 and onwards? I see three major shifts in the connections that link the Church and the faithful. Since these shifts are structural, a future restoration of authoritative bonds of the pre-1960-type is highly unlikely.

---

[26] See L. De Raeymaker, "Les Origines de l'Institut Supérieur de Philosophie de Louvain," *Revue Philosophique de Louvain*, no. 49 (1951): 505-633 for Louvain.

[27] On the reactions in Belgium, see A. Van Meerbeeck and A. Verlinden, "De Juni-Storm. Een Sociologische Doorlichting van Enkele Reacties Na Het Verschijnen van Ordinatio Sacerdotalis," *Tijdschrift Voor Sociologie* 16, no. 1 (1995): 5-29.

[28] D. Contreras, "Coverage of Complex Theoretical Content. The Case of 'Dominus Iesus,'" *Westminster Papers in Communication and Culture* 4, no. 1 (2007): 26-46.

First, the Church has become less relevant for the daily lives of people. While the 19th and early 20th centuries witnessed a rise in the functions the Church was directly and indirectly performing, most of these newly accrued functions were lost again after 1960. The Church is no longer the central wielding power of an extended Catholic world, pillar, or subculture. It is no longer considered by most people to be a guiding force in their handling of political, social, and cultural affairs. Even the Church's rulings on personal moral issues like contraception, divorce, and homosexuality, to which the Church attaches considerable importance, are ignored or openly defied. The Church has become confined, more or less, to its religious sphere. The loss of functions (on the political, socio-economic, cultural, and even moral levels) leaves the Church only with religious binding potential.

Second – and this is by far worse – there is an unmistakable loss in religious guidance potential too. The Church has become less able to sensitise people for the world of God. This constitutes the real crisis of the Church. Many people have left the Church without feeling that they have lost something valuable in doing so! Moreover, Catholics themselves are generally less surrounded by what I will call 'a religious offer' connected to the Church. Between 1850 and 1960, things like Catholic literature, daily prayers, fasting, devotional sodalities, dedication to a saint to which one felt particularly connected, the yearly celebration of the great religious feasts as markers of the calendar, the religious inner decoration of one's house, among many other things, made the Church religiously all-present to the believer. This is no longer the case. Of course, all things temporal have a temporary character. The problem nowadays, however, is the absence of new forms of religious offer with a similar impact on the daily lives of Catholics.

Last but not least, there is a third structural factor behind the changing bonds between the Church and its following: people now choose to remain or become Catholic and they also choose to what extent and in what form they are Catholic. The result is a complete power reversal: the faithful are no longer subject to the hierarchy; instead, the hierarchy has to prove useful in helping realise the religious longings of the people. Consequently, the faithful do not feel themselves bound by Church pronouncements. Nowadays, people in general, and no less so Catholics, feel free to judge the Church's pronouncements according to their own value system. With less enforcement power, the Catholic Church has to learn how to propose, and how to seduce people with an interesting offer and an appealing teaching.

Due to these structural shifts, which, in turn, are linked to structural changes in advanced modernity, the singular conjunction of the Church and the faithful present in the 19th and early 20th centuries has thus turned into a lasting disjunction. Accordingly, the Church hierarchy has lost the power it had built up in the 19th century to enforce its rulings and it has lost the authority of having the unquestionable right to be obeyed. Although successive popes and the Church hierarchy after 1967 have heightened the pressure to uphold the former teacher-learner relationship, this has resulted not in more commitment, but, on the contrary, in more resistance and alienation on the part of the faithful and the public.

CONJUNCTIONS AND DISJUNCTIONS

So far, we talked about the conjunction after 1800 and the disjunction after 1960 in the singular. However, they are both the end result of the presence or absence of a number of connections and, moreover, of different types of connections between the Church and the faithful. Let us now focus, in a more systematic way, on these connections. I, therefore, turn to the realm of political sciences and, especially, to the analogous issue of the channels that link political parties to voters. After all, the Catholic Church is not the only organisation with difficulties in reaching and binding a following. This has become a common problem for all major organisations in advanced modernity, for big corporations and banks, for trade unions, and, not in the least, for political parties. Political scientists have taken up this issue. The German-American political scientist Herbert Kitschelt[29] has devised an analytical catalogue of the ways political parties in the West may connect to citizens. I'll apply his scheme to our problem.

Kitschelt distinguishes between two fundamental classes of linkage types: affective and instrumental. Affective bonds can be created and reproduced in three ways: through common traits (ethnicity, gender, language, region), through party identification (tradition, collective mobilisation, corporate symbols, and narrative), and through charismatic leadership. There are also three types of instrumental linkages: voters may vote for a party because it is considered to be delivering desired valence goods (goods for everyone, like economic growth or crime reduction), highly attractive club goods or positional goods (like lower taxes for investors), or because a party builds upon clientelistic relations (goods for individuals or small groups, like providing contracts for particular companies).

Let us apply this analytical scheme of six possible types of linkages to the Catholic Church and its relations with the faithful. I start with the affective types of linkages.

1. Nowadays, affective linkages through common traits are pertinent only in the case of Catholic ethnic migrants and their migrant parishes. In these cases, the shared culture provides an easy platform for the building up of connections – but hinders, at the same time, their integration in the indigenous churches. In the past, the Catholic Church was often invoked in

---

[29] H. Kitschelt, "Linkages between Citizens and Politicians in Democratic Polities," *Comparative Political Studies* 33, no. 6-7 (2000): 845-79; H. Kitschelt, *Latin American Party Systems*, Cambridge Studies in Comparative Politics (Cambridge; New York: Cambridge University Press, 2010), 18-20.

an identity struggle which pitted whole regions against others, for example, the Catholic South and Southeast in the Netherlands against the Protestant Centre, or Catholic Poland against Protestant Sweden and Prussia and Orthodox Russia. This was even true for encounters between civilisations, e.g. during the Crusades, the Latin *christianitas* against the Muslim world. The 'culture wars' and the emergence of Catholic sub-societies in the 19th and early 20th centuries exhibit the continuing force of common traits in the first modernity. However, after 1960, trait linkages are no longer pervasive in the West. A residual role is still performed, though dwindling, in a number of countries (e.g. Catholic Poland). Only in contested territories, like in Northern Ireland or in the former Yugoslavia, is it still a lively identity marker.

2. Church identification by tradition was all-dominant in the past, but is, like in voting behaviour, declining in our age of volatility and choice. In the past, adherence to the Catholic Church was passed on from generation to generation, first of all within the family, second, through local or regional tradition, and, third, if possible, through the state. Once Catholicism had been established, there were thus few converts. The new ideal in advanced modernity, however, according to which each individual has to lead a personal, authentic life, questions adherence by tradition and demands that adherence to the Catholic Church be a conscious, individual choice. The demand is no less for the offspring of Catholics. Here, family traditions are still playing a role, but only in so far as the Catholic Church is able to make a lasting impression in the lead up to the choice of the individual person. A lasting impression often fails and a great many born Catholics leave the Church. On the other hand, an influx of converts becomes a possibility. Especially between 1800 and 1960, identification with the Church was also enhanced through frequent collective mobilisations. A variety of religious manifestations (Eucharist masses, 'rites de passage', processions, and pilgrimages) and an elaborated associational world buttressed identification. Moreover, in times of conflict, the Catholic Church was able to raise the rank and file in great numbers (cf. the culture wars at the end of the 19th century). The dualist corporate narrative, pitting "the cause of God" against "the terrible conspiracy of impious men",[30] equally bolstered identification by the faithful with the Church. After 1960, the forces of collective mobilisation and of the dualist narrative waned, but did not disappear. The Catholic Church is still strong in collective mobilisations (e.g. World Youth Days, papal voyages). The Catholic corporate narrative is still highly recognisable as well – and is retaining in conservative circles also a clearly dualistic nature – but without the former large-scale appeal.

3. Charismatic linkages are vital at the start of a religious movement. This was also the case with Christianity: undoubtedly, Jesus had great charismatic gifts. Nevertheless, as Max Weber pointed out already a century ago, early Christianity, in its drive for institutionalisation, very soon made a

---

[30] Gregorius XVI, "Mirari Vos," par. 6 resp. par. 1.

move away from the non-transferable qualities of personal charisma into the solid ground of charisma of the office. Personal charisma, joined to the office, was never dead though. It became even more salient after 1800. From Pius IX onwards, the popes were known and revered throughout the Catholic world. Since then, the charismatic authority of popes is, in part, staged. It is bestowed even on popes with little personal charisma (e.g. Benedict XVI). The combination of both personal and office charisma continues, however, to be potent. John Paul II and now Francis are obvious examples.

As is clear, affective bonds between the Church and the faithful were, and still are, though less than in the past, of major importance. Similar conclusions can be drawn for the instrumental class of linkage types.

1. Clientelistic linkages were in the past very significant. The clergy were, at one time and up until 1960, all-important power brokers. Nowadays, this is no longer the case.

2. 'Club goods' linkages were of major importance after 1800, when the Catholic Church was offering the Catholic faithful the benefits of modernity (education, health care, cultural goods, participation in politics, interest representation, and so on). After 1960, this type of bond declined due to the Church's loss of most of these functions. Where Catholic schools, hospitals, political parties, or interest organisations continued to exist, they had often already ceased for quite some time to function exclusively for Catholics. Yet, in numerous instances, Catholic social organisations are still functioning as channels linking people to the Catholic world, albeit in cursory ways.[31] In a number of non-Western Catholic churches, particularly in the 'failed states' of Africa (as in the Democratic Republic of the Congo), Catholic club goods are still vital for the population. In the West, also, smaller religious groups, such as migrant churches, provide club goods (e.g. job coaching and allocation, helping migrants with their papers and their integration into the host society). Moreover, in Western countries with few welfare state facilities, like the United States, so-called faith-based organisations have re-emerged as important civil carriers.[32] In sum, there is still a potential for 'club goods' linkages offering particular gains, but this is less prominent than in the past.

3. 'Valence goods' linkages result from the promise and offer of goods benefiting all people. In the past, the Catholic Church perceived itself as the institution *par excellence* offering universal social goods to society (e.g. ensuring social order, inculcating the right values and decent behaviour

---

[31] B. Fix and E. Fix, *Kirche Und Wohlfahrtsstaat. Soziale Arbeit Kirchlicher Wohlfahrtsorganisationen Im Westeuropäischen Vergleich* (Freiburg im Breisgau: Lambertus, 2005); K. Gabriel, *Caritas Und Sozialstaat Unter Veränderungsdruck* (Berlin: LIT Verlag, 2007).

[32] R. Wuthnow, *Saving America? Faith-Based Services and the Future of Civil Society* (Princeton and Oxford: Princeton University Press, 2004).

in all persons). However, today, as a minority church, it can no longer offer these goods as valence goods in a credible way, since the claim of offering these social goods to all people presupposes an institution that is acting as a sacred canopy on behalf of society. Nevertheless, the promise and offer of universal goods has not lost importance. After all, the core of Christianity, i.e. the promise of salvation in God and Christ, is a universal good, a promise for everyone. But it has to be translated and made effective in order for people to want to engage in the Church in the expectation of living a good and holy life.

CHRISTIAN FULFILMENT OF LIFE

Looking at the overall picture, it is quite clear that the Church has lost most of its former binding potential on its faithful. Two crucial affective linking mechanisms, namely, common traits and adherence by tradition, were most salient even in the recent past but are no longer so. Collective mobilisations and a corporate narrative retain some value but touch hearts and minds less so than in previous times. On the other hand, charismatic relations joined to the office of popes – and, to a far lesser extent, bishops – have gained in importance in modernity. Regarding instrumental linkages, the state of affairs is similar. Clientelistic linkages have, except in migrant parishes and for marginalised people, disappeared. Linkages springing from the promise of 'club goods' for Catholics – making the benefits of modernity available for Catholics – are still woven, but with far less intensity (again with the exceptions mentioned). This means that the Church nowadays is left to make its stance predominantly with its potential of 'valence goods' in the religious sphere. But, as religion has become a matter of personal choice and one framed in an ethics of authenticity, universal goods in general, including the promise of salvation, are now phrased in terms of personal fulfilment (Taylor, 1999). The outlook of leading a good life, a fulfilled life 'in God and in Christ' is what could be attracting people nowadays to Christianity. If the Catholic Church wants to gain new relevance, it is here – guiding people towards contact with God in order to live a fulfilled life – that convincing ideas and programs (in the form of spirituality, rituals, collective activities, social action, etc.) should be developed. However, viewed from this perspective, it is rather odd to find that the Church is, in effect, raising the conditions for full participation in a number of rituals, thereby turning what could be universal goods into club goods. Examples of this are denying communion to divorcees and non-married couples in a society with fewer first marriages and high rates of divorce, or the decision of the German Conference of Bishops in 2012 not to provide sacraments to people who do not pay their church tax (*'Kirchensteuer'*). Whether the Church will be able to reach people with the 'valence good' of the Gospel is, in my opinion, dependent on two conditions: creating a fitting religious offer and imagining the good life and the good society, which is where the *magisterium* comes in.

Let us first look at the religious offer. As has been indicated (see above § 4), after 1960, the religious offer declined because most old forms (sodalities, processions, parish activities, etc.) lost appeal and were not replaced by new forms that carried equivalent attraction. The Catholic Church in advanced modernity thus faces the challenge of elaborating, in line with the Catholic tradition, a new religious offer in such a way that it meets the cravings of contemporary people to lead a fulfilled life, bearing in mind that they can walk away at any moment. The elaboration of such a new, fitting religious offer is a huge task. It is, above all, a creative task and one that cannot simply be promulgated from on high because it has to build upon countless experiments, mostly from below, from which a small number of successful performances can be selected for fine-tuning and wider dissemination. To be fair, there has been widespread innovation, even after the waves of innovation of the 1960s had withered away (World Youth Days, new *movimenti*, spirituality centres, etc.),[33] but this has not been enough and what has been created has only had limited appeal. The Church's reluctance towards innovation and experimenting is certainly restraining the renewal. The really critical difficulty, though, is of another order: Will it be possible at all, given the absence of a Catholic state and (sub-)society and given the fact that secular goods nowadays can at most be provided peripherally, to attract major layers of the population with only a religious offer? After all, many seem to do well without religion or, at least, without demanding institutional religion.

Second, next to offering the opportunity of a religious practice, which promises to bring 'God's bliss and grace' into the personal life of the believer, comes the inspiring and, at the same time, reasonable imagining of the good life and the good society, and its intrinsic relations with God and Christianity. This is the imagining of what Taylor and Carroll call 'a Catholic modernity'.[34] Here, reflection, theory, theology, and the *magisterium* are at stake. With regard to the *magisterium*, however, a major stain becomes manifest: the teaching of the Church seems often to have been triggered and directed by negative energy, by apologetics, by the drive to demarcate oneself from heresies, to suppress errors. Gregory XVI and Pius IX seem, at times, only to issue magisterial documents when they want to suppress ideas and movements – culminating in the publication by Pius

---

[33] For an overview in Britain, see James Sweeney, "Catholicism in Britain: A Church in Search of Its Way," in *Towards a New Catholic Church in Advanced Modernity*, ed. S. Hellemans and J. Wissink (Vienna and Berlin: LIT Verlag, 2012), 147-76.

[34] Charles Taylor, "A Catholic Modernity," in *A Catholic Modernity? Charles Taylor's Marianist Award Lecture*, ed. J.L. Heft (Oxford: Oxford University Press, 1999), 13-37; A.J. Carroll, "A Catholic Program for Advanced Modernity," in *Towards a New Catholic Church in Advanced Modernity*, ed. S. Hellemans and J. Wissink (Vienna and Berlin: LIT Verlag, 2012), 51-77.

IX of the *Syllabus Errorum* in 1864. It is true that many later documents demonstrate a more positive attitude and present uplifting visions. Nevertheless, the negative interventions and imperative rulings remain frequent to this day, with the result that the Catholic Church in general and the *magisterium* in particular are, in the public mind – and also in the minds of many Catholics – nearly equated with ill dogmatism and insensitive condemnations. Since the conditions of advanced modernity are such that the Church can no longer enforce its will, it will have to be more prudent with bans and rulings and it will need to focus its teaching on the intimate positive relation between Christianity and the fulfilment of life. It is on this latter relation that Catholic social teaching is welcomed by so many, and also by those outside the Church, and that the documents of the Second Vatican Council are still regarded as a source of inspiration. Only if the *magisterium* and the Church appear to be conducive for people to lead a fulfilled life can it hope to regain some degree of authority. Vice versa, so long as the *magisterium* cannot shed its negative reputation, its teachings will not be received as inspiring.

Tilburg University, the Netherlands

CHAPTER IV

POST-METAPHYSICAL AUTHORITY

ANTHONY J. CARROLL

INTRODUCTION

Francis Oakley has argued that the contemporary exercise of magisterial authority in the church has been shaped by a rejection of historicity and a general tendency to take refuge in an uncommitted and abstract theology.[1] He also notes that these two factors have fostered an official church teaching style which tends towards an authoritarian annunciation of timeless certainties that demand obedience from the faithful. In this article, I explore the influence of the inability of the church to come to terms with both change and fallibility on these factors. Objectivist metaphysics derived from the classical traditions of Plato and Aristotle has provided the church with a model of God as the all-powerful and self-sufficient 'Supreme Being' and of an understanding of development, change, and fallibility which are seen in purely negative terms. Such metaphysical doctrines have been patterned in the image of unchanging structures of authority of the Church and its particular conception of the exercise of its moral and theological teaching role. The moral and theological teaching role is held to be substantially unchangeable because to change is to admit to a lack or a privation, to an unrealised potentiality and that would be to introduce uncertainty and incompleteness into the church's teaching, and hence to deny the objective and fully actualised status of divinely revealed truth, which the Magisterium is charged with transmitting and preserving faithfully.[2]

---

[1] See Francis Oakley, "Obedience and the Church's Teaching Authority", in Charles Taylor, José Casanova, and George McClean (eds.), *Church and People: Disjunctions in a Secular Age*, The Council for Research in Values and Philosophy, Washington, 2012, pp. 7-9. Daniel Decker's essay on "Subsidiarity" in the same volume also provides helpful reflections on the importance of subsidiarity in the internal workings of the Catholic Church, see Ibid., pp. 71-105. Both Francis Oakley's and Daniel Deckers' articles are reproduced at the end of this volume as Appendix I and II respectively. For more extended discussions of these issues, see Michael J. Lacey and Francis Oakley (eds.), *The Crisis of Authority in Catholic Modernity*, Oxford University Press, Oxford, 2011.

[2] Francis Oakley provides an excellent case study exemplifying this aversion to change in the understanding of doctrine in his account of the rise of a papalist master narrative of authority over against a conciliarist tradition of authority. He shows how in excising the Council of Constance (1414-1418)

However, I argue that, as the resignation of Pope Benedict XVI illustrates, change can be eminently sensible and even desirable. In adapting an abstract metaphysics for the purposes of thinking God and the church, the church has unnecessarily wedded itself to one approach to metaphysics that thinks of change negatively. It is this inability to think of change and fallibility as part and parcel of human reflection on God and morality, which I argue influences the church's aversion to historicity and its tendency to move into an abstract and uncommitted theology. The undesirable consequences of the church's current understanding of change and fallibility are both a diminishment of its credibility as it exercises its authority in ways that bypass necessary open discussion on complex moral issues and an overextension of the infallible teaching of the church to cover changing understandings of the human person and morality. It seems as if the "deposit of faith" has been stretched to include all currently held moral positions of the Catholic Church.

The importance of being able to think of both change and continuity in the context of the tradition of the church is that without this more rooted understanding tradition can be seen as either simply adherence to ancient customs and hence as having nothing to say to people of today or as remaining static and too dependent on the past to enable it to develop as new ideas gain general acceptance. For the sake of the vitality of the church, and inspired by the work of thinkers who really both inspired and took forward the work of the Second Vatican Council in this area (such as Yves Congar, Henri de Lubac, Karl Rahner, Joseph Ratzinger, and Edward Schillebeeckx) it is necessary to develop a nuanced conception of tradition which allows for continuity and progress, conservation and development in order to conceive of tradition as creative fidelity to the deposit of the faith transmitted from generation to generation and judged authentically by the magisterium.[3] Having the capacity to discern both necessary change and

---

from the narrative of the history of Church Councils an overly continuous account of doctrinal development has become the dominant one since Vatican I. This account portrays the rise of absolute papal authority as the singular instance of authority in the church and as gradually and continuously emerging through the ages. Yet, as Oakley notes, this continuity motif has lost credibility in the light of recent historical research which has recovered the importance of conciliar theory in the catholic tradition which even allowed for general ecumenical councils to have, in certain critical areas, a jurisdictional power superior to the pope. As Oakley notes, the consequence of this new catholic ecclesial consciousness is to force the issue of having to rethink this continuous doctrinal development account in the light of the historical reality of radically discontinuous change in doctrinal matters of central importance to the church's self-understanding. See Michael J. Lacey and Francis Oakley (eds.), op cit., pp. 29-56. See also Francis Oakley, *The Conciliarist Tradition: Constitutionalism in the Catholic Church 1300-1870*, Oxford University Press, Oxford, 2003.

[3] See, for example, Yves Congar, *The Meaning of Tradition*, Ignatius, San Francisco, 2004; Henri de Lubac, "Le Problème du développement due

faithful continuity is thus at the heart of what it means for the magisterium to exercise its authority credibly today.

The importance of being able to think fallible theological and moral teaching in the church is that when all church teaching is viewed as the infallible truth then any dissent from these teachings is tantamount to infidelity. Such "creeping infallibility" of the church has locked it into positions on a whole range of theological and moral issues, which have meant that they are unchangeable and hence beyond debate. The removal from office of Bishop William Morris of the Australian Toowoomba Diocese in 2011 over questions concerning the ordination of women is a case in point. Simply raising the issue of the possible future ordination of women in a pastoral letter dating back to 2006 seems to have been sufficient for him to be removed from office. In such a climate it is vital that the church reflect responsibly on the limits of its infallibility and perhaps as well as proclaiming itself to be infallible it ought to balance this claim by also reflecting on the theological significance of the fallible nature of the teaching authority of the ordinary and universal magisterium.

BEYOND METAPHYSICAL CONCEPTIONS OF AUTHORITY

The metaphysical model of the structure and function of authority in the church corresponded in the Middle Ages to a feudal and monarchical understanding of power and authority, which was mediated through the dual roles of the *sacerdotium* and the *regnum*, the priestly and the kingly offices of the church.[4] This led to what Francis Oakley has called a "sacral kingship" understanding of the papacy following the Gregorian era.[5] The transition from the medieval to the modern world has been, amongst a range of other changes, a move away from both the classical metaphysical traditions and the feudal political model at the level of structures of governance. In opposition to this modernisation, the Catholic Church has often resisted these changes in both its metaphysics and its own structures of governance. This oppositional stance provided a clear alternative to the secular structures of the modern world and provided the church with a distinctive identity. Entering the church was leaving the world and just as leaving one country and entering another often involves a change of

---

dogme," *Recherches de Science Religieuse* 35 (1948): 130-160; Karl Rahner, "Uberlegungen zur Dogmenentwicklung," *Schriften zur Theologie* 4 (1960): 11-50; Joseph Ratzinger, *Das Problem der Dogmengeschichte in der Sicht der katholischen Theologie* (Cologne: Opladen, 1966); Edward Schillebeeckx, "Recent Views in the Development of Dogma," *Concilium* (Special Issue) 21 (1967): 109-131.

[4] For an interesting discussion of authority and power, see Giorgio Agamben, *State of Exception*, University of Chicago Press, Chicago, 2005, pp. 74-88.

[5] See Oakley, op cit., 2012, p. 6.

language and culture, so too leaving the world and entering the church displayed similar changes.

Whilst this approach provided the church with a clear purpose and identity, its credibility was based on a certain idealisation of its authority and of its hierarchical representatives. The 1870 declaration of papal infallibility, whilst originally designed to circumscribe the authority of the pope in practice, gradually became a symbol of this idealisation with the pope as an absolute sovereign over the church.[6] Priests through the ontological transformation of their ordination and their promise of celibacy were lifted out of the ordinary realm of changing being, of work and family life, and placed in the heavenly and unchanging realm of Christ as his unique mediators on earth. As such, conditions of authority were shifted out of the day to day and placed in the realm of unchanging certainty. Such a model of authority had functional significance so long as this ontological dualism of the heavenly and the earthly structured people's imaginations.

This is no longer the case, at least not as it was in former times. Authority today is firmly rooted in the ordinary: in the capacity of people to provide good grounds for finding something credible. This need not be arguments, of course. It can be charitable actions, generosity, demonstration of insight and wisdom and so on. But it must be demonstrable in order for it to be credible. Systematic contradictions in this 'authoritative' behaviour provide evidence that such structures are not credible. The sexual abuse scandals have perhaps finally ended this metaphysically based model of authority. Shocked by the reality of the clerical sexual abuse scandals and the various forms of covering this up by the church, the idealised image of the hierarchy as having a "hotline to God" has lost its credibility.

In such a situation a number of alternatives present themselves. The first is one of denial. Characterisation of such failures as the result of sinful individuals rather than the systematic dysfunction of the structures of the church is one such alternative. This approach clearly has the advantage, at least from the point of view of the leadership of the church, of not requiring systematic reform in order to put this dysfunction right. However, for the medium and long term healthy continuation of the institution of the church this dysfunctionality will need to be put right at the structural level.

Perhaps at an even more serious level for the Catholic Church is the dissociation of faith and reason that is interfering with the articulation of the Catholic sacramental vision of reality. In one sense this is unsurprising. If modern forms of religion are increasingly following the trajectory that one would expect from Protestant patterns of modernisation then increased dissociation of the Catholic faith from rational argumentation bears a similarity to the growth of Protestant groups such as Pentecostalism in many

---

[6] See K. Schatz, *Papal Primacy*, Liturgical Press, Collegeville, 1996, pp. 167-68.

parts of the world.[7] Religion having been removed from the sphere of rationality is left homeless, placed outside in the sphere of the irrational, the realm of ultimate conviction or, for some, in the emotional realm. Max Weber's account of modernity paints this picture in terms of the historical trajectory of rationalisation in the West resulting in modern forms of religion that have been disenchanted or *entzaubert* (purified of magic): the emergence of Reformed Protestantism being the consequence of this process of rationalisation.[8] A religion that has emerged through the internal rationalisation of Christianity, and hence modernisation of religion, is one which accepts its place as that of the decision of ultimate conviction.

This choice between faith or reason leads to the removal of religion out of the spheres of rationality, out of the realm of science and into the conflictual realm of the clash between the "gods and the demons" of ultimate value commitments. One can interpret the current situation of the Catholic Church with respect to its position on authority in a similar light. Trapped within a classical metaphysical conception of objectivist rationality it has actually lost its ability to articulate this vision in a credible way to a Western post-metaphysical culture. Whilst it holds on to an authoritarian teaching style and condemns the post-metaphysical secular culture as relativist, it effectively removes itself from the public debate by declaring authoritative pronouncements based on its objectivist position. From the point of view of the Catholic hierarchy the fact that others do not accept this position is due to a relativism that has gripped hold of Western civilisation. This characterisation of secular rationality as relativist leaves the Catholic Church with the only option in debate of authoritatively declaring its position as objectively true without being able to offer credible arguments to those outside of its own worldview. Such a metaphysical conception of objectivist rationality corresponded to a classical and medieval philosophical and social framework. It does not correspond to the rationality the modern democratic world. This is why in declaring issues such as women's ordination as no longer open to debate, as having been infallibly defined in the 1998 document from the Congregation for the Doctrine of the Faith *Ad Tuendam Fidem* and Pope John Paul II's 1994 document on women's ordination *Ordinatio Sacerdotalis*, the impression is created of being in a medieval kingdom rather than in a modern Catholic Church.

The inability of the Catholic Church to modernise and to meet the problems and challenges of the modern age has resulted in it being locked into a former framework of rationality that it has absolutised as the only possible conception of itself and reality. This has pushed it into the irrational sphere of personal conviction, as Weber would describe it, and has paradoxically resulted in a 'protestantisation' of the Catholic Church. The

---

[7] See David Martin, *Pentecostalism: The World Their Parish*, Wiley-Blackwell, Malden, 2001.

[8] See Anthony J. Carroll, *Protestant Modernity. Weber, Secularisation, and Protestantism*, University of Scranton Press, Scranton, 2007, pp. 83-166.

general perception of faith and reason today is that these domains have become separated in this process and have left the Catholic Church unable to articulate its sacramental conception of reality in a way which makes sense to the wider society and indeed even to many within the Catholic Church today. This nostalgic move has of course its supporters and does have a powerful attraction for many. The longing for the former place of security and familiarity is a deep current in human experience and one which can result in a turning away from present reality and towards a real or imagined past. The Neo-Thomist turn in the modern Catholic tradition was a case in point and was a major factor in the short circuiting of important debates that emerged during the so-called "modernist crisis".[9]

But unless the Catholic Church faces up to the challenges presented to it today it will not be able to move forward outside of the option of being a community of resistance, closer in structure to that of a sect which stands against the modern world. Whilst this option may have the advantage of seeming to be heroic it actually negates the sacramental conception of the church and world relation that has normative roots in the Catholic tradition. The shift from a metaphysical conception of the exercise of authority, which is strong and self-sufficient, to a kenotic model is an important precondition of being able to face up to problems courageously and imaginatively. Only by entering into real dialogue concerning the fundamental challenges posed by our age will it be possible for the Catholic Church to discern the voice of the Holy Spirit speaking in the church and in the world today, and so to exercise its teaching authority with credibility.

Moreover, because of its structures and institutions the Catholic Church is in an important position to foster such dialogue as it has in the area of interreligious dialogue, for example.[10] It should also foster intercultural dialogue around the key issues of the age in a kenotic way which opens up spaces which are safe for people to enter and to enquire together about possible ways forward. The risk for the church is that it closes down such spaces of rational enquiry by a strategy of declaring unquestionable metaphysical truths, rather than through kenotically entering into the rational enquiry of the truth which emerges gradually through open and responsible dialogue.[11] Moreover, this is not simply a strategic change;

---

[9] See Anthony J. Carroll, "The philosophical foundations of Catholic Modernism", in Oliver Rafferty (ed.), *George Tyrrell and Catholic Modernism*, Four Courts Press, Dublin, 2010, pp. 38-55.

[10] On this issue see the article by Tomáš Halík and Anthony J. Carroll in Charles Taylor, José Casanova, and George McClean (eds.), *Church and People: Disjunctions in a Secular Age*, The Council for Research in Values and Philosophy, Washington, 2012, pp. 189-213

[11] See Louis Caruana's reflections on Charles Sanders Peirce's fourth method of settling opinion on contested issues in scientific enquiry in his essay, "Disagreement and Authority: Comparing Ecclesial and Scientific Practices" in this volume.

rather, it is because of faith that one can do this. Faith opens up the possibility of not clinging on to any metaphysical idols and of recognising the fact that we are always pilgrims on the way to a greater depth of understanding of God and God's presence in our world and in the church.[12] The danger of idolatry is thus not something of former times. It is an actual and very real danger of creating an image of God and the church in our own idealised likeness and image and fixed in metaphysical categories.

OVERCOMING IDOLATRY

The great protestant theologian Karl Barth took this critique of a certain metaphysical understanding of God as his point of departure for his dialectical theology. Central to Barth's project of rethinking theology in the twentieth century is the notion that thought about God had mirrored much too closely thought about a certain understanding of anthropology. The Feuerbachian notion of the isolated and self-concerned individual, the one who posits itself absolutely and who lives as if one could live for oneself alone, is both a false anthropology and a false theology for Barth. God is the one who decides from all eternity to be for humanity and in doing this constitutes humanity in grace as always a social animal, always for and with others. The atheistic rejection of God on the grounds of the alienation of the potential of humanity that is projected onto an illusory god is for Barth a false anthropological premise. God and humanity are intrinsically related and in reality neither lives in solitude from the other but rather in communion. The isolated individual is the alienated individual, alienated from God and other human beings. In relationship to God this alienation is removed and not constituted as it is in the anthropology of Feuerbach. As Barth puts it in his *Church Dogmatics*, "The solitary man is the potential, and in a more refined or blatant way the actual, enemy of all others".[13]

What Barth clearly saw in his theology was that the metaphysical inheritance of the all-powerful self-positing god was in the end an idol. A reflection of a false and idealised image of the human person which has been projected onto God and something which became the enemy of a modern humanity looking to liberate itself from all external encroachments on its own individual freedom. In the legitimate striving for freedom in the context of an increasingly materialistic and naturalistic worldview, modern anthropology shifted away from what Charles Taylor has called the "porous" understanding of the self to the "punctual" or "buffered" self.[14]

---

[12] On this point, see Nicholas Lash, *Theology for Pilgrims*, Dart, Longman and Todd Ltd., London, 2008.

[13] Karl Barth, *Die Kirchliche Dogmatik*, 4 vols., Zollikon, Zurich, 1936-68, Vol., 4/2., p. 474.

[14] See Charles Taylor, *Sources of The Self. The Making of Modern Identity*, Cambridge University Press, Cambridge, pp. 159-176; and *A Secular*

Isolated from its surroundings and alienated from the spiritual realm this separation became a necessary Freudian rupture from the father figure. The autonomous self, buffered from its surroundings, rejects the god of the first cause, the god who is the 'highest being' and instead sees itself as its own origin and law. Against this conception of the human person, Barth sees the God of Jesus Christ as the one who reveals the humanity of God and in so doing reveals that the human person is a person in relationship with God and it is through this relationship that human subjectivity is formed. Atheism in Barth's language is isolation. It negates the original constitution of human subjectivity in being with and for others in the original relationship to God. Rather than the unmoved mover, the essence of God is "Emmanuel, God with us". This turn to the self-emptying God of Jesus Christ is the revelation of God as love not as Supreme Being; or as Barth puts it, "There is no humanlessness in God".[15]

Barth saw atheism and Theism as caught in the same idolatrous trap. But whilst Theists worship this metaphysical idol beyond themselves atheists take on its very identity. They grasp this illusory independent being for themselves and in so doing may become enslaved to the non-being of isolation. Followers of Barth, such as Eberhard Jüngel, have developed convincing accounts of the modern dialectical genealogy of atheism and Theism that emerges out of this classical metaphysical conception of God.[16] Tracing the philosophical trajectory through the modernity of Theism and atheism, Jüngel outlines how this has led to an inability to think, speak, and worship this god for modern people. Concluding his work with a characteristically Barthian gesture towards a recovery of the humanity of God, he reminds us that it is the God of love who speaks to us, is with us, and to whom we pray and give praise that emerges after the death of this metaphysical idol in modernity.

An important question raised by Barth's theological enterprise is to what extent religion itself is guilty of creating and worshiping this metaphysical idol. In manufacturing a metaphysical idol and patterning this idolatry in institutional forms of religion, religion may itself be a major part of the cause of unbelief today. Paul Ricoeur makes this point in his 1966 Bampton Lectures entitled "Religion, Atheism, and Faith". Drawing on the inspiration of philosophers such as Feuerbach and Nietzsche, and theologians such as Barth and Bonhoeffer, Ricoeur explores the uneasy tension between religion and faith. He discusses the archaic roots of religion

---

Age, Belknap Press of Harvard University Press, Cambridge Mass., and London, 2007, pp. 37-42, 134-142, 300-307.

[15] Karl Barth, *Die Kirchliche Dogmatik*, 4 vols. Zollikon, Zurich, 1936-68, Vol., 4/1., p. 591. On this point, see also his classic essay, "The Humanity of God", in *The Humanity of God*, Collins, London, 1961, pp. 37-65.

[16] See E. Jüngel, *God as the Mystery of the World. On the Foundation of the Theology of the Crucified One in the Dispute between Theism and Atheism*, Eerdmans, Grand Rapids, 2008.

in two fundamental poles of religious feeling. The first is grounded in the taboo structure of religions. Here humanity is caught in fear due to the threat of divine punishment and expiation. Religion provides a way of dealing with this primal fear through various forms of appeasing god or the gods which feeds our basic desire for liberation from fear. The other primal feeling is that for protection. This is rooted in the desire to escape the contingency and vulnerability of existence which various offers of eternity provide. Religion, for Ricoeur, is formed in these primitive structures of life which always need to be overcome by faith if God is to occupy in an individual's life more than simply the functions of being an escape from punishment and a protection from insecurity. This is why, for Ricoeur, atheism can be important for people of faith. At its best it can unmask the primitive desires of our humanity which are responsible for the manufacturing of idols. Freud and Nietzsche, for example, do this for the taboo structures of religion. They both reveal aspects of religion as being mechanisms of fear and dependency, hidden motivations of piety, which deny life rather than affirm it. So, rather than seeing the atheistic critiques of such thinkers as Freud and Nietzsche, as being against faith, religious traditions should be discerningly open to the purifying of such primal idolatrous functions of religion that detract from the true meaning of faith as born of love and not of fear and the desire for security. In denying such idolatrous forms of religion it is the metaphysical god who dies in modernity, and the possibility of a faith after metaphysical forms of religion open up for Ricoeur beyond the modern dialectic of atheism and Theism.[17]

TOWARDS A KENOTIC EXERCISE OF MAGISTERIAL AUTHORITY

This divesting of ourselves of false idols has accompanied the monotheistic journey from its beginnings and has contemporary relevance with the recovery of the ancient tradition of negative theology of the Church Fathers such as Gregory of Nyssa and also in the turn to a phenomenology of the gift and giving in many areas of recent philosophy and theology. Whist this turn has been less evident in contemporary social and political theory this is perhaps due to the fact that democratic deliberation which characterises how modern democracies work has seen itself as anti-metaphysical and hence anti-religious. The "hence" here is the crux of the problem. The equation of religion with metaphysics has led modern political theory to think the political in terms of the "political not metaphysical" of John Rawls and the "post-metaphysical" deliberative democracy of Jürgen Habermas.[18] Both Rawls and Habermas were formed in a Protestant milieu

---

[17] See P. Ricoeur, "Religion, Atheism, and Faith", in *The Conflict in Interpretations*, Northwestern University Press, Evanston, 1974, pp. 440-467.

[18] Jürgen Habermas has developed his earlier thinking on postmetaphysical thought (*Nachmetaphysisches Denken,* 1988) in his recent

and share an instinctive reaction to the characteristically Catholic metaphysical approach.[19] Metaphysics here is a "discussion stopper", it is the bringing out of the "wild card" of the non-discursive authoritative dogma that forecloses rational debate. In this form, religion is incapable of democratic participation because it has preconceived ideas that are not open to justification, questioning, and revision.

The ideas that are relevant in the context of the Catholic Church's relation to the political sphere today are usually not core theological ideas such as the nature of the Trinity or the Sacraments and so on but rather the moral positions which influence behaviour and can directly affect legislation. It is the dogmatic core of unquestionable and un-revisable positions that are resistant to the democratic process of rational exchange that constitutes the inadequacy of metaphysical forms of religion for the democratic process. Rawls develops this position in his later work in terms of the "overlapping consensus" required from comprehensive doctrines to allow the democratic process to work in such a way that "ring fences" the undemocratic metaphysical dogmas from political debate. Habermas also performs a similar move in terms of his work on religion through the translation strategy that makes religious positions publically accessible in a secular rational language. In both cases the equation of metaphysical forms of religion with democratic inadequacy is characteristic of Protestant scepticism in matters of metaphysics and represents the form in which modern political theory has participated in the movement towards the death of the metaphysical conception of god.

On the side of the Roman Catholic Church such opposition to metaphysical positions has shaped a Catholic identity distinct from Protestantism. Resisting both external forces such as Protestantism, which move away from the metaphysical and towards a biblical basis of the faith, and internal forces which attempted to bring the Catholic tradition into dialogue with the modern world, the hierarchical structure of the church has often modelled itself on the metaphysical pattern of former feudal times in an attempt to secure a clear identity for itself in the modern world. One can see this in the Catholic version of identity politics that so often plays itself out in public debates over central moral issues today with the Catholic position being associated with the anti-gay rights position, for example. Representation of a Catholic view on the issue thus means being against gay

---

reflections on the continued importance of religion in post-secular societies. Although he sees no possibility of a return to a metaphysical (pre-Hegel) manner of thinking in late modernity, he nevertheless holds that post-metaphysical philosophy can neither replace nor repress the importance of religious thought and sentiment today. See his *Nachmetaphysisches Denken II. Aufsätze und Repliken*, Suhrkamp, Berlin, 2012.

[19] See Habermas 2012, op cit., p. 174 and John Rawls, *A Brief Inquiry into the Meaning of Sin and Faith with "on My Religion"*, edited by Thomas Nagel, Harvard University Press, Cambridge, Mass., 2009.

marriage or civil partnerships. There is little or no sense of real discussion within the Catholic Church on this issue because those in positions of authority are understandably afraid to appear unfaithful or even heretical. As a consequence few people are comfortable to enter public debates on these issues as Catholics. Those people who do usually follow the 'party line' and thus seem to be defending the church's unchanging and infallible moral position.[20]

The point here, however, is not that those who argue against gay marriage and the like should have no public forum. It is rather that the Catholic position on these matters is represented as if it were a part of the fixed deposit of the faith. Such a representation of the Catholic view on complex moral issues is a consequence of a stifling of internal debate and exchange of views that exist in the Catholic Church on such matters. Those priests and bishops who themselves are gay are often caught in a dilemma here. Unable to be open about their sexuality and afraid of speaking out of turn in the public forum they may remain silent or even, as we have seen recently, for a whole range of complex reasons, defend an abstract and uncommitted theology that Francis Oakley sees as characterising the teaching style of the church. But this means that the voice of the church in open discussion is absent from the public forum. Consequently, in many contexts the position of the church on such matters as gay relationships and gay marriage is represented as a dogmatic position adherence to which indicates orthodoxy. The extension of the understanding of the deposit of faith to such contentious matters without the necessary open exchange and consensus building has fostered an authoritarian style of exercising magisterial authority that lacks credibility. Furthermore, this illustrates the real danger of the so called 'creeping infallibility' in the Catholic Church: it has damagingly helped to foster a general perception of an absence of an internal connection between faith and reason in modern Western cultures.

In considering such matters as gay marriage the connection between the understanding of God and a certain model of authority in the church are displayed in a practical way. The metaphysical understanding of God has been patterned in the authoritarian structures of authority in the church. The omniscient, omnipotent God of the onto-theological tradition is mirrored in the absolutist monarchy of the papacy and in the inability of the church to allow genuine discussion over matters such as sexual morality. The inability of this classical metaphysical tradition to think change outside of inferiority

---

[20] The recent statements by Pope Francis on not judging gay clergy clearly soften a condemnatory tone in earlier documents on the formation of clergy. See, for example, the document of the Congregation for Catholic Education, "Instruction concerning the criteria for discernment of vocations with regard to persons with homosexual tendencies in view of their admission to the seminary and to holy orders": <http://www.vatican.va/roman_curia/congregations/ccatheduc/documents/rc_con_ccatheduc_doc_20051104_istruzione_en.html> accessed 14 August, 2013.

prevents an understanding of changing moral positions which develop as new insights and knowledge emerges.

Moreover, the issue of our changed and changing understanding of the human person and their sexuality need not involve the position *that God, after further reflection, has changed God's mind on particular issues*! Whilst debates with God especially in the Old Testament have taken place and represent God as changing his mind,[21] it is rather the issue here that our understanding of God and the human condition have evolved over time. The inability of the classical metaphysical tradition to think change outside of imperfection means that the evolution of Catholic moral theory is inhibited by the notion that moral positions are metaphysically fixed. The same issue is faced in terms of the ordination of women with the argument that the church has no power to change this as the ordination of men is the will of God objectively given and this cannot change. That we may have come to a new understanding of the nature of ministry is judged by this criterion as being simply a wrong understanding. The debate is once again closed and reasons why ministry should be restricted to men are simply defended by the argument from a purely fixed conception of tradition. And this argument from unchanging tradition is itself often grounded in an implicit conception of God objectively giving the fine details of human action. Such a metaphysical interpretation of the mediation of God's eternal law and our concrete actions has been translated into morality through an anti-Reformation apologetics which influenced the Neo-Thomist reception of natural law theory.

Yet, as a number of recent Thomist-inspired thinkers such as Michael Keeling and Russell Hittinger have noted, it would be wrong to lay the blame for this conception of natural law simply at the feet of St. Thomas Aquinas.[22] Natural law ethics, for Thomas, does not prescribe a detailed list of "do's and don'ts" for the moral life. Rather, it has been the teaching authorities of the church which have used it to provide an excessively detailed list of such rules and indeed have made "the definition of natural law an 'act of authority'" promulgated in the encyclical letter *Humanae Vitae* as a matter for the magisterium to define.[23] The fact that Thomas only considers a single question on natural law in the *secunda pars* (ST 1-2. 94) illustrates that it should not be treated in isolation. Rather, natural law should be understood in the context of his general considerations of the nature of divine providence and how our lives participate in this. As Pamela M. Hall argues, only by considering natural law in relation to how it draws us towards or away from God through our actions do we properly

---

[21] See, for example, Abraham's pleading with God for Sodom and Gomorrah in Genesis 18: 16-33.

[22] Fergus Kerr, *After Aquinas. Versions of Thomism*, Blackwell, London, 2002, pp. 97-113.

[23] See Kerr, 2002, op cit., p. 99.

understand Thomas's intentions in the *secunda pars*.[24] Isolated interpretations of this question tend towards producing moral algorithms and distort this wider purpose of how individual people reach happiness and holiness. This exercise of the magisterial teaching authority conflates its legitimate normative authority with an inappropriate degree of moral certainty that is difficult to reconcile with the positions of Aristotle and St. Thomas on these matters.

Reflection on such issues as homosexuality and the ordination of women illustrates the "democratic deficit" that is manifest in a traditional metaphysical understanding of the church; unchanging and unchangeable. The objectivist metaphysical conception of God and natural law provides a fixed set of categories which are by nature unchangeable. As such the role of the church having discovered these categories is to guard them for all eternity, to protect them from the introduction of error, and to transmit them to the passive faithful. Faith and morality become intrinsically connected in this manner through a metaphysics of being that is manifested in theological absolutes and objectivist moral categories.[25] The church culture which emerges in this situation is one which is unable to discuss openly contentious issues without accusing people of infidelity and heresy. This reinforces a peer pressure amongst the bishops to adhere to an over-determined conception of the deposit of faith and of moral prescriptions as a religious duty. The primal structures of religion that Paul Ricoeur noted also function at these levels of institutional organisation. On the one hand, they maintain a culture of fear and dependency in which individual bishops feel unable to speak their minds openly (at least during the active years of their ministry) without fear of being condemned and perhaps punished by being removed from office. Those 'aspiring' to such positions of authority in the church are thus socialised into a culture of conformity in which they know that to 'get ahead' one has to 'tow the party line'.

On the other hand, they provide a great security in following 'the party line' as this protects from a sense of vulnerability and isolation. The protection of the father figure, and indeed a whole culture of paternalism, from the insecurity of not knowing on matters of faith and morals, is very consoling! It also confers the consolation of being loyal and being part of the *esprit de corps* by which groups naturally bind individuals together through a whole range of conservative mechanisms and measures. But such a culture of conformism manifests more the archaic structures of religion rather than the open and courageous culture of faith. Without support and

---

[24] See Pamela M. Hall, *Narrative and the Natural Law: An Interpretation of Thomistic Ethics*, Notre Dame University Press, Notre Dame, 1994.

[25] Here, I am not denying a priori that there are universal principles to morality which can be known with certainty and that these principles can be applied to concrete situations. Rather, I am arguing that the metaphysical manner of elucidating and justifying such principles has become less than satisfactory today.

encouragement for bishops, and indeed the people in general, to speak openly and to allow for real differences of opinion a centralising and absolutist culture has emerged in the Catholic Church in which disagreement is viewed not as reasonable and mature but rather as disobedience requiring correction and even at times punishment.[26] Such a culture has encouraged a split between private opinions and public declarations which gives the false impression of homogeneity when it comes to contentious issues. As such a real enquiry into problems and challenges facing the church is often short circuited by a set of readymade and *presumed* objectivistic solutions that foreclose open and serious debate.[27] The danger with this situation is that as humanity develops its understanding of the world and of the human person the position of faith and moral enquiry can and indeed is becoming ever more detached from the position of reason, which by its nature is always situated in time, enquiring into new possibilities and options, and looking for solutions to emerging problems. Such a lack of open enquiry is in itself also a characteristic of non-kenotic ways of operating. It assumes that the truth is already known about a matter and that the task is simply for others to come to see this. But without a shift in the Catholic Church's understanding of how it should exercise its teaching authority to engage with open enquiry it is difficult to see how faith and reason will be reconnected in the general perception of many people in the modern world. And in the tradition of Catholic enquiry this is both bad for faith and bad for reason.

It is bad for faith because it reduces the general perception of faith to the affirmation of a set of propositional beliefs. This attitude views faith as less of a journey and rather as static, something to be tightly gripped. Yet, the actual dynamics of faith are much less like possessing something and rather more like moving (changing) forward in loving trust knowing that even though one does not know all the answers there is a fundamental goodness and truth that is discovered in the journey of faith. In fact, this not knowing characterises the journey of faith. It is the encounter with this darkness of unknowing that signals a maturation in faith and a deeper entry into the embrace of the loving God beyond all metaphysical idols. It is

---

[26] For a more helpful contribution to the issues surrounding disagreement, see Richard Feldman and Ted A. Warfield (eds.), *Disagreement*, Oxford University Press, Oxford, 2010; Christopher McMahon, *Reasonable Disagreement: A Theory of Political Morality*, Cambridge University Press, Cambridge, 2009; Linda T. Zagzebski, *Epistemic Authority: A Theory of Trust, Authority, and Autonomy in Belief*, Oxford University Press, Oxford, 2012.

[27] On this issue, see the interesting remarks of Joseph Ratzinger who in his debate with Jürgen Habermas in 2004 admitted that the assumption of agreement on "the notions of rational human nature and natural law" should not be presumed to be taken for granted prior to serious dialogue between cultures and religions, in Anthony J. Carroll, "Faith, reason and modernity", *The Tablet*, 30 September 2006, p. 11.

through this dynamic interplay between the active divesting of oneself of idols and the passive being drawn of oneself into the mystery of God that one grows in faith.

Ultimately this journey of faith is the journey of mystical love which leads to union and not only to an epistemological knowledge of metaphysical truths in which subject and object remain apart, as great works in the mystical tradition such as Gregory of Nyssa's *Life of Moses* have most eloquently expressed.[28] Perhaps part of the reason for the difficulty of the leadership of the church to pattern this now is due to the understandable anxiety that can arise with anyone, especially with those whose specific charge is that of leading others in challenging times, to themselves having to relinquish control of this process in faith. Yet, the dark night of the soul is also manifest in the dark night of the church and it is only in the courage of faith that one can enter this and relinquish former certainties in order to move more deeply and be moved more deeply into participation in the mystery of God.

Such general perceptions of the detachment of faith and reason are also bad for our common vision of reason because it allows for a conception of reason to grow that can more easily follow the desires of the ego, the desires for power, control and self-assertion that naturally follow when the self is placed in the centre rather than God. The decentring of reason that happens when allied with faith allows reason to function non-instrumentally and to pursue the common good. It liberates reason from an egocentric goal that appears realistic but is actually illusory and often self-destructive as many commentators on reason and rationality in the twentieth century have noted.[29] Faith thus opens out the way to a kenotic use of reason that is not full of itself nor intent on simply winning its own way but is really dedicated to finding the truth. It allows reason to find truth in inter-subjective deliberation as it can recognise the force of the better argument regardless of from whom this originates. It also allows reason to abandon positions formerly held because it is no longer tied to an absolutist conception of its own categories of understanding.

In St. Paul's letters, he seems to be attacking this way of using our human reason, or of doing philosophy, which he describes as *kata sarka*, according to the flesh, self-important, focussed on trouncing the opposing party by powerful and crushing argument that is merely destructive. Such "*sarkic*" philosophical practices are widespread in our culture today. Practitioners are more interested in the triumph of their own ideas than in the pursuit of wisdom (*Sophia*) or a constructive and collaborative attempt to advance human understanding. In the language of the Letter to the Philippians, the "mind of Christ", or one might venture to say a "Christian

---

[28] See Gregory of Nyssa, *The Life of Moses*, Paulist Press, New Jersey, 1978.

[29] See, for example, the now classic Max Horkheimer and Theodor Adorno, *Dialectic of Enlightenment*, Verso, London, 1979.

philosophy", is a form of "kenotic" or self-emptying philosophical practice. The power of such practice is not fleshly, worldly, or hubristic; it is divine in that it is manifest in what the proud think of as weakness. In this sense a Christian use of reason would not be dependent on a particular metaphysics or a specific method but rather on an attitude or an approach of mind and heart in which humility is a condition of the possibility of truth.[30]

Such a kenotic attitude is contrary to the metaphysical absolutist approaches which threaten to detach general perceptions of faith from reason. The dogmatic defence of such anti-kenotic positions actually becomes ideological in that they are no longer open to rational critique. But when such critique is fostered and encouraged there is a robust and healthy culture of enquiry that safeguards from both ideology and idolatry. Ideology and idolatry both resist rational critique because critique can reveal the irrational core of both and in this way it disempowers and de-sacralises them. The silencing of people in the church who speak out on controversial issues, often out of love for the church, is a sign of an understanding of critique that is operative in parts of the hierarchy of the church. Rather than operating in this punitive manner, it should be important in the exercise of the teaching authority of the church to safeguard open enquiry and to encourage voices to speak out in pursuit of the truth for which all people of good will should be striving.

In safeguarding such spaces of rational enquiry the church has an important role in the modern world which itself is often caught up in its own dogmatisms and idolatries. The freedom of faith is manifest in the ability to hear criticism and not to foreclose open debate and enquiry. In such freedom the exercise of reason can operate less instrumentally because it is liberated from the need to be right at all times. Like faith, the kenotic use of reason is on a journey of purgation towards union with God.

CONCLUSION

There can be little doubt that the exercise of magisterial authority in the church is viewed with suspicion by many within and most without the church at this moment of its history. If the church is to regain credibility in its magisterial teaching authority it will be necessary for it to rethink its way of operating so that it neither abandons its legitimate authority to be the guardian and teacher of the faith nor concludes that it can carry on the exercise of this authority in the manner that it has in the past. I have argued that an important part of the transformation required is to move towards a post-metaphysical exercise of its teaching authority in which it engages with appropriate forms of open deliberation that work towards consensus building. Moreover, the church also needs to develop a positive

---

[30] See Paul W. Gooch, "Paul, the Mind of Christ, and Philosophy," in Paul K. Moser, *Jesus and Philosophy*, Cambridge University Press, Cambridge, 2009, pp. 84-108.

understanding of the development of doctrine which allows for discontinuity as well as the currently dominant continuity model if it is to better correspond to the actual rather than the imagined developments of doctrine throughout church history.[31]

The inheritance of a metaphysically informed negative understanding of development and change has fostered an attitude in the magisterium which tends to view alterations to church teachings as deviation from the eternal truth rather than as the gradual and tentative discovery of it. Moreover, this rigid attitude has locked the magisterium into a corner of being unable to admit to mistakes. Without such a humane possibility of admitting the need for revisions it will remain prohibitively difficult for the magisterium to counterbalance the Vatican I defined assertion of its infallibility with an evangelically humble recognition of its own fallibility. A better working out of this constitutively humane relation between fallibility and infallibility could help to guard against what I have referred to as the "creeping infallibility" issue in the church today. The current overextension of the legitimate parameters of the deposit of the faith has undoubtedly been a result of this lack of equilibrium. The inability of the church to clarify these issues has led to it short circuiting the necessary open rational debate on contentious matters by dogmatic assertions of truth which lack credibility for most people socialised in modern democratic societies today.

Furthermore, the burden of not being able to admit that one has made errors has created an unhealthy culture in the church which is understandably but unnecessarily afraid to recognise mistakes for fear that the whole edifice collapse *like a house built on sand*.[32] This is a paradoxical situation given the evangelical importance of recognising oneself as a sinner and always in need of God's forgiveness and healing. Yet, this may well be due to an institutional manifestation of the inheritance of a legacy of the earlier structures of primal religion explicated in our time in contrasting and complementary ways by thinkers such as Paul Ricoeur, Robert Bellah, and Hans Joas.[33]

Clearly, something major needs to change in the manner of the exercise of magisterial authority if these issues are to be addressed in such a way which restores both credibility, and even more importantly, a healthy attitude to authority in the Catholic Church. I have argued that a significant change that needs to happen is the adoption of what I have called a "kenotic attitude" to the exercise of magisterial authority. Such a kenotic exercise of magisterial authority can foster a healthy attitude and restore credibility as it

---

[31] See Lacey and Oakley (eds.), 2012, op cit., p. 49.

[32] Cf., Matthew 7: 24-27.

[33] See Paul Ricoeur op cit., Robert Bellah, *Religion in Human Evolution. From the Paleolithic to the Axial Age*, Belknap Press of Harvard University Press, 2011. and Robert Bellah and Hans Joas, (eds.) *The Axial Age and Its Consequences*, Belknap Press of Harvard University Press, 2012.

reproduces the "mind of Christ" who "being in the very nature of God did not consider equality with God as something to be grasped but emptied himself taking the form of a slave..." (Phil. 2: 5-11). It is fundamentally the lack of congruence between the authority structures of the church and this "mind of Christ" which is manifesting a performative contradiction in the exercise of magisterial authority today and losing the church credibility as a witness of the gospel in the world.

No doubt, the belief that the church cannot err is grounded in the metaphysical conception of the omniscient God as representing the "mind of Christ" and it is this which translates into the *omniscient* church. But whilst one *should* hold to the omniscience of God it does not follow that this is manifested in the church at each moment of its history and in its complete fullness. The events of church history have revealed the church to be a pilgrim on this journey and not a fixed dweller in the *house of truth*. Rather, confident in the presence of the Holy Spirit guiding the church, it is rather faith in the fullness of truth as something which we are being led into and not something which we actually possess at any one moment in the history of the church that should animate an open and enquiring mind in the church. Without such an understanding of the discovery of truth humble enquiry has been replaced by dogmatic fiat and it is this vision of a 'realised eschatology' in the church which hinders the actual historical church in its search for ways forward. Being neither a free-floating relativism nor an absolutist rationalism such an understanding of the discovery of truth is consonant with our understanding of this process in scientific enquiry.[34] It is also grounded in the adventure of faith which rejects all forms of idolatry as less than the vision of truth shared with us by the living God throughout the ages.

If my argument is correct, the lack of congruence between the "mind of Christ" and the current exercise of magisterial authority is itself a product of a lack of faith in the God whom Anselm in his *Proslogion* knew to be at the dark edge of conceptual knowledge and whom, as St. Paul reminds us, is the one "who can do infinitely more than we can ask or imagine" (Eph. 3: 20).

Heythrop College, London, Great Britain

---

[34] On the congruence between religious and scientific enquiry, see Louis Caruana's paper in this volume.

CHAPTER V

DISAGREEMENT AND AUTHORITY: COMPARING ECCLESIAL AND SCIENTIFIC PRACTICES

LOUIS CARUANA, SJ

Within the context of faith, all authority is seen as deriving from God. God, as creator, is the source of the very existence and nature of things, including humans, the societies they constitute, and the proper functioning of such societies. Within the context of secular thinking, however, authority cannot be defined, accounted for, or explained in this way, but must be considered in other terms, for instance in terms of a social contract. What both contexts agree on is that authority structures should act always in line with, or for the sake of, the common good. There is of course a danger of circularity here: the common good that determines the degrees of freedom of the structures of authority is itself very often determined by those very same structures of authority. The system can therefore seriously malfunction, giving rise to periods of intense disagreement, especially if sections of the authority structure become purely self-referential. Now, in recent years, disagreement as a philosophical topic has started to attract considerable attention, giving rise to rich debates not only about disagreement in itself but also about specifically political and religious disagreement.[1] Moreover, in some recent official documents of the Catholic Church, we see a similar growing concern about how to deal with religious pluralism, with dialogue among religions, and with the tension that sometimes arises even within the Church between theologians and the Magisterium.[2] Such considerations are very often carried out without any reference to how disagreement is handled in the natural sciences. What lies behind this is, most probably, the assumption that the dynamics of inquiry within the natural sciences, with its special engagement with material reality

---

[1] Richard Feldman and Warfield, eds., *Disagreement* (Oxford: Oxford University Press, 2010); Christopher McMahon, *Reasonable Disagreement: A Theory of Political Morality* (Cambridge: Cambridge University Press, 2009); Linda Trinkaus Zagzebski, *Epistemic Authority: A Theory of Trust, Authority, and Autonomy in Belief* (Oxford; New York: Oxford University Press, 2012).

[2] International Theological Commission, "Theology Today: Perspectives, Principles and Criteria," 2012; Congregation for the Doctrine of the Faith, "Donum Veritatis: On the Ecclesial Vocation of the Theologian," 1990; Congregation for the Doctrine of the Faith, "Dominus Iesus: On the Unicity and Salvific Universality of Jesus Christ and the Church," 2000.

via experimentation, is totally different from that of the more human or religious areas of inquiry.

A new situation is however now becoming increasingly evident: the idea of a strict dichotomy between the dynamics of disagreement within science and that within other areas of inquiry is being undermined by various sociological studies of science and epistemology. What needs to be done therefore is to revisit the issue of ecclesial disagreement, together with the associated idea of doctrinal authority, with an eye on what happens in the sciences. Such a study can be a very useful starting point for further research in what may be called comparative methodology. The structure of this paper is very simple. The first section will focus on the dynamics of doctrinal authority within the Church; the second will focus on the same aspects within the scientific community; and the third will compare the two, ending with some suggestions. Since each area is vast, I will focus primarily on two particular influential authors and explore their ideas at some depth.

CHURCH AUTHORITY

The dynamics of theological inquiry within the Councils and within other kinds of meetings in the course of the history of the Church has been studied in innumerable ways, but one of the most profound, inspiring, and influential accounts remains that of John Henry Newman. Rather than present an overview of all the various currents of thought related to the Church's theological self-understanding, I will, as mentioned above, simplify the matter by focusing at first exclusively on some of Newman's contributions that are most relevant for this paper, referring mainly to his *A Grammar of Assent* and *An Essay on the Development of Christian Doctrine*. My understanding is that these contributions are typical of the very best the Church has to offer as regards the explicitation of the process whereby doctrinal inquiry and decision making happen within the ecclesial community.

We can start with the most general description of deliberation and assent. In this area, the key notion in Newman's thinking is what he called the illative sense, the sense that 'determines what science cannot determine, the limit of converging probabilities and the reasons sufficient for a proof'.[3] Newman was convinced that there is no step by step logical sequence that leads an individual from particular probabilistic judgements to certainty. What we see rather is a culmination of probabilities, which are 'independent of each other, arising out of the nature and circumstances of the particular case which is under review; probabilities too fine to avail separately, too subtle and circuitous to be convertible into syllogisms, to numerous and various for such a conversion'.[4] He postulated the illative sense to account

---

[3] John Henry Newman, *An Essay in Aid of a Grammar of Assent* (London: Longmans, 1903), ch 9, sec. 3; p. 360.
[4] Ibid., ch 8, sec. 2; p.288.

for the way individuals bridge the gap between probabilistic judgements and certainty. The gap is real because no amount of probabilities can add up to full certainty. In other words, adding probabilities can lead only to some other probability and never to certainty. Newman was aware of this issue and solved it by resorting to Isaac Newton who had argued that, in general, a limit of a series can indeed be different in kind from the elements of that series. For instance, for a series of regular polygons inscribed within a circle with increasing number of sides, the limit is the circumference of the circle, which is not itself a polygon. Newman argued that a series of probable judgements is like this series of regular polygons: it converges onto something that differs essentially from itself. It converges onto a judgement that is not itself probable but certain.[5] And the way we make this jump from probabilities to certainty is by exercising the illative sense.

This brief sketch is enough to show that Newman is not talking about a form of inference. The illative sense is not a logical procedure whereby a general proposition is justified by a finite number of exemplars – it is not induction. When Newman talks about the illative sense, he is exploring a particular aspect of human cognition, and what he refers to by the expression 'illative sense', even though related to logical processes that characterize thinking, is primarily a characteristic of human beings. What we have here, therefore, is a phenomenological study of the attaining of certitude. Moreover, because the illative sense is a characteristic of human beings that can lie dormant, as it were, when no occasion arises to manifest it, and can also be made better by frequent use, it can be called a virtue. It is clear that Newman is not describing here a cognitive characteristic that is specific to religious beliefs. The way a sequence of probable judgements can converge and can thereby enable the human person to arrive at a judgement that is not itself probable but certain occurs in the other areas of human intellectual activity. What happens in the religious sphere is a particularly clear case of such a process. One can see therefore that Newman's doctrine of the illative sense lies within the long tradition of Catholic thinking that adopts a naturalistic appreciation of the human spiritual vocation by highlighting how what is spiritual, in this case the act of faith, is not something inherently against what is material, but its perfection.

When considering a deliberation within the Church, an instance of doctrinal authority, we need of course to include a higher degree of complexity, especially because of the social nature of the event. Newman was aware that the illative sense works in different ways in different people: 'The inquirer has first of all to decide on the point from which he is to start in the presence of the received accounts; on what side, from what quarter he is to approach them; on what principles his discussion is to be conducted […] It is plain how incessant will be the call here or there for the exercise of

---

[5] Newman discusses this in a section on informal inference: Newman 1903, ch. 8, sec. 2, § 3.

a definite judgment, how little that judgement will be helped on by logic, and how intimately it will be dependent upon the intellectual complexion of the writer'.[6] For Newman the role of the illative sense is central. For him, agreement is assured not because there is an authority structure that checks all the logical steps one by one. It is assured because the illative sense can rise above all superficial differences. He writes: 'the fact remains, that, in any inquiry about things in the concrete, men differ from each other, not so much in the soundness of their reasoning as in the principles which govern its exercise, that those principles are of a personal character, that where there is no common measure of minds, there is no common measure of arguments, and that the validity of proof is determined not by any scientific test, but by the illative sense'.[7]

Is this enough to guarantee the attaining of truth? At one stage, Newman indicates that the illative sense is not enough. He thinks that, for attaining true certitudes, as opposed to false ones, we need divine intervention: 'this does suggest to us, that there is something deeper in our differences than the accident of external circumstances; and that we need the interposition of a Power, greater than human teaching and human argument, to make our beliefs true and our minds one'.[8]

We find many more interesting insights in his famous work *An Essay on the Development of Christian Doctrine*. Let me highlight two points that are of special importance for my inquiry. First, there is the claim that, since the development of ideas within the Christian community is inevitable, there must be a structure of authority. This dynamism emerges because divine revelation is not just operative but also acknowledged as such: 'Revelation has introduced a new law of divine governance over and above those laws which appear in the natural course of the world [...] As the Creator rested on the seventh day from the work which He had made, yet he "worketh hitherto"; so He gave the Creed once for all in the beginning, yet blesses its growth still, and provides for its increase'.[9] Newman's analogy involving organic life is already evident. He elaborates this point further by suggesting that church authority is within the believing community what conscience is within the individual. This parallelism has interesting consequences especially because individual conscience is not infallible. Newman develops Bellarmine's insight that just as we are obliged to obey our conscience even though we know that it is not infallible so also we are obliged to obey Church authority even when we do not see the point: 'as obedience to conscience, even supposing conscience ill-formed, tends to the improvement of our moral nature, and ultimately our knowledge, so obedience to our ecclesiastical superior may subserve our growth in

---

[6] Newman, *An Essay in Aid of a Grammar of Assent*, ch 9, sec 3; p.364.
[7] Ibid., ch 10, sec 2; p. 413.
[8] Ibid., ch 9, sec 3; p. 375.
[9] John Henry Newman, *Essay on the Development of Christian Doctrine*, 7th ed. (London: Longmans, 1890), 85.

illumination and sanctity, even though he should command what is extreme or inexpedient, or teach what is external to his legitimate province'.[10]

The second point worth highlighting is his famous list of criteria that distinguish genuine developments of an idea from corruptions. What lies behind all his criteria is the model of biological growth, such as that of a seed: 'it is plain, first of all, that a corruption is a word attaching to organised matters only; a stone may be crushed to powder, but it cannot be corrupted. Corruption, on the contrary, is the breaking up of life, preparatory to its termination'.[11] The criteria are seven. First, a development is genuine if it preserves the original idea's type (just as animals do not change their kind as they grow, so also ideas). Secondly, genuine development manifests the continuity of the original idea's principles (just as mathematics unfolds from a set of axioms and postulates, so also doctrines can be said to unfold from a set of principles that direct their development). Thirdly, genuine development is indicated when the original idea becomes capable of assimilating other ideas thus giving rise to a more extensive unity of comprehension. Fourthly, a genuine development is indicated when the later expression of an idea is linked to its earlier expression in a way that is logically consistent. Fifthly, the development of an idea is genuine when it realizes some of the anticipations inherent within the original idea. Sixthly, a genuine development conserves what was good in antecedent stages and adds to it; it does not correct comprehensively but corroborates. And lastly, a genuine development of an idea, unlike its corruption, is not violent and transient, but characterised by being peaceful and long lasting.[12]

These criteria together with the illative sense give a pretty good picture of how doctrinal authority should function according to Newman. Some may rightly point out that he does not do much to show how the illative sense operates within a community. For this we need to go to some of his other writings, such as *On Consulting the Faithful on Matters of Doctrine*. Here he explains that within a community of inquirers the illative sense functions not simply as a mere summation of the various individual illative senses but as a truly communal illative sense. What he calls the 'consensus fidelium' is a sort of collective virtue (what he calls 'phronema') in parallel with the individual virtue of practical reason ('phronesis'). To some scholars, these views indicate that Newman's position lies squarely within the current discussion on social epistemology, where belief-formation is not seen as an individual process but as a communal one that depends on the epistemic virtues shared by the members of that

---

[10] Ibid., 87.
[11] Ibid., 170.
[12] Newman explains and elaborates these criteria, which he describes as "Notes of varying cogency, independence and applicability", in chapter 5 of Newman, *Essay on the Development of Christian Doctrine*, and then discusses each at length in subsequent chapters.

community.[13] Once we speak of virtues within a community, we include the possibility that some individuals grow in such epistemic virtues more than others. This way allows an interesting and philosophically rich account of the role of the Magisterium within the Catholic hierarchy. Just as there is need for education as regards individual conscience, so also as regards the collective illative sense. This latter kind of education is realized through an ongoing interaction with the authority structure within the church community, involving Scripture, Tradition, and Magisterium.

With these ideas, Newman is rightly recognized as one of the most prominent theologians who defended a theological understanding, as opposed to a historicist understanding, of the development of Christian doctrine. Such a theological understanding, highlighting the supernatural nature of continuity within the process of development, and recalling that the deposit of faith is not only a set of propositions about God and the Church but also the divine mystery communicated by the indwelling Spirit, sees the historical unfolding of the deposit of faith as a coherent whole, where the implicit aspects are intimately connected to the explicit aspects. Other protagonists include Maurice Blondel, who described the development of doctrine as the shift from the implicitly lived to the explicitly known. Within the experience of the living Christian community there is much that remains subconscious, unrecognized, provisionally and partly irreducible to explicit thought.[14] Recent advances in philosophical hermeneutics have sustained such proposals, and the CDF arrived finally at a distinction between the meaning of a dogma, which always remains true, and the dogmatic formulations of the Church, which are true within the context of those who understand them, but remain open to further clarification and therefore changeable if needs arise: 'it often happens that ancient dogmatic formulas and others closely connected with them remain living and fruitful in the habitual usage of the Church, but with suitable expository and explanatory additions that maintain and clarify their original meaning. In addition, it has sometimes happened that in this habitual usage of the Church certain of these formulas gave way to new expressions which, proposed and approved by the Sacred Magisterium, presented more clearly or more completely the same meaning'[15].[16]

---

[13] Frederick D. Aquino, *Communities of Informed Judgement: Newman's Illative Sense and Accounts of Rationality* (Washington DC: Catholic University of America Press, 2004).

[14] Maurice Blondel, "Histoire et Dogme," in *Les Premiers Écrits de Maurice Blondel* (Paris: PUF, 1956), 210.

[15] Congregation for the Doctrine of the Faith, "Mysterium Ecclesiae," par. 5.

[16] Important theological works, within this tradition, about the development of Christian doctrine include: de Lubac 1948; Dhanis 1953; Rahner 1960; Poulat 1962; Ratzinger 1966; Schillebeeckx 1967.

SCIENTIFIC AUTHORITY

The way the theories proposed by natural science are, or should be, evaluated has been the object of intense study for hundreds of years. It is commonly believed that the issue is simply a matter of having recourse to a decisive experiment, but much more is involved. Although most philosophers involved in this area produced work that was primarily a specialized self-reflection and explicitation of their own scientific method and contributions (for instance Galileo and Newton), there were some who tried to see how the workings of science could affect and reform the entire discipline of philosophy. These latter thinkers had an enormous impact because they helped to transform what was in their time a somewhat restricted and specialized human activity into a way of thinking and a style of living for the masses, into a scientific *mentality*, with much broader implications than science itself. I will consider one of these latter thinkers for this section: Charles Sanders Peirce, famous for his launching of the philosophy of pragmatism, and arguably the philosopher whose ideas remain the most influential within current cultural trends that are becoming increasingly dominant within global economic and political transactions.[17]

In 1877, Peirce published a paper entitled 'The Fixation of Belief', one of six papers on the method of science, and it is this paper that supplies some of the clearest insights on how authority is conceived within scientific practice, and how such authority should extend to the full range of philosophical activity and indeed to all human practices. He starts by analysing belief and doubt. For him, they are not abstract descriptions of the state of an individual but, in a way, grades of satisfaction or inner calm. Doubt is a state associated with dissatisfaction from which we attempt to distance ourselves so as to arrive at the state of belief, thereby gaining a state of satisfaction and calm. Inquiry is nothing more than the struggle produced by the irritation of doubt, the struggle to return to the state of belief. This view explains how both individuals and groups tend to change their beliefs as little as possible, and then only when really obliged. With this background in place, he proceeds to articulate four different ways of how to settle opinion. These four ways are the most important aspect for our consideration.

According to the first way of retaining the peaceful state of belief, what he calls the method of tenacity, an individual retains his or her belief

---

[17] I focus only on Peirce mainly for convenience and to make this paper's line of argument clearer within the space available. Since Peirce, pragmatist ideas have had various champions, of one form or another, including for instance Richard Rorty, who sees the authority structure of science as just one of the many possible systems that can enable us to achieve our goals, and Hilary Putnam, who argues somewhat differently that, on a pragmatist understanding, science has the special role of offering the basis for the evaluation of human practices and for democracy.

come what may, by sheer willpower, somewhat like the ostrich, he says, that buries its head to avoid the anxiety of possible danger. What undermines this method is society itself, which is always full of a variety of different opinions that bombard the individual from all sides. But for an individual or group that retreats into isolation from others, the method of tenacity is always possible.

The second method, the method of authority, is the one he identifies with the Catholic Church. It involves the founding of an institution whose purpose is to keep correct doctrines before the entire group and to prevent contrary opinions from emerging and flourishing. The entire group endows this institution with the required degree of power to function in this way, which may include punishment and expulsion, or even torture and death. Peirce writes: 'This method has, from the earliest times, been one of the chief means of upholding correct theological and political doctrines, and of preserving their universal or catholic character. In Rome, especially, it has been practiced from the days of Numa Pompilius to those of Pius Nonus'.[18] He acknowledges that this method has been successful through the centuries and has had the most majestic results. He is even convinced that 'for the mass of mankind, then, there is perhaps no better method than this. If it is their highest impulse to be intellectual slaves, then slaves they ought to remain'.[19] He quickly adds that all such 'priest-ridden' groups of inquiry are unstable because they always contain some subgroup of individuals who want to think for themselves, and who thus brew doubt and disquiet.

His third method involves recourse to *a priori* truths. In order to pass from the irritating state of doubt to the stable state of belief and to secure agreement within a community of inquirers, instead of resorting to an established authority we can encourage everyone to figure out what is more in line with reason. Opinions will thus be progressively ironed out as the community moves increasingly towards more universal truths. For Peirce, this method is more intellectually respectable than the others but is still unsatisfactory. Although its use has given rise to impressive and influential metaphysical systems in the course of history, it actually makes 'inquiry something similar to the development of taste'.[20] He may be making a rhetorical flourish here, an exaggeration, but his main objection has a point. This method does not emphasize agreement with experience but consistency within a set of beliefs.

The fourth method, the one preferred by Peirce, is the method of scientific investigation. This assumes that 'there are real things, whose characters are entirely independent of our opinions about them; [...] and any man, if he have sufficient experience and reason enough about it, will be led

---

[18] C. S. Peirce, *The Essential Peirce: Selected Philosophical Writings*, ed. N. Houser and C. Kloesel, vol. 1 (1867-1893) (Indianapolis, IN: Indiana University Press, 1992), 117.

[19] Ibid., 1 (1867-1893):118.

[20] Ibid., 1 (1867-1893):119.

to the one true conclusion'.[21] Peirce concedes that the other methods have their advantages, but since they have no inherent tendency to ensure that opinion eventually converges onto fact, they remain inferior to this fourth method of the natural sciences.

This foundational paper which I just summarized is not the only place where Peirce compares authority structures within the Church with those within science. Overall, his attitude is certainly not one of wanting to debunk religion. He has his own argument for the existence of God, and defends a form of religion that dovetails smoothly with science as he understands it. There is truth in religious claims in so far as they are experiential even though vague. What he cannot stand is when 'theology pretends to be a science',[22] his reason being that this form of religion suffers from the vices that are inherent within the first three methods of inquiry mentioned above: tenacity, authority, and detachment from experience. For him, non-theologized religious claims are respectable because, being capable of generating doubt, they can indeed launch a genuine inquiry. He wants however to keep such religious claims at the level of practical guides that promote a good life; he wants to keep them away from the clutches of theologians who are ever prone to transform them into hypotheses within an inquiry. He justifies his position by referring to the never ending disputes among theologians.[23] Of course, one may object here that Peirce is somewhat inconsistent when he assumes that, for science, reasoning on experience can always make opinion converge onto fact while, for religion, reasoning can never accomplish the same thing. He seems to assume that reasoning is simply not sturdy enough to cope with the explicitation of religious claims.

For Peirce, the way forward is to have a theology-free church, which he describes as a religion of love, an agapistic evolutionary process.[24] In this way, the religious dimension of humanity will overcome its self-love, its self-seeking, just as the scientific community has done via the adoption of the genuine scientific method. The sacrifice scientists make in renouncing their presuppositions when faced with contrary evidence is the same kind of sacrifice genuine religious people need to make as regards religion. All in all, it is clear that for Peirce science can teach the Church how to grow towards perfection. His view guarantees that the religious person 'will gladly go forward, sure that the truth is not split into two warring doctrines, and that any change that knowledge can work in his faith can only affect its expression, not the deep mystery expressed'[25].[26]

---

[21] Ibid., 1 (1867-1893):120.
[22] Charles S Peirce, *Collected Papers of Charles Sanders Peirce*, ed. P. Weiss, C. Hartshorne, and A. Burks (London: Belknap Press of Harvard U.P, 1931), vol. 6, par. 3.
[23] Ibid., vol 6, par. 438.
[24] Ibid., vol 6, par 493.
[25] Ibid., vol. 6, par. 432.

COMPARISON

Although these two major thinkers formulated and published their work about a century ago, traces of their views are still with us today in some form or other. Newman is rightly acknowledged as a major influence behind Vatican II, and Peirce is viewed by many as the founding father of a pragmatic scientific attitude that is fast becoming global. Nevertheless, one needs to acknowledge that the 20th century has seen much further exploration in these areas and both positions need some serious amendments.

Newman's approach may be questioned because it simply draws a blanket over the very issue under investigation. If (and I emphasize the hypothetical form of my claim here) he is proposing the existence of the illative sense as an *explanation* of how an individual or a community arrives from a system of converging probabilities to a state of certainty, then he is vulnerable to the charge of empty explanation. He would in fact be explaining the way we arrive at certainty by merely saying that we have the potential to do it. But this is no explanation at all. It is just reiterating what we already know. Peirce's approach may be questioned because of his conviction that there is a world of facts available to everyone in a neutral way. Relatively recent work in the philosophy of science has produced compelling arguments and even historical evidence that such a view of science is at best naïve, at worst utterly mistaken.[27] No individual scientist or group of scientists can establish all the claims needed for the research engaged in. Scientific practice is not something that is linked to the bedrock of fact at every point. It is rather an activity associated with a fabric of interlocking, mutually supporting, knowledge-claims and hypotheses, a fabric within which we have the ineradicable roles of testimony and expertise, evident in questions like: Who is the real expert here? Who is to be trusted? On what grounds? In fact, what we nowadays call research programmes are units of scientific work made up of researchers who are meant to remain loyal to a set of core principles come what may.[28]

The point of these quick objections to both Newman and Peirce is not that their contributions are now outmoded. It is rather to draw two modest

---

[26] For more on Peirce's views of a Church based on agapistic love, see Douglas Anderson, "Peirce's Common Sense Marriage of Religion and Science," in *The Cambridge Companion to Peirce*, ed. Cheryl Misak (Cambridge: Cambridge University Press, 2004), 175-3.

[27] N.R. Hanson, *Patterns of Discovery* (Cambridge: Cambridge University Press, 1958); Thomas S Kuhn, *The Structure of Scientific Revolutions* (Chicago; London: The University of Chicago Press, 1996).

[28] Collins and Evans, *Rethinking Expertise*; Alvin Goldman, *Knowledge in a Social World* (Oxford: Oxford University Press, 1999); Imre Lakatos, *The Methodology of Scientific Research Programmes: Philosophical Papers*, vol. 1 (Cambridge: Cambridge University Press, 1978).

conclusions. The first is that, although the structures of authority and decision making within the Church and within the scientific community differ in their formal aspects, they turn out to be somewhat similar when considered more realistically, in other words when their practical dimension is highlighted.

The second conclusion deals more with the Church than with science. Newman and many other theologians after him who dealt with this issue rightly highlighted the role of the illative sense, especially in its collective dimension. The Church's system of doctrinal authority can easily slide into a situation in which coherence within the group is given priority over correspondence to the facts. Peirce reminds us that the scientific ideal, at least as he saw it, is to limit one's claims to what can be justified by correspondence to the facts. He thought that science has the upper edge because it limits itself to correspondence. Although somewhat naïve, this claim does indicate that the Church may profit from becoming more aware of the dangers associated with the coherence theory of truth. Of course, within the faith community, one can always resort to God, who, in His benevolence, will see to it that mutual agreement will lead to the truth. But even a faith community is obliged to do everything humanly possible to avoid an agreement that is nothing more than a convenient human construction. My basic suggestion therefore is that the Church should explore the role of 'correspondence to the facts' within its decision-making processes. Of course, the facts in this context are not of the same kind as those we find in the sciences. For the Church's field of operation, it seems that facts can be expressed primarily in terms of the *sensus fidelium*, in terms of Revelation, in terms of Tradition, or in terms of the various possible combinations of these three factors.

How can we explore this aspect further?

One way is to distinguish between dogmatic facts and particular religious facts. The former are taken to be elements of revealed truth that issue directly, in some clear sense, from the deposit of faith, while the latter are religiously significant states of affairs over which the Church does not enjoy infallibility. For instance, that the Second Vatican Council has the authority of an ecumenical council, is a dogmatic fact. On such a matter, and on others like it, the Magisterium has the competence to pronounce infallibly. As regards other facts, however, it does not. Particular religious facts, such as whether this particular marriage is valid or not, do not form part of the set of propositions for which the Church demands an act of faith. This distinction should not be taken as a clear dividing line. For further clarity, and responsible appreciation of the important nuances involved, this point should be explored in relation to the doctrine on the hierarchy of truths. What is essential for the inquiry presented in this paper is that the element or datum we can call a fact within the ecclesial context is one that demands absolute acceptance, or acceptance to a very high degree. Just as in science, a widely accepted experimental result is considered a datum that all future theories need to incorporate, so also in theology: a fact can be taken to be a datum that determines, in some clear sense, all possible future interpretations and all future developments of theological ideas and religious practices in that area.

Another possible way forward could be to consider theologically significant facts to be those widely accepted and genuinely justified sociological and anthropological empirical descriptions that are relevant to the way Christian doctrine should be applied in a particular context so as to arrive at clear principles of action. Such facts are indeed nothing more than empirical ones derived from the methods of the natural and human sciences, but they gain theological significance because of their role within the process of moral reasoning. For instance, various biological details concerning the early human embryo are rightly considered facts that should determine the way fundamental Christian principles of bioethics are formulated. Some features of social, political, and economic reality are rightly considered facts that determine the role the Church should play in the global context. Notice for instance how *Gaudium et Spes* starts by presenting and analysing the human condition, and then proceeding with the theological and moral reflection on the role of Christians in such conditions (§§ 4-10). These reflections show that, even though the Church may be concerned more with how to live in the world than how to describe it, even though the Church may differ essentially from the scientific community in being more concerned with the political than with the theoretical, the role of facts within the managing of ecclesial agreement and disagreement is not thereby diminished.

As can be seen from these suggestions, determining what a fact is for the ecclesial context is a difficult task, and determining what correspondence to such a fact means is probably an even more difficult task. In this paper, I have supplied only very sketchy guidelines on how to make these determinations. There is still more work to be done. The only result I can claim is a very modest one, namely the awareness that the dynamism of inquiry within the Church and the functioning of its structure of doctrinal authority can benefit considerably from a comparison with the dynamics of scientific inquiry, especially as regards the role of ecclesially-relevant facts within decision making.[29]

Gregorian University, Rome, Italy

---

[29] Useful studies for further research include: Richard Blackwell, *Science, Religion and Authority: Lessons from the Galileo Affair* (Milwaukee: Marquette University Press, 1998a); Richard Blackwell, "Could There Be Another Galileo Case?," in *The Cambridge Companion to Galileo*, ed. Peter Machamer (Cambridge: Cambridge University Press, 1998b), 348-66; Alexander Thomson, *Tradition and Authority in Science and Theology with Reference to the Thought of Michael Polanyi* (Edinburgh: Scottish Academic Press, 1987).

PART III

THEOLOGICAL PERSPECTIVES

CHAPTER VI

AUTHORITY IN THE CHURCH: AUTHENTIC AND EFFECTIVE?

JAMES SWEENEY, CP

INTRODUCTION

It has been said that *Humanae Vitae* triggered a crisis of ecclesial authority since Pope Paul VI felt constrained about changing the teaching on birth control in view of the explicit teaching of his predecessor Pius XI in *Casti Connubii*. In other words, he feared to undermine the credibility of the magisterium as a teaching authority by making the change recommended by his special commission[1]. Whatever the accuracy of this judgement on the Pope, it is arguably that much more significant that this papal act – the most far-reaching and penetrating exercise of papal authority of the last half century, directly and personally affecting the great majority of the laity – turned out to be almost completely ineffective. Most of the Catholic laity, after a period of anguish, simply ignored it, and made up their own minds how to regulate the size of their families.

Since then the argument has raged. On the one side, the refusal of reception of the teaching has been interpreted as the *sensus fidelium* in operation. On the other more noisy side of the argument, it has been seen as a signal failure of the Church at large. This was because, so it is said, theologians and pastors (bishops as well as priests) failed to give proper assent to the teaching, disputing it or quietly ignoring it; or because of the increasing sexualisation of society which the encyclical warned about, deafening people to the truth but at the same time rendering the Pope's action all the more 'prophetic'; or because of secularisation and a general weakening of faith and adherence to the gospel.

This chapter will not address, much less attempt to resolve, this or any other substantive point of ecclesial teaching. Its focus is on the *effectiveness* of ecclesial teaching and the tension between that and its *authenticity* or *credibility*. To put it simply: how can ecclesial authority be exercised in such a way as to have a real (and helpful) influence in people's lives and in society? This is not so straightforward and there is not one simple and obvious path to follow. The Church is called at times to be starkly prophetic with the magisterium sticking doggedly to truths that the culture discounts.

---

[1] See Carlo M. Martini and George Sporschill, *Night Conversations with Cardinal Martini: the Relevance of the Church for Tomorrow* (Mahwah, NJ: Paulist Press, 2012)

On occasion this is essential for validating the Church's evangelical authority and its credibility as witness to the Gospel; no one needs a church that simply apes the culture. But there are costs to prophetic confrontation, and one of these is in terms of actually being heard. This cost of discipleship should not, of course, be a deterrent. But it is still valid to ask whether a trade-off between authenticity and effectiveness does not sometimes take place. If, for example, the Church insisted on exceptionless adherence to the commandment 'Thou shalt not kill' it would arguably gain in authenticity as a witness to peace and the gospel injunction to 'turn the other cheek', but arguably it would be less effective in terms of restraining the evils of war, as Just War criteria attempt to do.

Setting terms for 'trade-off' is, of course, a crude way of speaking when dealing with the delicate skein of issues comprising: norms governing human behaviour; the responsibilities of ecclesial leaders in delivering an authentic interpretation of Gospel truth; the tasks of pastors in accompanying people on their journey of life; and the moral discernment and conscience of believers – all of which makes up the matrix within which ecclesial authority sits. Insofar as some form of 'trade-off' may be envisaged between this ecclesial frame and contemporary cultural circumstances, it concerns not just the values involved and how they are applied (e.g., the morality of homosexual practice, or laws liberalising or restricting it), but also the social processes in a democratic polity by which values come to be recognised and enshrined as social and legal norms. We shall examine this in greater detail later.

ECCLESIAL AUTHORITY – THE 'MAGISTERIUM'

But first, there is the actual authority structure in the Catholic Church, the magisterium. How do we imagine it? What does it look and feel like? Here's a quote from a senior cardinal writing shortly after Vatican II:

> The Catholic theologian…knows and has to bear in mind that Jesus has appointed a particular class of baptised persons who are endowed with a special supernatural charism to be the teachers and leaders of the Christian people, of all believers. He also knows that this universal magisterium of the Episcopal body or of the Roman pontiff rightly has the office and authority to transmit the faith integrally and to guard it from error and to pronounce the final word in the name of Christ in matters of faith and morals.[2]

---

[2] Giovanni Colombo, "Obedience to the Ordinary Magisterium" (1967) quoted in Gerard Mannion *et al*, *Readings in Church Authority* (Aldershot: Ashgate, 2003) 103.

What concerns us here is this *image* of the magisterium and its functioning – a 'class of persons'; a 'supernatural charism'; 'transmit the faith integrally'; 'guard it from error'; 'pronounce the final word'.

Cardinal Colombo was writing here about the work of theologians. Theirs is a distinct task with its own responsibilities and competences which he acknowledged but which, in his argument, must first be set in the context of 'the correct attitude of assent and obedience' that theologians must show, expressing a 'disposition of serene confidence in the teaching of the magisterium' (p. 102). Assent and obedience (these are not exactly the same) are acknowledged by the Cardinal as to some degree graduated – depending on 'the degree of authority and the obligation involved in the various forms in which the teaching authority is exercised' (p. 102). But this graduation, it would seem, is determined solely by the authoritativeness that official pronouncements attach to themselves, not by anything external that the theologian brings to them.

Colombo's text comes from the 1960s (and pre-*Humanae Vitae*) but not much has changed since then. The long column of theologians summoned by the Congregation of the Doctrine of the Faith, the recurring criticisms of its procedures, and the unease in the late 1990s about the revamped profession of faith that theologians must take on receiving a canonical mandate [3] tell of an enduring problem with the ecclesiastical discipline. Cardinal Colombo was representative of the official view and holds to an unmistakeably 'aristocratic' vision of a 'class of persons' claiming authority not by virtue of holding a specific office but because of being endowed with a 'supernatural charism'.[4] The magisterial office is portrayed as untrammelled by any structures or restraints except that of divine truth embodied in the Scriptures and the living tradition of the Church – but divine truth the expression of which the magisterial office is itself the sole arbiter.

Again, my intention here is not to enter into dispute about the substantive definition of magisterial authority as proposed by Cardinal Colombo. My question, rather, is operational – the imaginative hold of such a teaching office on minds and hearts; the detailed ways it functions; and whether a sketch of such details is actually necessary in order to understand magisterium aright.

CHURCH, SOCIETY AND HISTORY

That ecclesial authority is not fixed in one immutable form and that its exercise can change quite considerably can be seen from the shift in

---

[3] Congregation of the Doctrine of the Faith, *Instruction Donum Veritatis: Instruction on the Ecclesial Vocation of the Theologian* (Rome: Vatican Press, 1990).

[4] See Avery Dulles, *Models of the Church* (New York: Doubleday, 1987, p. 38).

religious orders since Vatican II from a military-style 'command and obey' model to one based on an understanding of the need for communal processes of discernment of God's will and purpose.[5] The matter here is the personal obediential relationship of religious to the authority of ecclesiastical superiors in discharge of Christ's 'kingly' or ruling function. But the same forces that brought about change in that context also affect the 'prophetic' or teaching (magisterial) office in the Church. Shifts in the operational models of authority have been generated by new understandings in ecclesiology and in Christology and the theology of Revelation, and – tied up with that – different social and cultural perceptions of freedom and autonomy, the dignity of the person, human rights, social equality, etc. In other words, history – the unfolding history of human and ecclesial society – calls forth change.

This history is a complex and tortuous subject. How to engage with the values of the modern world has been the recurrent challenge facing the Church at least since the Reformation and Enlightenment. Its default mode has been one of resistance. This gave way, if only briefly, at Vatican II when a more open attitude flowered. But this was just at the point when a new culture of modernity began making its mark (the 'postmodern' reaction or the 'high modern' apogee, depending on your point of view[6]). The controversy since Vatican II has been about how the Church should reposition itself, intellectually and practically, in the face of a new culture and society that is evolving at ever increasing pace.

One way of portraying the Church in relation to society is as its 'soul'. This transcends the overly-jurisdictional role it once occupied, but retains the claim to be the source of society's moral and social norms or the guardian of its conscience. It is a model of Church as a kind of 'spiritual director', even if of quite a strict kind! [7] The same notion is found with regard to human rights, espoused by Vatican II in something of a historical *volte face* in *Dignitatis Humanae*. The Church now claims to be their special guarantor, emphasising the key significance of freedom of religion in securing all other rights. A sense of spiritual-aristocracy once again attaches to the notion of magisterium.

However, portraying the Church as society's soul is becoming less and less convincing to modern ears. The fundamental problem lies deep in the growing disjunction between religious and secular world views – what

---

[5] See James Sweeney, "The Experience of Religious Orders", in Bernard Hoose (ed.) *Authority in the Roman Catholic Church: Theory and Practice* (London: Ashgate, 2002) 171-180.

[6] See A. Giddens, *Modernity and Self-Identity: Self and Society in the Late Modern* Age (Cambridge: Polity Press, 1991).

[7] On this image, see Pope John Paul II, *Ecclesia in Europa*, 2003, # 7; and, "Evangelising the soul of Europe" – theme of the November 2013 meeting of the Commission on Social Communications of the Council of European Bishops' Conferences (CCEE).

theologians have termed 'interruption'.[8] In itself this is nothing new; the abandonment of gospel values and practices and the alienation of significant sectors of society from the Church has been a feature of at least the last two centuries. Nevertheless, until relatively recently there was a tacit agreement that the religious and secular approaches retained something in common. Although bitterly divided about what was required and in strong competition, each knew (grudgingly) that the other's concern was for humanity; they could at least understand each other. Christians were still able to presume social acknowledgement that their life of faith, even when contested, was continuous with the life of society. There was continuity between evangelical values and social values, religious practices and social practices; religion was still socially significant and it fulfilled an effective social role. On this basis, churches flourished in significant new ways throughout the 19th century despite attacks from rationalists and atheists.

Today, however, this sense of continuity and cohesion has become strained and is overcome by a more radical pluriformity of belief systems and practices. Greater social and cultural diversity means that notions of what it is to be human, what human beings may aspire to, and the social practices in which to engage have less and less in common. These are now drawn from a very wide range of sources, far beyond the narratives and practices of the Christian tradition. The Bible is no longer taken for granted as a primary reference point, even for ethical standards; and it is not routinely accessible as it once was, or even comprehensible to modern ears.[9] This disrupts the sociological continuity between Gospel living and human living that held across previous centuries.

GOSPEL, CULTURE AND VALUES

The significant point I want to draw out here is not that society no longer accepts what the Church has to say on moral issues (which is true) but that the personal-social dynamics of adhering to the Gospel way and the processes of socio-cultural value production have become increasingly discordant and further and further out of alignment. Whereas the Church could once presume to be *the* agent in the production of social and moral values, and then was locked in competition with some few alternative philosophies, it is now caught in the postmodern maelstrom of claims portraying the far flung reaches of human aspiration. These postmodern cultural assumptions, fired-up by technological sophistication, find it easy to over-ride the sober judgments of faith.

The raw nature of this new situation was dramatically exposed over the civil partnership/same-sex marriage issue and the manner of the

---

[8] L. Boeve, *God Interrupts History: Theology in a Time of Upheaval* (London: Continuum, 2007).

[9] C. Brown, *The Death of Christian Britain: Understanding Secularisation, 1800-2000* (London: Routledge, 2000).

Church's interventions. The debate revolved around incommensurable basic conceptions of the meaning of marriage. What has become clear is that the values and arguments put forward by the proponents of change (which come down to equality and the rights of gay people) have widespread social purchase, whereas the arguments of opponents (reasonable and reasoned though they may be) lack compelling power for the majority of citizens, the young especially. A fundamental divergence of *moral perceptions* has become evident.

Now, to repeat, I'm not addressing the question of whether the moral values proposed by the Church are right or wrong or ought to be changed. What is at issue, rather, is the socio-cultural situation in which Church teaching is in competition with, and frequently vanquished by, *alternative values* generated within the diverse spheres which emerge in a complex society by the process of institutional differentiation. This is a well understood social process: as society becomes more complex its various fields – politics, economics, law, education, health care and, crucially, religion – separate out into their own autonomous domains, within which they generate their own operational norms and value perceptions. For as long as religion was socially enshrined as a 'sacred canopy'[10] over society it was able to influence and even dictate the values and norms of the other sectors; but with its restriction to its own tightly defined and separated sphere (which is the core meaning of secularisation) religion loses social purchase – all the more so if it is expunged politically from the social world or radically privatised.

Thus starkly stated, differentiation seems deterministic, an iron law of the social process which acts inevitably to restrict religion more and more. However, it has to be seen historically and contextually. Social reality does not evolve neatly; the many overlaps between the institutional spheres and new forces in play such as immigrant groups make the actual course of social change uncertain. What we need to note, however, is differentiation as a *process* rather than simply its structural end-point – that is to say, the social process by which norms are established and values produced. Institutional differentiation is both a matter of social structure and a cultural process. The era of modernity, spanning the Enlightenment to mid-20th century, saw the reorganisation and differentiation of the social structure. But this has been followed by the post-modern reaction to that era's rigidities. Now, the normative order that modernity established is newly open to question. A pervasive scepticism about institutions and established practices has taken over, and values have once again become fluid and diverse.

The postmodern contexts where social and cultural values are forged comprise the consumer economy, the media and the leisure industry. These are immensely powerful in furnishing us with images (which quickly become precepts) of the good life, of what to aspire to, how to behave, what

---

[10] P. Berger, *The Heretical Imperative* (London: Collins, 1980).

matters and what doesn't. In addition, the pluralism and cosmopolitan nature of late modern societies have a profound impact on our perception of the very nature of values. They are seen less as imposed than as chosen; less determined by the nature of things than socially constructed. So, as individuals are drawn into these new processes of value production they engage with a certain lightness or sense of freedom. But at the same time, they can be exposed to puzzlement and confusion. Why, if values are constructed, hold any value to be *true*? Why hold to *these* values? Alternatively, they may retreat atavistically into a defence of received, communally specific values. When values are thus up for questioning, the reactions of individuals span the spectrum from total relativism to dogmatic absolutism. Holding the middle ground, determining what are authentic values, keeping them in proper balance, holding the tension between freedom and commitment requires a sophisticated moral education.

These cultural dynamics are now the context within which ecclesial authority functions, whether that is in evangelisation, delivering Church teaching, declaring moral truths or making magisterial pronouncements. The believers and Church communities who receive such teaching are *already value-formed* by their immersion in postmodern living. It is by our *doing* more than by any philosophical or religious reflection that our values are learned; they are imbibed along with social practices such as consumer behaviour.[11] But of course values are also imbibed along with the discipleship practices which promote evangelisation, and whose goal is the ongoing transformation of our value perceptions in the light of the dawning Kingdom of God.

EFFECTIVE ECCLESIAL AUTHORITY

The critical issue in this light is *how* authority is to function in new social circumstances. There's more to authority than giving the correct answer or enunciating sound principles; effective authority means speaking authoritatively (Mt. 7:29). Evangelisation is more than preaching the Gospel; it means *commending* the Gospel, disclosing its truths as *good* news. It is all too easy to fall into the trap noted by one bishop with the wry comment: 'While the rulers of this age persuasively tell stories, we tend to issue documents, full of truth, but unread.'[12] The 'style' in which authority operates is about more than superficial differences of tone – as has been made clear by the example of Pope Francis; 'the medium' in a very real sense '*is* the message'.

Ecclesial authority is, of course, very properly concerned with holding on to and proclaiming the *truth* of the Gospel. But first of all it is required to

---

[11] V. Miller, *Consuming Religion: Christian Faith and Practice in a Consumer Culture* (London: Continuum, 2003).

[12] Archbishop of Toronto to the Convention of the Knights of Columbus, reported on Zenit, 09.08.12.

enquire into that truth; the *ecclesia docens* is also the *ecclesia discens*.[13] The magisterium is not the 'oracle of truth', but rather depends on the Church's living tradition, and it learns how to understand and present the one Gospel from the historical faith-experience and theological reflection of the Church community as a whole.[14] This is very evident in, for example, Catholic Social Teaching; the encyclicals do not just pronounce eternally-sourced general principles for practical application, but reflect the emerging faith-praxis and wisdom of the Church community.[15] This feature of the functioning of the magisterium is usually kept hidden – misguidedly, I suggest. The traditional manner, as well as aristocratic, has been Olympian – magisterial pronouncements framed as eternal verities, tracing a seamless continuity with all prior ecclesial declarations. But when magisterial documents refer only to previous magisterial documents and to classical theological sources in the Church Fathers and Doctors they risk becoming overly self-referential. Teaching gains immensely in credibility when it engages with a fuller range of conversation partners.[16]

Furthermore, authority becomes persuasive (as well as right) when it engages in a real, transparent and unthreatened conversation on the issues and concerns which affect those it addresses. The depth of the crisis after *Humanae Vitae* was due in large part to a disjunction between values-consultation (the special commission) and values-declaration (the encyclical), leaving a psychological sense of an abruptly terminated conversation.[17] In a previous more authority-compliant culture this wasn't a problem, and Pope Paul was clearly wrong-footed in this respect. Today, however, authority has to negotiate its way through very different and diverse perceptions. The issue is not about naively accommodating the values of the dominant culture, nor about haggling over what the true values are, but of negotiating a way through the social processes by which social

---

[13] See Gerard Mannion, "A Teaching Church that Learns?" in M.J. Lacey and F. Oakley, (eds) *The Crisis of Authority in Catholic Modernity* (Oxford: Oxford University Press, 2011).

[14] "For there is growth in the understanding of the realities and the words which have been handed down. This happens through the contemplation and study made by believers, who treasure these things in their hearts through a penetrating understanding of the spiritual realities which they experience, and through the preaching of those who have received through episcopal succession the sure gift of truth." (Vatican II, *Dei Verbum*, n. 13).

[15] Pope Paul VI, *Octogesima adveniens*, 1971.

[16] This was a characteristic of Benedict XVI"s *Deus caritas est*, 2005.

[17] The same could be said about the closure of discussion on the ordination of women (John Paul II, *Ordinatio Sacerdotalis*, 1994) and the subsequent statement from the CDF, echoing Vincent of Lerins, that this teaching is "to be held always, everywhere and by all as belonging to the deposit of faith" (Rome 1995). The attempt to stop discussion was ineffective except in the formal councils of the Church.

and cultural values are produced and absorbed. This does imply, of course, that values themselves are open to critique and clarification in the process.

This is a difficult and delicate exercise and means handling strong tensions and divergent expectations. An enquiry-based approach that develops through dialogue and conversation will always clash with an approach that sees its duty as simply proclaiming the truth 'in season and out of season' (2 Tim. 4: 2). This has come to the fore in preparations for the 2014 Synod of Bishops on the issues of family life. As the process got under way and in response to renewed questioning about the possibility of admitting divorced and re-married persons to the sacraments, the Prefect of the CDF published a document taking the line that this could not happen; but some of his fellow-German bishops took issue with him, and a questionnaire for a world-wide consultation covering these topics was published by the Synod Secretariat with Pope Francis's authority. Pre-synodal consultation is nothing new but its level and scope on this occasion are unprecedented. Much will hang on how well the Synod eventually manages to be a *communicative exercise*, not simply declaratory.

This all relates to the distinction famously made by Pope John XXIII at the opening of the Second Vatican Council:

> The substance of the ancient doctrine of the deposit of faith is one thing, and the way in which it is presented is another. And it is the latter that must be taken into great consideration with patience if necessary, everything being measured in the forms and proportions of a Magisterium which is predominantly pastoral in character.[18]

This distinction and what it implies have remained controversial. The notion of the 'substance' of doctrine – or, in the Latin, 'truths' (*veritates*) – and how to distinguish it from 'presentation' are difficult issues to tease out in analytical terms. However, it is worth noting that the papal statement points beyond such conceptual difficulties to the pastoral character of ecclesial authority as the locus where resolution is to be sought.

At the level of functioning – how ecclesial authority operates – the issue can be framed in terms of the purposes it serves. Is it the magisterium's purpose to ensure, in so far as it can, compliance with the norms which, in the light of the Gospel, guide human living? Or, is its purpose to lead people into full, free, conscious understanding of and adherence to the truth that the Gospel discloses about themselves and human living. Is the predominant aim to secure faithful behaviour; or to

---

[18] John XXIII, *Gaudet Mater Ecclesiae*, Address to the Opening Session of the Second Vatican Council, 11th October, 1962; "Est enim aliud ipsum depositum fidei, seu veritates, quae veneranda doctrina nostra continentur, aliud modus, quo eaedem enuntiantur", AAS 54 (1962), 792. Pope Francis refers to this principle in *Evangelii Gaudium*, 2013, #41.

help form persons as persons and to form consciences? These are often differentiated as teaching and pastoral aims – where the teaching has clear priority and determinative weight. But ecclesial teaching *is* pastoral – it conveys the saving message of the Gospel – and is to be judged in terms of the pastoral job it does. The magisterium is both 'teacher' and 'authority', and its dual aims cannot be separated. Both have to be kept in view as dependent upon one another. What is clear in the cultural circumstances of today's world is that the need is for the magisterium to be an *effective teacher* – putting the emphasis, therefore, on its pastoral, educative, communicative goals.

This is not to say, however, that the proper and authentic voice of authority can be marginalised or that it has become sociologically 'unrealistic'. On the contrary; when the postmodern person lays claim to autonomy in determining what is 'true for me', then the issue of what *is* true – and therefore authoritative – comes into prominence, is dramatised. If all determinations of truth are co-equal 'what is true' becomes privatised, and it then ceases to be a criterion of social or communal life. Consequently, humanity's philosophical and religious traditions of 'truth seeking' become mere resources, playthings in a game of lego-like self-referential reality construction. Society cannot proceed on such a basis, nor in the long run can personal life. Just as academic and scientific endeavour cannot proceed without due recognition of expertise and the authority that goes with it, so too social existence requires the dissemination of knowledge that is properly *validated*, and this requires *accredited* teachers who function with authority. The truth about our human existence and the truths embodied in a religious tradition, while they can be endlessly debated, cannot be socially sustained in the absence of some authoritative voice. If everyone is simply their own authority, there is no *authority*.

The issue here is authoritativeness. Ecclesial authority necessarily has a disciplinary function, but simple claims to authority as trumping all else ('Roma locuta est ...') are now not persuasive. If there is an absence of adequate supporting reasons, a teaching will lack credibility at the bar of cultural value production. It may be claimed, in defence of religious pronouncements, that religious faith is *more than* a cultural production, and so *over-rides* the requirements of cultural credibility. But that would be to portray faith as non-incarnational and even irrational. Teachings have to be *believe-able*; and authority has to attend to the reasonable grounds of its own credibility and publicly attest to the validity of its actions; otherwise it lapses into authoritarianism and simple power.

In addition, ecclesial authority depends upon the openness and goodwill of those it addresses. It appeals, in the end, to the faith of believers – their capacity to perceive the religious and moral teaching proposed as coherent with and implied in the Good News revealed in Jesus Christ. Ecclesial teaching and faith response are completely bound up with each other. This is what shows the essential nature of Christian authority as 'not lording it over others' (Mt. 20:25) but existing in a mutually dependent relationship with believers' faith. The teaching authority has the duty not only to declare the truth but also to work to awaken the faith on which acceptance of its teaching depends. Faith-education is an inherent aspect of ecclesial authority; it must nurture the theological understanding on which its own teaching rests. It must also be properly communicative. Ecclesial teaching is pastoral in intent – delivered *for the good of* person and community – and it will only be received as such if it is delivered in the appropriate mode of life-giving communication, not as cold law (or as a 'scold'!). These features are more than incidental add-ons to the magisterium's essential role, and are part of its central operation.

Postscript – a Kairos?

How would ecclesial authority operating transparently in this manner be received by contemporary, postmodern people, not only in the Church but in the wider secular world? The surprise today is the openness to the new voice of authority emanating from the papacy – prompted by the tone the new Pope has struck. We might say that this moment in the life of the Church, with Pope Francis's election, is a *kairos* – a moment that stands out from the routine flow of time, offering some special opportunity, and somehow revelatory. The Pope has both delighted and unsettled people in the Church by the change he's brought to the papal office. The way his personal charisma has appealed and his capacity to break through even to the sceptical and the secular minded has shown that openings do exist for sharing the Christian message. Despite much despondency among believers as they see their contemporaries desert the Church, a 'new evangelization' suddenly seems realistic. A determining feature of this *kairos* is Francis's call at the very start of his papacy for 'a poor Church, for the poor', and his own striking personal witness on this point.

What is happening to the Church? How is the Spirit forming it anew? Is the Church being readied for a new time of mission? And how will authority function in this new time? There are, as we know, deep structural reforms planned which will re-shape the episcopal office at its different levels, and these will be much more than a re-jigging of the ecclesiastical bureaucracy. People in authority, as this *kairos* time is making abundantly clear, are persuasive if their lives ring true to the truths they announce. But this witness must be conveyed by more than personal charisma, or by a new Pope – inevitably briefly serving – and has to be embedded in the routine, everyday life of the Church. Here, the defining mark of 'a poor Church, for the poor' will be critical.

While caution is needed about exaggerated expectations of papal initiatives, the freshness of Pope Francis's approach suggests some deep transformation at work. There is a deep logic here in that the whole Church community, and in particular those called to the service of authority, are being summoned once more to a life and witness of self-emptying – of *kenosis* – leaving aside all semblance of power and dominance and taking on a humbler tone. Fifty years after Vatican II called for 'aggiornamento' the task has to be taken up once again, this time learning from the accumulated experience, negative as well as positive, of the post-conciliar years, and firm now in the settled intention to be 'a poor Church, for the poor'.

To be re-called to the great ideal of poverty that Francis of Assisi embraced in the twelfth century and to the way of *kenosis* is to take a particular pathway through postmodern times, with profound implications for how its challenges are to be met. The postmodern shift in culture is something we have all absorbed in different ways. It has been a cumulative process which first got under way around the 1960s when settled traditions began to be swept aside, followed quickly by a deeper rejection of aspects of modernity itself. The effect has been a de-stabilising of social structures and authority regimes in all their forms, not just the ecclesial or political. These cultural perturbations coincided with the post-conciliar era in the Church and were instrumental in making it uniquely confusing, with communities caught in reaction and counter-reaction.

Pope Francis now arrives as the first distinctively post-conciliar pope – the first pope not to have been involved in the actual event of Vatican II. But his religious life and his whole priestly and episcopal experience have been marked by the struggles of those times, and especially the crisis of authority – and, as he freely admits, by the mistakes he himself made, a candid admission that only enhances his authority. The *kairos* that is the new papacy may turn out to be the maturing of post-conciliar Catholicism as the lessons of experience come to be drawn, just as Francis himself was forced to draw difficult lessons about his own exercise of authority.

While there are many positive features of the post-conciliar period, it has also shown the disconnectedness, and even pathology, that can overcome the ecclesial community. These decades have seen great disputes over the beliefs, values and fundamental orientations of Catholicism – 'conservatives' versus 'liberals' (i.e. the labels ascribed to one's opponents) or 'orthodox' versus 'open' (self-ascribed labels) – with one side intent on preserving the 'deposit of faith', the other with meeting the contemporary world. In this post-modern culture, communities are easily rent by disagreements and *communio* dissolved.

It is to be hoped that in the new *kairos* of the Church such tensions can be superseded and the squabbles of the culture warriors settle down. *Kenosis* would chart a radically different path. It is not wedded to some fixity of view as to how the Church should line up for mission. It is more astringent, open, and even apophatic in approach. So it can unlock the fixity of the neo-conservative/orthodox position and its beguiling prospect of a simple restoration of received values and practices; it can unlock the fixity of the open/liberal camp, long frustrated by the stalling of their project. *Kenosis* shares something of post-modernity's scepticism of the grand totalising tendency of those who see their own view of things as 'the one true way'. It is open to giftedness and to receive, whether from tradition or from what is newly emerging in history. *Kenosis* is the readiness to discover truth rather than pretend to possess it. As a characteristic of ecclesial authority *kenosis* builds bridges to those it addresses rather than taking its stand on some lofty distant ground.

Heythrop College, London, Great Britain

CHAPTER VII

AUTHORITY AND MAGISTERIUM: A LESSON FROM THE SEVENTH CENTURY

RICHARD PRICE

THE MONOTHELETE CONTROVERSY IN CURRENT RESEARCH

The current official dialogue between the Catholic and the Orthodox Churches is centred on the question of the appropriate role for the pope in a reunited Church. Hopes have been expressed that an answer may be found by going back to the first millennium, before the schism between the two communions. How in this period was papal primacy understood? What role did the popes play in the universal Church, and in particular in the life of the churches of the East? What authority did they claim? What authority was universally recognized? How did they exercise their magisterium? Particular attention has been paid to the role of the popes vis-à-vis the early ecumenical councils, all of which were held in the eastern provinces of the Roman Empire under the aegis of the emperor at Constantinople.

I shall concentrate on a single controversy, where the role of the popes was both dramatic and decisive, and this is the monoenergist-monothelete controversy of the seventh century. It reached its climax at the Third Council of Constantinople, or Sixth Ecumenical Council (680-1), where the weight attributed to Roman documents and the influence exerted by papal representatives were higher than at any other eastern council.[1]

The seventh century was a period of acute crisis in the Mediterranean world. It had been the dream of the Sassanians in Persia, ever since they toppled the comparatively benign Parthian kingdom in the early third century, to restore the great Achaemenid Empire of Darius and Xerxes by reconquering what we call the Near East – Anatolia, Syria and Egypt. In the 610s and 620s they almost achieved this goal, with not only a temporary loss of Byzantine control over these regions, but a permanent dislocation of city life in the Greek East, spelling the end of the antique world. There was a general sense in the empire that the divisions in Christendom had contributed to this disaster, and the decade of the 630s saw an

---

[1] The following discussion follows a revisionist account of the monoenergist-monothelete controversy that is currently being developed by a number of scholars, including W. Brandes, H. Ohme, Bronwen Neil, and Marek Jankowiak. My own contribution will appear shortly in translations (with commentary) of the Acts of the Lateran Synod of 649 and the Third Council of Constantinople, to be published by the Liverpool University Press.

unprecedented series of church reunions (sadly short-lived), as great numbers of non-Chalcedonian Christians (Copts, Syrians and Armenians) returned to communion with the imperial church.

These unions were made possible by the clarification of the Christology of the Council of Chalcedon that had been largely accomplished by the emperor Justinian and the Fifth Ecumenical Council in the middle of the sixth century.[2] Whatever the ambiguities of the wording of the Chalcedonian Definition, it had become manifest that the imperial church followed Cyril of Alexandria, and not Nestorius, in its teaching of the one person and hypostasis in Christ. Together with the emphasis on God the Word as the one personal subject in Christ went a recognition of his unity in will and activity. Pope Leo had been pilloried by the non-Chalcedonians for a single sentence in his famous Tome, where he apparently attributed a distinct agency to Christ's manhood over against his Godhead – 'Each form does, in communion with the other, what is proper to itself' –, but in later and more careful writing he had stated that Christ 'did human things divinely and divine things humanly', in other words that the Godhead and the manhood never acted independently.[3] Dionysius the Areopagite had written of 'a new theandric [divine-human] operation' in Christ, and a number of theologians were ready to speak of a single operation in Christ, both human and divine; these included Pope Vigilius and Patriarch Menas of Constantinople in the middle of the sixth century.[4] The phrase 'a single operation' featured in the dogmatic statement that accompanied the reunion of the churches at Alexandria, though with no special prominence. Who could raise an objection? Yet protest was made by a leading Palestinian monk, Sophronius the Sophist, soon to be elected Patriarch of Jerusalem; he had inherited a Palestinian tradition of strict adherence to the letter of Chalcedon. The irenic Patriarch Sergius of Constantinople agreed on a compromise by which both expressions, 'one operation' and 'two operations' in Christ, were to be avoided. In his *Ekthesis* (or *Exposition*) of 638, issued under the name of the emperor, this compromise was reasserted, together with a statement of unity of will in Christ. Precisely the same language had been employed, shortly before, by Pope Honorius.[5]

---

[2] See Price, *The Acts of the Council of Constantinople of 553* (Liverpool 2007), vol. 1, 59-75.

[3] See Price, "Monotheletism: A Heresy or a Form of Words?", *Studia Patristica* 48 (2010), 222-3.

[4] Ps.-Dionysius, Letter 4. The monoenergist pronouncements by Vigilius and Menas were rejected as forgeries at the Third Council of Constantinople, Sessions III and XIV, but modern scholars do not doubt their authenticity.

[5] An English translation of all the relevant documents can be found in Pauline Allen, *Sophronius of Jerusalem and Seventh-Century Heresy* (Oxford 2009).

There the matter might have rested, but for military disaster before the Arab tribes now united under the new faith of Islam. Why had God abandoned the Christian Empire? A number of disciples of Sophronius, led by Maximus the Confessor (acknowledged today as the greatest of late antique Greek theologians), decided that the only plausible answer was that the *Ekthesis* was heretical and had excited God's anger. Had it not imposed the novel heresy of one will in Christ, implying that he lacked a human faculty of will? Both Sergius and Honorius had spoken of one will of Christ entirely incidentally, without any sense that they were defining anything or saying anything controversial; neither they nor any of the later defenders of 'monotheletism' or oneness of will in Christ had any intention of denying volition to Christ's manhood. But Maximus insisted on misinterpreting them. He moved to Rome and gained the ear of Pope Theodore, a fellow Palestinian. Preparations were made for a synod that would condemn monotheletism. The carpet was pulled from under their feet by the issuing by the emperor Heraclius in 648 of a new document, the *Typos*, which forbade the assertion of either one will or two wills in Christ. Neither this nor Theodore's death, however, put a stop to the Roman plans. Theodore's successor Pope Martin I went ahead with a synod in 649, which condemned the *Typos* for implying, with its condemnation of both monotheletism and dyotheletism, that Christ has neither one will nor two wills, that is, that he has no will at all; it condemned for heresy at the same time a whole series of patriarchs of Constantinople, including Sergius. Not surprisingly, these divisive and tendentious decrees were ignored in the East. Martin proceeded to send agents to Palestine and Syria, with the task of consecrating new bishops, who would accept the Roman decrees and be under Roman jurisdiction; this was a grossly uncanonical attempt to abolish the patriarchates of Antioch and Jerusalem. He also gave his support to two attempted usurpations against the Byzantine emperor by military commanders in Italy and Africa. When the Byzantines recovered control of Rome, he was arrested and sent for trial in Constantinople. Condemned for treason, and abandoned by Rome (which elected a new pope in his place), he died in exile.[6]

Rome remained hostile to the *Typos*, though without pressing the issue. By the end of the 650s the East had moved on to a position that simultaneously asserted the presence in Christ of both one will and two wills; as Christ is one person and hypostasis out of two natures, so he has one will and one operation, compounded out of two wills and two operations. This position was accepted as reasonable by Pope Vitalian in 658. Maximus the Confessor, however, remained obdurate, rejecting the

---

[6] Historians used to dismiss the condemnations of Pope Martin and Maximus the Confessor on treason charges as "show trials", but see now W. Brandes, "'Juristische' Krisenbewältigung im 7. Jahrhundert? Die Prozesse gegen Papst Martin I. und Maximos Homologetes", *Fontes Minores* 10 (Frankfurt am Main 1998), 141-212.

position just described as 'tritheletism' (the assertion of three wills in Christ), and even came to make the startling claim that eucharists celebrated by clergy who did not condemn monotheletism were invalid. This, and his previous support for usurpers, led to his trial, conviction and death in 662, viewed by now as an heroic but almost isolated figure.[7]

In the 670s, however, Rome reverted to its strongly dyothelete position, and in 678 the emperor Constantine IV wrote to the pope in quest of a resolution of the long-standing theological dispute. The result was the Sixth Ecumenical Council of 680-1, where the Roman delegates maintained a firm dyothelete position, and the emperor (who chaired most of the sessions of the council in person) gave them his decisive support.[8] At the same time he allowed the representatives of a strict monothelete position every opportunity to put their case, manifestly because the emperor's new policy was unpopular in both the Byzantine Church and the Byzantine army, less (perhaps) because of the theological niceties than because it represented humiliation for the see of Constantinople. The Lateran Synod of 649, however, remained unmentioned, and so did Maximus the Confessor. The council concluded with the approval of a dyoenergist and dyothelete definition, asserting two operations and two wills in Christ, which made no use of the Christology of Maximus, and reverted to an understanding of volition in Christ expressed by Athanasius and Cyril of Alexandria.[9]

To see the definition, therefore, as many do, as a return to the so-called Chalcedonian balance and a correction of the Cyrillian Christology approved at the previous ecumenical council (Constantinople II, 553) would be a mistake. The definition included an anathematization of the so-called originators of the monothelete heresy – four previous patriarchs of Constantinople (though not the most recent ones) and Pope Honorius –, none of whom (in fact) had formally defined the doctrine for which they were condemned. The emperor's aim in restoring unity in the Church in this way was to recover divine favour for the empire after decades of crisis and moments of near-extinction. As a first test of God's favour, while the

---

[7] See Marek Jankowiak, *Essai d'histoire politique du monothélisme* (doctoral thesis Paris/Warsaw 2009, publication forthcoming), ch. 3.3.

[8] See H.G. Thümmel, "Zur Phämenologie von Konzilien: Das 6. Ökumenische Konzil 680/1", *Annuarium Historiae Conciliorum* 40 (2008), 85-98.

[9] In the words of the Definition: "Likewise we also proclaim two natural wills, which are not contrary (God forbid!), as the impious heretics asserted, but his human will follows and does not oppose or resist, but is instead subject to, his divine and omnipotent will. For "it was necessary for the will of the flesh to be moved and yet subjected to the divine will", according to the all-wise Athanasius", *Acta Conciliorum Oecumenicorum*, Series II (*ACO²*), II.2 (Berlin 1992), p. 774, 22-6. The teaching is Athanasian, even if the citation is from a pseudepigraphal work.

council was still meeting, he conducted a completely needless campaign against the Bulgarians, which ended in a resounding defeat.[10]

In all, the true story of the so-called monothelete controversy is less than edifying. So far from it being a case of the valiant defence of orthodoxy by the Roman see against a novel heresy concocted for political reasons (as older treatments invariably treated it), it represented the condemnation of a heresy that was the invention of its opponents, who pursued their campaign through the misrepresentation of their enemies, tendentious appeals to the patristic tradition, infringement of the canons, and high treason. At the same time, the story is significant for the claims to unique authority made in the course of it by the Roman see. Pope Martin not only held a synod that defied the ecclesiastical policy of the emperor, but published and circulated its acts in a way that had hitherto been reserved for ecumenical councils.[11] Maximus the Confessor went so far as to call the synod (attended almost exclusively by Italian bishops) an ecumenical council; hitherto, however, only emperors had summoned ecumenical councils. We have noted how Martin attempted to set up a new ecclesiastical hierarchy in Syria and Palestine, implying that the bishops already there (unless they submitted to Rome) were no longer valid holders of their sees and that Roman jurisdiction had no territorial limits. Finally, Pope Agatho, both in his own name and in that of a synod he held in Rome, responded to an invitation to dialogue from the emperor with long epistles in which he claimed to settle the doctrinal dispute on his own authority. These letters were received with respect at the council of 680-1, and even though the council carried out at length its own discussion of the issues, it concluded by abandoning the position with most support in the East and approving the teaching of the Roman see. The council marked a high point in the influence of Rome in the East. No other genuinely ecumenical council, until the Council of Florence, was equally receptive to the voice and authority of the Roman see.[12]

ROMAN AUTHORITY AND THE CRITERIA OF ORTHODOXY

My reason for choosing this episode in the history of the papacy lies not, however, in the evidence it gives of papal claims to a fullness of authority long before the Great Schism, let alone before Ultramontanism, but because of the way in which in the course of the controversy Rome sought to establish and vindicate its version of orthodoxy. How did Pope

---

[10] See Jankowiak, *Essai d'histoire*, ch. 4.1.4.

[11] See Price, "Aspects of the composition of the Acts of the Lateran Synod of 649", *Annuarium Historiae Conciliorum* 42 (2010), 51-8.

[12] Chalcedon (451) in approving the Tome of Leo and echoing it in its Definition came nearest, but the adoption of dyotheletism had strong support in the East and was not a capitulation to Rome.

Martin in 649 and Pope Agatho in 680 present their position? We have full acts for both these councils. What do these documents reveal?

The Acts of the Lateran Synod contain a number of letters from local churches (largely in Roman Africa) that express a clear acknowledgement of the unique authority of the Roman See. For example, a letter from Bishop Stephen of Dor, claiming to represent the patriarchate of Jerusalem, refers to Rome as 'the see that rules and presides over all others', and continues:[13]

> It has been accustomed to perform this authoritatively from the first and from of old, on the basis of its apostolic and canonical authority, for the reason, evidently, that the truly great Peter, the head of the apostles, was deemed worthy not only to be entrusted, alone out of all, with the keys of the kingdom of heaven for both opening them [the gates] deservedly to those who believe and shutting them justly to those who do not believe in the gospel of grace, but also because he was the first to be entrusted with shepherding the sheep of the whole catholic church. As the text runs, 'Peter, do you love me? Shepherd my sheep.' And again, because he possessed more than all others, in an exceptional and unique way, firm and unshakeable faith in our Lord, [he was deemed worthy] to turn and strengthen his comrades and spiritual brethren when they were wavering, since providentially he had been adorned by the God who became incarnate for our sake with power and priestly authority over them all.

This expresses the papalist theory that St Peter had unique authority among the apostles and that his role was fully and uniquely inherited by the popes of Rome. This theory was accepted in the East to the extent that it recognized that the popes had a special responsibility to stand up for the truth, but not in the sense that they were believed to possess a charism of truth in virtue of which their rulings were to be accepted without question or debate. The emperor Constantine IV, communicating to Pope Leo II the results of the sixth ecumenical council in December 681, reports how the council accepted the doctrinal report sent by Pope Agatho *after* 'setting against the report the decrees and definitions of the holy and ecumenical councils, comparing the citations it contained with the works of the fathers, and finding nothing discordant'.[14]

Equally significant for our topic is how the papal decrees were expressed and issued. It is first to be noted that neither Pope Martin in 649 nor Pope Agatho when preparing for the council of 680 issued decrees purely on their own authority. Instead, both of them summoned synods to discuss and issue an appropriate resolution. This practice arose from a

---

[13] *ACO*² I (Berlin 1984), pp. 38,43-40,10.
[14] *ACO*² II.2, p. 896, 2-5.

general principle in the Church that those in authority, at whatever level, should have a council and consult it regularly. Presbyters, or priests, were in the origin the members of the diocesan council that advised the bishop; only gradually did they come to be defined instead by their liturgical role. Metropolitan bishops, in charge of provinces, were required by canon law to summon and consult councils of their suffragans twice a year (Nicaea, Canon 5). Likewise, Roman pontiffs regularly summoned councils of Italian bishops before taking important decisions. Towards the end of the first millennium Roman cardinals emerged, who formed a consistory that advised popes in the same way. This system continued till 1588 when Sixtus V created fifteen separate congregations to conduct business. Each one was to deal with the pope separately, and so they could not unite to restrain him. In the words of J.N.D. Kelly, 'This arrangement reduced the importance of the consistory and thereby the claims of the sacred college to co-rule with the pope.'[15]

At the Lateran Synod of 649 Pope Martin chaired the sessions and directed the council in its examination of the doctrinal controversy in question. At the end of the council a decree was presented to the assembled bishops, which they all signed, with the pope's subscription coming first, but in an identical form to those that followed.[16] Nothing was said about the pope's special role or his unique authority.

The documentation sent from Rome to the Sixth Ecumenical Council was different in form. It consisted of two documents – a letter (styled *anaphora*, or 'report') from the pope personally, and a similar 'report' from the pope together with the bishops he had summoned to a synod at Rome to discuss the question with him. How in his own letter does the pope describe his own authority? He certainly stresses the unique authority of St Peter, and thereby (by implication) of himself as Peter's successor: 'His authority as the prince of all the apostles has always been embraced and followed in all respects by the whole catholic church and the universal synods, and his apostolic doctrine has been embraced by all the venerable fathers'.[17] Of the Roman see, styled 'the Apostolic Church of Christ', he writes: 'Through the grace of almighty God she will be proved never to have strayed from the path of the apostolic tradition, nor has she ever yielded to distortion by heretical novelties, but just as from the beginning of the Christian faith she received it from her founders the princes of the apostles of Christ, so she continues unstained till the end'.[18] Nevertheless, the pope does not presume to dictate the line the emperor is to follow, for he says to him: 'May therefore the height of your clemency appointed by God, with the inward eye of that discernment which, through the illumination of divine grace, you

---

[15] J.N.D. Kelly, *The Oxford Dictionary of Popes* (Oxford 1986 and 2006), 272.

[16] *ACO²* I, 391.

[17] *ACO²* II.1 (Berlin 1990), p. 63, 15-18.

[18] *ACO²* II.1, p. 65, 7-10.

were privileged to receive for the directing of the Christian congregations, consider which one of these teachers the Christian people should choose to follow, and the teaching of which of them it ought to embrace in order to be saved.'[19]

But the most revealing and representative statement is perhaps the following, from the same letter, with reference to the legates the pope is sending to the council:[20]

> Therefore, my most Christian lords and sons, fulfilling the pious command of your gentleness, protected by God, in accordance with the obedience we owe, though not out of assurance as to the knowledge of those we are sending, we have taken care with suppliant devotion of heart to give instructions to our fellow servants here present [the legates are then named]. How among men placed in the midst of the tribes [the Lombards in Italy] and seeking their daily sustenance with the greatest difficulty from bodily labour can knowledge of the scriptures be found to the full? All we can do is to preserve, with simplicity of heart and without any doubts about the faith handed down by our fathers and formally defined by our holy and apostolic predecessors and the venerable five councils, while we hope and endeavour always to possess one particular blessing, that on the matters that have been formally defined there is to be no subtraction and no alteration or addition, but that the same things are to be kept inviolate in both wording and meaning. To these messengers we have entrusted the testimonies of certain holy fathers acknowledged by this apostolic church of Christ, together with their books, so that, on receiving from the most benign rule of your Christianity the opportunity to make proposals, they may endeavour to give satisfaction at least from these books (when your imperial gentleness so directs) as to what this spiritual mother of your rule protected by God, the apostolic church of Christ, believes and preaches.

The pope is confident of his own authority, and happy to admit the defective learning of his legates, because he is making no addition to the apostolic faith, and can prove his fidelity to the tradition by citing 'the testimonies of certain holy fathers'.

It is precisely this mode of proof that was adopted at the Lateran Synod of 649. At the final and decisive session no fewer than 166 passages were read out, mainly from orthodox Fathers, but a few from heretics – in order to prove that monotheletism had been invented by theologians acknowledged to be heretical. Arguments by recourse to reason played

---

[19] *ACO²* II.1, p. 111, 17-20.
[20] *ACO²* II.1, p. 57, 4-24.

some part at the synod, but the dominant mode of argument was to show that monoenergism and monotheletism were innovations, and thereby of necessity contrary to the authentic faith, preached by the Apostles and transmitted by the Fathers of the Church. Likewise, in Pope Agatho's letter to the emperor of 680, the argument is dominated by patristic citations, and the accompanying commentary is concerned to justify the pope's understanding of these citations, not to prove by theological analysis that the Fathers got it right, for that is simply taken for granted. The conclusion is as follows: 'What remains is for the truth to shine forth, crowned with a wreath of victory by the pious support of your clemency crowned by God, and for the novelty of error, together with its concoctors and those whose doctrine they followed, to pay the penalty of their presumption, and for them to be expelled from the midst of the orthodox priests because of the heretical depravity of their innovation.'[21] Just as tradition is evidence of truth, so novelty and innovation are proof of error.

The trouble with the papal position, in this case, was that the claim that the tradition was solidly dyoenergist and dyothelete, and that monoenergism and monotheletism were innovations, was not successfully made out. As one of the members of the opposition at the Sixth Ecumenical Council pointed out correctly, the Fathers had spoken of activity and volition in Christ, but had not been concerned to count them.[22] The exceptions were few, and as often asserted oneness in Christ as duality – indeed more often. The claim that monoenergism and monotheletism were heretical depended on claiming that the passages in orthodox Fathers that gave them some support were either interpolations or at least wrongly interpreted, and on wilfully misinterpreting the monotheletes as holding tenets that manifestly contradicted the Chalcedonian faith in two natures, divine and human, in Christ.

The fact that the argument from tradition was therefore defective makes it all the more significant that it was this argument on which the papacy based its position. In all, claims for the unique authority of the magisterium, as vested in the see of Peter, did not allege a unique charism of truth, a special grace of the Holy Spirit; it attempted, instead, to prove papal infallibility not by recourse to theoretical arguments but by an appeal to history – by the claim that it could be shown that popes had always been faithful to the tradition. It remained the tradition that was the guarantor of truth. This tradition was stable and unalterable. This did not exclude advances in theology; it did not forbid theologians from propounding new ideas. But a teaching that was only a development could not claim to the full authority accorded to Scripture and the creeds, whose teaching was not *developed* but *preserved* by the decrees and definitions of councils. This, then, was the faith of the undivided Church of the first millennium, the faith that the Catholic Church needs to reaffirm, if she is to receive into her

---

[21] *ACO²* II.1, p. 115, 17-21.
[22] Theodore of Melitene at *ACO²* II.1, p. 202, 13-19.

embrace the communions and denominations that in the course of history became estranged from her.

FURTHER REFLECTIONS

Am I claiming, you may wonder, that full authority pertains only to doctrine that was formulated and approved in the early centuries? Where does this leave the magisterium – the continuing teaching authority of pope and bishops? Is 'tradition' necessarily so static?

In this context reference is often made nowadays to the notions of 'living tradition' or of 'development of doctrine'. In the words of the decree of the Second Vatican Council on divine revelation, 'this tradition which comes from the Apostles makes progress (*proficit*) in the Church with the help of the Holy Spirit. For there is a growth (*crescit*) in the understanding of the realities and the words which have been handed down.'[23]

But this notion needs to be treated with care. Not only was the notion of a development that goes beyond logical deduction a novelty in official teaching, but it is open to a variety of tendentious interpretations: it enables radical theologians to dress up innovation in a guise of continuity, and yet it is equally open to exploitation by integrists, who wish to make everything we have inherited immune to change. John Henry Newman's famous *Essay on the Development of Doctrine* (1845) was not concerned to encourage innovation, but to defend the developed doctrines of the Catholic Church from the charge of departing from the original apostolic proclamation. He admitted that the teaching of Nicaea and Chalcedon, not to mention Trent, was not to be found unambiguously expressed or universally asserted in the first three centuries, but argued that it was present *implicitly* in the faith of the Church right from the beginning, as an 'idea' communicated by God to the mind and heart of the Church. This is simultaneously to admit and to deny the reality of historical change, a typical example of that mental habit that Newman's admirers praise as subtlety and his detractors deplore as sophistry.

What Newman meant by an 'idea' has been, and will be, endlessly debated, for the notion was not clearly defined in his own mind. A summary by Owen Chadwick is as good as any:[24]

> The revelation was given as a unity, as a totality, addressing itself to the hearts and feelings and consciences as well as to the minds of men. It was given partly in the form of propositions. And partly, Christian thinkers have needed to draw out and formulate, not only the intellectual consequence of the given

---

[23] *Dei Verbum* 8, in *Sacrosanctum Oecumenicum Concilium Vaticanum II: Constitutiones, Decreta, Declarationes* (Vatican City 1966), 429-30.

[24] Owen Chadwick, *From Bossuet to Newman: The Idea of Doctrinal Development* (Cambridge 1957), 153.

propositions, but the rational expression of what at first they experienced wordlessly, and which could be formulated as their feelings and experiences encountered opposition, error, pagan philosophy, or evangelistic success.

This notion of an 'idea' communicated to us by God in the age of the apostles in the form of imperfect propositions (imprecise and capable of misunderstanding), accompanied by wordless feelings and intuitions, which gradually develop, with growth but without change, into the full clarity of Catholic doctrine will seem to the critical mind to be a myth – an imaginative story, intended to assert an identity between the first dim lineaments of a belief and its final expression in word and worship. But in what is this 'identity' supposed to consist, beyond the bald assertion that the final product is 'the same' (in some indefinable sense) as the original revelation?

It is true, of course, that ideas and beliefs 'develop' in the sense that there is intellectual continuity between early doctrine and that later teaching which takes the early doctrine as its starting point and does not consciously or deliberately alter or correct it; we can indeed talk of 'development' as something different from 'supersession'. But there cannot be actual identity between the original apostolic teaching and later doctrine. At the same time the Church has always firmly rejected the notion of continuing revelation. Strictly, revelation ceased with the passing away of the Apostles. We may, however, with some legitimacy extend the period of doctrinal formulation with full apostolic authority down into the fourth century, when the Nicene Creed was composed and revised, till it attained the form in which it is used by all the Churches.[25] And a proper understanding of the creed requires reverent attention to the 'Nicene Fathers', a group that extends beyond the bishops who attended the Council of Nicaea to later Fathers such as Basil the Great and Cyril of Alexandria, who shared the same mindset and expressed the Nicene faith in its fullness. But beyond this point we reach a broad plane where different roads lead in different directions. The claim of the Catholic Church that certain later pronouncements satisfy the requirements for infallibility defined at Vatican I does not secure inerrancy for the whole range of current church teaching.

Recognition that Scripture and the early tradition enjoy an authority that is unique to them and cannot be claimed for later developments may seem too conservative, and in danger of fettering the magisterium. Would it

---

[25] The Nicene Creed was not at first a fixed text, but could accommodate a range of variations. The version that came to be universally used was composed in the 370s and was accorded canonical authority by the Council of Chalcedon (451), which attributed it (with very doubtful accuracy) to the Council of Constantinople of 381. See A.M. Ritter in G. Alberigo, ed., *Conciliorum Oecumenicorum Generaliumque Decreta, I: The Oecumenical Councils from Nicaea I to Nicaea II (325-787)* (Turnhout, 2006), 47-9.

tie the Church forever to outdated and untenable positions on certain notorious issues (such as the standing of the Jews in God's sight), while depriving her of the ability to provide any answers at all to questions that are new and were not addressed in the tradition?

My own conclusion, however, would be different – namely, that new questions do indeed require new answers, but that these answers cannot lay claim to infallibility. Take the question of in vitro fertilization. Catholic unease about the importation of intrusive technology into a sphere where natural means of procreation seem part of the definition of 'male' and 'female' is wholly understandable, but once the technology is available, it is not obvious that it cannot be used to compensate for defects that appear to be accidental rather than part of the divine plan. Or take the imminent development of medication that can stave off the physical process of ageing: is this to be welcomed as a fruit of that great divine gift which is human intelligence and our ability to shift the frontiers of physical vulnerability, or is it a refusal to accept the God-given cycle of life and death, and of the passing of the generations? Answers are needed to such questions, and must attempt to unite the contemporary context and scientific developments with principles derived from the tradition. This is the proper task of the magisterium. But it would be temerarious to claim that arguments along these lines can ever possess a degree of certainty that leaves no room for doubt and no scope for dissent.

The richness of developed Catholic doctrine is one of the glories of the Church. But to attribute full apostolic authority to the whole range of currently standard doctrine, as if it were all part of divine revelation, goes against the basic principle that guided the early ecumenical councils and the popes who contributed to their work – that, while new ideas are often commendable and even necessary, the Church should require unconditional assent only to what is explicit in the tradition, as contained in Scripture and the Fathers, and only condemn as heretical what contradicts this tradition. A vast range of fruitful ideas lies outside this range and is not to be neglected; nor should the Church through her magisterium hesitate to address new questions and find new answers. But she needs to proceed with humility and prudence, neither presuming inerrancy nor condemning dissent, but praying to God that he may use our decisions, unimpeachable or questionable, for the ultimate good of the Church and the final attainment of the Kingdom.

Heythrop College, London, Great Britain

CHAPTER VIII

BE SUBJECT TO EVERY HUMAN CREATURE FOR GOD'S SAKE: ST FRANCIS OF ASSISI AND THE EXPERIENCE OF AUTHORITY

PAUL ROUT

You are an archbishop or a bishop. So you wish to find grace? Then humble yourself. If we do not humble ourselves we are robbers.[1]

So wrote the seventh Minister General of the Franciscan Order in the year 1268. St Bonaventure had held this position since 1257 and saw as one of his main projects for the Order the recapturing of the spirit of its founder, St Francis of Assisi. He had commented earlier that of all the virtues he saw in the life of Francis, the one that impressed him the most was his humility.[2] Humility lay at the heart of Francis' radical living out of the gospel of Christ, it characterised the quality of Francis' experience of God who had revealed himself in the poor and suffering Christ. Consequently it was vital for Bonaventure that those who professed to follow the path of Christ in the service of the gospel should live and express lives of profound gospel humility. Even more so should this apply for the leaders of those who follow Christ: bishops, archbishops, all who exercise authority within the Church.

In this chapter I wish to explore the understanding of the nature and purpose of authority that arose within the early Franciscan tradition. Part 1 will be concerned not so much with theory as with experience. I shall begin with an examination of the inspirational foundation that can be discerned within the life experience of St Francis of Assisi. Focusing on a selection of episodes within the accounts we have of his life, I shall seek to put forward a number of principles that are operative within his understanding of the nature and purpose of authority within his own Order, within the Church and within the wider world with which he came to engage.

---

[1] Bonaventure "Collations on the Gifts of the Holy Spirit" 1.10 in *St Bonaventure's Collations on the Gifts of the Holy Spirit*, trans. by Zachary Hayes, Works of St Bonaventure, ed. by Robert Karris, Vol 14 (St Bonaventure, NY: The Franciscan Institute, 2008) p.35.

[2] Eric Doyle *The Disciple and the Master: St Bonaventure's Sermons on St Francis of Assisi*, trans. and ed. by Eric Doyle (Chicago: Franciscan Herald Press, 1983) p.3.

Part 2 will look at the theological implications of the experience of St Francis as developed in the theological/ spiritual writings of St Bonaventure. Beginning with Bonaventure's own theological departure point of the nature of God who is Trinity, this section will move on to explore what this has to say for questions concerning the nature of the human person, the nature and purpose of the moral life and the individual's relation to wider society and to the world. It is only in the light of these fundamental issues that we can then appreciate Bonaventure's understanding of the nature and purpose of authority, particularly the exercise of authority within the Church.

The final section of the paper will argue that what emerges from this analysis of 'authority' within the early Franciscan tradition has relevance for our contemporary discussion concerning the nature of authority within a kenotic Church. The question of authority is not a theoretical question. Authority and its exercise have practical implications for people's life-experience; consequently, discussions concerning authority cannot remain in the world of theory but need to be rooted in human experience. The early Franciscan theological tradition is grounded in experience and from that experience there developed a theology. This is the way by which I shall proceed in this chapter.

THE EXPERIENCE

St Francis was born in the central Italian city of Assisi in 1182. At that period in history, Assisi, like much of central Italy, was undergoing profound changes. The old authority structure of the feudal nobility had been overthrown and the new locus of authority was to be found in the city burghers, the emerging wealthy merchant class. As the son of a clothing merchant, Francis enjoyed the wealth and status that came with belonging to the privileged group, the *maiores*. Although in the year 1200, the citizens of Assisi may have overthrown one oppressive authority structure, it was not long before the new authority structure ensured that once again Assisi became divided between the *maiores*, and the *minores* – the poor, the needy, the uneducated, who stood as the polar opposites of the rich, the powerful, and the learned.

Although born among the *maiores*, in October 1226 Francis was to die among the *minores*. At the very beginning of his *Testament* which he composed some six months before his death, he attributed this fact to an event that occurred some twenty years earlier:

> While I was in sin, it seemed very bitter to me to see lepers. And
> the Lord himself led me among them and I had mercy upon them.

And when I left them that which seemed bitter to me was changed into sweetness of soul and body.[1]

This encounter with a leper was pivotal in bringing about a fundamental reorientation in Francis' awareness of how he stood in relation to the other. He understood this encounter as divine revelation which moved him from a horizon that focussed on privilege and self-interest to a horizon that focussed on mutual encounter with the other, especially the other who was most wounded and broken.[2] No longer did he relate from above as a *maior*, but now alongside and in reciprocal relationship, as a *minor*.

Francis' conversion experience unfolded within his growing realisation of the nature of the God who is revealed in Jesus Christ. The Prologue to his Rule of Life of 1221 described the Rule as "the life of the Gospel of Jesus Christ".[3] What the life of the Gospel was to entail for the Brothers is expressed in Chapter 9, "All the brothers should strive to follow the humility and the poverty of our Lord Jesus Christ."[4] The Gospel values that Francis constantly focussed upon were the kenotic values of humility and poverty. Likewise, when Francis contemplated the Eucharistic presence, what he experienced above all was the paradox of the humility of God.

> Let the whole of humanity tremble, the whole world shake and the heavens exult when Christ the Son of the living God, is present on the altar in the hands of a priest. O admirable heights and sublime lowliness! O sublime humility! O humble sublimity! That the Lord of the universe, God and the Son of God, so humbles himself that for our salvation He hides himself under the little form of bread.

In response to such divine humility, the brothers were called to be humble themselves through lives that were expressions of self-emptying, kenotic generosity.

> Look, brothers, at the humility of God and pour out your hearts before Him! Humble yourselves as well, that you may be exalted by Him. Therefore hold back nothing of yourselves for

---

[1] Francis of Assisi, "The Testament" 1 in *Francis and Clare: The Complete Works* trans. by Regis Armstrong and Ignatius Brady, Classics of Western Spirituality Series (New York: Paulist Press, 1982), p. 154.

[2] *Writings of Francis of Assisi: Rules, Testament and Admonitions*, ed. by Michael Blastic, Jay Hammond and J.A. Wayne Hellmann (St Bonaventure, NY: Franciscan Institute Publications, 2011), p. 244.

[3] Francis of Assisi, "The Earlier Rule" Prologue 2 in *Francis and Clare: The Complete Works*, p. 108.

[4] Francis of Assisi, "The Earlier Rule" 9.1 in *Francis and Clare: The Complete Works*, p. 117.

yourselves so that He who gives Himself totally to you may receive you totally.[5]

It is significant that this meditation on Eucharistic humility was placed in that section of his Letter where he addressed in particular the brothers who were priests. The Letter was written by Francis after his return from the Middle East in 1220. In his Commentary on the Letter, Michael Blastic notes "Some brother-priests were seemingly bringing into the brotherhood attitudes and values connected to the hierarchical role and position of the priest in the church and world of those times. This affected the internal relationships among the brothers, perhaps suggesting a kind of class distinction."[6] Francis' Letter addressed these concerns. He recognized that "the Lord God has honoured you [brother-priests] above all other persons because of this ministry", but reminded his brother priests that their ministry was to be exercised as one of humility and service.[7]

Within the life of the brotherhood, Francis urged that the exercise of authority should result in the practice of reciprocal obedience. Chapter 4 of the Rule of 1221 speaks of the relationship between the *Minister* (in Chapter 6 of the same Rule Francis specifies 'no one should be called Prior but all generally should be called Friars Minor') and the other brothers. The brothers are called to "diligently obey them [the ministers] in those matters which concern the well-being of their soul and which are not contrary to our life." Ministers are called to "...remember what the Lord says: I have come not to be served but to serve." It is important to note that in Chapter 5, he extends the notion of obedience to include the obedience of the Minister to the brothers. Francis exhorts the brothers who are "subjects" to "diligently consider the actions of the ministers". Should it be seen that the ministers are not living in accordance with the "integrity of our life", the subjects ought to admonish the ministers. He moves on to remind the brothers, ministers and subjects, "...all the brothers in this regard should not hold power or dominion...for the Lord says...Whoever is the greater among you should become like the lesser."[8]

Such a vision of authority and obedience necessitated an awareness of the part of all that they stood not over others as *maiores*, but alongside each other, called to different ministries within the community, but also called to mutual encounter in the light of a way of life that had been revealed in the

---

[5] Francis of Assisi, "A Letter to the Entire Order" 26-29 in *Francis and Clare: The Complete Works*, p. 58.

[6] *Writings of Francis of Assisi: Letters and Prayers*, ed. by Michael Blastic, Jay Hammond and J.A. Wayne Hellmann (St Bonaventure, NY: Franciscan Institute Publications, 2010), p. 133.

[7] Francis of Assisi, "A Letter to the Entire Order" 23 in *Francis and Clare: The Complete Works*, p. 57.

[8] Francis of Assisi, "The Earlier Rule" 4.3, 6;5.9,11; 6.3 in *Francis and Clare: The Complete Works*, pp. 112-4.

Gospel. This was an awareness that had so powerfully come to Francis in his embrace of the leper when he was drawn out of himself through compassion for the other. His approach to authority and obedience was shaped dramatically through this experience.

As preachers of the Gospel who were officially approved by the Church, the brothers were involved in the exercise of spiritual authority. Their words and actions were to impact upon those to whom they were sent on mission. When Francis instructed the brothers on how they should carry out their mission, the influence of his 'leper experience' is once again evident. Chapter 9 of the Rule of 1221 urged the brothers, "[You] must rejoice when [you] live among people [who are considered to be] of little worth and who are looked down upon, among the poor and the powerless, the sick and the lepers."[9] The English 'live among' is the translation of the Latin *conversantur*. During the Middle Ages, the Latin verb *conversari* "...implied movement and familiarity; it communicated a notion of dynamism and relationship."[10] The brothers' mission was to involve dynamic movement outwards to the other, to 'live with' the other, and its authority was to be derived from their familiarity and relationship with those to whom they ministered.

Francis' own mission extended to the Islamic world, as evidenced in his meeting with Sultan al-Malek al-Kamil, near Damietta in Egypt in 1219. This took place during the Fifth Crusade, at a time when in much of the Christian world Muslims were regarded as enemies of God, as evil. I have argued elsewhere that the process of conversion that began with Francis' embrace of the leper led him to a continuing transformation in his life that forced him to assess all of his relationships, especially with those whom he had previously regarded as outcasts or enemies.[11] It would appear that his journey to Damietta was a further unfolding of this. It is evident after his return from Egypt that his encounter with the Sultan and the world of Islam had made a deep spiritual impact upon him.

What is relevant here are the instructions Francis provided in Chapter 16 of the Rule of 1221 for those of his brothers who felt called to missionary activity among the Muslim people. He decreed that the brothers

---

[9] Francis of Assisi, "The Earlier Rule" 9.2 in *Francis and Clare: The Complete Works*, p. 117.

[10] Keith Warner, "Pilgrims and Strangers: the evangelical ministry of itinerancy of the early Franciscan friars", in *True Followers of Justice: identity, insertion and itinerancy among the early Franciscans*, ed. by Elise Saggau, Spirit and Life: a journal of contemporary Franciscanism 10 (St Bonaventure, NY: The Franciscan Institute, 2000), p.149.

[11] Paul Rout, "St Francis of Assisi and Islam: A Theological Perspective on a Christian-Muslim Encounter", *Al-Masaq: Islam and the Medieval Mediterranean*, 23 (2011), 205-215.

were to live "spiritually" among the Saracens.[12] This is a theme that frequently occurred in Francis' writings, that the brothers are to live 'in the Spirit of the Lord'. For Francis, a presence 'in the spirit of the Lord' was a presence which expressed the qualities of the life lived by Jesus Christ, especially, for Francis, the qualities of humility and peace.[13] Consequently, as he urged in Chapter 16, they were not to engage in arguments or disputes, but were to be "subject to every human creature" as Christ himself was subject. This notion of 'being subject' is crucial and marked a new approach in Christian attitudes towards Muslims. Warren notes: "This was not only a radical departure from the practice of the day, it was in direct opposition to Canon Law. Several decrees regarding relations between Christians and Saracens, composed between 1188 and 1217, presupposed or even stated explicitly that Christians may not be subject to Saracens."[14]

Anton Rotzetter comments that the aim of subjection is brotherliness: a new way of dealing with people and with the world, not on the basis of violence and power, but in a spirit of love and tenderness. The humility of Jesus was for the purpose of ushering in the new creation. So for Francis and the brothers, submission was not simply humility for humility's sake, but for the radical aim of introducing a new approach to people which was opposed to the use of domineering power which so often characterised the nature of relationships in the society of his day – and so often still does.[15] To live as 'subject to' is a way of ministering and relating to the other that finds expression in a spirit of love and humility. It can be seen as an alternative way of exercising authority, which is essentially kenotic in nature.

What is evident in the life of Francis is the reality of a profound experience of interpersonal encounter which he understood to be an occasion of divine revelation. This encounter with the poor and suffering other was to dramatically alter his world view. It brought about within him a reversal of values, leading him to abandon the world of privilege, status and power, the world of the *maior*, in order to embrace the life style of the *minor*, the lesser one. His motivation was religious, that of the Gospel, through which he came to believe that the way to human fulfilment was the way of *kenosis*, the way of Christ as seen in his poverty and humility. Humility was to find expression in his refusal to stand in positions of dominance over another, but through compassion to be drawn out beyond

---

[12] Francis of Assisi, "The Earlier Rule" 16.5 in *Francis and Clare: The Complete Works*, p. 121.

[13] Dominic Monti, "The Experience of the Spirit in our Franciscan Tradition" *The Cord,* 49 (1999), 114-129, (p.124).

[14] Kathleen Warren, *Francis of Assisi Encounters Sultan Malik al-Kamil* (St Bonaventure, NY: Franciscan Institute, 2003), p.74ll.

[15] Anton Rotzetter, "The Missionary Dimension of the Franciscan Charism" in *Mission in the Franciscan Tradition* ed. by Anselm Moons and Flavius Walsh (St Bonaventure, NY: Franciscan Institute, 1993), pp.51-2.

self to stand alongside, in mutual relationship with the other. This fundamental life conviction was to find expression in his understanding of the nature and exercise of authority within his Order and in the wider world.

THE THEOLOGY

When we consider the theological writings of Saint Bonaventure, we need to recognize the central place in his thought of the life experience of the saint who so inspired and shaped the particular theological approach of the Seraphic Doctor, Saint Francis of Assisi. Bonaventure was born in 1217, Francis died in 1226, so their two worlds were temporally intertwined. Bonaventure, after eight years of study at the University of Paris, was to join the Order that Francis had founded, the *Fratres Minores*, a decision made on the grounds of the inspiration that he received from those early young and enthusiastic followers of Francis whom he encountered at the University.[16] As his theological style developed, it increasingly displayed what Bonaventure believed to be the wider implications of the religious experience of this Poor Man of Assisi who had made such a powerful impact upon the world of his time. Balthasar comments, "When we speak of this event, we have at last mentioned the living, organising centre of Bonaventure's intellectual world...Bonaventure does not only take Francis as his centre: he is his own sun and his mission."[17]

It is not surprising to find, then, that Bonaventure's theological vision is in keeping with the central elements of Francis' experience. Bonaventure's theology began with the Trinitarian God of Christian revelation and saw all else, including the life of the Church, in the light of his understanding of the nature of God. Francis' profound insight that the life of God who is revealed in Jesus Christ is a life that found expression in kenotic humility was captured by Bonaventure in his Trinitarian theology.

Bonaventure understood the nature of God to be essentially Trinitarian goodness. Chapters 5 and 6 of his *Itinerarium* are contemplations upon the nature of God. It is important to note the structure of these two Chapters. Chapter 5 is a contemplation of the name *God* in its philosophical sense, which is Being. Chapter 6 is a contemplation of God in the theological sense, God as Trinity, with the primary name of God being 'Good'. Bonaventure symbolizes these two ways of contemplating God through the image of the two Cherubim who stand on the ends of the Throne of Mercy that rests on top of the Ark in the Holy of Holies in the Temple:

---

[16] For an extended chronology of the life of Bonaventure, see Jacques Bougerol, *Introduction to the Works of Bonaventure* (Paterson, NJ: St Anthony Guild Press, 1964) pp. 171-177; John Quinn "Chronology of St Bonaventure (1217-1257)" *Greyfriars Review* 32 (1972), 168-186.

[17] Hans Urs von Balthasar *The Glory of the Lord: A Theological Aesthetics* ed. by John Riches, trans. by Andrew Louth and others, 7 vols (Edinburgh: T&T Clark, 1982-1991), II (1984), p. 262.

"Enter with the high priest into the Holy of Holies where the Cherubim of glory stand over the ark overshadowing the Mercy Seat. By these Cherubim we understand the two modes or stages of contemplating the invisible and eternal things of God."[18]

Bonaventure's Trinitarian theology drew upon the thought of Pseudo-Dionysius, who himself utilised Neoplatonic thought. This is evident in Bonaventure's *Breviloquium* where he identifies the Neoplatonic One with the Father: "The Father is properly the One without an originator, the unbegotten One; the Principle who proceeds from no other; the Father as such."[19] The Father as Unbegotten is the fertile source of the life of the Trinity. Moreover, as the fullness of the good, (the *fontalis plenitudo*) the Father is necessarily self-communicating. "The more primary a thing is, the more fecund it is and the principle of others." [20] As the Unbegotten and the fertile source, and also as the self-communicating good, the Father begets the Son. Such *begetting* is portrayed as a movement that is a complete outpouring of self – God's self-communication holds back nothing but pours itself out entirely to the other: "Because the whole is communicated and not merely part, whatever is possessed is given, and given completely."[21] The reciprocal outpouring by the Son towards the Father creates a union that is expressed in the person of the Holy Spirit. It is possible then to speak of the Trinitarian processions as *kenotic* in nature.

It is important to note that within Bonaventure's Trinitarian theology, the term 'Father' is not meant to be understood in a patriarchal way, implying concepts of domination and subordination. The Father is not the one who rules over but rather the one who, as fertile source of the good, gives totally of that good. The fatherhood of God is to be understood as total self-giving love. What is witnessed in the generation of the Son is the self-emptying of the Father. When Bonaventure speaks of the Father as primary, he understands such primacy in terms of an original source of self-giving and life-giving goodness and love. He offers no suggestion of the Father as a ruling male monarch. As Ilia Delio points out, he does not think of 'Father' as a literal name (i.e. that God is primarily a male patriarchal entity) but rather as a relational concept which signifies the principle that the source of Trinitarian life, the source of the Godhead, is dynamic and personal.[22]

---

[18] Bonaventure, "The Soul's Journey into God" 5.1 in *Bonaventure. The Soul's Journey into God, The Tree of Life, The Life of St Francis* trans. by Ewert Cousins, Classics of Western Spirituality Series (New York: Paulist Press, 1978), p. 94.

[19] Bonaventure *Breviloquium* 1.3,7, trans. by Jose de Vinck, The Works of St Bonaventure, Vol. 2 (Paterson, NJ: St Anthony Guild Press, 1963) p.39.

[20] Bonaventure "First Book of Sentences" d.27, p. 1, a.u., q.2 in Ilia Delio "Bonaventure's Metaphysics of the Good", *Theological Studies*, 60 (1999), 228-246, (p. 237).

[21] Bonaventure, "The Soul's Journey into God" 6.3, p. 105.

[22] Delio, "Bonaventure's Metaphysics", p. 237.

Bonaventure's understanding of the nature and purpose of human life must be seen in relation to his Trinitarian theology. His theological notion of *exemplarity* enables him to develop an anthropology that springs from his conviction concerning the relational nature of all created reality. "The universe is like a book reflecting, representing and describing its Maker, the Trinity."[23] All created realities can be seen as *vestiges* (traces) of the divine, human beings as rational creatures are *images* of the divine. The human person is primarily understood as 'image' of God, hence as image of the Trinity. Since the life of the Trinity is one of relational goodness and love, such is the fundamental calling of humanity. Relationality lies at the heart of Bonaventure's vision of human life.[24] It is a relationality ordered towards the expression of love and consequently any ordering within human communities must exist for the sake of the promotion of relational love – as does the *ordering* within the life of the Trinity.

An ordering of relational love is one in which unity can rejoice in diversity, as the oneness of the Godhead rejoices in the individuality of the Persons. Such is the ordering Bonaventure saw as desirable within the life of the Church. Trinitarian life is revealed in the Incarnation of the Word who becomes the "exemplar and mirror of all graces, virtues and merits." All created ordering flows from in its origin in the Incarnate Word and must serve to enhance in its members imitation of the qualities that are found in the life of Christ, the exemplar.

Diverse states, degrees and orders are derived from him according to the various distribution of the gifts and the various manners in which the Exemplar is to be imitated. To them the manifold perfection of Christ is distributed according to a multiform participation in such a way that it is found at the same time in all things. And yet it does not shine in any one of them in the fullness of its universal plenitude, but each state and degree receives the influence from such exemplarity and moves forward to imitate it.[25]

The ordering that Bonaventure called for required that all participate in the attitude of Christ who brought salvation through his condescension, his *kenosis*. Speaking of Christ's incarnation, he uses the words, "Likewise the Son of God, the very small and poor and humble one, assuming our earth and made of earth...."[26] In his *Collations on the Ten Commandments*, Bonaventure spoke in detail of the 'condescension' of Christ, stressing that through such a way of life, he "...liberated us and brought us from death to life and from

---

[23] Bonaventure *Breviloquium*, 2.12,1.
[24] Zachary Hayes *Bonaventure: Mystical Writings* (New York: Crossroad, 1999), p. 62.
[25] Bonaventure, "Defence of the Mendicants" 2.12, in *St Bonaventure's Defence of the Mendicants*, trans. by Jose de Vinck and Robert Karris, Works of St Bonaventure Vol. 15 (St Bonaventure, NY: Franciscan Institute, 2010), p. 62.
[26] Bonaventure, *Collations on the Six Days* 1.22, trans. by Jose de Vinck, The Works of Bonaventure Vol. 5 (Paterson, NJ: St Anthony Guild Press, 1970), p. 12.

darkness to light."[27] The function of ordering within the life of the Church is to mediate salvation, to liberate, to bring from death to life, from darkness to light. In order to achieve this, what is called for on the part of all is an asceticism of condescension, of kenosis.

It is appropriate, then, that Bonaventure speaks of the operation of hierarchy within the Church in terms that speak more of the acquisition and mediation of spiritual, 'Godlike' qualities, rather than in terms of the power dominance of one group over others. Drawing on Pseudo-Dionysius, he notes that the concept of hierarchy has its origins not in the language of power structures but in the language of spirituality and life with God.

> The goal of a hierarchy, then, is to enable beings to be as like as possible to God and to be at one with him. A hierarchy has God as it leader of all understanding and action....Hierarchy causes its members to be images of God in all respects, to be clear and spotless mirrors reflecting the glow of primordial light and indeed of God himself. It ensures that when its members have received this full and divine splendour they can then pass on this light generously.[28]

The whole Church, not just one group within the Church, constitutes the hierarchy. Any institutional 'hierarchy' fulfils its purpose only when it promotes the qualities of hierarchy that are firstly found within what Bonaventure terms 'the hierarchised soul', qualities by means of which the members of the Church come to resemble God in their dispositions and actions. "The third part of hierarchy consists in considering the hierarchised human soul. And this is understood through the light of the stars, which indeed has a radiation that is faithful, beautiful and joyful. The soul, when it enjoys these three, is hierarchised."[29] Hierarchy is concerned with the states of a being of a person in terms of relationship with God. The human person is 'hierarchised' in manifesting the spiritual qualities of constancy, beauty and joy; the Church is hierarchised when it enables the flourishing and expression of such qualities. As I have commented elsewhere.

The Church is hierarchical in nature. This does not mean that the Church has an elite who are the hierarchy. On the contrary, *all* people within the Church are called to be hierarchised. Understood in this way, the Church's hierarchical structure is not a static reality, but rather a challenge. To be a

---

[27] Bonaventure, "Collations on the Ten Commandments" 7.17 in *St Bonaventure's Collations on the Ten Commandments*, trans. by Paul Spaeth, Works of St Bonaventure, ed. by F. Edward Coughlin, Vol. 6 (St Bonaventure, NY: The Franciscan Institute,1995), p. 101.

[28] Pseudo-Dionysius "The Celestial Hierarchy" 3.2 in *Pseudo-Dionysius: The Complete Works*, trans. by Colm Luibheid and Paul Rorem, Classics of Western Spirituality (London: SPCK, 1987), p.154.

[29] Bonaventure, *Collations on the Six Days* 20.22, p. 312.

hierarchical Church should have nothing at all to do with power and control. Any group within the Church which claims hierarchical power can only rightly substantiate that claim when the statements which are issued in the name of that authority are permeated with attitudes of constancy, beauty and joy, and facilitate the growth of those same attitudes within the life of the community. To speak of the Church as hierarchical is a challenge to the Church as a community to live in such a way that God's world is able to be uplifted through the witness of lives which, like the life of Francis of Assisi, are constant, beautiful, and joyful.[30]

Hellmann notes Bonaventure's insistence that "all that exists comes forth from the ordered First and thereby reflects the divine order."[31] The divine order is the order of Trinitarian creative, ecstatic love in which the dynamic principle could be spoken of in terms of movement of Persons beyond self towards the other. Bonaventure incorporates the notion of *ecstatic knowledge* into the heart of his theology. Once again his inspiration was the experience of St Francis. This is seen, when in Chapter 7 of the *Itinerarium*, he refers to the Stigmata of St Francis, "This was shown also to blessed Francis when in ecstatic contemplation on the height of the mountain there appeared to him a six-winged Seraph fastened to a cross."[32]

It is interesting to see how Bonaventure speaks of this state of ecstasy when he writes about the Stigmata of Francis in Chapter 13 of his *Life of St Francis*. The Stigmata is not an isolated incident, but is presented within the framework of a continuous circular pattern of movement, the pattern of ascent/descent. He begins this Chapter, "Francis had made it his habit never to relax in his pursuit of the good. Rather, like the heavenly spirits on Jacob's ladder he either ascended to God or descended to his neighbour."[33] Francis ascends Mount La Verna and encounters God in the ecstatic contemplative experience of the Stigmata and then descends the mountain to continue his ministry among lepers. He is taken out of himself, seized by rapture, in contemplation and continues this movement beyond self in focussing his attention not on self, but on the other, in his embrace of the leper. In his Stigmata, there is ecstasy in contemplation, in his leper ministry, there is ecstasy in compassion. Both are ways in which Francis engages in what we can call an ecstatic way of knowing.

Bonaventure's understanding of ecstatic knowledge incorporated the Dionysian language of ecstasy, *ecstasis*, to mean 'standing outside oneself', standing outside our customary way of understanding in order to be able to

---

[30] Paul Rout *Francis and Bonaventure* (Liguori, Missouri: Triumph, 1997), p. 75.

[31] J.A. Wayne Hellmann *Divine and Created Order in Bonaventure's Theology*, trans. and ed. by Jay Hammond (St Bonaventure, NY: The Franciscan Institute, 2001), p. 4.

[32] Bonaventure "The Soul's Journey into God" 7.3, p. 112.

[33] Bonaventure "The Life of St Francis" 13.1 in *Bonaventure. The Soul's Journey into God, The Tree of Life, The Life of St Francis*, p. 303.

receive a new understanding that is shaped by the experience of the other. In the Epilogue to *De Scientia Christi,* he describes ecstatic knowledge as "...that ultimate and most exalted form of knowledge".[34]

What implications might this ecstatic way of knowing have for the question of the nature of authority within the Church? What is fundamental here is the pivotal place of 'relationship' within this epistemology. An ecstatic way of knowing always involves relationship between the knower and the other that is known. The nature of this relationship is not that of control or possession of the known by the knower. Rather, in an ecstatic way of knowing, the knower *stands outside oneself*, stands outside one's customary way of understanding in order to be able to receive a new understanding that is shaped by the experience of the other. All knowing is essentially relational and the knower comes to deeper understanding through an encounter with the reality of the other, an encounter which does not control the other but which enables the knower to be drawn by the other to deeper and newer ways of knowing and understanding.

Some of the difficulties that arise within the context of the actual practice of authority within the Church can be traced back to a situation where authority is seen in terms of enforcing a particular understanding or even world view that belongs to the one who has been given authority but not necessarily to those whom that person encounters. A key question becomes, How does the authority figure 'know' the other who is encountered? Here lies the value of an ecstatic way of knowing. In an ecstatic way of knowing, the other is not seen as one to be controlled, but as one with whom the authority figure enters into relationship, so as to allow the understanding of both to be deepened through mutual encounter. It allows both to move into new horizons of understanding and knowledge.

This in keeping with what Bernard Lonergan speaks of as an "about-face...a new sequence that can keep revealing ever greater depth and breadth and wealth. Such an about-face and new beginning is what is meant by conversion."[35] For Lonergan, conversion is central to theology. What enhances the possibility of conversion is 'encounter': "Encounter is meeting persons, appreciating the values they represent, criticising their defects, and allowing one's living to be challenged at its very roots by their words and by their deeds...encounter is the one way in which self-understanding and horizon can be put to the test."[36] Conversion was also central to the life experience of St Francis of Assisi and it is an experience in which all who profess to live the gospel of Christ are called to engage.

---

[34] Bonaventure, "Disputed Questions on the Knowledge of Christ", Epilogue, in *St Bonaventure's Disputed Questions on the Knowledge of Christ* trans. by Zachary Hayes, Works of St Bonaventure Vol. 3 (St Bonaventure, NY: Franciscan Institute, 1992), p. 195.

[35] Bernard Lonergan, *Method in Theology* (Toronto: University of Toronto Press, 1999), p. 236.

[36] Lonergan *Method*, pp. 237-8.

What facilitates such a process is for the knower to be engaged in an ecstatic way of knowing, rather than a comprehensive way of knowing. Problems can arise in the exercise of authority when too much attention is given to comprehensive knowledge, to intellectual speculation and propositions, and too little attention is given to ecstatic knowledge, to personal encounter with the other and a willingness to allow oneself to be changed through that encounter. An ecstatic way of knowing incorporates genuine dialogue. Perhaps this 'ecstatic way of knowing' is what Gregory Baum hinted at when he wrote: "An unintended consequence of the [Second Vatican] Council was its effect on the perception of the Magisterium by ordinary Churchgoing Catholics. They understood that in seeking fidelity to the Gospel in various historical situations, the Magisterium relies on dialogue with the experience and the thought of the faithful."[37]

Francis of Assisi's understanding of authority was shaped by his encounter with the poor and humble Christ and found expression in a ministry of humility and service. Within the brotherhood, the exercise of authority entailed a reciprocal relationship between the brothers and the Minister. All exercised different ministries but all stood alongside each other, called to mutual encounter in the light of a gospel way of life. Spiritual authority entailed familiarity and relationship, being subject to the other as Christ was subject to. Drawing on Francis for his inspiration, Bonaventure developed an ecclesiology which, in keeping with its Trinitarian foundation, called for a relational ordering of the community in which unity rejoices in diversity. Within the heart of such an ordering must lie an ecstatic way of knowing, entailing a surrender of the desire to control the other and a willingness to deepen understanding through dialogue and mutual encounter.

In the relatively short time since his election, Pope Francis appears to have embodied in his ministry many of the qualities associated here with his patron, St Francis of Assisi. Leonardo Boff observed: "One of the first things Pope Francis said was, 'how I would like a Church that is poor, for the poor'. This idea is in consonance with the spirit of St Francis, called the Poverello, the Little Poor Man of Assisi."[38] Pope Francis has issued a call to humility, "We have to be humble but with real humility from head to toe."[39] In his ministry, which he refers to as the ministry of the bishop of Rome, he has emphasised simplicity, wearing the simple pectoral cross of iron, rather than ornamental gold. Eschewing the Vatican Palace, he has opted to live with ordinary people and his daily celebration of Eucharist is attended by

---

[37] Gregory Baum, "My Vatican II" *The Tablet*, 19 January 2013, p.12.

[38] Leonardo Boff, "To be radically poor so as to be fully a brother", https://www.facebook.com/New Catholic Times/posts/5312247336107657 [accessed 9 August 2013].

[39] Pope Francis, "Homily at Morning Mass in the Chapel of Saint Martha's House. 14 June 2013" in http://www.catholicnewsagency.com/news/be-humble-from-head-to-toe-pope-francis-says/ [accessed 9 August 2013].

Vatican workers. In resonance with Francis' use of the term *conversari* ('familiarity with') he urges the ministers of the church to learn poverty by being "with the humble, the poor, the sick and all those who are on the existential peripheries of life. Theoretical poverty is of no use to us."[40]

In April 2013 Pope Francis selected a group of Cardinals from around the world to form a council to advise him in the governance of the Church. At the time of writing the Council has yet to meet, but this decision by Francis can be seen as a movement towards greater collegiality within the Church. In a recent address to the Bishops of Brazil, he stressed, "Central bureaucracy is not sufficient; there is also a need for increased collegiality and solidarity."[41] Certainly this appears to be a move towards a Church ordering that reflects Bonaventure's concept of relational ordering, modelled on the relational life of the Trinity. It is significant that on the night of his election, Francis never once referred to himself by the title of 'Pope', but used exclusively the title 'Bishop of Rome'. "This emphasizes Rome's particular role: Rome also is a local church within the community of churches. Nevertheless it presides over all the churches....He has this place within a network of churches which are in communion with each other and with him and he fosters that communion."[42] The emphasis in Pope Francis' exercise of authority appears to be placed on dialogue and reciprocal relationship. In an address to clergy, religious and seminarians at Rio de Janeiro's Cathedral of Saint Sebastian, he exhorted the congregation, "Be servants of communion and of the culture of encounter! Permit me to say that we must be almost obsessive in this matter. We do not want to be presumptuous, imposing 'our truths'"[43]

At the heart of the new Pope's addresses to the world is the call to practice mercy. Speaking to Brazil's cardinals and bishops on 27 July 2013, he addressed them with the words, "We need a Church capable of rediscovering the maternal womb of mercy. Without mercy we have little chance nowadays of becoming part of a world of 'wounded' persons in need of understanding, forgiveness and love."[44]

---

[40] Pope Francis, "Address to the International Union of Superiors General 8 May 2013" http://www.vatican.va/holy_father/francesco/speeches/2013/may/-documents/papa-francesco_20130508_visg_en.html [accessed 9 August 2013].

[41] Pope Francis, "Address of the Holy Father meeting with the Bishops of Brazil" in http://en.radiovaticana.va/news/2013/07/27/pope_francis_to_brazili-an_bishops/ [accessed 9 August 2013].

[42] Annemarie C. Mayer, "Pope Francis: a pastor according to the heart of Christ", in *International Journal for the Study of the Christian Churches* 13:2 (2013), 147-160, (p.152).

[43] Pope Francis, "Homily in the Cathedral of Saint Sebastian, Rio de Janeiro, 27 July 2013" in http://www.news.va/en/news/pope-to-clergy-religious-seminarians-respond-to-go [accessed 2 August 2013].

[44] Pope Francis, "Address to Brazil's cardinals and bishops, 27 July in Rio de Janeiro's St Sebastian Cathedral" in *The Tablet* 3 August 2013, p. 5.

When Francis of Assisi embraced the leper, it was this ecstatic experience of 'a heart full of mercy' that initiated the continuing process of conversion within his life. Pope Francis' call for the practice of mercy is also the call to grow into an ecstatic way of knowing. The poor and humble Francis of Assisi, in his kenotic and ecstatic way of encountering the other, ushered in a new age for the Church of his time. If the Church of our time is able to follow the path along which Pope Francis is leading, then once again might be heard the words from the Book of Revelation, "Behold, I am making all things new." (Rev. 21:5)

Heythrop College, London, Great Britain

CHAPTER IX

IMAGINING AUTHORITY IN A KENOTIC CHURCH: MAGISTERIUM IN THE CONTEMPORARY CHURCH

GEMMA SIMMONDS

"Your strength lies in your God and your conscience".[1]

In his earliest sermons Newman taught that the laity, whatever their status or level of education, are called to holiness and entrusted with baptismal responsibilities. This belief is echoed in chapter 5 of the Second Vatican Council's constitution on the church, *Lumen Gentium*. Newman referred repeatedly to the laity during the Nicene period as being well catechised and faithful to their baptismal promises. He became increasingly sure that the maintenance of the faith is the responsibility of the laity, though he never elaborated what he saw as their rightful role in the governance of the Church. Newman held that there were three offices or 'authorities' in the church to which the faithful owe obedience. The office of government is vested in the hierarchy which has charge of tradition, the authority of truth is largely in the care of the thinkers of the church and the authority of 'devotion' is invested in the whole people of God. Each of these is necessary, but can become corrupted when perceived or exercised without reference to the other two: "Each has to find room for the claims of the other two; and each will find its own line of action influenced and modified by the others."[2]

Newman taught that if reason became absolute it would result in arid rationalism. If devotion or experiential religion became absolute it would result in superstition and if government of the church became absolute it would result in ambition and tyranny. It is the perceived disjunction between the more recent exercise of the church's magisterium and the sense of responsible critical dissent which has arisen in our time among the faithful, among theologians and even occasionally among bishops that lies at the heart of this study.

The centripetal tendency within the church, largely espoused in ahistorical and anachronistic ways by neo-conservative elements within it, cites 'the Magisterium' as the ultimate source of authority without always having a clear idea of who or what constitutes it in its fullest sense. *Lumen Gentium* indicates, at least by implication, that the teaching role of bishops

---

[1] J.H. Newman, *Lectures on the Present Position of Catholics in England*, ed. by Andrew Nash (Gracewing, Herefordshire and University of Notre Dame Press, Notre Dame 2000), p. 388.

[2] http://www.newmanreader.org/Works/viamedia/volume1/preface3.html.

includes the principle of subsidiarity and of local particularity, and that the richness that comes from localized consultation should be brought to bear in both teaching and governance.[3] This suggests that context plays a strong role in the interpretation and understanding of doctrine. Yet the centralization of all authority in Rome, a relatively recent development in ecclesiology, would appear to negate the magisterial role of bishops informed by the circumstances of their local church and the experience of the local faithful.[4]

It is a point of considerable interest that the first non-European pope in centuries has been keen to point this out and to shift the balance of power from the centre to the periphery again, both in his decision to bypass the curia with an appointed international council of cardinals and in his constant reference to the authority of local bishops and to himself as bishop of Rome. Even more striking has been his insistence on the experience of the poor not only as objects of charity but as the agents of revelation as they teach the rest of the church, in a very particular way, an experience-based understanding of the Gospel, which the teachers of the faithful have often managed to avoid.[5] At local level, however, there may be little sense that the lay faithful have any role to play except that of obedient acquiescence in the faith and practice enjoined on them by 'the Magisterium', a role epitomised, somewhat cynically, under the slogan 'Pray, Pay and Obey'. Questions and practices arising from contexts found 'on the ground' have at times earned the condemnation of a given theologian, writer or pastoral practitioner when rejected by central authority. This censure has extended as far as bishops themselves.[6]

Like all theological terms 'magisterium' as both a name and a function has developed over time. In the patristic era and the Middle Ages a *magister* was a scholar or theological authority who functioned in a teaching role. Since being introduced in its current sense in the nineteenth century in an encyclical defending the church's teaching authority, it has been used to refer to that authority, to the person holding it and to what is taught. It did not, in its earliest sense, apply in an automatic sense to the pope or to

---

[3] See *Christus Dominus,* 36-38, *Lumen Gentium,* 13, 23.

[4] See Mary McAleese, Quo Vadis?: *Collegiality in the Code of Canon Law* (Dublin, Columba, 2012).

[5] J.M. Bergoglio, *Nell cuore dell'Uomo: Utopia e Impegno* (Milan, Bompiani, 2013), p. 23 and Pope Francis, *La Mia Porta è Sempre Aperta: una Conversazione con Antonio Spadaro* (Milan, Rizzoli, 2013), pp.86 ff and p.117, where he quotes former Jesuit General Superior Pedro Arrupe on this point.

[6] Cf. the removal from office of Bishop Bill Morris of Toowoomba in 2013 and the highly critical letter of protest written by Bishop Reinhold Stecher on his retirement from the see of Innsbruck in 1997 http://archive.thetablet.co.uk/page/20th-december-1997/48.

bishops.[7] One has only to think of the influence of Albert the Great, Aquinas and Bonaventure or Peter Lombard to realise the extent to which individual theologians and university faculties exercised influence in church teaching authority in the Middle Ages. This was also true of early Jesuit theologians who attended the Council of Trent, and the likes of St. Robert Bellarmine.[8] This collaboration between theologians and council fathers would be repeated at Vatican II and provides a positive example of the best kind of collaboration between theologians and magisterium.[9]

If we are to imagine authority in a kenotic church, we need to begin by exploring the way in which we perceive Jesus as exercising authority kenotically, since the authority claimed by the church originates in that of Christ himself. Jesus' exercise of authority was thoroughly sacramental – it effected what it signified. A kenotic theology of authority must in this sense be a sacramental theology of authority and vice versa, particularly within a church which is to be understood 'as a sacrament…[both] of intimate union with God and of the unity of all humanity.'[10] If the church is a sacrament of the unity of all humanity, then the experience that all sectors of humanity within the faith community bring to bear in their reflection on the life of faith, lived in concrete reality, must have a voice in the articulation of the church's decision-making processes and in the way it speaks in the name of God. 'The Magisterium' is frequently quoted as an autonomous entity within the church which bears little relationship to the mass of the faithful and their experience of life and ecclesial belonging. The dissonance this brings about is a matter of increasing concern and the reason for which many have ceased to practise their faith in any observant sense.[11] More recently still, in response to the remarkably rapid canonisation of Pope John Paul II, a new reinforcement of this approach has emerged with reference to 'the Magisterium of St. John Paul II', as if this were an even more ultimate, turbo-charged form of papal authority. When the teaching office within the church becomes separated from the life of believers and a sacramental notion of reality embedded in lived experience (as being an outward sign of inward grace), the authority which it carries is crucially diminished. This has strong theological and practical implications for the exercise of

---

[7] Yves Congar, "Pour une histoire sémantique de terme «magisterium»", *Revue des Sciences Philosophiques et Théologiques* 60 (1976), 85-98.

[8] Hubert Jedin, "Theologie und Lehramt" in R. Bäumer, ed., *Lehramt und Theologie im 16. Jahrhundert* (Münster 1976), 10-52.

[9] Francis Sullivan, *Magisterium: Teaching Authority in the Catholic Church* (Mahwah, 1983), p. 217.

[10] *Lumen Gentium*, 1.

[11] Reports so far suggest that this is emerging clearly from answers to the recent survey on the Church's teaching on family life. See http://www.thejournal.ie/acchbishop-diarmuid-martin-survey-church-papal-synod-1337112-Feb2014/.

magisterial authority. If we look briefly at the question of authority in the life of Jesus himself we see a different picture.

Where there is contention in the Gospels about his authority Jesus always answers his challengers, whether friend or foe, in a way that both establishes his rightful authority and bears his particular hallmark, 'My kingdom is not of this world', 'you must call no one on earth Rabbi', 'I am among you as one who serves'. His claims to authority are simultaneously claims that establish his identity as the Messiah sent by God. This identity, while hidden from those claiming religious authority and even from his disciples, is immediately apprehended by the demons over whom he exercises power (Mk. 1:24). His identity/authority is tested in the desert and questioned by John the Baptist (Mt.4:1-11, Mt.11:2-6) who finds it difficult to square the person and work of Jesus with the Messiah of his expectations. In the face of John's doubts Jesus responds cryptically, with a reference to the authority of his works rather than that of any claim to leadership. This claim to authority through authenticating praxis is repeated in his confrontation with the Pharisees in Jn. 10:37-38, and is a signpost for those who follow him. Those who love him are to keep his word (Jn. 14:23), and it is through this fidelity that they will be given the power through the Spirit to act authoritatively (Jn. 14:11-17). Jesus acknowledges the proper authority that is his due while refusing to wield it as power over against others. Fidelity to his words and works promises to be the origin and source of authority for his followers. This will be the model for authority posited in this study.

The exercise of authority within the Catholic church has often been perceived and experienced as less than Christ-like and less than sacramental – it signifies and articulates one thing, at least in theory, but effects quite another. The sacraments, from Baptism and Eucharist through all the others, are fundamentally kenotic. The outpouring of God's grace and the signs of God's presence are signified in humble signs of human agency. This is especially true with the priesthood, in its claims to represent, in ordinary human lives, Christ who was both priest and self-giving sacrifice. Thus a kenotic theology of authority which imitates Jesus must be a 'sacramental' theology in this sense, authority being exercised with appropriate confidence, but also with a deep sense of humility and service. The scriptures emphasize the obedience of Jesus to the Father in service of the truth. Jesus prays that his followers will be 'consecrated in the truth' (Jn. 17:7), so the church's pursuit and practice of the truth will properly be modelled on the obedience of Jesus. The root of the word obedience is Latin *ob* and *audire*, to listen attentively. This attentive listening is part of the relational dynamic of the Trinity ('Father...I know that you always hear me', Jn. 11:41-42) which the church must model within its own dynamics and structures if it is to be true to its founder. It models it when the listening is mutual between the teaching and the learning parts of the church, so that all become, in their different ways, teachers and learners of the faith.

There is a difference between teaching authority and governance but the two cannot be entirely separated. In a kenotic understanding of the magisterium the truth of revelation is not an abstract set of faith propositions imposed upon the lived practice and experience of the faithful. It is the result of a dynamic conversation between doctrine and life which takes seriously the experience of Christians. When doctrinal truth and the church discipline upon which it is based are predicated almost exclusively upon the life experience of a male, unmarried priesthood, they will inevitably be coloured by the limitations this entails. It will only serve to perpetuate a clericalist mindset based on a fundamental disconnect between experience and belief on the one hand and doctrine and procedures on the other.

One of four disjunctions between the Catholic Church and modern society, identified by Charles Taylor and others lies between 'those who bring a modern sense of personal responsibility to Church teaching in search of critical convergence [and] the Church as a jurisdictional authority to which is due obedience'. This includes understanding ethical and moral praxis as part of the human, fallible and historical endeavour for meaning as opposed to something abstract, unchanging and universal built on an essentialist interpretation of natural law morality. Part of this disjunction is also the separating out, in practice, of any notions of the *sensus fidelium* and reception by the faithful from the authority of the magisterium as binding and normative.[12]

Newman's understanding of the laity's role in the reception of doctrine means that those governing the church and exercising its teaching authority must do so in the light of continuous dialogue with those they govern and teach: 'If we wish to become exact and fully furnished in any branch of knowledge [...] we must consult the living man and listen to his living voice.'[13] This dialogue makes it possible to admit mistakes in governance and in the teaching coloured by particular styles of governance without fearing that the church and its doctrines will be engulfed in rampant relativism. The lived experience of the faithful is of course not in and of itself an infallible source of a new revelation, but must not be treated as an irrelevance in the development of doctrine. A kenotic understanding of magisterial authority places itself in dialogue with the belief and experiences of the whole church without leaving the faith community trapped in an exclusive opposition of two dictatorships, one of relativism and one of the magisterium. When we think of divine power and authority we are dealing with one which operates in a radically different way from human attempts at coercion or power 'over against.'

---

[12] Charles Taylor, José Casanova and George F. McLean eds., *Church and People: Disjunctions in a Secular Age*, http://www.crvp.org/book/-Series08/128710%20ChurchPeople.pdf.

[13] J.H. Newman, *The Present Position of Catholics in England* (Longmans, Green and Co., London, 1868-81), p. 325.

Sarah Coakley describes divine power as 'the subtle but enabling presence of a God who neither shouts nor forces, let alone 'obliterates'. She presents Christ as the incarnate God in whom non-bullying divine power is found together with self-effaced humanity in a 'unique intersection of vulnerable, "non-grasping" humanity and authentic divine power.' While this makes Christ voluntarily vulnerable this is not 'an invitation to be battered' but a complete openness to the transformative effect of God's Spirit who works within humanity beyond any familiar human power dynamics of coercive control.[14] St. Paul, in his great hymn to the kenotic Christ, urges us to 'put on the mind of Christ' (Phil.2:5). By doing so we yield to a divine power which, paradoxically, frees us to become more fully human. The Spirit of God brings 'new non-coercive power to a receptive person', by appropriating 'the available motivational power of God's Spirit' which 'empowers us to love as God loves'. We do this in imitation of Jesus as God's fully obedient Son in whom is perfectly manifested the 'power of divine self-giving love'.[15]

How, then, do we bring together putting on the mind of Christ in terms of personal conversion and truth-seeking and membership of a community within whose structures of authority lies a deposit of truth? The closing words of Matthew's Gospel and Mt. 16.18 assure us that Christ's church and its fidelity to his Gospel are divinely assured until the end of time. This is embedded in the Christian creed. In John's farewell discourses Jesus promises that the Spirit of truth will come upon the gathered community of believers as a Counsellor (Jn.14:16f). This assurance stands in contrast to evidence in Acts and the Epistles and Gospels of individuals and groups within the early church who fall away into false beliefs and practices. Any notion of the indefectibility of the church lying within the body of the faithful cannot be predicated on perfect behaviour and belief among its members, but must therefore accept that it is a mixture of saints and sinners. *Lumen Gentium* states that: 'The body of the faithful as a whole, anointed as they are in the Holy One, cannot err in matters of belief'.[16]

While this is reassuring it does not solve the problem of our struggle to articulate the truth, susceptible as it is to change and development, given our finitary predicament. The church is *semper reformanda*. The whole truth of the revelation of God in Christ is something that 'subsists' in the church but can never be grasped in its entirety.[17] Vatican II's *Dei Verbum* posits a view of the church constantly moving forward towards the complete

---

[14] Sarah Coakley, "Kenōsis and Subversion", in *Powers and Submissions: Spirituality, Philosophy and Gender* (Oxford: Blackwell, 2002), pp. 3-39.

[15] Paul K. Moser, *The Elusive God: Reorienting Religious Epistemology* (New York, Cambridge University Press, 2008), pp.146-147.

[16] *Lumen Gentium,* 12.

[17] *Lumen Gentium,* 8.

fulfilment of God's word within the community.[18] This move may not always be in a straight direction, however. Henri de Lubac's monumental study *Corpus Mysticum* shows how the shift in meaning of the same words and concepts down the centuries can change doctrine and practice for ill as well as good, and a certain work of recuperation may at times be necessary to remind the church of a nuance or a practice that has been lost in translation. This happened in the case of the *ressourcement* movement in the years prior to Vatican II, in which de Lubac was heavily involved. A return to the sources of the past allowed for the development in the twentieth century of a more dynamic view of reception as experienced in the church of the first millennium.[19]

Along with belief in the church's inerrancy runs a whole concept and tradition of ecclesial reception – the process by which some teaching, liturgical practice or law is assimilated into church life.[20] The patristic and medieval concept of reception has been described as 'a tributary of the dominant ecclesiology of that age: a communion ecclesiology'.[21] In the church of that period reception was a dynamic process between pastors, teachers and taught. A council would propose some article of faith, liturgical rite or disciplinary practice and this would in time make its way into the thought and practice of local churches and be assimilated by the faithful even though it did not originally emerge from among their specific community. The faithful participated in the life of the church in ways that included either assimilation or rejection of what was received. This assimilation of doctrines or practices became a transformative process through which the community grew in spiritual maturity and identity. Whether conscious or not, the submission of the community to such developments can be seen as a kenotic act of obedience to the Spirit of God speaking and acting upon it through the development of doctrine and practice. In an ecclesiology of communion modelled on this mutual, attentive listening the deposit of faith is understood as the living, revealed word of God sustained by the life of the church itself.

In this context reception is not a passive acquiescence but the active appropriation of the revealed word of God and the praxis it inspires which in turn becomes the foundation of ecclesial life. The *sensus fidelium*

---

[18] *Dei Verbum,* 8-12.

[19] See Laurence Paul Hemming and Susan Frank Parsons eds., *Henri de Lubac, Corpus Mysticum: the Eucharist and the Church in the Middle Age,* (London, SCM Press, 2006); and Richard Gaillardetz, *Teaching with Authority: a Theology of the Magisterium in the Church* (Collegeville, Liturgical Press, 1997), p. 229.

[20] The arguments and references that follow throughout this study owe a heavy debt to Gaillardetz, *Teaching with Authority,* pp. 228ff.

[21] Edward Kilmartin, "Reception in History: an Ecclesiological Phenomenon and its Significance" *Journal of Ecumenical Studies* (21), 1984, 34-54.

denoting the inerrancy of faith is based on the centrality of the witness of the whole community of believers. This places a primacy on the role of conscience and requires the teaching magisterium to be in constant dialogue with the lay faithful. This is echoed by Newman's conviction that, during the Arian controversy, orthodoxy was preserved not by the episcopate but by the faithful: 'In that time of immense confusion the divine dogma of our Lord's divinity was proclaimed, enforced, maintained, and (humanly speaking) preserved, far more by the *Ecclesia docta* than by the *Ecclesia docens*, [...] the body of the episcopate was unfaithful to its commission, while the body of the laity was faithful to its baptism....'[22]

While Newman's interpretation of the Arian controversy is strongly contested by today's patristic scholars, his understanding of the importance of reception points to a dynamic hermeneutical circle between teaching, taught and article of faith or religious practice. The beliefs and spiritual life of the faithful based on their lived experience work in harmony with the authoritative teaching of the ecclesiastical magisterium. Believers articulate their Christian faith through their life of discipleship, expressing their personal and corporate devotion through the liturgy. In turn the ecclesiastical magisterium discerns what is articulated in the faith of the baptized and authoritatively represents it in propositional form. The response to this is reception, whereby the faithful recognize (or not) the faith that is authoritatively proclaimed as their own, which in turn influences the articulation of faith and the inclusion of this articulation in the content of belief.[23] In this hermeneutical circle it is the effectiveness of the teaching which is tested by its reception as well as its juridical validity or truth.[24] Reception, as it were, makes the church, since attention to the experience of contemporary Christians whose lives are shaped by the signs of the times is the means by which the church discerns what the Spirit is saying to the churches today.[25]

When this earlier theological view of reception came to be replaced by a juridical notion of obedience extending to the entire teaching ministry of the church the emphasis shifted to a pyramidal view of the community of believers. Here the faith and practice of the mass of believers is entirely

---

[22] John Coulson, ed., *John Henry Newman, On Consulting the Faithful in Matters of Doctrine* (London, Collins, 1986), p. 41.

[23] Jeremy Miller, *John Henry Newman on the Idea of the Church* (Shepherdstown: Patmos, 1987), pp. 151-52.

[24] See H. Bacht, "Vom Lehramt der Kirche und in der Kirche" *Catholica* 25 (1971), pp. 144-67, esp. 157 ff.

[25] Ormond Rush, *The Eyes of Faith: the Sense of the Faithful and the Church's Reception of Revelation* (Washington, Catholic University of America Press, 2009), p. 295. See also Joseph Komonchak "The Epistemology of Reception" in Hervé Legrand, Julio Manzanares and Antonio García y García eds., *Reception and Communion among Churches* (Washington, Catholic University of America Press, 1997), pp. 180-203, 193.

ruled by its hierarchical summit, the Holy Spirit acting as the guarantor of the infallibility of its judgements.[26] This is one reason why the recent 'reforms' of the liturgy, with little or no reference to the mind of the faithful or the judgement of local bishops has been seen by many as such a violation of the principle of ecclesial reception.

Teaching authority is kenotic when the teachers show themselves also willing to be learners and the *sensus fidelium* of the pastors enters into conversation with the experience of ordinary believers and they are transformed by the encounter. A marked example of this is found in the case of Archbishop Oscar Romero of El Salvador, whose previously conservative approach to the task of leadership was transformed into a prophetic office by his encounter with the suffering poor. Something similar can be seen in the life of Pope Francis, and he has been at pains to urge openness to this transformation on bishops, pastors and the faithful. In a letter to Archbishop Vincent Nichols publishing his elevation to the consistory of cardinals, the pope writes: 'The cardinalate is not a promotion, an honour or an award; it is simply a service which calls for a broader vision and a more expansive heart. Although it may seem paradoxical, this ability to see farther and have a greater, universal love can only be achieved by following the same path which the Lord himself took: the path of abasement and humility, in the form of a servant (cf. Phil2:5-8). For this reason I would ask you please to receive this appointment with simplicity and humility of heart.'[27]

Lumen Gentium sees the prophetic office of Christ himself being fulfilled: 'not only through the hierarchy who teach in his name and by his power but also through the laity whom he constitutes his witnesses and equips with an understanding of the faith and a grace of speech precisely so that the power of the gospel may shine forth in the daily life of family and society'.[28]

This does not automatically validate all the beliefs, practices and devotions of the laity. Pope Benedict XVI was at pains to point out, in the Congregation for the Doctrine of the Faith's *Instruction on the Ecclesial Vocation of the Theologian* of 1990, that the weight of public opinion and the pressure brought to bear by the media do not of themselves guarantee theological coherence in service of the truth.[29] History has produced some

---

[26] See Yves Congar, "Reception as an Ecclesiological Reality" in Giuseppe Alberigo and Anton Weiler, eds., *Election and Consensus in the Church*, Concilium 77 (New York, Herder, 1972), 43-68.

[27] Letter of Pope Francis to Archbishop Vincent Nichols, 12 January 2014, published in the order of service for the Mass of Welcome in Westminster Cathedral, 28.2.2014.

[28] *Lumen Gentium*, 35.

[29] See CDF, *Instruction on the Ecclesial Vocation of the Theologian*: http://www.vatican.va/roman_curia/congregations/cfaith/documents/rc_con_cfa ith_doc_19900524_theologian-vocation_en.html.

remarkable aberrations in faith at local levels, including the veneration of a saint who turned out to have been a dog.[30] But attention to reception as a constant source of renewal in the church's articulation and practice of faith is no recent invention and goes back as far as the second century, when St. Irenaeus observed: 'Unceasingly, through the action of the Spirit of God, such a deposit of great price enclosed in an excellent vessel rejuvenates and causes a rejuvenation of the very vessel which contains it.'[31]

The need for inculturation of the Gospel message, whether in terms of ethnic or social culture, was recognized at Vatican II in *Gaudium et Spes*.[32] The Gospel has never been proclaimed in a 'pure' fashion that ignores the historical and cultural context into which it is being brought, as we see in St. Paul's attempt to evangelize the Athenians with reference to their own religious horizon.[33] Evangelization and the articulation of the content of faith at the level of the teaching magisterium can only be successful in dialogue with the modes of discourse and thought of the prevailing culture in which it occurs. Attempts to impose disciplines of liturgy, pastoral practice or theological articulation irrespective of the context and culture in which they are to be received cannot be a good foundation for faith. A kenotic exercise of the magisterium requires a genuine exchange between the concerns and preoccupations of the receiving community and the content of faith as mediated by the tradition of the church. If the concerns of the faithful do not match the tradition of the church, this is not automatic proof either of the weakness of their faith or of error within the tradition, but both must be reassessed in a spirit of openness and informed respect. This openness may generate conflict, as we see in instances such as the Chinese Rites controversy of the eighteenth century, when Jesuit missionaries fell foul of Rome for appearing to assimilate the Christian faith too closely to the culture and religious understanding of their Chinese hosts.[34]

Many commentators have remarked on the disconnect that exists between the current teaching magisterium and ordinary people in terms of sexual morality, whether this means issues of reproductive health, homosexuality or the laws pertaining to marriage. While there are undoubtedly many sensitive and painful issues around sexuality and authority there is, perhaps, a deeper underlying issue here about the relationship between sex and power. The continued insistence on the imposition of celibacy on priests in the Latin rite, despite the increasing population of married ex-Anglican or Lutheran clergy within the church, and the exclusion of women from all forms of ordained ministry are issues of a theological construct of sexuality and gender but they are also

---

[30] St. Guinfort.

[31] Irenaeus *Ad. Haer*, II, 241.

[32] *Gaudium et Spes,* 53 and Robert Schreiter, *Constructing Local Theologies* (Maryknoll, Orbis, 1985), pp. 6-21 esp.10.

[33] Acts 17:16-34.

[34] See http://www.fordham.edu/halsall/mod/1715chineserites.asp.

perceived by many as issues of power. As long as most of the decision-making processes in the church are reserved to the ordained they will be the privileged preserve of celibate men. That this has a serious impact on the orientation and contextual articulation of much that emanates from the sources of authority within the church is beyond doubt. The answer to this need not necessitate the indiscriminate admission of married men or women to the ranks of the ordained, but it does require an urgent rethinking of the access of the laity to decision-making positions within the faith community, the importance given to their experience of lived faith and the exercise of authority in a way that is experienced as non-coercive.

Today 'magisterium' as a term is hardly used at all except to denote the teaching office of the hierarchy or the hierarchy itself as both bearer and defender of the truth. Francis Sullivan points to the addition of the word 'authentic' to magisterium as denoting 'genuine' rather than the original Latin *authenticum* which more correctly denotes 'authoritative'.[35] The crowds who flocked to hear Jesus commented that he spoke 'as one having authority, and not as their scribes' (Mt.7:28-29). They recognized his authority not only because his words carried conviction but because his works paralleled his words. In that sense his authority was linked to his authenticity: what they saw was what they got. The current public fascination with Pope Francis lies not so much in his pronouncements, fine and stirring though these have been, but in his actions, loaded as they are with symbolic significance. When he washes the feet of women or of a Muslim, or kisses the face of a man with terrifying disfigurements, he is showing a deeply sacramental understanding of the human condition which makes his teaching more convincing to the ordinary faithful.

While in many parts of the church and outside its borders there is much public enthusiasm for the warm and kenotic style of Pope Francis, there are obvious inconsistencies involved in pinning hopes of church reform excessively on him alone. While some decisions, such as the reform of the curia, can probably only come from above, the treatment of the pope as superstar, whoever occupies the see of Peter, will not encourage the assumption of adult responsibility on the part of the faithful. It is encouraging to hear the pope himself speak of the need to reform the papacy, but a kenotic exercise of the magisterium involves more than the pope himself.[36]

The disconnect between authority and the life of the faithful is not only experienced at ground level. Avery Dulles, the great ecclesiologist of the twentieth century, has observed that between the nineteenth to the mid-twentieth century the magisterium of popes and bishops became 'more

---

[35] Francis Sullivan, *Magisterium: Teaching Authority in the Catholic Church* (Mahwah, 1983), p. 27.

[36] See Pope Francis, *Evangelii Gaudium*, 32.

authoritarian, absolutist, abstractionist and backward-looking'.[37] The result of this has been a growing tension between the notion of authoritative magisterial statement and the authority that is proper to theologians as part of their academic expertise. The promulgation of *Humanae Vitae* in 1968 provoked widespread dissent among bishops, theologians and the ordinary faithful. Over six hundred Catholic theologians in the United States of America dissented publicly against what they perceived as the wrongful identification of the Church's teaching function with hierarchy alone.[38] For many this raised a conflict between the exercise of the papal magisterium and the nature and authority of the ordinary universal magisterium. It also appeared to raise a conflict between theological reasoning and the ecclesial responsibility of theologians on the one hand and magisterial statement on the other. The term 'dissent' has become increasingly one of censure within the church, leaving little room for open and honest questioning as part of the proper exercise of theological investigation or pastoral practice.[39] The laity of the past would mostly have had neither the theological education nor the confidence to question the way in which the teaching authority of the church is exercised. A higher level of theologically-informed education and the confidence that stems from fifty years of post-conciliar insistence on the role of the laity has allowed for a greater critical awareness among them when pastoral roles and the teaching office within the church fall short. John Sullivan, professor of Christian Education at Liverpool Hope University, writes passionately about the way such questioning, on the part of young people, is often treated as a sign of weak faith and a lack of humility and deference on their part, or as an indicator of poor teaching in their Catholic schools, or as evidence of the failure of their parents to give strong examples of a lived faith. He argues instead for the need to respect the gap discerned by young people between ideals and reality, and 'to stand willingly, if vulnerably, in the heat of their interrogation'. This is what he understands by the kenotic exercise of the magisterium.

If the attentive listening that is central to authentic obedience is only a one-way street, and mutuality in its exercise is not modelled by those in ecclesial authority, it will be hard for those who feel that their voices go unheard to offer uncritical obedience in their turn. Sullivan refers to a letter in the *Tablet* in response to a statement from Cardinal Napier about the need for obedience in the church, in which the author replies: 'Unquestioning obedience to authority is neither a sign of faith in, nor respect for, that

---

[37] Avery Dulles, *The Survival of Dogma* (Crossroad, New York, 1971), p. 114.

[38] See Charles Curran, *Faithful Dissent*, (Sheed & Ward, London, 1986).

[39] See the open letter of Professor Tina Beattie on http://home.sandiego.edu/~baber/trouble/Documents/Publicstatementonmytheologicalpositions_TinaBeattie.docx.pdf.

authority. Failure to ask relevant questions is no sign of trust but a sign of a malfunctioning conscience'.[40]

When authority is neither transparent nor accountable it weakens its own claims. When there are painful dissonances between pastoral experience and magisterial teaching it becomes virtually impossible to present that teaching in a comprehensible fashion to the faithful. Daniel Speed Thompson's study of theologian Edward Schillebeeckx argues for a 'more decentralized, egalitarian, participatory, and experiential ecclesiology' and recommends the exercise of dissent within a healthy church.[41] This is not dissent for its own sake, or as an expression of grandiose self-justification on the part of disobedient theologians, laity or clergy, but a desire to offer the insights of more varied experience to those placed to comment on it in the name of the Gospel. This allows the Holy Spirit to be operative at every level, and the relation to be mutually enriching.

Vatican II's *Dei Verbum* presents the tradition handed down by the apostles as developing in the church by the help of the Holy Spirit through a growth in understanding of the realities and words handed down: 'This happens through the contemplation and study made by believers, who treasure these things in their hearts (see Luke, 2:19, 51) through a penetrating understanding of the spiritual realities which they experience, and through the preaching of those who have received through Episcopal succession the sure gift of truth.'[42]

The faith seeking understanding of which the constitution speaks is a dynamic movement towards the fullness of divine truth which cannot be had in this world. If the exercise of the magisterium is to be kenotic, it is also to be incarnational and eschatological. It must be based on the penetrating understanding of the spiritual but also the practical, human realities experienced by the faithful and seen as part of a pilgrimage towards ultimate truth in which the whole church is involved. An understanding of this truth is given to the church in trust, but is still awaiting fulfilment. When theologians and practitioners are investigated by the Congregation for the Doctrine of the Faith in opaque processes that are not open to challenge, the teaching office of the church is discredited, not defended. When the disconnect lies not only between the magisterium and the laity but between the magisterium, theologians and bishops themselves, the discrediting

---

[40] The preceding section is based on John W. Sullivan, "Critical Fidelity and Catholic School Leadership" in the forthcoming *International Handbook on Faith-Based Learning, Teaching and Leadership* to be published by Springer.

[41] Daniel Speed Thompson, *The Language of Dissent: Edward Schillebeeckx on the Crisis of Authority in the Catholic Church* (Notre Dame, University of Notre Dame Press, 2003).

[42] *Dei Verbum*, 8.

becomes dangerously toxic.[43] The church is not a people's democracy, and assimilation to the ways of the world has not always stood it in good stead. But there is health and virtue in some secular values such as the tolerance of difference and the call for transparency in governance. Tolerance cannot override the need to uphold and teach divine revelation authoritatively, but when teaching authority becomes punitive and coercive it defeats its own object.

Theologies of liberation largely emerged in the 1970s and onwards as a result of two emphases to be found in Vatican II's ecclesiology. One was on the need for inculturation, urging a sensitivity to local culture, concerns and forms of expression when it came to evangelization. The subsequent marriage between formal theology and Marxist-inspired social analysis in Latin America is well known, but liberation theology was also the result of attempts to give an authentically indigenous voice to faith communities outside Europe, which reflected not only their culture but also the social, political and economic contexts within which they lived. Theologians like Clódovis Boff and Gustavo Gutierrez saw the need for theology to put itself at the service of the poor, to empty itself of its magisterial status, while always serving the revealed truth of God, and to submit instead to the authoritative voice of the lived experience of the poor and suffering. Only in this way would it become the transformative and liberating force that it was meant to be, the articulation of a Gospel which would both comfort the afflicted and afflict the comfortable. As time went on this also became the case in feminist and all other contextual theologies which sought to find space for the authoritative voice of experience in the dialogue between doctrine and lived reality.

Tensions that have existed between inculturated and contextualized theologies of all sorts and the magisterium as proclaimed and imposed from Rome stem from the dissonance between these local voices and one which appears to see all forms of contextualization or inculturation of church teaching as a pernicious form of relativism. A more open and kenotic note has sounded of late in documents like Pope Francis' *Evangelii Gaudium*, which echoes some of the theologies of Latin America: 'An evangelizing community gets involved by word and deed in people's daily lives; it bridges distances, it is willing to abase itself if necessary, and it embraces human life, touching the suffering flesh of Christ in others. Evangelizers thus take on the "smell of the sheep" and the sheep are willing to hear their voice.'[44]

Another source of a more kenotic concept of authority in the current papacy may stem from the fact the Pope Francis is the first religious in over

---

[43] Anthony J. Figueiredo, *The Magisterium-Theology Relationship: Contemporary Theological Conceptions in the Light of Universal Church Teaching since 1835 and the Pronouncements of the Bishops of the United States* (Editrice Pontificia Università Gregoriana, Rome, 2011), pp. 14-16.

[44] Pope Francis, *Evangelii Gaudium*, 24.

a hundred years to become pope. In recent times the virtual disappearance of religious life as an authoritative voice in the church has deprived the faith community of regular access to a major traditional source of alternative patterns of authority. While hierarchies inevitably exist within all rules of religious life, they nevertheless contain embedded within them the principle of subsidiarity and a kenotic theology and spirituality of leadership through service. The Benedictine Rule insists on the entire community, including the youngest member, being consulted on major decisions while minor decisions are left to the abbot and his council. 'Whenever any important business has to be done in the monastery, let the Abbot call together the whole community and state the matter to be acted upon. [...] The reason we have said that all should be called for counsel is that the Lord often reveals to the younger what is best.' It would be interesting to see something like this methodology operative within the church, where it often feels as if the wisdom and experience of the lay faithful, especially women, the young and those considered marginal in some way is ignored by those in charge of making decisions. This sensitivity to the potential wisdom within different voices carries a challenge for all within the body: 'Let the brethren give their advice with all the deference required by humility, and not presume stubbornly to defend their opinions [...] Let no one in the monastery follow his own heart's fancy [...] At the same time, the Abbot himself should do all things in the fear of God and in observance of the Rule, knowing that beyond a doubt he will have to render an account of all his decisions to God, the most just Judge.'[45]

The Ignatian *Spiritual Exercises*, warning against 'disordered affections' especially with regard to power and status, encourage interior freedom. In the Constitutions of the Society of Jesus Ignatius builds in the understanding that different contexts may require different choices, actions, or articulations of a given idea that he himself, or the superior giving an order, may not have foreseen. This level of discernment requires a considerable level of inner freedom and maturity, but it is more likely to develop outside infantilizing structures of disordered authority. The Augustinian Rule also points to a kenotic understanding of authority: 'In your eyes [superiors] shall hold the first place among you by the dignity of their office, but in God's sight let them lie beneath your feet in fear [...] It is by willing obedience, therefore, that you show mercy not only toward yourselves, but also toward superiors, whose higher rank among you exposes them all the more to greater peril.'[46]

---

[45] Selections above from *Saint Benedict's Rule for Monasteries*, translated from the Latin by Leonard J. Doyle OblSB, of Saint John's Abbey (© Copyright 1948, 2001, by the Order of Saint Benedict, Collegeville, MN 56321).

[46] See http://www.midwestaugustinians.org/prayerrule.html).

A reclaiming of these alternative patterns of authority and obedience would serve as an effective counterbalance to more imperial forms of governance within the church.

French philosopher Maurice Blondel was named as a source from the floor of the Vatican Council more than sixty times. He stressed the role of a living tradition within theology rather than of timeless, immutable dogmas, making a clear link between consensual faith, authority and lived experience: 'Nothing can impose itself on a man; nothing can demand the consent of his intellect or the consent of his will which does not in some way find its source in man himself'.[47]

Much of the work of *ressourcement* theologians like Henri de Lubac and Yves Congar and of later liberation theologians bears the imprint of Blondel's 'principle of immanence', which stresses the importance of an understanding of how the divine will is manifested within the conscience of the individual or a group of individuals acting in mutuality. God does not manifest the divine will exclusively from outside the human self by means of an extrinsic authority, since this would involve the contradiction of God creating human beings free while redeeming them in a way that negates their freedom. Divine revelation perfects human freedom rather than negating it. We are led to understand and receive it through our inner conscience, which directs the values that serve as our guide and sanction. Blondel sees action determining thought rather than thought action, and implies an attitude of openness and trust in the life experience of the believer. This echoes much of what we find in the Ignatian *Spiritual Exercises*, so it is not surprising to find similar thinking in the work of Jesuit theologians de Lubac and Rahner as well as such post-Conciliar phenomena as the Worker Priest movement and liberation theologies.

The primacy of the baptismal vocation as found in *Lumen Gentium* and the outline of the role of the laity found in *Gaudium et Spes* are in part the fruit of Blondel and Newman's ideas on conscience and action and have developed since into widespread understandings of the sources of authority among the faithful that have been at variance with prevailing notions of authority at the church's hierarchical centre.

It is the whole people of God who are the primary receivers of the revelation with which the church is entrusted by the Holy Spirit as the content of its evangelical mission. The nature and mission of the entire church are contained in the threefold office of Christ as prophet, priest and king in which all the baptised take part.[48] As Cardinal Ratzinger, Pope Benedict XVI was at pains to point out that theology is not the private idea of the theologian. It is a communal exercise, undertaken for the good of the

---

[47] Maurice Blondel, *The Letter on Apologetics, and History and Dogma* (London, Harvill Press, 1964), pp. 60-61.

[48] See Ormond Rush, *The Eyes of Faith: the Sense of the Faithful and the Church's Reception of Revelation* (Washington, Catholic University of America Press, 2009).

whole community. Neither the theologian nor any individual Christian can assume that because they hold a particular belief with passion, it is necessarily correct, since 'conscience is not an independent and infallible faculty'.[49] Nevertheless at a press conference introducing the Congregation for the Doctrine of the Faith's *Instruction on the Ecclesial Vocation of the Theologian* he also stated that 'truth is located in the communitarian subject of the People of God, the Church.' Rather than being a binary relationship between God and the theological expert, theology is a triangular relationship between God, theologian and people of God as bearers of the *sensus fidelium*.

Joseph Komonchak offered a penetrating critique of the *Instruction* shortly after its publication.[50] In it he points out that the interpretations of the role of the magisterium and of the theologian are unhelpfully narrow and that there is an almost uniformly negative view of the laity's capacity to discern matters of faith. More importantly, he highlights the fact that no space is given for the kind of kenotic, open discussion whereby matters of faith and practice might be discerned in mutual dialogue. Without this dialogue there is little hope of voices being heard which may contribute to a breaking of the many *impasses* in which the teaching magisterium now finds itself. To challenge this is a sign neither of weak faith, poor theology or loose morals. It is a call for the entire body of the faithful to listen to the voice of the Holy Spirit speaking through the signs of the times.

Heythrop College, London, Great Britain

---

[49] See CDF, *Instruction on the Ecclesial Vocation of the Theologian:* http://www.vatican.va/roman_curia/congregations/cfaith/documents/rc_con_cfaith_doc_19900524_theologian-vocation_en.html, 38.

[50] Joseph Komonchak, "The Magisterium and Theologians", in *Chicago Studies* 29 (Nov. 1990), 307-29.

CHAPTER X

THE "UGLY BROAD DITCH": AUTHORITY IN A KENOTIC CHURCH

MICHAEL KIRWAN, SJ

INTRODUCTION

This volume addresses the crisis of legitimacy arising out of a disjunction between the Church as an authoritative teacher of doctrine, and the acceptance of doctrinal pronouncements (that is, their 'reception') by the lay faithful; and whether it is possible to heal the disjunction by envisioning a 'kenotic' Church. The sociologist of religion, José Casanova, describes the crisis as follows: 'the perception of an increasing and, in my view, dangerous disjunction between societal morality and church morality on issues of gender and sexual mores', a disjunction which creates difficulties on both sides.[1] From a faith perspective, he reminds us, the Catholic Church is a sacramental, eschatological sign of the Kingdom of God; sociologically, however, it is a socio-historical institution in the *saeculum*, a 'religious regime' that belongs to the City of Man, analogous in many respects to polities and economies.

I intend to affirm the theological slant of Casanova's sociological analysis, by attending to the themes implicitly or explicitly treated in his address: firstly, the practice of theological discernment which *Gaudium et Spes* referred to as 'reading the signs of the times'; secondly, the status of the Church as an 'eschatological' sign of the Kingdom of God; thirdly, the appeal to an Augustinian 'Two Cities' deployment of history and politics, which, among other things, offers a distinctive understanding of the 'division of labour' between theology and the social sciences.

I will undertake this theological consolidation with the help of two other contemporary thinkers: Giorgio Agamben, an Italian philosopher (whose own books he describes as 'confrontations with theology'), and the British Catholic theologian James Alison, as well as a number of other commentators. Giorgio Agamben has worked extensively with the proposition, familiar from the writings of Carl Schmitt, Walter Benjamin and others, that 'all significant political concepts are secularized theological concepts'. James Alison is one of the leading theological exponents of the Mimetic Theory of René Girard, which asserts a collusion between

---

[1] Jose Casanova, "The Church in the World: The Theological Responsibility of a Lay Sociologist; on the Contemporary Disjunction between Societal Morality" (Lecture on the occasion of the reception of the Theological Prize of the Salzburger Hochschulwochen, Salzburg, August 8, 2012).

articulations of the 'sacred' and structures of social exclusion or victimization – what Girard has termed the 'scapegoat mechanism'.

As we shall see, both Agamben and Alison identify 'eschatology' as a hermeneutical key. In different ways, each diagnoses in the current crisis a false consciousness: for Agamben, the Church's forgetfulness of its eschatological mission – an amnesia which makes apparent an unacknowledged tension between rival forms of theo-political existence. For Alison (following Girard) the crisis lies in *méconnaisance,* the misrecognition which is crucial to the smooth operation of the scapegoat mechanism, and whose defining symptom is a paralyzing culture of dishonesty and double-think, among those who 'know not what they do'.[2]

The divergence of the two perspectives, which Casanova alludes to as the difference between the City of God and the City of Man, makes apparent an 'ugly broad ditch' between social and ecclesial morality.[3] Above all, the implications of social equality – now firmly established in secular political and moral frameworks – have continually wrong-footed the Church, which has been slow to read the 'signs of the times': historically, in the abolitionist movement, and in the articulation of individual human rights, including the right of religious freedom. The 'ditch', between an evolving secular morality and a resistant Church morality, means that the dynamic of *aggiornamento* – such an important guiding principle of the Second Vatican Council – is forever a matter of 'catching up'. Casanova identifies three areas of doctrinal disjunction, arising out of this bifurcation of faith and society. The first two (the issue of women's ordination, the official pronouncements of the Church hierarchy on issues of gender and sexual morality) highlight his analogy between the urgency in our day of the 'gender question' and the 'social question' of the nineteenth century. The third example of disjunction is the scandal and shock occasioned by the clerical child sex abuse (CSA) crisis.

---

[2] René Girard is a "hedgehog theorist" who for fifty years has focused, somewhat obsessively, on the dynamics of group victimization, understood as a process of sacral legitimation. As he has argued in his classic work *Violence and the Sacred* (French original, 1972), the social configuration of a majority group against an individual or a minority of individuals, is all too recognizable, as the everyday phenomenon we call "scapegoating". Girard identifies this as the most fundamental and archaic of social interactions. In pre-state societies, where there is no other protection against the ravages of unchecked violence, the "scapegoat mechanism" has an apotropaic function: it "wards off" the threat of a catastrophically unlimited and all-destructive violence by a limited strike against a vulnerable victim. Hence, for Girard, the origins of "sacrifice"; hence the shocking aphorism which sums up his thesis, that "violence is the heart and secret soul of the sacred".

[3] Gotthold Lessing's "ugly broad ditch" (*der garstige breite Graben*) denotes the unbridgeable gap between history and eternal truths.

Following Casanova, therefore, we are justified in examining the third of these as an example of doctrinal and societal disjunction. Attempts have been made to quarantine the crisis, to proceed as if the structure and validity of Catholic teaching and discipline are unaltered by the failings of individual perpetrators (not to mention their superiors who responded inadequately and inappropriately). Such denial is, for the most part, unconvincing. There is widespread and vocal demand for a recognition of systemic and structural, and not just individual culpability; and for an acknowledgement of the possibility (at least) of a connection between the CSA meltdown and the more general disjunction of doctrinal authority and its lay reception.[4]

GIORGIO AGAMBEN: 'THE CHURCH AND THE KINGDOM'

Casanova argues that 'the church can maintain a critical, indeed prophetic, relationship to secular cultural only if it can differentiate its eschatological principles from their irremediable historical embeddedness in particular traditional historical cultures.' The eschatological tension between the City of God and the City of Man is historically unsustainable if it is predicated upon the unreflexive defence of a traditionalist, naturalist position, unheeding of moral historical development. It is interesting to hear Casanova's intuitions echoed by the Italian philosopher, Giorgio Agamben, who is best known for his diagnosis of the problematic aspects of contemporary political legitimacy, above all in his analysis of 'states of exception'. Much of Agamben's work is an excursus into classical philology and legal theory, and yet he himself has maintained that '[M]y books...are confrontations with theology. I think that it is only through metaphysical religious and theological paradigms that one can truly approach the contemporary and political situation.'[5]

In March 2009, Agamben was invited by the Bishop of Paris to deliver an address to the French hierarchy in the cathedral of Notre-Dame. This talk, published subsequently as *The Church and the Kingdom*, draws

---

[4] The UN report in February 2014, which severely condemned the Vatican for its inadequate treatment of perpetrators of abuse, and for historic cases such as the tragedy of the Magdalene sisters in Ireland, understood itself in possession of a remit to go further, and question the Catholic Church's teaching on abortion, contraception and homosexuality, insofar as these impact on the rights of minors. Much as a testy response from the Vatican may challenge the legitimacy of this criticism, there can be no doubt about the undermining of the Church's credibility in the wake of the crisis. http://uk.reuters.com/article/2014-/02/05/uk-vatican-abuse-un-idUKBREA140LM20140205 accessed 7th February 2014.

[5] Agamben: to name just two books which illustrate this "genealogy" of political concepts, *Homo Sacer* (1995) and *The State of Exception* (2005).

on his understanding of messianic time and political economy, in order to deliver a challenging critique of the institutional Church and what he regards as its lost sense of purpose. The Church's disorientation, he suggests, is best conveyed by reflecting on the Greek term *paroikousa*, or 'sojourning'. This is the manner in which foreigners and those in exile dwell; Christians are called to live as sojourners in the world. This displacement also implies a distinctive experience of time, specifically of time as *messianic*. We are not talking about the duration of time, but time which contracts and begins to end: the 'time that remains'. This is 'a time that pulses and moves within chronological time', transforming it from within.

To experience this time implies 'an integral transformation of ourselves and of our ways of living.'[6] At stake here is a proper relation between the ultimate and the penultimate: a rejection, therefore, of any radicalism which would separate them and require us to live solely with the ultimate. An ultimate experience entails experiencing penultimate things differently, not destroying or negating them, but rendering them inoperative (Paul's term: *katargein*) in a gesture of deactivation or suspension. Only in this time, and only in experiencing this time, does the Church exist:

> Where do we find an experience of time in today's Church? That is the question that I have come, here and now, to pose to the Church of Christ sojourning in Paris. An evocation of final things, of ultimate things, has so completely disappeared from the statements of the Church that it has been said, not without irony, that the Roman Church has closed its eschatological window.

Agamben here calls into question the Church's capacity to 'read the signs of the times' (Mt 16.3); specifically her ability to discern the presence of the messiah in the course of history, the 'signature of the economy of salvation.' This history is a field traversed by two opposing forces: the first is Law or State (the *katēchon* – the maintenance and deferral of the end along a linear and homogenous line: cf. 2 Thessalonians). This force is dedicated to economy, the indefinite governance of the world. The second vector is 'messiah or Church', the economy of salvation. Only a dialectical tension between these poles can enable a community to form and persevere over time.

---

[6] Agamben, p. 13: citing Paul in 1 Corinthians 7. Agamben draws on Walter Benjamin for the concept of the "messianic vocation": Benjamin asserts that the present "now time" is charged with "splinters of the messianic". For both Benjamin and Agamben, "the sole possibility we have to truly grasp the present is to conceive of it as the end...the paradigm for the understanding of the present is messianic time."

And yet it is precisely this tension which seems today to have disappeared. With the weakening and elimination of a sense of the 'economy of salvation' in historical time, the economy extends its blind and derisive dominion to every aspect of social life. Eschatological urgency, no longer present in the Church, reappears in the form of secularized parody, in the states of permanent exception and emergency, and an unprecedented 'hypertrophy of law.'

> [N]owhere on earth today is a legitimate power to be found; even the powerful are convinced of their own illegitimacy. The complete juridification and commodification of human relations – the confusions between what we might believe, hope and love and that which we are obliged to do or not to do, say or not say – are signs not only of crises of law and state but also, and above all, of crises of the Church. The reason for this is that the Church can be a living institution only on the condition that it maintains an immediate relation to its end.

If the Church loses this relation, 'it cannot but lose itself in time':

> Will the Church finally grasp the historical occasion and recover its messianic vocation? If it does not, the risk is clear enough: it will be swept away by the disaster menacing every government and every institution on earth.

THE NEED FOR A NEW ECCLESIAL DISCOURSE

With Agamben's warning in mind – that the Church is in real danger of forgetting its messianic calling, and conducting itself instead like any other institution – we turn to the CSA scandal, which has certainly placed the Church, as institution, under intolerable scrutiny. As Casanova describes it, the scandal has tended to take a threefold form, with shock and dismay being experienced on three counts: first of all, the clerical sexual abuse of children itself; secondly, the widespread and persistent cover-up by bishops and by curial officials; thirdly, the totally inappropriate character of so many public statements and rationales offered by ecclesial authorities. Casanova notes the irony that the scandal has been most ferociously expressed in countries where sexual activity has been most liberalised – the sexual abuse of minors being the last taboo, as it were. Indeed such sense of shock and moral outrage is, according to Durkheim, the typical societal response to the sacrilegious profanation of any taboo.

In any case, secular society and public opinion appeared once again to be ahead of the Church on an important moral issue. One overriding external factor has contributed to the sudden and rapid decline of CSA in recent decades: a change in secular societal morality which led to the criminalization of the sexual abuse of women and children. Casanova proclaims that feminists should be acknowledged as the main carriers of this secular moral revolution; the elevation of the sacred dignity of children, and their protection from adult sexual abuse, are primarily the moral consequence of this same feminist movement. This is a sobering thought for those in the Church who see the resistance of feminist ideology as one of the primary fields of combat in the Church's culture-wars. As noted above, much of the shock and outrage has been generated, not by the cases of abuse themselves, but by institutional complicity in terms of episcopal dereliction of responsibility, and by the complete lack of a properly ecclesial language or discourse which is in any way adequate to the scale of the crisis. These defects have exposed deep fault-lines in the Church's credibility. In response to damning conclusions from reports which too often read like the findings of Truth and Reconciliation Commissions, official ecclesial statements have at times been astonishingly naïve and over-spiritualised. The Church has been 'possessed by Satan', or needs to be 'swept clean' of the filth that has infested it. In his Christmas address to the Curia on 20th December 2010, Pope Benedict spoke of abusive priests who 'twist the sacrament into its antithesis', and while he acknowledged with real sorrow the dreadful suffering that has been visited upon the victims, the main part of his reflection is more ethereal, citing a vision of Saint Hildegard of Bingen from 1170. The mystic perceives the Church as a woman, beautiful and dazzling:

> But her face was stained with dust, her robe was ripped down the right side, her cloak had lost its sheen of beauty and her shoes had been blackened. And she herself, in a voice loud with sorrow, was calling to the heights of heaven, saying, 'Hear, heaven, how my face is sullied; mourn, earth, that my robe is torn; tremble, abyss, because my shoes are blackened....And Christ's wounds remain open because of the sins of priests. They tear my robe, since they are violators of the Law, the Gospel and their own priesthood; they darken my cloak by neglecting, in every way, the precepts which they are meant to uphold; my shoes too are blackened, since priests do not keep to the straight paths of justice, which are hard and rugged, or set good examples to those beneath them. Nevertheless, in some of them I find the splendour of truth.

Benedict urges the Church to accept this humiliation 'as an exhortation to truth and a call to renewal'. He calls for ways of repairing the injustice, asking 'what was wrong in our proclamation, in our whole way of living the Christian life, to allow such a thing to happen?' Finally, he thanks those who stand alongside and work with victims, as well as the many good priests who 'amid the devastations, bear witness to the unforfeited beauty of the priesthood'.

Pope Benedict goes on to offer a diagnosis which focuses not on ecclesial dysfunction, but upon those external contributing factors in contemporary society, such as the apparent social acceptance of child pornography, sexual tourism, the 'octopus tentacles' of drug abuse and the dominance of mammon. Once again, a cosmic image is invoked, this time the city of Babylon and its commodification of bodies and souls.[7] Such problems are rooted in 'a fatal misunderstanding of freedom' which actually undermines and destroys human freedom. The ideological foundation of this misunderstanding is to be found in the 1970s, when a moral relativism, arising out of consequentialist and situationist systems of ethics which even infiltrated Catholic theology, created a climate where paedophilia was judged to be a way of human flourishing. He urges a return to the 1983 encyclical of Pope John Paul, *Veritatis Splendor*, in which these false ethical pathways were condemned.

In support of Pope Benedict's analysis, there does indeed appear to be evidence of external societal factors in the 1960s and 1970s, insofar as the two reports presented to the U.S. Bishops linked the worst phase of the abuse crisis to the countercultural experiments and the general anomic attitudes and behaviour of liberal Western societies during these decades. At the same time, as Casanova points out, this evidence can too easily reinforce the dangerously misleading impression that the abuse was due to social and external factors: "rotten apples" within the Church were contaminated by secular moral degeneration.

In any case, what requires attention here is not the range of possibilities for apportioning blame, but the disjunction between official ecclesial articulations to the crisis, and what the situation actually calls for. There is no reason to doubt Pope Benedict when he says that 'we are well aware of the particular gravity of this sin' and of 'our corresponding responsibility'. Nevertheless, it is hard not to be conscious of the limitations of a kind of official discourse which has too often lacked a direct, second-person address of the victim, and has usually fallen short of formal apology. The exclusive emphasis on sin, rather than criminality, must surely have been a further provocation for some victims, especially in those instances where non-cooperation with civil authorities has been catastrophic. The emotive intensity and metaphorical euphemism of the Hildegard vision, and the unsettling Manichaean appeal to the Book of Revelation, suggest an incapacity to speak a reasoned language of communal responsibility, beyond formulaic expressions of repentance or rarified spiritual lamentation. To put this in Casanova's terms, the tension between a

---

[7] "No one will buy their cinnamon, spices, incense, myrrh, frankincense, wine, olive oil, fine flour, wheat, cattle, sheep, horses, chariots, slaves, and other humans." (Revelation 18:13).

theological description and a realistically sociological description is in danger of being lost, and the ugly ditch becoming broader.

Above all, one may point, here and elsewhere, to the aching absence of an ecclesiology which recognizes the structural and systemic aspects of abuse, as well as the personal failures of individuals. In a previous address on Hildegard, once again (8th September 2010), Pope Benedict commended her harsh reprimand of the German Cathars; in demanding radical reform of clergy abuse they were 'seeking to subvert the very nature of the Church' since true renewal lies in 'a sincere spirit of repentance and a demanding process of conversion, rather than with a change of structures.'

This preference for personal rather than structural explanation explains something of the Church's inability to draw straightforwardly on her own discourses of structural sin; two of which have been marginalized, though for different reasons: firstly, the Church's own tradition of Catholic Social Thought (CST) and secondly, the Theology of Liberation (ToL). CST is regarded as a treasured resource by which political systems are judged according to their adherence to principles of solidarity and subsidiarity, and to their promotion of the common good. Notoriously, however, these principles are non-reflexive: Richard McBrien notes that 'there are only two places in the entire corpus of Catholic social teaching where the teaching on social justice and human rights are explicitly applied to the church itself'.[8]

The second discourse, theology of liberation, remains marginalised by the official Church because of its alleged reductionism and inappropriate reliance on Marxist analysis. The official critique in 1984 of 'certain aspects of liberation theology'[9] takes ToL to task for its overemphasis on structural sin, rather than affirming that all sin is rooted in the human person. A rejection of such concepts as 'structural sin' has left the church bereft of a coherent way of articulating the communal dimensions of the present crisis, other than Manichaean formulae of 'possession', or needing to be 'swept clean' or (more mystically, as with Hildegard) needing to be re-clothed.[10]

---

[8] McBrien, 2009: 154. The two references are from *Iusticia in Mundo* (Justice in the World, ch. 3), from the 1971 Synod of Bishops, and the U.S. Bishops pastoral letter, *Economic Justice for All*, no.347, 1986. There are further instances, in Pius XI on subsidiarity, and in the 1983 *Revised Code of Canon Law*.

[9] *Instruction on "Certain Aspects of Liberation Theology"*, issued by the Congregation for the Doctrine of the Faith, in 1984, under the signature of Cardinal Joseph Ratzinger.

[10] To be fair, it is not surprising that recent studies find it hard to be dispassionate. *The Dark Night of the Catholic Church: Examining the Child Sexual Abuse Scandal* (Brendan Geary and Joanne Marie Greer, eds., *The Dark Night of the Catholic Church: Gender, Power and Organisational Culture* (Oxford: Oxford University Press, 2011) cites in its title a classical of the Carmelite mystical tradition, thereby (albeit unintentionally) "spiritualising" the

In short, the consequence of marginalizing these two discourses has been a severe impoverishment of the church's ability to think and speak about its own systemic and structural disfigurement.

Here it is worth considering the curious case of Fr. Cantalamessa and his Good Friday homily of 2nd April, 2010. The intervention is worth recalling at length because Fr. Cantalamessa seeks to apply a Girardian framework, even if the attempt goes unfortunately awry. Fr. Cantalamessa is a Franciscan priest and was the official preacher to Pope Benedict. On Good Friday he preached on the Letter to the Hebrews, specifically on the great High Priest who has passed through the heavens, and on the nature of Christ's sacrifice and priesthood of Christ. He then cited 'a famous French thinker' who announced in 1972 that 'violence is the heart and secret spirit of the sacred', and proceeded to give a thorough exposition of Girard's theory, spelling out its implications for the Christian doctrine of the atonement, and for our current defence of victims.

In applying this Girardian reflection, however, Fr. Cantalamessa makes two further moves – the second of which provoked public outcry. Firstly, in speaking powerfully about our culture's simultaneous condemnation and exaltation of violence, Cantalamessa goes on to focus, not on violence against children, since 'of that there is sufficient talk outside of here', but against women, especially in domestic situations, often with a sexual background. He affirms both the systemic nature of such violence in society, and its unacceptability. What caused the media storm were his subsequent comments, addressing and greeting our Jewish brothers on the occasion of Easter and Passover coinciding. Jews 'know from experience what it means to be victims of collective violence and also because of this they are quick to recognize the recurring symptoms'. He then cites a Jewish friend who had written privately to him, condemning:

> ...the violent and concentric attacks against the Church, the Pope and all the faithful by the whole world. The use of stereotypes, the passing from personal responsibility and guilt to a collective guilt remind me of the more shameful aspects of anti-Semitism.

Cantalamessa was widely criticised for entertaining the possibility that virulent attacks on the Church could in any way be equated with the excesses of anti-Semitism – despite the fact that his correspondent who drew the comparison was Jewish. To draw such an analogy on Good Friday was seen as especially insensitive. The case is worth dwelling upon, because it illustrates both the awkwardness of many recent ecclesial

---

crisis. At least one journalist has described the situation in Ireland as "the Irish holocaust", a tendency which Marie Keenan finds understandable but unhelpful. (Marie Keenan, *Child Sexual Abuse and the Catholic Church: Gender, Power and Organisational Culture* (Oxford: Oxford University Press, 2012), xii.).

pronouncements, and also many of the dynamics of Girard's mimetic theory, to the point of being a kind of 'case study'. Fr. Cantalamessa uses Girardian theory to castigate our culture and its hypocritical fascination with violence. Referring to successive frenzied media images as a 'palimpsest', he names the mechanisms of displacement and evasion familiar to practitioners of mimetic theory. Violence disguises itself. It 'changes the subject' so as to divert attention from the victim. However, the wheels come off when Fr. Cantalamessa falls into the same trap: firstly, by rather pointedly choosing to discuss the 'safe' topic of violence against women, rather than the child abuse crisis; secondly, and more dramatically, by urging victimhood status for the Church, when he proposes the parallel with the scapegoating of the Jewish people.

What is especially problematic is the assertion that the passage from personal responsibility to collective guilt is illegitimate. Such an extension of culpability is compared, implicitly, to the 'blood libel' according to which the Jewish people were held collectively responsible for the death of Christ. To repeat: the Church's refusal or inability to describe the CSA crisis as a collective, systematic failure of responsibility, rather than the fruit of individual sinfulness, is for many people the most shocking and dispiriting aspect of its handling of the crisis.

The Cantalamessa incident demonstrates the value of mimetic theory in providing insights into the 'ruses' of victimisation, but also the difficulty of applying a Girardian hermeneutic consistently. Once the privileged status of the victim has been acknowledged – *vox victima, vox Dei* – it is hard to resist the magnetic pull towards this magical victim status. The specific temptation for the Church is to 'sacralise' the public criticism directed towards it – either by dismissing it as an example of *odium Christi*, or even (as Fr. Cantalamessa does here) to align the Church's unpopularity with the terrible mystery of Jewish suffering.

'CHANGING THE SUBJECT'

Despite the pitfalls illustrated in Fr. Cantalamessa's homily, the Mimetic Theory of René Girard holds promise of being the kind of discourse which has been lacking up to now. Its attentiveness to the processes and mechanisms of victimization is clearly of value. Girard's 'interdividual' psychology seeks to overcome unproductive polarities of individual and group, person and structure. Above all, because it offers a theologically-inflected wisdom about human beings, an 'intelligence of the victim', Girardian theory proposes a more fruitful alignment of theology and the human sciences than has been possible up to now; a set of conceptual tools which will help to bridge the 'ugly broad ditch'.

James Alison is one of the foremost theologians working out of a Girardian commitment. Before examining his contribution, two authors, Marie Keenan, and Robert Orsi will be considered, both for their insights (from psychological and socio-cultural analysis) into the CSA crisis, and to show how such insights point towards an integration in terms of Girardian mimetic theory.

Marie Keenan's book, *Child Sexual Abuse and the Catholic Church* (2012) is described by the publishers as an 'inside look' at the CSA crisis. It includes interviews with abusive priests as well as survivors, and seeks to propose a new way of thinking about clerical sexual offenders. Keenan locates the problem of child sexual abuse not exclusively in individual pathology, but also in the coalescence of a 'prefect storm' of systemic factors: the institution of priesthood itself, the process of formation for priesthood and religious life, the governance structures of the Church, and Catholic perspectives on sexuality, clerical culture, and power relations. Noteworthy in Keenan's study is her intention to unite 'insider' and 'outsider' perspectives on global and local levels, so that 'that the individual, the organization, and the institutional dimensions are actually influencing each other and bound together in particular dynamic relations' (xviii), in a way that breaks down the classic macro/micro distinction. Also important is her attempt to move beyond 'totalizing' categories of "perpetrator" and "victim"; even when this might incur the appalled opposition of those who assume that to seek to understand is the same as to forgive.

Robert Orsi, a scholar of American history and Catholic Studies, is the author of a disturbing and provocative article entitled 'A Crisis about the Theology of Children'[11]. Orsi wants to ask about the theological stories we tell about children: about their 'innocence' or their 'depravity', and the kinds of relationships that ensue between children and adults (celibate or otherwise) in church contexts. The power and authority which is asserted over children in these contexts renders them strangely 'double', simultaneously *present* and *absent* to the moral imaginations of both perpetrators and church officials, both at diocesan level and in the Vatican.

Is this linked, asks Orsi, to the ambivalence that Christianity has always had about children? For Augustine and medieval authors, the alleged depravity of children alternates with the ideal of the child as holy innocent. Within Catholicism, recent centuries have seen the privileged access of children to the holy: in the 'spiritual childhood' of saints such as Theresa of the Little Flower and the saints of Lourdes and Fatima. The innocence and purity of children are, for Pius X, speaking in 1912, 'a mirror of the divine'. But this innocence, like every mirror, is empty. This is a discourse which 'denies children any existence at all', leaving the child immensely vulnerable because of the ease with which adult desire can be projected into this empty space. Such idealism alternates with the fantasy of the dark teenager, and (in religious terms) the fear that accompanies catechesis, if we do not hand on or transmit the faith to the young (meaning: if we fail to replicate religious meanings of the adult world in theirs). Genuine

---

[11] Robert A. Orsi, "A Crisis about the Theology of Children," *Harvard Divinity Bulletin* 30, no. 4 (2002): 27-30.

protection against the 'hollowing dynamics' of innocence means granting children autonomy, to ensure that children are not extensions of their parents' religious worlds.

Marie Keenan's extensive study of the 'perfect storm' of the CSA catastrophe; Robert Orsi's unsettling thesis about the 'endlessly spinning modern Christian dialectic of children's absence/presence'; and even the awkwardly expressed argument of Fr. Cantalamessa, all point in the same direction as Girard's theory. Each alerts us to the systematic mechanisms of deflection and displacement which cause us to look in the wrong place, and to construct inadequate diagnoses. Girard's analysis is fundamentally Johannine: no knowledge or science is possible which does not take into account the human tendency to 'prefer the darkness'. Our capacity for systematic self-deception is so pervasive that the author of the Fourth Gospel has to describe it in cosmic terms: Satan, the 'father of Lies' is also the 'Prince of this world', and his fatherhood has distorted even the historical memory of Israel's religious leaders.

JAMES ALISON: A JOYFUL 'ANTHROPOPHANY'

The range of analyses in the last section concur in the judgment that simply to identify someone to blame is an inadequate response to the CSA crisis. This is especially so, where scapegoating leaves untouched more disturbing and wide-ranging questions. Such euphemism and displacement leaves us enthralled in what Girardians would characterise as the 'sacrificial sacred'. In James Alison's terminology (to be explained below), this would be to work out of an 'an-ecclesial hypostasis' rather than an 'ecclesial' one.

James Alison is one of the foremost Girardian theologians seeking to work in the light of 'the intelligence of the victim'.[12] In his work on original sin, *The Joy of Being Wrong*[13], he draws attention to the distinction (from Maximus the Confessor, via the Orthodox theologian John Zizoulas) of two modes of existence, the hypostasis of 'biological existence' and the hypostasis of 'ecclesial existence'. Alison himself recasts the distinction as 'ecclesial' and 'an-ecclesial' hypostases. The first of these is the only possible perspective – an eschatological, theological one – from which our entanglement in structures of mimetic desires can be discovered. This latter is the anthropological reality which the Church has traditionally described as original sin, and which Alison has explicated in terms of Girard's

---

[12] He speaks as a gay man, called to the vocation of Catholic theologian as well as to priestly ministry. No single one of his books is dedicated to the Church as such, nor does he offer a fully worked-out ecclesiology; this he declares an "open-ended task for the future". Nevertheless, it is possible to discern such an ecclesiology in the creative threads running through his writings.

[13] James Alison, *The Joy of Being Wrong: Original Sin through Easter Eyes* (New York: Crossroad, 1998).

theory.[14] Ecclesial existence is understood as a continuous process of undistorting, of learning to receive an identity rather than assert oneself over against others. The contrast between the two modes of existence is reaffirmed in key New Testament sayings and images: the rock of Jesus' words, rather than sand (Mt. 7: 24-7); Jesus as the true vine (Jn. 15: 17); and the Lucan perception that in Jesus God gathers rather than scatters (Lk. 11:23), with the Pentecost event described in Acts 2 as an undoing of Babel.

The 'ecclesial hypostasis' refers to the process by which the human being is set free from the reality of original sin: Alison follows Robert Hamerton-Kelly[15] in seeing such a process at the heart of Paul's conversion, with the insistence on justification by grace through faith as precisely an opening oneself up to God's gratuitous self-gift. Alison is keen to stress that this process is not simply a passage from particularity into 'universality', such that contingent, particular existence is now left behind; rather, the journey is carried out in a particular context, and with a specific understanding of how the undistorting of desire and the pacific imitation of Christ are to be enacted, through the sacramental life of baptism and Eucharist.

As indicated, this ecclesial hypostasis is 'eschatological', a term which Alison contrasts with 'apocalyptic' in the following way. He ascribes to Jesus an 'eschatological imagination': a new understanding of identity founded on God's gratuitous gift, which is slowly and painfully worked out in the life of the early Church. The Acts of the Apostles and the epistles of Paul make clear the conflict and scandal involved in breaking down structures of particularity, above all around the question of Jewish and Christian identity (218-9). One aspect of this scandal is the expectation of an immediate return of Christ, especially within vulnerable, threatened groups; insofar as their expectation was fixed upon patterns of retributive violence, their worldview is 'apocalyptic'. As the eschatological imagination comes to replace the apocalyptic, new continuities and new possibilities for human life open up, not least in relation to time:

> This of course means that as the eschatological imagination emerged, a certain sort of participation in time and history came to be seen as redundant or futile: the original sin from which we have been set free can be seen, on our way out of it, as being so deeply anterior to us that it involves us in living memory, time and history in a radically distorted way. (219)

---

[14] Ibid.

[15] Robert Hamerton-Kelly, "A Girardian Interpretation of Paul: Rivalry, Mimesis and Victimage in the Corinthian Correspondence," *Semeia*, no. 33 (1985): 65-81; Robert Hamerton-Kelly, *Sacred Violence: The Hermeneutic of the Cross in the Theology of Paul* (Minneapolis, MN: Fortress Press, 1992).

Alison agrees with Giorgio Agamben, therefore, that the readjustment of earliest Christian expectations in the face of the delayed return of Christ is not to be understood as an embarrassed recalibration, but as more to do with a transformed experience of time, with what Agamben calls 'messianic time' implying 'an integral transformation of ourselves and of our ways of living.' Alison continues the task of proposing a 'non-rivalrous ecclesiology' in the second edition of his work on eschatology, *Raising Abel*.[16] For the Church to be the community where this eschatological reality is lived out, a difficult 'ecclesial secondary naïveté' is required, in order to negotiate the huge 'shift from within' of the relationships between authority, teaching, belonging and witness.

> How are we to live as ecclesial signs of the incidence of God's axis-shifting act of communication in the midst of the human race? And how are we to do so in communion with, not in rivalry with, and not mimetically burdened by, the ecclesiastical carapace that weighs heavily on us all, office-holders included? (207)

Such an ecclesiology rests on the anthropological discovery, which can be referred to as an 'anthropophany'. Alison does not offer a *logos* about human beings, so much as bear witness to a process of discovery, exemplified in his and Girard's respective biographies as conversion, an awareness of 'the joy of being wrong'.

Insofar as the process can be spoken of objectively it is a dismantling of the Durkheimian social other (an order established on sacralised violence), so that the authentic sacred may be manifest.

This seems to converge with Agamben's idea of the two vectors or forces: Law or force (*katēchon*), and messiah or Church. A tension between these poles must be maintained if a community is to survive, and the Church is taken to task for not 'living in the end time', for not bearing witness to the messianic pole. Alison argues that it is the 'katechonic' force which has been 'rendered inoperative'; in this he follows Girard, especially in Girard's latest 'apocalyptic' phase, in which he argues that there has been an 'escalation of extremes'; we are faced with an array of potentially destructive forces, and deprived of the institutions (such as, for example, limited, codified warfare) which used to give us some kind of protection. A social order which has survived by legitimating and sacralizing violence can no longer do so; this includes the crisis of political legitimacy to which Giorgio Agamben refers. Only by means of an authentic turning to the gospel can we hope to survive. Alison refers us once again to an apparent

---

[16] James Alison, *Raising Abel: The Recovery of the Eschatological Imagination* (London: SPCK, 2010).

choice to be made, between an apocalyptical and eschatological imagination:[17]

> The apocalyptic imagination is the increasingly fear-laden and violent dualistic way of thinking in which God and the violence of our world are confused together. By the eschatological imagination, I meant Jesus' imagination fixed on God, which is entirely without violence, and which he taught and teaches us.

A 'PAULINE BOLDNESS'

This chapter has explored from a range of perspectives and disciplines – sociology, political theory and cultural anthropology – the disjunction of social morality and theological doctrine.

José Casanova has provided a point of departure in his insistence that only a theologically-sensitive social science can be entrusted with this task; due respect must be paid, as it were, to each of the Two Cities.

Giorgio Agamben, whose philosophy is a continuous 'confrontation' with theology, argues in similar vein. As noted above, his work is guided by the intuition that secular political concepts have their origins in theological ones; he locates the disjunction within classical theology itself, as a tension between two strands of political theology, stressing 'glory' and the 'economy'. His address to the French bishops characterizes the disjunction between Church as institution and the Kingdom of God in terms of two different experiences of time which need to be held in tension: *messianic* and *katechonic*.

James Alison's nascent ecclesiology proceeds on the basis of his commitment to a Girardian theological anthropology, whose scientific credentials he accepts. The 'two Cities' motif is recast here as a distinction between two modes of existence, the 'ecclesial' and the 'an-ecclesial', and between the two conceptions of the 'end' to which they correspond: the eschatological and the apocalyptic respectively. If these categories do indeed map onto Agamben's *messianic* and *katechonic*, then the two authors differ, insofar as Alison (like Girard) understands the world to have exhausted its *katechonic* possibilities; i.e. it is no longer capable of holding back or restraining 'what is to come'.

Robert Orsi asks whether a certain theological culture, profoundly ambivalent towards children, has contributed to the crisis; even Marie Keenan's extensive socio-psychological study of the Child Sex Abuse crisis contains a theological postscript in which she asserts 'the need for a more

---

[17] *Raising Abel*, p. 203. "Apparent", because the "kachechonic" option is no longer genuinely available to us. It should be noted that Girard also speaks of "apocalypse", most clearly in his final book *Battling to the End*, but does not attribute to it the negative valency which Alison does.

critical theology' (citing Karl Rahner and Johann Baptist Metz) to address the tension between divine message and human institution. Keenan calls for a fresh engagement with the ecclesiology of Vatican II and its aborted promise of a reform of church governance; and yet, given the ambiguities and mixed ecclesiology of the conciliar documents, she wonders whether perhaps nothing short of a Third Vatican Council will suffice.

At this point, it may be worth proposing a final theological postscript. This is Karl Rahner's paradigm of the 'three epochs' of the Church, which he offers as a fundamental theological framework for understanding the Second Vatican Council.[18]

Rahner's typology is audacious, arguing for an analogy between the traumatic surrender of identity, implied in the emergence of the church from a Jewish matrix in order to be a church for the nations, and the transition from a *de facto* European church to a truly global one. These two ruptures denote crises of 'otherness', in which the Church has had to confront competing self-identity claims, in order to become what she truly is. In addressing, simultaneously, the Jewish people and the 'world of today' (in the documents *Nostra Aetate* and *Gaudium et Spes* respectively), the Council fathers were urging the Church to recognize its own face in these mirrors. Against exclusivist interpretations of the dogma *extra ecclesia nulla salus*, two *loci* of God's saving action, external to the confines of the visible Church, now had to be explicitly acknowledged.

James Alison describes the Christian mode of existence as the slow-burning corrosion of rivalistic, 'an-ecclesial' existence by the ecclesial. Is it possible to identify precisely this process as the dynamic element of Rahner's fundamental theological scheme: the subversion of the 'apocalyptic' imagination by the 'eschatological'? The Council conducted itself above all as a pastoral council, seeking to dialogue rather than condemn (no *anathemas* were issued by the Council fathers). With regard to the transformed understanding of the destiny of the Jewish people, which we read in *Nostra Aetate*; one has to insist that this immense theological *rapprochement* would not have been possible without the horrific persecution of the Jewish people in the Holocaust (*Shoah*) twenty years

---

[18] Briefly, Rahner proposes that there have been three great "theological" epochs of Church history: firstly, the short period of Jewish Christianity, up to approx. AD 50. The second epoch, when the existence of a "world church" for all the nations is theoretical, though historically the Church becomes, culturally, a predominantly Hellenist and European phenomenon, which is then exported, from the sixteenth-century onwards, to the rest of the globe. In the third epoch, it is the entire world which is the sphere of the Church's activity. However, only with Vatican II and its gathering of indigenous bishops from all continents (1962-65), do we discern the emergent traces of a genuinely global church. Karl Rahner, "Towards a Fundamental Theological Interpretation of Vatican II" (1979).

earlier. Fascinating also, is the way this recognition of a religious legitimacy is extended, as it were, to other faiths: 'The Catholic Church rejects nothing that is true and holy in these religions' (*NA* 2).

What this reading requires us to do is to view the *Shoah* as certainly one of the 'signs of the times' which had to be read by the Second Vatican Council. This 'sign', for all its unspeakable mysterious horror and shame, bore extraordinary theological fruit: for the first time, the Church appreciates and acknowledges God's mysterious continuing Covenant with his chosen people. *Nostra Aetate* sees a definitive renunciation of Christian supersessionism and of blood libel against the Jewish people: attitudes which had sustained, over millennia, the 'an-ecclesial' identity of the Church over against its Israelite sibling.

As indicated above, it is profoundly unhelpful to compare the clerical abuse of children, for all its horror, to the Jewish *Shoah* at the hands of the Nazis. It is possible, even so, to ask whether the analogy holds, insofar as this is another 'sign of the times' which might lead to a similar conversion and rejuvenation. The disjunctions which concern this volume depict a Catholic Christianity having to encounter, to an unprecedented degree, its own internal otherness. In her 'ecclesial' becoming, the Church learns to discern once again, with astonishment and joy, her own face in those who had become alien: in God's mysterious dispensation with the Jews, in the 'world of today', in those in irregular sexual relationships – agonizingly, even our own children.

It is striking that so many of the authors discussed in this chapter appeal to St. Paul as the symbol of this anguish and of this transformation. Rahner's close analogy of the ruptures between the epochs (from Jewish, then to Hellenistic, finally to global Church) leads him to call for a 'Pauline boldness'. Alison reads Paul's conversion and mission in terms of Jesus' 'eschatological imagination'. And Agamben has taken Paul as the theologian *par excellence* of the 'State of Exception' – our guide to what happens when the law is seen to have failed.

Paul holds fast to the Crucified One, as the key to all understanding: *vox victima, vox Dei*. The real challenge of the 'ugly broad ditch' is revealed, as more than a requirement for interdisciplinary conversation between theology and the human sciences, or bringing together discordant ecclesial voices. 'There is a great gulf fixed between us; no one can cross it from our side to reach you, and none may pass from your side to us' (Lk. 16: 26); the gap between persecutor and victim, which only in God's own messianic time, can find healing.

Heythrop College, London, Great Britain

CHAPTER XI

RESPONSIBLE, CRITICAL ASSENT

KAREN KILBY

Authority can at times be rather amorphous and hard to pin down. Someone who takes on the leadership of a group – a committee, a town council, an academic department – can acquire a distinct aura of authority even if the exact nature of their powers is never articulated. A parent has a certain authority in relation to his children, though there are probably few families where its exact degree and contours are spelled out. One might become aware of the authority, in fact, only when one finds oneself incensed at its breach – whether by a provocative teenager or an insubordinate colleague.

For the past 150 years and more, the hierarchy of the Roman Catholic Church has sought to disambiguate the nature and extent of its own authority – it has sought to become maximally, or at least highly, explicit about the weight of authority carried by papal and other 'magisterial' teaching. And as a corollary, quite a precise system has arisen about the appropriate *response* to this authority, including in particular when it comes to what is to be believed – the degree and nature of the 'assent' that is to be made to what church teaching proposes.

For those, including most Catholics, not educated into this system, to begin to explore it is to move into what can seem quite a strange world. One comes across distinctions between the 'extraordinary' magisterium and the 'universal and ordinary magisterium' (both equally infallible); between 'irreformable' and 'authentic' teachings of the magisterium (the latter are lower down in the scale); between that which is infallibly taught and that which is infallibly taught as belonging to revelation (though both must be believed, two different kinds of response are required). One can find, since 1989 at least, a three-fold distinction between that which is 'believed with firm faith', that which is 'firmly accepted and held' and that which one 'adheres to with religious submission of will and intellect' (this last, though it may sound to the uninitiated the most fearsome, is in fact the weakest level of assent). One finds, more generally, a language suggestive of quite precise calibrations of authority of different documents and even of different components within documents, to which must then correspond an equally finely calibrated response in terms of firmness of assent on the part of the faithful – or at least on the part of faithful theologians.

What, then, should we make of this strange world?

I

There has been substantial scholarly discussion in the last few decades around what one might call this 'magisterial teaching on the magisterium'. Some of the scholarship has been concerned to set this relatively recent set of ideas in a broader historical context, and some to probe it theologically. A brief glance at both sides of this work may help us understand the sense of strangeness and dislocation that the uninitiated – even, or in particular, uninitiated Catholics – can feel when encountering these expectations on their 'assent'.

Both historians and theologians have noted, as one dimension of this oddness, a certain incongruity between the very limited power that the Church in our period actually has on the one hand and the mode in which the hierarchy often claim authority on the other.[1] What to make of a situation in which an institution with little coercive power 'insists peremptorily on outright obedience'? One might want to insist that it reflects the unique, transcendent quality of the Roman Catholic Church amongst all human institutions, but the situation can also, and perhaps more plausibly, be understood as the result of concrete and quite contingent historical developments.

Francis Oakley makes this case effectively in his 'Obedience and the church's teaching authority: the burden of the past'. Among other things, he points to the development, not from the very beginnings but at a particular moment in the Middle Ages, of a divide between laity and clergy which is 'clear and hierarchically ordered' in which the 'superiority and monopoly of sacrality' on the part of the clergy was established: to a gradual emergence of an understanding of church office in legal and governmental terms – 'in an essentially political vocabulary drawn from Roman law and connecting with the type of relationship prevailing in the world at large between rulers and those ruled'; to the rise of the papacy to a non-traditional 'position of overwhelming preponderance in the Church'; and to the development of an imperial understanding of the papacy, reaching its peak in the 12th and 13th centuries, so that the pope was installed in a coronation ceremony, was alone allowed to use the imperial regalia, was described as the 'true emperor' and *pontifex maximus*. In short, the popes 'came not only to rule a highly politicized church via a centralized bureaucracy in accordance with a law modelled on...that of the Roman Empire, but they did so also with a marked degree of imperial grandeur'. The papacy is 'the last of the truly great sacral monarchies,' and it is, at least in part, he suggests, the hangover from this, the ongoing reverberations of this imperial self-understanding,

---

[1] This is a point made very effectively by Oakley in the paper reprinted in this volume, for instance, and by Karl Rahner in "The Teaching Office of the Church in the Present Day Crisis in Authority," *Theological Investigations* 12 (London: Darton, Longman and Todd, 1974).

which we hear in the demand and expectation of obedience and assent to church teachings.

More recent history also surely plays a part. A full narrative of the origins of our present situation would include, among other things, attention to struggles between different parties at the Second Vatican Council and to the re-emergence in the 1980s and 1990s of a sensibility which had been to some extent sidelined during the Council.[2] It seems to be out of the renewed assertion of a kind of neo-scholasticism that the three-fold distinction mentioned above (believing with a firm faith, firmly accepting and holding, religious submission of will and intellect) emerged in 1989.

Whatever the historical origins of the current magisterial teaching on the magisterium, in any case, the reflections of systematic theologians can help direct us towards the possibility of a certain oddness in the underlying *logic* of the position. This has to do with the status of the authority of the teaching office relative to the status of that which is taught.

Suppose we imagine a more or less ideal Catholic believer, as envisioned by mainstream Catholic theology. Among the things we can expect her to believe is of course something about the authority of pope and bishops, but we would not expect this to be the very root and source of her faith: 'according to fundamental theology and the interpretation of the faith of the Catholic Church', writes Karl Rahner, 'the formal authority of the teaching office is not the first and most fundamental *datum* in the content of the faith,' but is 'based upon certain more radical truths of faith'.[3] Belief in God, Christ, grace and resurrection are a more primary and central part of Christian faith than belief in the authority of the teaching office. It is more the case that belief in the authority of the magisterium follows from these fundamental beliefs than vice versa. The situation becomes somewhat odd, then, if it is supposed that a high level of assent – an assent to something that must therefore be very central to faith – is to be given to particular teachings on the basis of the formal authority of the teaching office. There is something odd, that is to say, on supposing that one can base the more

---

[2] Christof Theobald, in any case, makes an argument along these lines. He suggests that the *Professio Fidei* – which was published in 1989 and subsequently incorporated into canon law, and which develops some of the distinctions mentioned above between classes of truths and the corresponding levels of response required – in fact reproduces "the broad outline" of a 1962 preparatory document for the Second Vatican Council, a document that was quite deliberately *rejected* by the Council. Cf. Christof Theobald, "The "Definitive" discourse of the magisterium: why be afraid of a creative reception?" in Mannion, Gerard et al., eds., *Readings in Church Authority: Gifts and Challenges for contemporary Catholicism* (Aldershot: Ashgate, 2003).

[3] "The Teaching Office of the Church in the Present-Day Crisis of Authority" in *Theological Investigations*, vol 12 (London: Darton, Longman and Todd, 1974), p. 24.

central aspects of the faith on the more peripheral, items which are higher in the 'hierarchy of truths' than those which are lower.

II

Determining the appropriate kind of 'assent' to make to church teaching authority seems at first sight to be a very specifically Catholic problem, not something about which we could hope to get much help from Protestant colleagues. But in fact I think the body of work which has come to be known as 'Reformed Epistemology' can cast a degree of light on the situation in which Catholics currently find themselves.

A central focus of Reformed Epistemology, and in particular of thinkers such as Alvin Plantinga and Nicholas Wolterstorff[4], has been the rationality of religious belief. They are concerned to repudiate the widespread assumption that for belief in God to be intellectually justifiable, it needs to be based on adequate evidence – the common supposition, in other words, that to be rational a believer would have to rest their belief on proofs of the existence of God, or, if indisputable proof is unavailable, at least on evidence establishing that God's existence is more probable than not. It is important to be clear that Plantinga and Wolterstorff's aim is to offer not an apologia for the *irrationality* of faith – although people often mistake it for that at first sight – but a reconsideration of what it means for faith to be rational.

Of course it seems commonsensical to suppose that if belief in God is to be rational, it would need to be based on some sort of argument or evidence. Plantinga and especially Wolterstorff put a name to this common sense (the 'evidentialist challenge to belief', or just 'evidentialism'), trace its source to a distinct moment in the history of modernity, and open up the possibility of thinking differently about the requirements of rationality.

Both philosophers place the starting point of evidentialism in John Locke, who insisted that 'the not entertaining any proposition with greater assurance than the proofs it is built upon will warrant'[5] is the one mark of being a genuine lover of truth. Locke's concern about balancing one's degree of assurance with the quantity of evidence arises out of his antipathy to the 'enthusiasts' of his day who were claiming divine revelations. Wolterstorff is keen to make the point that something genuinely *new* is introduced in Locke: while medieval thinkers like Anselm and Aquinas may have explored proofs for the existence of God, they did it for a very

---

[4] The third key figure usually associated with Reformed Epistemology is William Alston, but I will here confine myself to the position set out by Plantinga and Wolterstorff in the key early volume they jointly edited. (Alvin Plantinga and Nicholas Wolterstorff, eds, *Faith and Rationality*, Notre Dame: University of Notre Dame Press, 1984).

[5] Plantinga quotes Locke without citing the original text, in his essay in *Faith and Rationality*. "Reason and Belief in God" (p. 24).

different reason than Enlightenment figures – they were seeking to lift their minds to the contemplation of God, not to respond to an apologetic need by the provision evidence for belief. But the position that Locke first set out, others took up and repeated: Plantinga cites Hume ('A wise man...proportions his belief to the evidence'), Clifford ('it is wrong always, everywhere and for anyone to believe anything upon insufficient evidence') and Russell ('Give to any hypothesis which is worth your while to consider...just that degree of credence which the evidence warrants'), among others.

Both Plantinga and Wolterstorff reject evidentialism. Plantinga makes a case that evidentialism is itself rooted in classical foundationalism, and argues that classical foundationalism is not only wrong but incoherent. Wolterstorff takes a more constructive route: he offers an alternative vision of what it means to be rational, a vision which draws on the 18th century common sense philosophy of Thomas Reid and which attends to how we do in fact tend to come by our beliefs (which is, one realizes as soon as one comes to think about it, *not* by a process of systematically weighing up evidence). A shorthand description of Wolterstorff's position is that he takes our beliefs to be 'innocent until proven guilty': there are a range of different mechanisms by which we, quite properly, come to the beliefs we hold, and as long as we have arrived at a belief by such a non-culpable mechanism, and have not come across good reason to *cease* holding the belief, then we can be considered rational in our believing.

So what use is all this? What can Protestant-inspired philosophical reflection on rationality have to do with a knotty area of Catholic theology in which obedience to the requirements of rationality is not the issue – indeed, a hostile observer might imagine that in this area the issue here is precisely to *override* any claims to rationality in favour of obedience to the demands of authority. At first glance there seems little connection. And yet the obedience that we owe to the demands of rationality according to the evidentialist, and the obedience we owe to the teaching of the magisterium according to the official Catholic position, seem to bear an eerie resemblance to one another. In each case it is a question of the regulation of our assent. In each case it seems to be supposed that we can somehow fine-tune this assent at will. And in each case the fine-tuning is to be done by weighing up the evidence – in one instance evidence in general, in the other, evidence of the exact status and weight of authority of a given statement or document. Francis Sullivan, for instance, lists four different considerations in determining just how much authority is exercised in an 'authoritative but non-definitive teaching' of the magisterium – one has to take into account who is exercising the magisterium, what sort of document they are using, what kind of intervention they intend to make, and what sort of language they use – and then concludes, in a phrase heavily suggestive of Locke et al, that 'the response which a Catholic gives to such teaching should be proportionate to the degree of authority that is exercised'[6].

Both the historical contextualizing of 'evidentialism' and the critique that Reformed Epistemology develop, then, may be of some use in thinking about our current system of magisterial teaching on the magisterium. To the historical narrative sketched in section I, first of all, we can now perhaps add another layer. It may be that the Church's contemporary conception of its authority is shaped not only by the memory and habits of an imperial past, but also by the absorption of certain Enlightenment conceptions of rationality and belief. Insistence on submission to authority is itself a rejection of Enlightenment rationality, of course, but the *pattern* through which this insistence on submission is presented seems very much 'Enlightenment-shaped'. The Enlightenment, perhaps, has found its way into the very centre of Catholic understanding of magisterial authority, in spite of the best efforts of the magisterium.

So how can the criticism of evidentialism developed by Reformed Epistemologists be of use? Wolterstorff's critique is particularly helpful insofar as he turns our attention to the question of how we do in fact come by our beliefs.[7] If one looks at all the belief-forming mechanisms that are actually at work in us, it becomes clear that deciding to believe something because one has weighed up the evidence for it is, while possible, very much a marginal case. Wolterstorff follows Reid in suggesting that in fact we have a whole range of belief dispositions. We tend to believe certain things about the external world when we have certain kinds of physical sensations, and we tend to believe certain things about the past when we have memory experiences, and we have a 'credulity' disposition – "we are all so constituted as to be disposed in certain circumstances to believe what we apprehend people as telling us". We tend to believe in the consistency of

---

[6] Francis A. Sullivan, S.J., *Creative Fidelity: Weighing and Interpreting Documents of the Magisterium* (Dublin: Gill and MacMillan, 1996), p.141. Sullivan himself does not, it should be noted, think we can directly control our assent, or calibrate it to different degrees. We either assent or we don't. What we must rather calibrate, on his account, is the level of *effort* we make to persuade ourselves of that which is proposed to us with authority. He makes the case well, but his interpretation of the magisterial language about assent to magisterial teaching is not the most natural one. Essentially, he makes a case that this language *cannot* mean what it seems on the surface to mean, since what it seems to mean would involve asking us to do something impossible.

[7] The attempt to get away from the abstraction characteristic of most philosophy and pay attention to the actual psychological mechanisms of believing and reasoning also marks John Henry Newman thought in *The Grammar of Assent*. I think it is arguable, though, that Newman remains somewhat captured by a Lockian and evidentialist epistemology. The whole worry which drives *The Grammar,* for instance, is how it can be that the firmness of assent can (apparently) exceed what can be justified by the weight of the evidence.

things in a way which gives rise to induction: we have "a natural, original and unaccountable propensity to believe, that the connections which we have observed in times past, will continue in time to come"[8]. Wolterstorff suggests, though Reid did not, that we have also some distinctly 'ignoble' belief dispositions, such as a 'disposition to believe that which gives us security' or 'to believe that which serves to perpetuate our positions of economic privilege'. Over the course of a life the dispositions are modified, and we have, on a second level, Wolterstorff suggests, a certain power to *govern* our belief-forming dispositions: we can turn our attention to certain things, making it more likely that we will form certain beliefs; we can resolve to resist in particular circumstances our natural inclination to believe in certain ways (Wolterstorff gives as an example here the decision to resist one's credulity disposition and form no beliefs until one has heard from both parties in a marital dispute).

So the picture is far more complex than for the evidentialist: we don't just have one (legitimate) belief-forming mechanism – that of weighing evidence – but a whole host of them, which change and develop over the course of our lives, and which we can to a limited degree take steps to shape.

Presumably a similar complexity is involved in the way that the beliefs which are part of a Catholic's faith are formed. Trusting people – trusting those from whom one learns the faith, and trusting priests, bishops, councils, popes – is certainly somewhere in the mix, but this is likely to be in a complex, tangled, and, depending on the individual, very varied way. It should not be surprising, then, that the uninitiated, even those who are not inclined to cynicism or distrust of church authority, should feel a great sense of strangeness when they come across the system according to which the response of the believer should be finely calibrated and proportioned to the level of authority exhibited in a particular pronouncement or document. The sense of dislocation comes from being told one is supposed to govern one's belief in a way which seems unnatural and unfamiliar, a way which just does not resonate with the experience of believing.

III

How, then, shall we proceed? How *ought* we in fact to think about 'responsible, critical assent,' to use the full title of the chapter?

One approach would be to aim for a kind of damage limitation. Useful work has been undertaken by Catholic theologians in the cause of protecting against inflationary pressures on magisterial authority, resisting, at its most extreme, 'creeping infallibilism'. One can be very clear and insistent about how rarely the strenuous requirements for infallibility are fulfilled, and one can draw attention to the limited nature of most exercises of authority. So

---

[8] Wolterstorff, "Can belief in God be rational if it has no foundations?" in *Faith and Rationality*, p. 150. Wolterstorff is quoting from Reid.

although the rhetoric may at times sound as though the institution is, in the words of Francis Oakley, 'insist[ing] peremptorily on outright obedience,' one can show through a close study of the system of gradations of authority and through a close study of particular documents, that really this is not so – or at least not quite so much as it might first seem.

Such work I think is necessary and important, but it is also, in a sense, merely tinkering around the edges. One is still left with a sense of a strange world of careful gradations of authority and response, a world which seems not much linked to the rest of the life of faith. In fact this 'damage limitation' approach only takes us *deeper* into this strangeness, asking us to pay *more* attention to the whole rather improbable business of carefully weighing up evidence and carefully proportioning our response to it.

Perhaps, then, in order best to think about authority and assent, Catholic theology needs to start somewhere *other* than the relatively recent attempts of those who hold authority to become explicit about its nature.[9]

IV

It is in the nature of Christian faith to acknowledge an authority prior to and larger than one's own whims and preferences, and even than one's own rational capacities. There is a certain givenness of things, and we know that we stand under judgment. Christ speaks to us from the Gospels with authority, and Christian life is, among other things, an acknowledgment of this authority. The faith is not to be thought of, then, at its most fundamental level, as some option we exercise, a preference we assert, a free selection of beliefs and practices we make, but as an obedient response to a call.

Ultimately, then, the authority to which Christians respond is the authority of Christ and of God, and the assent we make is to the message of the Gospel. But what does this mean, concretely? How is it played out in actual Christian lives? How is it experienced? One might suppose that if authority is to mean anything, it needs to express itself in a quite specific way, to make some clear, identifiable demands and a clear, identifiable difference.

We might be tempted to say, for a Protestant this authority becomes concrete and particular and really binding in the authority of Scripture, and for a Catholic, in the authority of the magisterium. But this kind of opposition would, I think, be a mistake.

---

[9] It is worth saying that what is involved in my argument as a whole is not so much an examination of the *truth* of the 'this' or 'that' element within the current magisterial teaching on the magisterium, but an examination of the *helpfulness* of the system as a whole. Fergus Kerr, in *Twentieth Century Catholic Theology*, writes of the "creative amnesia" of the Church, and if my argument holds, what it points towards will not be the repudiation of particular claims within the current pattern of thinking about the magisterium, but the appropriateness of such a creative amnesia towards this whole style of thinking.

There is indeed an impulse in certain forms of Protestantism on the one hand to reject any concrete mediation of authority other than Scripture, and on the other to ensure that this authority of Scripture is highly specified, that it has some real teeth, that it cannot be evaded. It is an impulse which we can see at work in doctrines of inerrancy and so on. But we are not obliged to understand Catholicism as a mirror image to such forms of Protestantism, nor to locate its defining centre by reference to precisely what Protestantism rejects.

We might instead see what is distinctive in Roman Catholicism as a certain confident and optimistic *holism*. I meet Christ in and through the Church, and this means that I encounter his authority in all kinds of ways: in those who introduce me to the faith (parents, catechists); in liturgy and sacrament; in Scripture (which is the Church's book); in engagement with my fellow Christians; in the study of theology or encounter with the monastic tradition, or in the sufferings of the poor or in a conversation with a bishop or in the teachings of the Pope. And the list is not a tidy or an ordered one – these things are all highly entangled. In the liturgy I hear Scripture; the Pope might direct me to attend to the authority of Christ that I encounter in the poor; from my parents I learn a certain demeanor towards priest or bishop. And so on.

This is not to say of course that none of this can ever go wrong, that the Church is always entirely successful in its mediation of the authority of Christ. Manifestly many things can and do go wrong. But the Catholic response to the possibility and reality of things going wrong is not to insist on finding a single utterly pure mediation of the authority of Christ – whether one thinks of this as Scripture or infallible teachings of the magisterium – and then to reject or denigrate or downgrade the rest. The response is instead to be confident that when things go astray in one strand, the resources will be available for correction and repair from others. The Catholic may not have in her possession, in other words, a tidy formula for orchestrating the interplay between the various strands which mediate authority to her, but she has disposition to trust that within the whole lie the resources for its own correction.[10]

V

What then shall we say, more particularly, of the status of the teachings of Popes, councils, bishops? How should they be received? How are we to conceive 'critical, responsible assent' to such teachings?

---

[10] To say that the Catholic should not reach for infallible teachings of the magisterium the way a certain sort of Protestant might reach for the inerrancy of the Bible is not, incidentally, to dismiss papal infallibility, although it does involve rejecting an understanding of the Catholic faith which would make papal infallibility somehow pivotal or foundational.

We can learn something here from one of the key points that Nicholas Wolterstorff makes with regard to the rationality of belief. It is necessary to ask, he insists, not how rational a particular belief is considered generally, but how rational a given person, of a given age and set of circumstances, is in believing it. So a 10-year-old may be perfectly rationally justified in her belief in God even if she would have no answer to make to the critique of a Freudian or a Marxist, whereas a 25-year-old intellectual who finds herself in the same position would not be.

In a similar vein, it seems to me, we need to acknowledge that what constitutes appropriate response to magisterial teaching will vary according to the position and circumstances of the one who encounters this teaching.

In general, it follows from the broadly trusting and optimistic approach that Catholicism takes towards the Church as mediator of the authority of Christ, that we can expect ordinary Catholics to attend to the teachings of popes and bishops, insofar as they come across them, in a positive way. These are our leaders. We naturally absorb a sense of their authority from the way they are dressed and addressed, and from the way others treat them. We pray for them regularly in the mass. We suppose they have a good deal of expertise to draw on, that they have had the time to think through matters that we have not, that they were selected at least partly for their suitability. It is for all these kinds of reasons – not because of a formal theory of magisterial authority, but because of the place of bishops and pope in the whole economy of the Church as we experience it – that the default position is to presume that bishops and popes know what they are talking about, that they can teach us of the faith, that they can be trusted. People may depart from this default position, of course, to the degree that they have experience suggestive of a lack of sanctity or probity or good sense in their bishops (this is perhaps the situation in countries where sex abuse scandals and their handling by bishops have been shocking). Or people may depart from the default position if what the bishops are saying lacks all resonance with their faith as a whole. But a basic presumption of trust is still, in the absence of concrete reasons to doubt, the default position.

The situation of theologians is a little different. The theologian may well, on a range of questions, have more substantial intellectual resources at hand – a richer knowledge of theological tradition or biblical scholarship, a quicker mind, a wider awareness of the available options – than many of the bishops he or she encounters. In this sense the natural response to a pronouncement of a bishop might be more to entertain it as a hypothesis to be examined, than to accept it as a teaching of the faith. The particularly rich contact the theologian has with some of the other strands through which Christ's authority is mediated to the Church, we might say, will naturally tend to shape their reception of this particular strand.

Out of a certain respect, nevertheless, theologians ought generally take seriously, and look for ways to accept whenever possible, the teachings of the hierarchy. What is important to realise is that the respect that is needed here is not respect for the hierarchy so much as respect for the laity.

The vast majority of the laity quite rightly, we have said, when all is going more or less as it should, give a prima facie credence to what is proposed to them by bishops and popes. It is not the *only* way in which the authority of Christ is mediated to them, but it is one of the ways. So the theologian, if she wants to be of service to the laity, needs to work with and not against the normal situation in which the ordinary lay person finds herself

Something like this, it seems to me, can be seen at work in the writings of a liberation theologian such as Gustavo Gutierrez. It is striking how often Gutierrez will appeal to the authority of Vatican documents or of documents of Bishops' conferences, when exactly the same points can in fact be found in, and may well have been derived *from*, his own earlier work. Quite often, indeed, these points can be found in his own earlier work in a stronger or clearer or more powerful way than they appear in the official documents. If one were functioning only in a normal academic mode, the proper thing to do here would clearly be to demonstrate how the Vatican had both taken on and watered down one's own earlier ideas. But such an exercise would be of little use to ordinary Catholics. If Gutierrez is concerned that the theology itself should be of use to the Church in the broadest sense, then working with rather than against the normal channels of (hierarchical) authority in the church is the natural thing to do.

VI

But what, then, of the critical dimension? Is there a role for criticism in one's response to authoritative teaching? Is there a role for dissent?

I hope it will be clear from all that has gone before that there is of course such a role. The gently optimistic disposition that I am suggesting Catholics ought to have about the Church is as much as anything an optimism that when things go wrong in one dimension, the Church as a whole will have resources for its correction in another. And if the default position of a Catholic theologian, I've suggested, should be to respect the teaching of the hierarchy out of respect for the situation of the laity, it can nevertheless also at times be the duty of Catholic theologians to help the laity work out how to resist hierarchical teaching gone wrong.

What is particularly important to realise is that the two things – assenting to the teachings of the hierarchy, and dissenting from them – can be seen, on the most fundamental level, as arising from a single source. It might seem otherwise. It might seem obvious that Catholics find themselves caught between competing norms – fidelity and obedience on the one hand, intellectual liberty or freedom of conscience on the other – and that they have to work out how to reconcile, or balance, or choose between them. Shall I follow my freedom and disagree with the hierarchy, or shall I take the path of obedience and assent? But if we allow that the authority of the Gospel and our assent to it begin at a deeper and more fundamental level than our response to the magisterium, and that the response to the magisterium is only one of the ways in which the more fundamental assent to the authority of the Gospel is expressed, then a different view becomes possible. It becomes possible to see that the need for reflection, for struggle, for wrestling with difficulties, arises *within* a fundamental obedience of faith, and not in opposition to it. And this means in turn that criticism and dissent can be conceived of as a possible outcome of this fundamental obedience – they should not be thought of as the normal, the *standard* outcome of this obedience, but they can nevertheless under certain circumstances be its most perfect expression.

Durham University, Durham, Great Britain

APPENDIX I

OBEDIENCE AND THE CHURCH'S TEACHING AUTHORITY: THE BURDEN OF THE PAST

FRANCIS OAKLEY

The trouble about history is that we take it too much for granted. – HughTrevor-Roper

Historians are the professional remembrancers of what their fellow-citizens would like to forget. – Eric Hobsbawn

One of the oddities of the current ecclesiastical scene almost half a century after the Second Vatican Council's *aggiornamento* is the contrast between the *status* of the church in the world and the stance it expects of the faithful in response to its magisterial pronouncements. Since the council the church has come, self-confessedly, to accept its status at law as a voluntary association, one that has put behind it not only medieval dreams of universal empire, temporal no less than spiritual, but also the modern regime of concordats with the secular state, one that is bereft, accordingly, of even an indirect public coercive power, and one that must necessarily depend for the discharge of its religious mission upon its ability to touch and shape the consciences of the faithful via a process of exhortation and persuasion.[1] And yet, in connection with the exercise of its magisterial power on matters of faith and morals, matters that surely call for a response firmly grounded in the conscience of the individual believer, it still insists peremptorily upon outright obedience – or, as the "Formula for the Profession of Faith" puts it, "religious submission of will and intellect."[2] Its model, in effect, is an

---

[1] Though admittedly tempted at times to deploy a type of sectarian psychological coercion. See, e.g., Peter Berger, *The Sacred Canopy: Elements of a Sociological Theory of Religion* (Garden City, NY: Doubleday and Company, Inc., 1969), pp. 29-51, 148-33, where he notes that those who, in a thoroughly secularized world "continue to adhere to the world as defined by the religious traditions...find themselves in the position of cognitive minorities – a status that has social-psychological as well as theoretical problems." Cf. Peter L. Berger and Thomas Luckmann, *The Social Construction of Reality: A Treatise in the Sociology of Knowledge* (Garden City, NY: Doubleday and Company, Inc., 1967), pp. 126-27.

[2] This, the successor to the anti-modernist oath required of all clergy until 1967 and "now required of all persons, clerical or lay, who have any official responsibilities in the church" – thus Lacey in the prologue to *The Crisis of Authority in Catholic Modernity*, ed. Michael J. Lacey and Francis Oakley (New York: Oxford University Press, 2011), p. 23, n.7.

authoritarian one involving the affirmation of allegedly timeless certainties rather than something more supple in nature that may call, certainly, for a species of respect and religious attentiveness but does not preclude on the part of the faithful anxious hesitancy, probing discussion, frank admission of doubt and uncertainty, perhaps even, at the end of the line, what has been called "loyal" or "faithful" dissent.[3] That the former model of authority calling so bluntly for obedience came to establish itself so firmly in the Catholic consciousness and experience that it has persisted on into the post-Vatican II era reflects, I believe, the burden of the past that continues to weigh so heavily on our ecclesiastical authorities as they go about the discharge of their onerous duties. It calls, therefore, for an historically-conditioned effort at understanding.

In mounting such an effort, it is my presumption that we should not take the dominance and persistence of the "obedience model of authority" simply for granted. There is nothing "natural" or "inevitable" about it. It is, instead, the deliverance of a whole concatenation of contingent historical developments, most of them originating no further back than the high or central Middle Ages. Things could well have turned out other than they did. I cannot aspire to tell any full, counter-factual story of why they did not do so, but in any attempt to tell such a story I do believe that the following half-dozen, complexly-interrelated, factors would prove to be central. They concern conceptions of clerical status and ecclesiastical authority in general, notions of papal authority in particular, and the degree to which the official ecclesiological consciousness of our day continues to be informed by a deeply-ingrained aversion to historicity and shaped by a theological practice that I would reluctantly categorize as essentially *uncommitted*. And they are as follows:

1. First, what one may refer to as the "clericalization" of the Church. Even if one prescinds from any debate swirling around claims to the effect that the emergence in Christian antiquity of a separate priestly caste "after pagan and Judaic patterns, standing between God and men and barring direct access to God which the whole priestly people should enjoy" was "contrary to the New Testament message of the one mediator and high priest Jesus Christ and that of the priesthood of all Christians,"[4] – even if one brackets any such debate, the fact remains that the existence of a distinct clerical order laying proud claim to a higher ontological status than

---

[3] See Charles E. Curran, *Loyal Dissent* (Washington, DC: Georgetown University Press, 2002).

[4] Thus Hans Küng, *The Church*, trans. Ray and Rosaleen Ockenden (New York: Sheed and Ward, 1968), p. 383. See the whole section on the "priesthood of all believers," pp. 363-87. Cf. the carefully nuanced discussion in Miguel M. Garijo-Guembe, *Communion of the Saints: Foundation Nature and Structure of the Church*, trans. Patrick Madigan, S.J. (Collegeville, MN: *The Liturgical Press*, 1994) and the extensive literature referred to therein.

that occupied by mere lay folk was not taken either in the ancient or in the early-medieval Church as any sort of given. In the course of the twelfth century, it is true, leading figures like the canonist Gratian (d.c. 1160) or the early scholastic theologian Hugh of St. Victor (d. 1141) did come to insist that among Christians there are basically two types of people, clergy and laity, the former superior in dignity and power to the latter.[5] But as late as 1100, the intriguing figure whom we know only as the Anglo-Norman Anonymous, stressing the priesthood of all believers and the overriding importance of the sacrament of baptism (which, for him could be said in some sense to comprehend all the other sacraments, priestly ordination not excluded), could reject even the application to lay folk of the term *laicus*, which he himself viewed as derogatory and equated with the *vulgar* (*popularis sive publicanus*).[6]

During the earlier medieval centuries, then, although tentative efforts were made to establish a clear and hierarchically-ordered divide between clergy and laity, they had been doomed to remain in the realm of aspiration. During those centuries it appears to have been less common to see society as divided simply between clerical and lay orders than to see it divided among lay folk, monks, and bishops or, in another tripartite classification, between those who prayed, those who fought, and those who worked.[7] During those centuries, too, kings and emperors, inheritors in biblicized form of the archaic pagan vision of sacral kingship that had left so profound an imprint on the Hebraic notion of monarchy, and themselves anointed

---

[5] *Decretum Gratiani*, (12, qu. 1, c. 7; in *Corpus Juris Canonici*, ed. A. Friedberg, 2 vols. (Leipzig: B. Tauchnitz, 1879-80), 1:678. Hugh of St. Victor, *De sacramentis Christianae fidei*, II, pars 2, c. 4; in *Patrologiae cursus completus: Series Latina*, ed. J.-P. Migne, 221 vols. (Paris: Migne, 1884-1904), 176:418.

[6] For he who is baptized, putting on as he does the very sacerdotal nature of Jesus Christ, is transformed by that sacramental moment into a species of priest or cleric. See his *De consecratione pontificum et regum et de regimine eorum in ecclesia sancta*, 24c; in Karl Pellens, ed., *Die texte des Normannischen Anonymous* (Wiesbaden: Franz Steiner Verlag, 1966), 201. Pertinent to this passage is a comment which George Williams, *The Norman Anonymous of 1100 A.D.* (Cambridge, MA: Harvard University Press, 1951), 14, makes in relation to one of the other *Tractates* by the Anonymous, namely that the latter was "intent on effacing the barrier which the Gregorian Reform would set up between the clergy and the laity, to the disparagement of the latter." Cf. the discussion of the Anonymous's thinking in Francis Oakley, *Empty Bottles of Gentilism: Kingship and the Divine in Late Antiquity and the Early Middle Ages* (*to 1050*) (New Haven and London: Yale University Press, 2010), pp. 167-76.

[7] I.S. Robinson, "Church and Papacy," in *The Cambridge History of Medieval Political Thought c. 350 – c. 1450*, ed. J.H. Burns (Cambridge, Cambridge University Press, 1988), 263-66; G. Duby, *Les Trois ordres au l'imaginaire du feudalisme* (Paris: Gallimard, 1978).

with chrism in a liturgical ceremony akin to episcopal consecration that was viewed as conferring a sacrament, were understood to be possessed of a sacred, quasi-sacerdotal aura. Only with the partial triumph in the late-eleventh and early-twelfth centuries of the Gregorian movement of ecclesiastical reform was the greater dignity of the clerical *ordo* secured, a sharp line drawn between it and the lay *ordo*, and its superiority and monopoly of sacrality vindicated.[8] The German emperor Henry IV was bluntly dismissed as "a layman and nothing more" and "the age of priest-kings and emperor-pontiffs" was proclaimed to be a thing of the past. With that, moreover, went the related move finally to vindicate within the clerical *ordo*, and in terms that permitted of no ambiguity, an hierarchical structure analogous to that believed to prevail among the celestial choirs of angels and one that culminated on earth, at least, in the monarchical supremacy of the man known as the vicar of St. Peter, the pope or bishop of Rome.[9]

The tone was thus set for the centuries ensuing and down, perhaps astonishingly, to the present. The teaching of the priesthood of all believers was not altogether lost sight of in the scholastic theology of the High Middle Ages though it amounted to little more than a minor perturbation on the outermost orbit of an essentially clericalist ecclesiological consciousness. Moreover, after the provocative use made of that teaching by Martin Luther, it appears to have more or less disappeared from Catholic ecclesiology until its partial recuperation by the liturgical movement of the twentieth century and its reaffirmation by the Second Vatican Council in *Lumen gentium*. That official reaffirmation, however, was accompanied by a cautious admonition to the effect that "the common priesthood of the faithful and the ministerial or hierarchical priesthood [of the clergy]," though interrelated, "differ from one another in essence and not simply in degree,"[10] and one gets the distinct impression that, in any practical terms at

---

[8] It was the clear purpose of the Gregorians to redraw "the boundaries between the secular and the sacred" and to claim "the latter as the exclusive domain of the clergy" – thus Mayke de Jong, "Religion," in *The Early Middle Ages: Europe, 400-1000*, ed. Rosamund McKitterick (Oxford: Oxford University Press, 2001), 161-62; Robinson, "Church and Papacy," in *The Cambridge History of Medieval Political Thought*, ed. Burns, 261-66.

[9] For this development, see Oakley, *Empty Bottles of Gentilism*, pp. 200-219, and Oakley, *The Mortgage of the Past: Reshaping the Ancient Political Inheritance 1050-1300* (New Haven and London: Yale University Press, forthcoming in 2012).

[10] See *Lumen gentium* (*The Dogmatic Constitution on the Church*) 2:10; cf. the affiliated allusions in 4:30 and 4:34; in Giuseppe Alberigo and Norman P. Tanner, eds. *Decrees of the Ecumenical Councils*, 2 vols. (London and Washington, D.C.: Sheed and Ward and Georgetown University Press, 1990), 2:857; cf. 4:874-75, 877. Cf. *The Church in Our Day: A Collective Pastoral of the American Hierarchy on the Mystery of the Church* (Washington, DC: United States Catholic Conference, 1968), a set of reflections focused largely on the two opening chapters of *Lumen gentium* which makes only passing

least, the doctrine of the priesthood of all believers, having resurfaced in our own day, has survived as little more than an *inert* piece of theorizing, in this analogous to a chemically inactive "noble metal" like platinum. It is something quite alien certainly, to the more clericalist, even "cultic" self-perception of the generation of clergy sometimes labeled as "John Paul II" priests.[11] That being so, the form of clericalism that took strong root in the Catholic mentality during the twelfth century appears, in effect, to remain alive and well in our own day. In its absence, indeed, one would be hard pressed to make any sense at all of the truly disastrous way in which our ecclesiastical authorities have responded (or failed to respond) to the sexual abuse crisis.

2. Second, the politicization and juridification of ecclesiastical power. If by the thirteenth century, the clergy had come to see themselves as a distinct *ordo*, superior to the laity not only in dignity but also in power, the question arises as to how, precisely, they came to understand that power. By that time the Church had come to be distinguished from the secular states within the boundaries of which it functioned as a separate entity, juridically self-sufficient and governmentally autonomous, a "perfect society" to which the term "Christian commonwealth," "ecclesiastical commonwealth," "ecclesiastical polity," "ecclesiastical kingdom," had come to be attached. All of that witnessed eloquently to the fact that, over the course of the centuries preceding, a profound change had taken place in the typical understanding of the notion of ecclesiastical office itself. By the twelfth century, the New Testament understanding of that office as ministerial in nature and grounded in love of others had long since been nudged to one side or, at least transformed, by a very different mode of understanding

---

references to the common priesthood of all believers, and then with the worried comment that many of the bishops saw "an unfortunate eclipse of the clear and separate status of ordained priesthood." "The historic development in the Council of the doctrine of the priesthood of the laity should prove a blessing to all the Church," the pastoral says (p. 49). But it goes on to warn that "the fruits of that blessing could be diminished, even lost, if the heightened awareness of the general priesthood in the Church lowered, even momentarily, a true appreciation of the necessary roles of the particular vocation special to the priest called apart and ordained for men in the things that pertain to God." All of this incorporated in a section of the letter (pp. 48-50) entitled, significantly enough, "Apartness" and emphasizing the "essential difference between priest and people."

[11] For the growing generational ecclesiological differences between "so-called Vatican II priests and John Paul II priests," see Katarina Schuth, "Assessing the Education of Priests and Lay Ministers: Content and Consequences," in Lacey and Oakley, eds., *The Crisis of Authority in Catholic Modernity*, 317-47, esp. at 326, 338-39, and Dean R. Hoge and Jacqueline E. Wenger, *Evolving Visions of Priesthood: Changes from Vatican II to the Turn of the New Century* (Collegeville, MN: Liturgical Press, 2003), esp. 47-59.

which found expression in an essentially political vocabulary drawn from the Roman law and connecting with the type of relationship prevailing in the world at large between rulers and those ruled. Already by the seventh century the word *jurisdictio* had been taken into canonistic usage from the civil law, and over the following centuries it had come to be used intermittently to denote the general administrative activity of ecclesiastical government. By the mid-twelfth century, with the marked growth of papal governmental activity and the great flowering of legal studies both civil and canonistic, the process of juridification had already become so marked as to evoke from St. Bernard of Clairvaux his celebrated admonition to Pope Eugenius III to the effect that the pope should properly be the successor of Peter, not of Constantine, and that at Rome the laws of Christ should not be supplanted by "the laws of Justinian."[12] And by the following century, with the process of juridification having if anything accelerated, the canonists had subjected ecclesiastical power to a probing legal analysis and had come in the process to deploy a crucial distinction that was destined to play a central role in the delineation and understanding of ecclesiastical power all the way down to the Second Vatican Council when, for the first time in eight centuries, it began finally to lose ground.[13]

The distinction in question was that between the power of ecclesiastical jurisdiction or government (*potestas jurisdictionis*) and that sacramental power or power of order (*potestas ordinis*) which priests and bishops possessed by virtue of having received the sacrament of holy orders. Within the power of jurisdiction, in turn, it had become customary to distinguish a double modality, one pertaining to the internal and the other the external forum. The former (*potestas jurisdictionis in foro interiori*) concerned the domain of the individual conscience. It was a power exercised quintessentially through the sacrament of penance, it was exercised only over those who voluntarily submitted themselves to its sway, and it was directed to the private good. This was not the case, however, with the power of jurisdiction in the external forum or public sphere (*potestas jurisdictionis in foro exteriori*), which was a coercive power pertaining to a public authority, exercised even over the unwilling and directed to the common good of the faithful. Unlike the power wielded officially or at law by ecclesiastical bodies today or in the pre-Constantinian era (in both cases powers wielded over essentially private societies whose membership is no less voluntary than that, say, of modern universities or trade unions), it was a truly governmental power akin to that wielded today by what we call the

---

[12] St. Bernard, *De consideratione*, I, 4, 4, 3; in *Patrologiae cursus completus...series Latina*, ed. J.-P. Migne, 331 vols. (Paris: 1884-1904), 182:732, 776.

[13] See Francis Oakley, *The Conciliarist Tradition: Constitutionalism in the Catholic Church 1303-1870* (Oxford: Oxford University Press, 2003), pp. 5-13.

via that complex pattern of collaborative episcopal governance and synodal activity which stands out as so marked a feature of the Church's earliest centuries and which was to find its culmination at the level of the universal Church in the great succession of ecumenical councils stretching from Nicaea I in 325 to Nicaea II in 787. In the second half of the eleventh century, with their vigorous leadership first of the Gregorian reform and, later, of the crusading movement, the popes began to undertake a more than intermittent exercise of judicial authority and of truly governmental power over the entire Latin Church. Only in the thirteenth century, with the rapid expansion of that governmental role, did they come to be viewed as credible claimants to the *plenitudo potestatis*, the fullness of jurisdictional authority over that entire Church. And even then, partly by way of reaction to papal centralization, partly because of the crisis and scandal caused by the outbreak of the Great Schism of the West, the conciliar ideal, framed now with greater legal precision and clothed with all the accoutrements of canonistic corporation theory, rose once more to prominence and precipitated in the fifteenth century the historic constitutional legislation asserting the superiority in certain critical cases of general council to pope and providing for the regular and automatic assembly of such councils. By the end of the fifteenth century, it is true, the papacy had regained the initiative and the attempted conciliarist, constitutionalist revolution had proved abortive. But the historical scholarship of the past century has made it clear that the conciliarist ecclesiology was destined to remain alive and well right across northern Europe, from Paris to Cracow, down into the nineteenth century, at the beginning of which the English historian Henry Hallam, describing it as embodying "the Whig principles of the Catholic Church," had called the Constance superiority decree *Haec sancta* as one of "the great pillars of that moderate theory with respect to papal authority which…is embraced by almost all laymen and the major part of ecclesiastics on this [i.e. the northern] side of the Alps."[22] It was only after the triumph of ultramontane views in 1870 at Vatican I that a subtle ecclesiastical politics of oblivion took over, that the whole Conciliar episode came to be stuffed down some sort of Orwellian memory hole, that its history came to be rewritten, and the whole regrettable business dismissed as nothing more than a stutter, hiccup, or momentary interruption in the long and essential continuity of the Latin Catholic Church. So far as I can make out, and historical revisionism to the contrary, that still appears today to be the official "take" on conciliarism.[23] And in the degree to which, via

---

[22] Henry Hallam, *View of the State of Europe in the Middle Ages*, 3 vols. (London: 1901; first published in 1818), 3:243-45.

[23] For all of this I venture to refer to Oakley, *The Conciliarist Tradition*, and for a synoptic introduction to the historical debate on the matter, Francis Oakley, "History and the Return of the Repressed in Catholic Modernity: The Dilemma posed by Constance," in Lacey and Oakley eds., *The Crisis of Authority in Catholic Modernity*, pp. 29-56.

effectively centralized governmental agencies, mechanisms, procedures and instrumentalities of communication, the papacy is actually able on a day-to-day basis to impose its sovereign will on the provincial churches of Roman Catholic Christendom, the contemporary papacy may well stand today at the historical peak of its prestige and at the very apex of its effective power within the Church.

4. Fourth, the degree to which the papacy continues today to behave in practice, though it can no longer claim to be such in theory, as the earthly fount and source of the jurisdictional power wielded via a process of delegation by all other ecclesiastical agencies and officials, the bishops themselves not excluded. That understanding of the Church's constitution had come powerfully to the fore in the context of the seemingly recondite dispute that broke out in mid-thirteenth century at the University of Paris between the mendicant and secular masters – that is, between those theologians who belonged to the great, international orders of friars, mainly Dominicans and Franciscans, and those drawn from the ranks of the secular clergy.[24] Pope Innocent III had extended official approbation to those two mendicant orders, and to their members were subsequently accorded an array of privileges as a result of which, without seeking approbation from local bishops, they could intrude into the normal parish life of Latin Christendom. Those privileges authorized them, in effect, to preach, teach, administer the sacraments, bury the dead, and collect any offerings normally attaching to such activities. In effect, it has been said, the popes had used "their sovereign authority as heads of the church to set up a new pastoral structure alongside the old one."[25] The overt strife that broke out at Paris in 1252 reflected, in general, a reaction on the part of the bishops and their supporters among the secular clergy against the growing centralization of power in the hands of the papal monarch that the grant of such privileges dramatized. After 1256, however, it came to focus in particular on matters more fundamental than pastoral structures, matters, indeed, that were essentially constitutional in nature. It did so after a Franciscan friar, Thomas of York, had bluntly claimed that the grant of papal privileges to the friars was no more than a particular manifestation of the fact that the pope was the

---

[24] The classic study of the controversy is that of Yves Congar, "Aspects ecclésiologiques de la querelle entre mendiants et séculiers dans la seconde moitié du XIIIe siècle et la début du XIVe," *Archives d'histoire doctrinale et littéraire du moyen âge*, 28(1961), 35-151. See, more recently, Kenneth Pennington, *The Pope and the Bishops: The Papal Monarchy in the Twelfth and Thirteenth Centuries* (Philadelphia: University of Pennsylvania Press, 1984), pp. 4-6, 186-89.

[25] Brian Tierney, *Religion, Law, and the Growth of Constitutional Thought: 1450-1650* (Cambridge: Cambridge University Press, 1982), p. 61, where he adds that "some theologians came to see this as subversive of all right order in the Christian community."

source of all jurisdictional power in the church, not excluding the power wielded by lesser prelates such as bishops. That claim is one of great and essentially constitutional importance. It had the effect of undercutting the ancient and hallowed view that "the church's constitution consisted of a collection of rights and duties, some established by Christ, others created by custom,"[26] and that each bishop wielded *by divine right and concession* a measure of autonomous authority grounded in the church's fundamental law. As a result, the salience of the "derivational" theory of ecclesiastical jurisdiction cleared "the way for a theory of absolute monarchy" which eventually "became the foundation of absolute monarchy in the modern church."[27]

No more than equal to the other bishops though the pope might be so far as the power of order is concerned, he was now to be viewed, nonetheless, as the very "fount and origin" of all the jurisdictional or governmental powers wielded by the other members of the clerical hierarchy, all of which derive from him alone. As Augustinus Triumphus put it at the start of the fourteenth century, the pope represents the person of Peter, so that in Matthew 16

> when Christ, therefore, granted the power of jurisdiction, he spoke not in the plural but in the singular, saying to Peter alone, "I shall give thee the keys of the kingdom of heaven," as if clearly to say, although I shall have given the power of order to all the apostles, I give thus to you alone your power of jurisdiction, to be dispensed and distributed by you to all the others.[28]

Although this was to be the point of view echoed influentially by Juan de Torquemada in the fifteenth century, by Thomas de Vio, Cardinal Cajetan, in the sixteenth, by the Jesuit theologians Francisco Suarez and Robert, Cardinal Bellarmine in the seventeenth, and was to remain the dominant ecclesiological view in the *Roman* (though not the Gallican) theological school right down into the nineteenth century, it never quite succeeded in carrying the day. It was endorsed neither by the Council of Trent nor (perhaps more surprisingly) by Vatican I, and it was finally precluded by Vatican II's historic teaching on episcopal collegiality.[29] But

---

[26] Pennington, *The Pope and the Bishops*, p. 188.

[27] Pennington, *The Pope and the Bishops*, p. 189 (italics mine). He adds: "It was an important turning point in the history of political thought."

[28] Augustinus Triumphus, *Tractatus brevis*, in Richard Scholz, ed. *Die Publizistik zur Zeit Philipps des Schönen und Bonifaz VIII* (Stuttgart: F. Enke, 1903), p. 492.

[29] See William Henn, "Historical-Theological Synthesis of the Relation between Primacy and Episcopacy during the Second Millennium," in *Il primato del successore di Pietro*, pp. 222-273; Schatz, *Papal Primacy*, pp. 128-74. For

while precluded in theory, it has certainly not been dislodged from the established routines of curial practice or, indeed, from the Roman Catholic imaginary at large. Speaking, indeed, of the way in which things ecclesiological have developed in the century and more since Vatican I, and noting that "the dogma of infallibility has not...[turned out to have had] the significance attributed to it in 1870 by its supporters or opponents," Klaus Schatz has insisted that it is "the papal primacy of jurisdiction [which] has acquired a greater scope than it actually had in 1870." As a result, especially in relation to the nomination of bishops and their selection in such a way as to promote the cause of specific papal policies, "by the eve of Vatican II Rome ruled the Church in a much stronger fashion and interfered in its life everywhere to a much greater degree than had been the case in 1870."[30] And, during the past half century, despite the summoning of successive episcopal synods and the currency of high-minded talk about episcopal collegiality, that trend towards tighter central control has, if anything, intensified. It has done so to such a degree, indeed, that, whatever the official theological stance, it is hard to envisage the bishops in practice as being anything other than subordinate wielders of a delegated power derived from Rome.

5. Fifth, the fact that, having during the Gregorian era launched a frontal assault on the sacral status of the emperors and kings of the day, the papacy went on itself to succumb to the age-old allure of sacral kingship. That ancient complex of notions cast a very long shadow across its own ambitions for supremacy in Christian society. Had it not done so, indeed, it would be hard to explain how the popes of the High Middle Ages permitted themselves to emerge as fully-fledged sacral monarchs in their own right. Brooding about the ubiquity of sacral kingship and about the close parallel between royal and episcopal unction, the anthropologist A.M. Hocart was once moved to observe that "the king and priest are branches of the same stem."[31] And it is certainly the case that over the course of the twelfth and thirteenth centuries the bishops of Rome moved authoritatively to the forefront as the true (or, at least, most convincing) successors to the erstwhile Roman emperors.

Thus they came not only to rule a highly politicized church via a centralized bureaucracy in accordance with a law modelled on (and

---

the difficulty the Council of Trent experienced with this highly-fraught issue, see Hubert Jedin *Geschichte des Konzils von Trient*, 4 vols., in 5 (Freiburg: Herder, 1948-78), 4/2.

[30] Schatz, *Papal Primacy*, pp. 167-68, adding "a systematic policy for the nomination of bishops in the sense of promoting specific trends and in the service of positions taken by the magisterium has only manifested itself in our time."

[31] A.M. Hocart, *Kingship* (London: Oxford University Press, 1927), p. 128.

creatively extended from) that of the Roman Empire, but they did so also with a marked degree of imperial grandeur. They called themselves "true emperor" or "celestial emperor" and deployed the old pagan Roman republican and imperial title of *pontifex maximus*. Like Justinian himself they claimed the prerogative of being a *lex animata* or "living law" and, at least from the time of Nicholas II (1058-61) onwards, they were crowned in a ceremony "that was meant to signify by visible, easily comprehensible and familiar means the monarchic status of the pope."[32] So far as regalia, costume and ceremonial went, already in the mid-eighth century the forged Donation of Constantine (later to be incorporated influentially into the *Corpus Juris Canonici*) had taken pains to depict the bishop of Rome as entering into possession of the imperial regalia, of the red imperial cloak (or *cappa rubea*) with which popes eventually came to be "enmantled" at their investiture, and of the Byzantine *phrygium* or tall white hat, which was to evolve, on the one hand, into the mitre worn by all bishops and, on the other, into the triple crown (or *Triregnum*) worn as a symbol of their sovereign power by all popes down into the 1960s.[33] If that eighth-century depiction was well ahead of the actual ceremonial realities of the day, the introduction in the mid-eleventh century of a coronation ceremony (eventually to include also a ceremonial enthronement followed by homage),[34] as well as the blunt stipulation in Gregory VII's *Dictatus papae* (1075) that the pope alone might "use the imperial regalia,"[35] launched a process that was to reach its culmination in the thirteenth century and to leave a legacy that has endured down to our own day. For then it was that "all the symbols of empire were to become attached to the papacy," and Innocent III could assert that he wore the mitre as a sign of his pontifical position but the crown or tiara as a sign of his imperial power, and that "popes like Gregory IX (1222-41) and Boniface VIII (1294-1303)...[were]

---

[32] Walter Ullmann, *A Short History of the Papacy in the Middle Ages* (London: Methuen, 1872), pp. 139-40, where, asserting that "in this the papacy borrowed one more element from royal and imperial symbolism," he notes that the very purpose of the coronation ceremony was "declarative" rather than "constitutive" in that it was election and his acceptance of that election that made a man pope.

[33] When Pope Paul VI, though himself crowned with it, went on to set aside that papal crown and other symbolic trappings of papal regality.

[34] A development that was not without its marked oddities. See the interpretation given to the practice of seating the newly-crowned pope on the *sedes stercoraria* (night commode) by Sergio Bertelli, *The King's Body: Sacral Rituals of Power in Medieval and Early Modern Europe*, trans. R. Burr Litchfield (University Park, PA: Pennsylvania University Press, 2001), pp. 177-90.

[35] Erich Caspar ed., *Das Register Gregors VII*, 2 vols. (Berlin: Weidmannsche Buchhandlung, 1955), 1:201-208. English translation in Brian Tierney, *The Crisis of Church and State 1050-1300* (Englewood Cliffs, NJ: Prentice Hall, Inc., 1964), pp. 49-50 (No. 8).

seen in every respect as successors of Constantine."[36] We cannot know how accurate the chronicler's description of Boniface VIII's reception in 1298 of the ambassadors of the claimant to the imperial throne may have been, but whatever the case contemporaries themselves would hardly have been surprised by his depiction of the scene:

> Sitting on a throne, wearing on his head the diadem of Constantine, his right hand on the hilt of the sword with which he was girt, he [the pope] cried out "Am I not the supreme pontiff? Is this throne not the pulpit of Peter? Is it not my duty to watch over the rights of the Empire? It is I who am Caesar, it is I who am emperor.[37]

Paul VI may have retired to museum status the papal crown, the *sedia gestatoria*, and other conspicuous trappings of papal royalty. But he relinquished none of the imperial power attaching to his ancient high office, and its royal past continues to weigh heavily on that office. Though it would doubtless try to shrug off the designation, it remains the case that the papacy, which a thousand years ago launched a frontal assault on the sacral pretensions of the German Emperors, stands out in solitary splendor today as itself the last of the truly great European sacral monarchies. And that fact almost inevitably affects the way in which it interacts with the faithful and expects its teachings to be received by them. As one historian has put it, in an era in which "vast Catholic populations [had] become irrevocably committed to political democracy the Roman see remained wedded to the improbable task of governing a world-wide Church through the institutional apparatus of a petty baroque despotism."[38] In his *Leviathan*, the seventeenth-century English philosopher Thomas Hobbes was moved to describe the papacy as "no other than the ghost of the deceased *Roman empire* sitting crowned in the grave thereof."[39] I believe we should forthrightly acknowledge that that observation is no less accurate in its fundamental perception for being derisive in its conscious intent.

6. There was nothing inevitable about any of the five historical developments described above. Things could well have turned out otherwise. But they did not, and antiquated though those developments may

---

[36] Robert Folz, *The Concept of Empire in Western Europe from the Fifth to the Fourteenth Century*, trans. Sylvia Ann Ogilvie (New York: Harper and Row, 1969), p. 79; cf. pp. 201-3.

[37] The Chronicle of Francesco Pippino cited from Folz, *Concept of Empire*, p. 207.

[38] Thus Brian Tierney, "Medieval Canon Law and Western Constitutionalism," *Catholic Historical Review* 52 (No. 1, 1966), 15.

[39] Thomas Hobbes, *Leviathan*, Pt. 4, ch. 47; ed. Michael Oakeshott (Oxford: Basil Blackwell, 1946), p. 457.

well seem, they are not altogether redundant. They continue in ways both obvious and subtle to shape the institutional climate in which church teachings are proclaimed and to frame hierarchical expectations about how the faithful should receive such teachings. And their impact is reinforced, finally and in the sixth place, by two further features which, I believe, characterize the contemporary exercise of the official magisterial authority and help to lock it into the authoritarian model in which timeless certainties are enunciated and nothing less than outright obedience and religious submission of will and intellect demanded of the faithful. Hence the all-or-nothing mentality informing so much of Church teaching and distancing it so sharply from the contextual pluralism, the shifting crosscurrents, the sea of turbulent contingency that the faithful at large must try to navigate as they struggle onwards in the stubborn attempt to lead decent Christian lives.

The first is that aversion to or, at least, discomfort with historicity which, in an extreme form, was so marked a feature of the anti-Modernist campaign which did so much intellectual damage in the Catholic world during the first half of the twentieth century, remaining in play, after all, right down to the very eve of Vatican II. I doubt if any cardinals today bear on their coats of arms the motto *Semper Idem*, as I believe Cardinal Ottaviani did fifty years ago, but official pronouncement by ecclesiastical authorities rarely convey any marked consciousness of the church's embeddedness in the turbulent flow of time, or the degree to which it is buffeted by the shifting winds and treacherous crosscurrents it inevitably encounters, shaped willy-nilly by the sometimes startling contingencies that go with historicity, subject accordingly to change, and change that has not always proved to be gradual or evolutionary. Instead, one still encounters echoes of that persistent strain in traditional Catholic thinking which has sometimes been described as a species of ecclesiological monophysitism, the tendency, that is, in thinking about the church and its teaching function to focus too exclusively on its divine dimension – eternal, stable, and unchanging – and to underestimate (or repress) the degree of confusion, variability, and sinfulness that goes with its human embodiment as it forges its way onward amid the rocks and shoals of time. That fear of history is surely reflected in those advocates of a seamless ecclesiological continuity who continue to bridle at any suggestion that the work of the Second Vatican Council might conceivably have involved some moments of significant, non-continuous change in the life of the church, change affecting the way in which the ordinary member of the faithful must work out his or her moral and spiritual destiny.[40] And, so far as the interpretation

---

[40] For an example see the essays contained in Matthew L. Lamb and Matthew Levering eds., *Vatican II: Renewal within* Tradition (New York: Oxford University Press, 2008). Cf. Oakley, "History and the Return of the Repressed in Catholic Modernity," in Lacey and Oakley, eds., *The Crisis of Authority in Catholic Modernity*, pp. 29-56 (at 29-32); cf. idem, "Epilogue, pp. 349-55 (at 350-52).

of Vatican II goes, that fear of history is surely not without its harmonics in the somewhat anxious distinction Benedict XVI himself drew in 2005 between what he portrayed as a confusing "hermeneutic of discontinuity or rupture" and a fruitful "hermeneutic of reform."[41]

The second thing that I believe to be characteristic at least of official ecclesiological discourse is a related tendency to seek refuge in abstraction, to deploy a species of theology that seems essentially uncommitted in that it lacks the impetus to translate into concrete reality the implications of its noble but remotely theoretical premises. Here I am endorsing the relevance to our present ecclesiastical discontents of something that the English theologian Charles Davis had to say more than forty years ago in his book *A Question of Conscience* – in effect, his *apologia pro vita sua* seeking to explain and defend his break with the Roman Catholic church. "The present time," he said, and he could well be talking about the early twenty-first century,

> The present time...is characterized by an escape into theology....We are dazzled by what is fundamentally an uncommitted theology, deluged with a spate of theoretical ideas that are not thought through consistently to their ecclesiastical, social and political consequences.[42]

The fate of Vatican II's teaching on episcopal collegiality is a case in point: high-minded affirmations in theory followed by bland denials in practice. That Paul VI should have chosen, for example, and by simple papal fiat, to deny to the bishops assembled at Vatican II, who were

---

[41] "Address of His Holiness Benedict XVI to the Roman Curia," Thursday, December 22, 2005, 5-8. The text is available at http://vatican.va/holy_father/benedict_xvi/speeches/2005/december/documents/hf_ben_xvi_spe_20051222_roman-curia_en.html.

Commenting, not on this particular statement but on "the sociohistorical consequences, intended or unintended, unleashed by the publication and widespread internalization" of Vatican II's *Dignitatis Humanae, Gaudium et Spes, Lumen gentium*, and *Christus Dominus*, the sociologist José Casanova has argued that there is no better confirmation of the significance of those consequences than "the very emergence of a project of Catholic "restoration" based on the premise that" they were "the unexpected and undesired result of a misinterpretation of the original Vatican intent." In that connection, he also claims that the "Ratzinger restoration is trying to revise the meaning of these four documents by stressing," among other things, and "against doctrinal relativism and moral subjectivism," "the duty of the individual conscience to submit to revealed truth and to the objective moral order" – *Public Religions in the Modern World* (Chicago: University of Chicago Press, 1994), pp. 72-73 and 254 n. 3.

[42] Charles Davis, *A Question of Conscience* (London: Hodder and Stoughton, Limited, 1967), p. 236.

possessed of an incomparably rich trove of pastoral experience, the right to decide on matters with such practical pastoral consequences as clerical celibacy and birth control is, in this connection, truly revealing. So, too, is the decision right from the start to treat the Synod of Bishops not as a practical manifestation of collegiality but as a merely advisory assembly, with "its potential deliberative (decision-making) function" deriving not "from God through the episcopal consecration of its members, but from the pope." As such, it hardly fulfils the requirements of "a truly collegial act," as that is defined in the provisions of *Lumen gentium*.[43] If so little leeway is accorded to the college of bishops which, united with its papal head is, according to Vatican II, endowed with supreme ecclesiastical authority in the church,[44] should we really be surprised that what continues to be expected of the ordinary faithful in response to an exercise of the magisterial authority is nothing less than dutiful obedience and religious submission of will and intellect?

President Emeritus
Williams College
Williamstown, Massachusetts
U.S.A.

---

[43] This is the view expressed at Rome in 1967 by Giuseppe Alberigo; see Francis X. Murphy and Gary MacEoin, *Synod 67: A New Sound in Rome* (Milwaukee: 1968), pp. 18-19. Cf. *Apostolica Sollicitudo* Pope Paul's *motu proprio* of September 15, 1965, establishing the Synod of Bishops (printed in Walter M. Abbott, S.J., *The Documents of Vatican II* (New York: Guild Press, 1966), pp. 720-24. Sect. II of that document reads as follows: "By its very nature it is the task of the Synod of Bishops to inform and give advice. It may also have deliberative power, *when such power is conferred on it by the Sovereign Pontiff* (italics mine).

[44] *Lumen gentium*, ch. 3, §22; in Alberigo and Tanner, eds., *Decrees of the Ecumenical Councils*, 2:865-66.

APPENDIX II

SUBSIDIARITY: DOES IT APPLY ALSO TO THE LIFE OF THE CHURCH?

DANIEL DECKERS

AVANT PROPOS[1]

An essay by the emeritus professor in Sociology at Bielefeld, Franz-Xaver-Kaufmann, was published in the April 26, 2010 "Frankfurter Allgemeinen Zeitung." Under the impression wrought by the revelations of countless sexual abuses practiced by clergy on children and others under their protection in the Catholic Church, Kaufmann, one of Germany's most famous sociologists, a member, in the 1960s, of the Joint Synod of the bishoprics in the Federal Republic of Germany, entered into the debate with a provocative thesis about the constitution of the Catholic Church:

> The current media debacle of the Catholic Church threatens to end up as a moral debacle. The moral problem is not the misuse of the children as such, and not the, by today's standards, apparently barbaric forms of discipline, which were in no way typical of the church. It is the Church's inability to recognize or interpret its own pathogenic structures and the consequences of its clerical cover-ups, and thus to draw the practical consequences.[2]

Kaufman does not hesitate to make it clear to his reader just what "pathogenic structures" make revision pressingly necessary. Much must be attributed to the Church's antiquated structure and understanding of itself, the basis of which reaches back to the high Middle Ages, and in which the spirit of absolutism has yet to be overcome. The jurisdiction of the pope and bishops (which remains without veto) has long lost its organizational purpose, and with the growing network of the world-church has become more and more irritating in terms of the lack of an ordered system of governance. The lack of anything resembling a cabinet and the corresponding cabinet disciple is all the more grave as the tasks of the

---

[1] The reworked draft of a text that first appeared under the title: "Subsidiarität in der Kirche. Eine theologiegeschichtliche Skizze" in Jean-Pierre Wils/Michael Zahner (Editors), Theologische Ethik zwischen Tradition und Modernitätsanspruch (FS Holderegger), Freiburg 2005, 269-295.

[2] Franz-Xaver Kaufmann, Moralische Lethargie in der Kirche, [Moral Lethargy in the Church] in: Frankfurter Allgemeine Zeitung 26. April 2010, p. 8.

World Church becomes ever more complex. The current crisis in confidence with regard to the Catholic Church is not so much about its personnel, who have probably never before in history been so qualified and perhaps even morally competent. It concerns the Church as a social institution: "its centralism, its monarchical self-image, its clerical mentality, the inefficiency of its organisation, still operating like a royal court, and the lack of guarantees of rights and fairness in the face of conflictual developments."[3]

Of course, Kaufmann's diagnosis is neither new nor original. The sociologist is, rather, articulating an impression of the idea uniting many of the Church's educated scorners with many passionate Catholics: that the quasi-absolutist constitution of the Catholic Church and its hierarchical governance cannot be, to a large extent, integrated with the legally based cultural structures, at the very least, of Western societies. Or to cite the words of the Canadian philosopher, Charles Taylor:

> The Catholic Church today is in several ways out of phase with the world is wants to speak to.…The disjunction is very evident in the model of authority which the official Church seems to hold to. In spite of the work of Vatican II, there seems to be a regression to a concentration of power and authority at the centre more reminiscent of the Age of Absolutism.[4]

But how could we tackle this regressive lack of development? And do this in such a way that it accords with the doctrine of the Church, or in any case does not come across as in contradiction with its tradition? The magical word that applies here is: subsidiarity.

TRIAD

The Catholic Church recognizes three social principles. They are personality, solidarity and subsidiarity. The meaning of the first two elements is easy to guess. Yet what of the cumbersome term, "subsidiarity" that closes this triad? To what does it apply?

In the past, or more exactly, in 1931, it read: "Just as it is wrong to take from an individual and to give to a group what private enterprise and industry can accomplish, so, too, it is an injustice, a grave evil and a disturbance of right order for a larger and higher organization to arrogate to itself functions which can be performed efficiently by smaller and lower bodies. Every society is, by its nature, subsidiary; the true aim of all social activity should be to help members of the social body, and never to absorb

---

[3] Ibid.
[4] Charles Taylor at the Conference "The Church and the World," Vienna, June 12th, 2011.

or destroy them." So it stands in the encyclical, "Quadragesimo Anno," Number 79.

If the doctrine seems new, for the times it was not. Soviet communism and Italian fascism and soon German National Socialism made masses out of the people and an omnipotent machinery out of the state that pulled the whole world down into ruin. It was then that the hour of subsidiarity struck. Liberal economists and Catholic social ethicists made fruitful use of the concept of the social market society in West Germany.

The belief in the primacy of the smaller unities and the duty of the greater to provide assistance did not, in the meantime, remain merely a German affair. Even in the transformation wrought by Maastricht of the organisation of the European Economic Community (EEC)[5] into a transnationally organized European Union endowed with superior capabilities over the 25 member nations, subsidiarity was gradually adopted as a "regulative idea."[6] The treaty on all religious or confessional elements that was part of the constitution the European nations and presidents signed in December 2004 mentions the originally "Catholic" subsidiarity principle in Article I-11 in a significant context: "Under the principle of subsidiarity, in areas which do not fall within its exclusive competence, the Union shall act only if and insofar as the objectives of the proposed action cannot be sufficiently achieved by the Member States, either at central level or at regional and local level, but can rather, by reason of the scale or effects of the proposed action, be better achieved at Union level."

This all sounds so good that it has already occurred to many people that what the Church, looking at the organisation of the state and society, holds to be sensible and just might also be applied to the Church itself as well. As a 'structural principle', subsidiarity offers an ecclesiology not only from the often pejoratively mentioned pre-conciliar era that speaks of the Church in the image of a societas or of a "corpus Christi mysticum." The affinity of these principles seems not less great to the doctrine of a Church that utilizes the metaphor of the "people of God" or "communion" about itself. And finally, the late Pope John Paul II's doctrinal pronouncement of April 2005 came near to recourse to the subsidiarity principle. Because

---

[5] For more, see Helmut Lecheler, Das Subsidiaritätsprinzip. Strukturprinzip einer europäischen Union, Berlin 1993.

[6] See Frank Ronge, Legitimität durch Subsidiarität: Der Beitrag des Subsidiaritätsprinzips zu Legitimation einer überstaatlichen politischen Ordnung in Europa, Baden-Baden 1998. Since the change of the legal code for Germany that was put into place on December 21 1992, the concept of subsidiarity occurs in article 23, paragraph 1, sentence 1 as follows: "The German Republic cooperates in the realization of a united Europe through the development of the European Union that is committed to the principles of democracy, federalism, social responsibility and the rule of law, and the principle of subsidiarity that provides protection for fundamental rights essentially comparable to that provided for by this basic law."

according to the classic social doctrine of the Church, solidarity together with subsidiarity guarantees the value of the human person. The value of the person holds a place at the center of the approximately 27 years of papal pronouncements on social issues and is the starting point of his commitment to a "culture of life."

Yet what, in theory, should represent a logically compulsory binding of the church's doctrine on social issues and the doctrine of the church is not realized in practice. It looks almost as though the increasing recognition of the subsidiarity principle outside of the Church corresponds to a lessening influence of the principle within it in the area of Church law.

ROMA LOCUTA

The idea of creating a subsidiarity principle that would apply not only in state and society, but also in the Church, is not at all new. It does not stand in the shadows of the controversies over the hermeneutics of the Second Vatican Council and its doctrine concerning the Church. The demand that a higher social community should show "as much restraint as possible, and as much support as necessary" towards a lower one,[7] is in the proper sense not only pre-Vatican II, but not even a theological insight. Oswald von Nell-Breuning, who is seen as the Nestor of Catholic social issues doctrine, defines the general applicability of the subsidiarity principle as follows: As a "rule of responsibility" it is not a "truth of revelation," but an expression of a "primitive idea of reason and experience of the human race."[8]

The principle proclaims the help rendered by the community to its members as a 'duty' ('subsidiarium officium'!) and demands, more specifically, that this aid [s]hould be real and authentic aid, helpful aid, and must not patronize the members or put their autonomy in question, but should rather help lead them to the full unfolding of their God-given talents and capabilities; and thus the aid should, as much as possible, lead to self-help.[9]

From this angle it appeared completely logical that Pope Pius XII in 1946 should make it clear succinctly and bindingly that the subsidiarity principle applied within the Church. In his discourse to the new members of the College of Cardinals, February 20, 1946, he expressed himself in reference to his predecessor Pius XI's encyclical on social teaching:

---

[7] According to Ad Leys striking phrase in Structuring Communion. The Importance of the Principle of Subsidiarity, in: The Jurist 58 (1998), 84-123, here 85.

[8] Oswald von Nell-Breuning, Subsidiarität in der Kirche, in: StZ 204 (1986), 147-157, here 147.

[9] Ibid.

It operates in the heart of humankind, in man's personal dignity as a free creature, in his infinitely elevated dignity as a child of God. The church shapes and educates this man, because only he, developing in harmony with his natural and supernatural life, in the ordered development of his drives and inclinations, his rich resources and his manifold capacities, only he is the origin and at the same time the goal of the life of the human community, and thus even the principle of its equilibrium. Therefore, Paul, the apostle of the people, proclaims that man is no longer an "immature child," going with shaky steps within human society. Our predecessor of blessed memory, Pius XI, in his circular letter concerning the social order, *Quadragesimo anno*, drew from the same thought a practical conclusion, when he gave expression to a universally applicable principle: whatever the individual person can do out of his own initiative and with his own powers, should not be taken from him, and the community should be held to a principle that applies as much to the smaller and subordinate communities and to the greater and higher ones. Because – the wise Pope continues – all social activity is according to its nature subsidiary; it should support the members of the social body, which should never be broken up or absorbed; truly illuminating words that apply to life in all of its stages, and even to the life of the Church, without harming its hierarchical structure.[10]

Lack of any report prevents us from reconstructing how the Cardinals listened to the Pope's discourse – in any case in as much as it related to the theme of subsidiarity. Pius XII, in his discourses to the College of Cardinals pronounced a few months after the end of the Second World War, had called on three German bishops to reject the thesis of the collective guilt of the Germans.[11] This eminently political message really superimposed itself, distantly, on the no less political expressions about subsidiarity in the Church. Thus it is not to be wondered at, that the imaginative impulse of the Pope was taken up primarily not by the bishops so much as by the theologians.

---

[10] Pius XII, Ansprache an das Heilige Kollegium aus Anlaß der Inthronisation der neuen Kardinäle, in: AAS 38 (1946), 141-151, here 144, German: A.F. Utz-J.F.Groner, "Aufbau und Entfaltung des gesellschaftlichen Lebens. Soziale Summe Pius" XII., Bd. 2, Freiburg i.Ue. 1954, Nr. 4080-4111, here 4094.

[11] On the reaction of the Cologne Archbishop Josef Frings, see Norbert Trippen, Josef Kardinal Frings (1887-1978), 2 Bände, Paderborn 2003-2005, Band I, 146f.

Was it because of this that Pius XII came back to this thematic once again ten years later in his remark, on October 5, 1957, in an address to the Second World Congress of the Lay Apostolate?

Furthermore, aside from the small number of priests the relations between the Church and the world require the intervention of lay apostles....In this matter ecclesiastical authorities should apply the general principle of subsidiarity and complementarity. They should entrust the layman with tasks that he can perform as well or even better than the priest and allow him to act freely and exercise personal responsibility within the limits set for his work or demanded by the common welfare of the Church.[12]

We do not know, and we cannot reconstruct the basis for it.

EX NIHILO

It is easy to fill in what post-war theology made out of the Pope's version of subsidiarity as it related to the Church: nothing, or in any case mostly nothing. Arthur-Fridolen Utz OP, the social ethicist in Freiburg, is symptomatic. He lists the occasional expressions of the Pope faithfully in his "Social Summa" of Pius XII, which finally grew to three volumes. He obviously does not make these suggestions his own – in any case not to the point that would give space in his publications to the theme of subsidiarity in the Church. Even the Jesuit Oswald von Nell-Breuning, with Gustav Gundlach an author of the Encyclical "Quadragesimo Anno," did not give any countenance to the idea that the subsidiarity principle applied to the Church. The silence of the theologians was not limited to Germany. Even in the United States, the argument of Pius XII did not seem to strike anybody's fancy.[13]

Were the social ethicists all still caught up in the idea that the connection of subsidiarity was, if not de facto, at least de jure excluded? Or were they unwilling to go forward into mined territory in a climate that did not encourage the kind of free thought in which one could bandy about arguments concerning authority? Or were they so obsessed with the structure of the state and society that they did not have the leisure to think through the effects of the subsidiarity principle on the organization of the Church? A simple answer, one which is even halfway plausible, does not force itself upon us. Only one thing is certain: that on the point of contact between social ethics and systematic theology, no theological debate was kindled, and it seems that in fifty years, hardly anybody seriously bothered.

---

[12] Pius XII, Ansprache an den Zweiten Weltkongreß des Laienapostolats, in: AAS 39 (1957), 922-939, here 926, German: A.F. Utz-J.F.Groner, Soziale Summe (Anm. 10) Bd. 3, Freiburg i.Ue. 1961, Nr. 5980-6012, here 5992.

[13] Compare Joseph A. Komonchak, Subsidiarity in the church: the state of the question, in: The Jurist 48 (1988), 298-349. The 1946 address of the Pope to the newly named Cardinals was even published in an English translation: (The Catholic Mind 44, April 1946).

Otherwise, it would hardly be explicable that young social ethicists like the German Jesuit Anton Rauscher, a student of Gundlach's, saw no occasion to make the teaching of social ethical principles of the Church fruitful for its own self-organisation.[14]

Yet why poke further into the fog of Catholic social teachings to see if back then some ecclesiastical lawyer was concerned to gain some clarity on the issue, remembering that today it is often not much different? And this one was not even in some distant corner of this world, but just a few kilometers from the Vatican. Wilhelm Bertrams SJ, who taught ecclesiastical law in the years after World War II at the Papal University Gregoriana, pushed (in a certain measure ex nihilo) in 1957 in three publications for "the subsidiarity principle in the Church."[15] With a lack of restraint that was nourished not by naiveté, but by a sovereign view of the position of the Church, Bertrams spoke of the philosophical-theological basis of subsidiarity as the "jurisdictional principle of communities," taking as self-evident that it couldn't actually be doubted that this principle was generally applicable within the Church. The social character of the Church as the "social body of Christ" thus had no need to be proven on its own.

And how might this relate to the "proper" character of the Church as a subnatural community, and with the corresponding hierarchical structure of the church?

As according to this the common well-being demands the subsumption and subordination of believers in the church, the

---

[14] Anton Rauscher's article, Subsidiarität-Staat-Kirche, in: StdZ 172 (1962/1963), 124-137 served to rebut evangelical social ethicist Trutz Rendtorf's reproach that the subsidiarity principle was "the representative Catholic social principle in a secularized society," validating the tendency to "observe and secure" the traditional Christian claim to "natural law" as "the right of Church institutions and organizations in particular to self rule." Trutz Rendtorff, Kritische Erwägungen zum Subsidiaritätsprinzip), in: Der Staat 1 (1962), 405-430. Here Rauscher does not explain the pro and contra for the application of the subsidiarity principle in the Church. Seven years later he complained on this score: "unfortunately the emphasis on the subsidiarity principle in the Church that occurred almost two decades before Vatican II did not unleash among Christian sociologists nor within the field of ecclesiology some greater resonance leading to reflection upon its material meaning and consequences for the life of the Church. There even occurred an opposite striving that expanded in the preparatory commissions before the Council." *Anton Rauscher*, Das Subsidiaritätsprinzip in der Kirche, in: JCSW 10 (1969), 301-316, here 303.

[15] De principio subsidiaritatis in iure canonico, in: Periodica de re morali canonical liturgica XLVI (1957), 3-65; Vom Sinn der Subsidiaritätsgesetze, in: Orientierung 21 (1957), 76-79; Das Subsidiaritätsprinzip in der Kirche, in: StZ 160 (1956/1957), 252-267.

narrower community in the more extensive one, the common well-being of the Church thus limits even this subsumption and subordination. The church does not constitute a supernatural community as a totalitarian collective, which extinguishes the self-standing and the independent life of its members.[16]

Almost fifty years after its publication, this thought sounds self-evident, even banal. Yet how must it have seemed in the last years of Pius XII's pontificate, as the Second Vatican Council and the reform of the Codex Iuris Canonici of 1917 was only a bold dream?

But what follows from this? Bertrams formulated a unilateral rule of application: "The more 'intensive' is the supernatural character of a sphere of Church activity, the less does the subsidiarity principle apply; the less the supernatural character is, and the more it is a question of activity of an organisational kind, the more the subsidiarity principle applies."[17] This means: the administration of the material goods of the Church must be the most subsidiarally organized, for instance in the forefront the duties on parish or diocese churches, and the organisational interventions of the Church in the lives of believers and narrower communities like dioceses, parishes or orders are allowed out only in as much as it is a question of the insuring of the "supernatural" life.

That much in the Church, like the ordering of the liturgy, falls to the Holy Chair was, for Bertrams, only logical. This is explained by "the great meaning that the celebration of the liturgy has for the unity of the world church, in truth and in love." A priori, the prescriptions of the universal church have nothing in common with "centralism" – even this pejorative word turns up here in 1957. And centralism in general. In Bertrams' words, that there is a central power like the pope's in the Catholic church is in every respect "a great blessing" – as an effective guarantee of the unity of the Church not less than as a defense against all violence that may befall, for instance, a functionary of the Church. Otherwise, however, the Church only contains as much centralisation as "we ourselves bring about." Yet it would be much more fruitful, according to the clever canonist, "to do away with real grievances in one's own sphere of responsibility oneself, and not wait until a higher power sees itself forced to intervene – in accordance with the subsidiarity principle!"[18] To avoid centralism, this almost prophetic being announces, "is proper to the spirit of personal responsibility, and above all to the readiness for taking on odium and becoming unpopular."[19]

This readiness also distinguished Bertrams, in as much as he presented these thoughts in the journal, "Stimmen der Zeit," to a broad readership. They understood the message well. An impressive sign of the

---

[16] Ibid. 258.
[17] Ibid. 261.
[18] Ibid. 265.
[19] Ibid.

regard that the subsidiarity principle enjoyed among believers as well as thinking Catholics on the eve of the Council is offered by a questionnaire given to 81 Catholic lay people and theologians. This was done by the journal "Wort und Wahrheit" in the German linguistic sphere at the beginning of the sixties of the last century, shortly before the beginning of the advisory preliminary to the Second Vatican Council.[20]

ST PAUL

Goetz, who in 1934 fled the Gestapo to a position at Georgetown University in Washington D.C., where he taught social politics, sociology and social philosophy, wrote, for instance, a letter bluntly demanding "higher flexibility in the church's organisation, with the decentralisation of everything that can be decentralized – for the principle of subsidiarity applies even inside the Church!"[21] Otto von Habsburg-Lothringen was of the same opinion, even if he did not explicitly call upon the subsidiarity principle: "The Church is worldwide. But it is much too defined by centralism. Even in non-Western concerns, it is often aligned with the Roman schema. This results in serious problems. It would thus be desirable that the regions and dioceses be guaranteed the greatest possible autonomy."[22] The youngest son of the last Emperor of the Austro-Hungarian empire made similar arguments – and in order to take two examples from the German sphere, so did the Dean of Cologne, Robert Grosche, a confidante of Cardinal Frings, and Anton Roesen, one of the prominent members of the Archbishop of Cologne Diocese's committee. Grosche brightly opined:

> The work going into the realization of Catholicity will force us to rethink the question of the nature of the 'unity' of the Church. Concern about preserving the unity of the Church ought not to level it down to uniformity, but should, alternatively, also not endanger unity through the strong approach of the oncoming "greatest possible pluralism." It falls especially on those who desire to strengthen the bishop's office and to give greater independence to the dioceses to take care that the connection with the whole is preserved, that the office of St. Peter as the symbol and guarantee of unity is secured and made effective. (…) The monarchical and collegial principles in the leadership

---

[20] Umfrage zum Konzil. Enquete der Zeitschrift Wort und Wahrheit, Freiburg i.Br. 1961.

[21] Ibid. 583.

[22] Ibid. 601. Otto von Habsburg spoke out following this for lifting the celibacy rule in Latin America and consecrating viri probati everywhere as priests. His reasoning consisted in this: "Isn't the survival of the endangered faith more important than disciplinary forms?"

of the church must be mutually bound together in an authentic manner.[23]

For his part, Roesen, in one sentence, grasped the conjunction of the ideas of the mission and decentralisation, pluralistic society and lay associations: "To me it seems that it lies in the power of the Council to seriously impose the subsidiarity principle within the Church."[24] In short: the "sensus fidelium" was obviously completely more "papal" than the theologians and the greater part of the hierarchy.

For it turns out that only a few cardinals and bishops put their weight expressly behind the subsidiarity principle before and during the advisory sessions of the Second Vatican Council.[25] We recall the case of the Cologne Cardinal Frings in particular, who had gratefully taken up the rejection of the collective guilt thesis from Pius XII and in the following years always came back to this expression, a good year before the beginning of the Council sessions, still taking it that the word of the pope defined the application of the subsidiarity principle within the Church. In his pastoral Lenten letter of 1961,[26] which was about "burning social questions," Frings wrote about the life of the Church on the eve of the Second Vatican Council:

> What has been said previously about the necessary cooperation of personality and community (vide over subsidiarity in the state and society), applies analogously to the domain of Church life. The constitution of the Church stems from Christ himself and is therefore untouchable. It is essentially hierarchical, that is, ordered from above to below, but does not renounce democratic elements.

---

[23] Ibid. 595.
[24] Ibid. 661.
[25] Compare what follows to, among others, Komonchak, Subsidiarity (Anm. 13).
[26] Kirchlicher Anzeiger für die Erzdiözese Köln 101 (1961), Nr. 4, 25-35. "The highest pastoral word," according to the afterword, "is to read the Septuagesima and Sexagesima on all holy masses every Sunday. If some abbreviation of the Sexagesima is necessitated on account of Lent in some holy Masses, the sections II and III (and thus not the prescriptions concerning subsidiarity in the Church, D.D.) or one or the other can be left out. In these cases the content of the sections can be briefly announced and reference be made to the possibility of reading them in the Church newsletter." Ibid 35. For the neglect of these important and in the literature up to now not sufficiently utilized texts I thank Dr. Ulrich Helbach, Director of the Historical Archive for the Archbishopric of Cologne.

As a proof Frings referenced the same places in Paul's epistles that Pius XII had used to prove that the subsidiarity principle applies within the Church as well:

> St. Paul in the Letter to the Ephesians expressly underlined the fact that the individual Christian was no longer an immature child, but had come fully into adulthood, to measured by the age in which Christ came into the fullness of his estate. Simultaneously he emphasizes the necessity of community, when he speaks of the building of the body of Christ, through which the particular task of the apostles, prophets, teachers and shepherds, revealed through the spirit, is allotted to the individual. Christ himself however is the head, to whom all must grow, and through whom the whole body is bound together and supported.[27]

Frings did not just leave this point to biblical injunctions, but instead came directly to the point: "The principle of subsidiarity must also apply in the life of the Church, as Pope Pius XII once explained,"[28] he says – and the footnote references the address to the newly appointed Cardinals. But what does it mean? "The Pope alone is not supposed to rule God's Church. Even the bishops have a right to action within the order, as is confirmed in doctrine and practice. They do this firstly in their allotted parish, the diocese. But as to how the bishops, according to a sentence of Pius XII's, are supposed to feel co-responsible for the task of the world wide mission of the Church – they are also called to co-govern the whole Church, which occurs through their participation in the order that assigns them their doctrinal office in the church, as when they cooperate in a general council." What Frings wrote to the "dear members of his arch-diocese" was unambiguously clear. For the Cologne Cardinal not only held up a mirror before "Rome," but also before himself:

> Even the Bishop cannot and should not govern his diocese in a purely patriarchal and unlimited manner....The more the congregation is given responsibility, the better it is for its religious life....If the priest is seen in his teaching and shepherding activities only as an assistant of the Bishop, they still have, in their office, great freedom and self-responsibility....[29]

---

[27] Ibid. 28
[28] Ibid. 28f.
[29] Ibid. 29

ST PAUL

While Bishop Gargitter von Bozen advocated the principle of the decentralisation of the Church in the field before the Council, the Archbishop of Freiberg, Hermann Schäufele, demanded, under the cover of a reference to Pius XII's ideas, more rights for the diocesan bishops as well as for the Bishops' conferences, and Bishop Josef Schoiswohl von Graz-Seckau warned that the Church, declaring the subsidiarity principle binding on society, let it be ineffective for itself.

Most German bishops, meanwhile, conspicuously restrained themselves. The Bishop of Munster, Joseph Höffner, previously the holder of the chair for Christian Social Doctrine at the University of Münster, always referred to the subsidiarity principle in connection with its role and place among the laity.[30] Cardinal Frings, who, from 1960 to 1962, belonged to the Central Preparation Commission of the Council,[31] along with the Münich Cardinal Julius Döpfner, who was one of the four moderators of the Council from September 1963 onward, no longer expressly invoked the subsidiarity principle "within the Church," or at least as far as could be seen.[32]

Still, by the end of the Council there could be found numerous materials in the Council texts that came from the subsidiarity friendly faction, chiefly in the documents about the office of the Bishop (Christus Dominus) and about the Church (Lumen gentium).[33] Yet, the almost classic

---

[30] Joseph Höffner, Laienapostolat und Subsidiaritätsprinzip, in: Yves Congar u.a. (Hgg.), Konzilsreden, Deutsche Übersetzung von Christa Hempel, Einsiedeln 1964, 66-67.

[31] See Trippen, Frings (Anm. 11), Band II, 230-299.

[32] Of course it is still worthwhile to follow in the traces of Dopfner's "Archivinventars der Dokumente zum Zweiten Vatikanischen Konzil," which appeared in 2004, edited by *Guido Treffler* und *Peter Pfister* as Tome 6 of "Schriften des Archivs des Erzbistums München und Freising." For the entry "Subsidiaritity, principle of" the index shows 16 instances.

[33] Chiefly Christus Dominus 8 (The role of the Bishops in the Universal Church) and Lumen Gentium 23 (Relations of particular Churches/Universal Church with the famous "subsistit"-phrasing). Otto Karrer, the theologian, goes so far as to write, with regard to the Church constitution, that subsidiarity moves through the collective text as a guiding idea – "if not in word, then through the thing itself." His analysis of the Council documents, then, is crowded with references to "subsidiarity" features without raising the question even in approximate form; what motive could there have been to basically avoid the concept of subsidiarity? (Otto Karrer, Das Subsidiaritätsprinzip in der Kirche, in: G. Baraúna (Hg.), De Ecclesia. Beiträge zur Konstitution "Über die Kirche" des Zweiten Vatikanischen Konzils, Bd.1, Freiburg i. Br. 1966, 520-546, here 520).

principle of the social order was expressly not related to the Church.[34] Evil to him who evil thinks....

There is no comfort to be found in the fact that two texts expressly mention a structuring principle of state and society: twice in the "Declaration concerning Christian education"[35], and once in the "Pastoral constitution on the Church in the modern world."[36] This was about leaving well enough alone – even though, or perhaps just because, there were among the Conciliar Fathers many a Cardinal who were among the newly named whom Pius XII in 1946 had shocked with his remarks about subsidiarity within the Church. But it was, in any case, hardly a healthy shock.

Also, it did not help things that the Church lawyer, Matthäus Kaiser, who later taught for many years in Regensburg, had, in the epoch of the Council, affirmed the principle of subsidiarity as a "basic structure within the Church" in a lecture in Munich:

> The principle...does not limit the full might of the Church in regard to enforceability, but instead organizes in all cases its competence in the allowed exercise of ecclesiastical authority. It thereby spurs the smaller communities and even the individual members of the church to activity. The realization of the principle of subsidiarity in the constitution of the church can encourage life in the Church and thus serve for the well-being of all.[37]

Yet this goal was not even seen by the Council fathers as being particularly pressing. Or they believed one would be able to achieve it by other means, or even achieve it better. Or it was simply that the majority thought it wiser to refrain from naming the principle of subsidiarity as such, in order not to shock the minority even more – the "institutional-critical

---

[34] Pavel Mikluscák, Einheit und Freiheit. Subsidiarität in der Kirche als Anliegen des Zweiten Vatikanischen Konzils, Würzburg 1995. The book is based on a dissertation under the direction of the dogmatist Peter Walter (Freiburg i.Br.).

[35] Gravissimum educationis 3 (Hilfe der Gesellschaft und des Staate bei der Erfüllung der Erziehungsaufgabe der Eltern) und 6 (Berücksichtung des Subsidiaritätsprinzips in der Organisation des Schulwesens).

[36] In Gaudium et Spes 86 it is written among other things about the international community "under consideration of the principle of subsidiarity we are to order economic relationships globally so that they develop according to the norms of justice."

[37] Matthäus Kaiser, Das Prinzip der Subsidiarität in der Verfassung der Kirche, in: AkKR (1964), 3-13, here 13. The argument is clearly influenced by Wilhelm Bertrams' contribution (Anm. 15).

dynamic,"[38] and the invitation not just to critique of society, but even of the Church, was finally unmistakable.

Who would have wanted to contradict them? The editor of the second edition of the Lexicon for Theology and the Church, among them Karl Rahner SJ, did not even hold it to be advisable, in the nine volumes that appeared in 1964, to include an entry under "subsidiarity." One was referred to the article on "social teachings."[39] The author, Franz Kübler, did not just ignore the meaning of the principle of subsidiarity for the church as an issue, but even ignored the concept. And that, too, is the politics of science.

IN ECCLESIA APPLICANDUM

Thus, the astonishment must have been all the greater when the subsidiarity principle was rediscovered two years after the end of the Council – and once again in Rome. Consultants for that Commission, who were preparing the revision of the 1917 CIC, as requested by Pope Paul VI, now counted this principle of Catholic social teachings among the guiding principles orienting the re-edition of the Codex – a project Pope John XXIII had announced on January 25, 1959, along with the Second Vatican Council. In October 1967, at the suggestion of Pope Paul VI, the document with its guiding principles was submitted by the Codex reform commission to participants of the first annual Bishops' synod under Cardinal Pericle Felici.[40]

Even today it is astonishing what the reformers included: "So that in the *care of souls* the *supreme lawgiver* and the *bishops* may work together and the pastoral role may appear in a more positive light, those faculties to dispense from general laws, which up to now have been extraordinary, shall become ordinary, with reservations to the supreme power of the universal church or other higher authorities only those areas which require an

---

[38] According to Walter Kasper, Zum Subsidiaritätsprinzip in der Kirche, in: IKaZ 18 (1989), 155-162, here 155, referencing to Walter Kerber, Die Geltung des Subsidiaritätsprinzips in der Kirche, in: StZ 202 (1984), 662-672.

[39] LThK2 IX, Sp. 917-920 (Freiburg i.Br. 1964); in the third edition of LThK, Bd. 9, Sp. 1075f. (Alois Baumgartner) it is expressed as always, if also shamefully: "As a social ethical structure and process principle, subsidiarity is formulated firstly as regards the relation of the state and society, with the critical intent, to oppose a totalitarian or even excessive state activities or organizations of the providential kind and support intermediary societal formations. But its approach also requires respect within society and within social sub-systems, including the Church."

[40] Compare Peter Huizing's Subsidiariät in: Conc 22 (1986), 486-490, particularly 487f. and John G. Johnson, Subsidiarity and the synod of the bishops, in: The Jurist 50 (1990), 488-523, esp. 491ff.

exception because of the common good, requires an exception," reads the fourth guiding principle.[41]

The fifth is immediately joined to it conceptually:

> *Careful attention is to be given to the greater application of the so-called principle of subsidiarity within the Church.* It is a principle which is rooted in a higher one because the office of bishops with its attached powers is a reality of divine law. In virtue of this principle one may defend the appropriateness and even the necessity of providing for the welfare especially of individual institutes through particular laws and the recognition of a healthy autonomy for particular executive powers while legislative unity and universal and general law are observed. On the basis of the same principle, the new Code entrusts either to particular laws or executive power whatever is not necessary for the unity of the discipline of the universal Church so that appropriate provision is made for a healthy 'decentralization' while avoiding the danger of division into, or the establishment of national churches.[42]

It is not known even today what set of persons phrased this guiding principle. Thus we cannot also reconstruct how it was composed at that time, or at whose instigation the subsidiarity principle arrived in this guiding text.[43] In any case, we cannot fall back on the texts of the Second Vatican – the council postulated the subsidiarity principle for state and society, but did not apply it to the Church. In spite of which it reappears in Cardinal Frings' sense as a mediating principle between the just autonomy of the Diocesan bishops as the descendants of the apostles and the power of the Pope.[44]

Yet, whatever the bishops wished to communicate, for many, even if the lesser number, the open naming of the subsidiarity principle was a poke in the eye. Why did Cardinal Felici in his address only insist on the limits and dangers, but not the opportunities that could be opened up by the application of the subsidiarity principle to the Church? Did he want to calm down possible opponents? Or did he want to signal that the opponents of subsidiarity in the Church would always find a hearing with him? We do not

---

[41] CIC 1983 Preface, XLIII.
[42] Ibid.
[43] In the preparation phase of Codex Reform Wilhelm Bertrams' "Quaestiones fundamentales Iuris Canonici," Rome 1969, particularly 545-562 is overruled, as well as the contribution of French canonist René Metz "De principio subsidiaritatis in iure canonico," in: Acta Concentus Internationalis Canonistarum Romae diebus 20-25 May 1968 celebrati, Vatican City 1970, 297-310. In 1972 Metz submitted an expanded version of his thesis in French.
[44] Johnson, Synod (Anm. 40) 492.

know. We do know that collectively twelve verbal amendments were given to this theme.[45] It is also certain that the nearly unanimous votes of the succeeding synod left no doubt about this guiding principle, for the subsidiarity principle in the proposed revisions of the book of Canon law was certainly taken into account.

Already in the following year, the Vatican raised the fear that the subsidiarity principle could be applied too far and would make for a pluralism not only in the question of belief and morals, but even in the sacraments, liturgy and church discipline. Endangering the unconditional indivisibility of the Catholic Church. No lesser personage than Pope Paul VI expressed himself in this sense during the first extraordinary Bishops' Synod and demanded at the end of the session further research into the applicability of the subsidiarity principle to the Church.[46] Did not he or his co-workers pay any heed to the pertinent work of Bertrams and the Canonists of the Gregoriana? Or to the "Baugesetze der Gesellschaft" (1968) of Oswald von Nell-Breuning SJ, the specialist in the Church's social teachings, with its small section on subsidiarity in the Church?[47] Note well that the "parole of the laity," "dynamics of movement" – this is all not genuine post-Vatican II social ethical thinking, but instead can be found as a motif even in the pre-Council texts of Canon lawyer Bertrams. Even the sentence was not original by which the subsidiarity concept corresponds "most exactly" to those provisions "which help all to bring all governing powers to their fullest unfolding and to their most effective implementation."[48]

It should thus have been clear to the Pope as well as to all the bishops and to many a theologian what fundamental questions around the subsidiarity principle awaited an answer. Nell-Breuning expressed himself uninhibitedly: "On what occasions the central Roman office must rule unilaterally for the entire Church, and what others fall to individual bishops or bishops' conferences, according to the different relations and needs of the different bishoprics, is not fixed for all time, but constantly changes."[49] It is on this account that, at the request of the Pope, the full session of the Fall 1969 Bishops' synod took up the question of the relationship of the new Bishops' conferences with the Holy See.

CIRCULI MINORI

As one cannot but expect in the face of the little experience of most

---

[45] Komonchak, Subsidiarity (Anm.13), 316.

[46] See on the trajectory and result of Synod deliberations, Johnson, Synod (Anm. 40), 504-513.

[47] Oswald von Nell-Breuning, Baugesetze der Gesellschaft, Freiburg i.Br. 1968, 133-142.

[48] Ibid. 140.

[49] Ibid. 141.

bishops with this new form of collegiality, and with the dogmatic controversialness of this theme, and with the opinions concerning all the questions of the ecclesiological status of Bishops' conferences in relation to how they related to the Holy See, there was also disagreement about the extent to which the properties of these new institutions would diminish the rights of the Diocesan bishops.[50] All such considerations did no harm to the idea of the applicability of the subsidiarity principle. At the end, after strictly formal debates in the plenary session and consultations within the small, linguistically distinct groups ("circuli minori"), the participants of the synod united around not only theoretically recognizing the subsidiarity principle, but even having it observed in the communications of the Holy See with the bishops' conferences and the individual dioceses, for instance through participation in the preparations for Rome's decisions.[51]

One way or another, then – the hour seemed propitious to help to apply the subsidiarity principle in the Church theoretically as well as practically, in all forms. Only it was not used. In systematic theology, in social ethics as well as in the episcopacy, the post-Council call for deeper study of the subsidiarity principle resounded, unheard. Joseph Höffner, who was by now Cardinal and Archbishop of Cologne, did not publicly advocate this suggestion. Also the German Conciliar theologians, from Karl Rahner to Joseph Ratzinger, did not take up Paul VI's proposal.

Instead of which, in April 1970, approximately, Joseph Ratzinger, after brief academic posts in Freising, Münster, Bonn and Tübingen and now Ordinarius in Regensburg, and the Munich political scientist and later Bavarian Minister of Religion and President of the Central Committee of German Catholics, Hans Maier, disputed over "Democracy in the Church."[52] The concept of "subsidiarity" did not appear in the dispute. Instead of this, Ratzinger denounced "Fraternity, the functional understanding of offices, charisma, collegiality, synodochiality, the people of God" as "slogans of conciliar ecclesiology" and at the same time "half way points for the democratisation thesis."[53] Against this, Maier took up for the "assimilation of democracy throughout the Church" for which he had spoken for years[54] – yet even he did not base his argument on Catholic social principles nor did he advocate for the proposal of Pius XII that the subsidiarity principle must apply within the Church.

In contrast, Gustav Ermecke, whose theological morality was deeply rooted in so-called pre-Vatican II thinking, took Paul VI at his word. In 1972 he proposed "thoughts" concerning research into and "current

---

[50] Johnson, Synod (Anm. 40), 507.

[51] Ibid. 513.

[52] The lectures of Ratzinger and Maier before the Catholic society of Publicists were read, newly edited, in 2000: J. Ratzinger/H. Maier, Demokratie in der Kirche. Möglichkeiten und Grenzen, Limburg-Kevelaer 2000.

[53] Ibid. 23.

[54] Ibid. 49.

application" of "the social-philosophical help principle of subsidiarity" within the Church. It even, or so it was said in his article for the magazine, "Neue Ordnung," supported the "principle of universality and membership, from which we draw our conclusion of the validity of subsidiarity and the principle of subsidiarity both in regard to lay and independent orientations."[55]

Ermecke did not even line up against understanding of the principle of subsidiarity as the "principle of decentralization" – valid for the modern state as well as for the Church. "But the tendency to the enlargement of administration and thus the tendency to an "administered world" and the great unlearning of the habit of correctly using one's freedom is simply a symptom of sickness in the Western world," he pessimistically wrote. The Church did not seem to be immune to this sickness, even if it was now on the way to improvement:

> In the Church today we now recognize (unfortunately, rather late) the significance (sic) of regions as independent, long standing forms of the one Catholic credo. Even here the subsidiarity principle has a decisive meaning, with of course different emphases according to its lay or independent orientation.[56]

At the same time in France and Spain two solitary authors dared to take that Pope at his word – and the subsidiarity principle as well. In Spain it was the Canon lawyer José Luis Gutiérrez,[57] in France the Canon lawyer René Metz, who, like Wilhelm Bertrams, was a clever man, an observer schooled within the realities of the Church.[58]

JEU NORMAL

Tensions in the Church between the Pope and the Bishops, the center and the periphery? Nothing could be better! "Le jeu normal de ces tensions est un signe de santé et un facteur d'enrichissement pour l'Eglise."[59] [The

---

[55] Gustav Ermecke, Das Subsidiaritätsprinzip. Gedanken zu seiner Erforschung und heutigen Anwendung, in: NO 26 (1972), 211-221, here 218.

[56] Ibid. 219f. Look also at the author's Subsidiarität und Auxiliarität in der Kirche, in: JCSW 17 (1976), 81-90. On page 89 is found a notable affirmation of the validity of the subsidiarity principle within the Church: "This requires...more basic reflection. Here we, as social theologians in the CST (Christian social teachings), and in ecclesiology, stand at the beginnings."

[57] José Luis Gutiérrez, El princípio de la subsidiaridad y la igualdad radical de los fieles, in: JC 11 (1971), 413-444.

[58] René Metz, La subsidiarité, principe regulateur des tensions dans l'Eglise, in: RDC 22 (1972), 155-176.

[59] Ibid. 173.

normal play of these tensions is a sign of health and a driver of enrichment for the Church.] It is not tensions in the Church as such that are evil, but rather their suppression and refusal to assimilate the living play of forces of the always new historical realities. "Le phénomène actuel de décentralisation que nous constatons dans l'Eglise tend simplement à rétablir l'equilibre des tensions,"[60] [The actual phenomenon of decentralisation that we observe in the Church simply tends to re-establish the equilibrium of tensions], Metz assures his reader at the end of his coolly instructive article, and holds it thus to be only fitting to anchor the subsidiarity principle as a "regulative principle" of that "Lex Fundamentalis" which, at the time, was imagined to be at the core of the Codex reform.

Yes, this was how it really was: Under Wilhelm Aymans and Klaus Mörsdorf the Munich Canon School, as influential as it was tradition conscious, had developed the concept of a Lex Ecclesiae Fundamentalis, a codification of the common law of the universal Catholic Church, under which there was possible space for the legal circles of other traditions such as the united Eastern Churches and the Latin Church, and possibly even for further denominational differences.[61] But here the subsidiarity principle was supposed to become very concrete, for instance in the supplying of the missing elements, traceable "everywhere in the Church," constructing administrative courts on the diocesan and super-diocesan level, "by which the defense of the fundamental rights of believers would have their proper hearing, in order to overcome any suspicion as to the arbitrariness of ecclesiastical acts of administration through their directing agencies."[62]

No sooner said than done: The General Synod of the Bishops of West Germany asked the Pope on November 19, 1975, by an overwhelming majority, "to permit a framework for ecclesiastical administrative court or to invest the German Bishops' Conference with express power to organise an ecclesiastical administrative court."[63] There follows correspondingly articles for incorporating the court of, all together, 128 paragraphs.

---

[60] Ibid. 176.

[61] See the retrospective and the wide-ranging bibliography in W. Aymans, Das Projekt einer Lex Ecclesiae Fundementalis, In: HdbKathKR, 65-71, as well as – post festum reconsidering a "fundamental law" for the Church – Peter Krämer, Universales und partikulares Kirchenrecht, in: Kramer. (Ed.), Universales und partikulares Recht in der Kirche, Paderborn 1999, 47-69.

[62] Dominikus Maier, Verwaltungsgerichte für die Kirche in Deutschland? Von der gemeinsamen Synode 1975 zum Codex Iuris Canonici 1983, Essen 2001 (BzMK 28), 1, and Daniel Deckers, Würdig und recht. Verwaltungsgerichte in der Kirche, in: Frankfurter Allgemeine Zeitung, 21 July 2003, 10.

[63] Gemeinsame Synode der Bistümer in der Bundesrepublik Deutschland, Offizielle Gesamtausgabe, Freiburg 1976, 734-763.

Yet the members of the German synod, the Munich canonists, René Metz and even Gustav Ermecke had all, in the end, backed the wrong horse. Subsidiarity in the Church? Not with Paul VI, and also not with Pope John Paul II. The schema of Lex Ecclesiae Fundamentalis was superceded by the "Schema Novissimum," which was transmitted to John Paul II to implement on April 22 1982.[64] And as the Pope promulgated the new Codex three quarters of a year later with the Apostolic Constitution "Sacrae Disciplinae," the Canons of 1736 to 1763 (Schema novissimum) had been stripped out of Book VII "De processionibus." Together with some confidantes, among whom were Cardinal State Secretary, Agostino Casaroli, Canonists Eugenio Corecco and Zenon Grocholewski, and, as well, German Curia Cardinal Joseph Ratzinger,[65] the Pope had "proofed" the last draft of the new Codex.[66] Which means: the Pope and the Cardinals went through the draft canon by canon and changed, marked through or even composed completely anew numerous definitions – a process that scorned, if not subsidiarity, at least all collegiality.

Subsidiarity as a principle in order to regulate tensions in the Church? Nobody demanded that the work performed by different reform commissions over almost twenty years could bind de jure the Pope and his co-workers. But that John Paul II did not even feel, de facto, bound to the will of the last representatives of the reform commission of the many Bishops' conferences says more about the mentality of this Pope and the influence of the Vatican Curia than all the pleasant sounding oaths of allegiance to the spirit of the Council.

But even if not in practice, did the theory of collegiality, and even subsidiarity stand better in theory? Or in other words: did the legal working of the Latin Church stand within the framework laid down by the Bishops' Synod of 1967, with its guiding principles? A foolish question for it requires that dogmatists, fundamental theologians, or even social ethicists undertook an exhaustive analysis of the new lawbook from the viewpoint of its claims and reality. Nothing lay farther from their minds, be it because they knew no better, or be it because they did not want to know any better.

In his Ph.D. dissertation, Canonist Georg Bier in 2001[67] for the first time put into question the dominant opinion that the 1983 CIC contained central material in the spirit of the Council and strengthened the legal position of the Diocesan bishops. His thesis: "The general codical

---

[64] In the Preface to the CIC/1983 (LXI) it is simply (by omission) meant that the Canons of the LEF schema had to be incorporated "by reason of the condition of the material" into the Codex.

[65] See Maier, Verwaltungsgerichte (Anm. 62), 69.

[66] "The Pope proofed it in his eminent person with the help of some experts and under the injunction of the proposition of the Papal Commission for the revision of the Codex Iuris Canonici ..." CIC 1983/Preface LXI.

[67] Georg Bier, Die Rechtsstellung des Diözesanbischofs nach dem Codex Iuris Canonici von 1983, Würzburg 2001 (FKRW 32).

definitions concerning the Episcopacy and the office of the diocesan bishop as well as the normative elaboration of these offices in the codical definitions designate the diocesan bishop legally as the Papal officer."[68] Here, the canonist takes his ground against the ruling consensus in systematic theology. Yet his arguments cannot be dismissed out of hand. Did not circumstances alone make one suspicious about the fact that the Codex's subsidiarity principle was not introduced anywhere but in the 1967 guiding principles, much less defined as norma nomans? As so often in theology, here, too, the wish was father to the thought.

Already in 1988, five years after the promulgation of the CIC, the American canonist Thomas J. Green had reconstructed the fundamental features of the history of this increasing suppression.[69] In a first evaluation of the treatment of the subsidiarity principle during the revision phase of the ecclesiastical canon, he showed that the work of the reform commissions as well as on the Codex itself must have assumed that the validity of the subsidiarity principle within the Church was never, "in principle," put into question. But in the meantime, during the course of deliberations, the upper hand was gained by those who saw in the comprehensiveness granted to this social principle a danger for the unity of the Church.[70] In the end, this group had Pope John Paul II on their side, who after taking office in October 1978 had sufficient time to put his stamp on the Codex Reform. And not only this: in looking back over the Pontificate of John Paul II it is evident that centralisation and not respect for subsidiarity is simply its signature. Because not only the new book of canon law, but even the post-codical law, which Pope John Paul II implemented either personally or had Roman Curia do in his name, can hardly satisfy the claim to having carried out subsidiarity or the subsidiarity principle as the structural principle of the Church.

CAUSA FINITA?

A collection of essays in commemoration of the 70th birthday of Josef Homeyer, Bishop of Hildesheim, appeared in the fall of 1999. Walter Kasper, the long-time professor of dogmatics in Münster and Tübingen and, for almost a decade, the Bishop of Rottenburg-Stuttgart, also contributed a text.[71] In the first part of his contribution Kasper dealt with the theology of the Bishop's office according to Aquinas; in the second part he dealt the

---

[68] Ibid. 376.

[69] T. J. Green, Subsidiarity during the Code revision process: Some initial reflection, in: The Jurist 48 (1988), 771-799.

[70] According to the conclusion I drew from Green's accurate presentation, Code revision (Anm. 69).

[71] Walter Kasper, Zur Theologie und Praxis des bischöflichen Amtes, in: Werner Schreer/Georg Steins (Hg.), Auf neue Art Kirche sein (FS Homeyer), München 1999, 32-48.

current tendencies of ecclesiastical governance under Pope John Paul II. Kasper presented the thesis that the Catholic Church had undertaken a "theological restoration of Roman centralism" at the end of the 20th century.[72] A hard judgment that, according to its reprinting in the "Frankfurter Allgemeinen Zeitung"[73] called attention in multiple ways to Joseph Ratzinger, the prefect of the Vatican Congregation for the Doctrine of the Faith.[74]

Yet Kasper, who had at this point been the Bishop of Rottenburg-Stuttgart for ten years, knew of what he spoke. Fourteen years had gone by since the fall of 1985, when he had, for instance, taken part as a private secretary in the Extraordinary Synod of Bishops that, in carrying out the wish of the Pope, dealt with the end of Vatican II exactly twenty years before, with the theme "communion" in the Church.[75] Even then the subsidiarity principle was debated – but in a paradoxical manner. In the final report of the synod there is a reference to Pope Pius XII's talk before the new Cardinals in 1946, reading: "It is recommended to begin a research program over the question of whether the subsidiarity principle that applies in human society also finds application within the Church, and, if so, to what extent and with what sense the application is possible and eventually necessary."

Thus, the subject that a Pope affirmed in 1946 ("that" the subsidiarity principle must be valid in Church), is represented by the members of the 1985 Bishops' Synod as a possibility – and so we can jump around with learned statements when it suits us. Or...not? The Canon lawyer Peter Huizing[76] has sought to solve this paradox with the suggestion that the formulation of the Synod could be so read that the proponents of the subsidiarity principle could always posit against the sceptics or the manifest opponents that they also openly clung to the possibility that it also possessed validity in the Church, while more extensive formulations would obviously not obtain a consensus – and, before everything else, were not desired, at least by the Roman Curia. In a lecture before the Cardinals immediately before the opening of the Bishops' synod, did not Jerome Hamer, the long-time secretary of the Congregation for the Doctrine of the Faith, represent the principle of subsidiarity as tendentially irreconcilable

---

[72] Ibid. 44.

[73] Daniel Deckers, Restauration des römischen Zentralismus, in: Frankfurter Allgemeine Zeitung, 31 December 1999, p. 12.

[74] See chiefly Joseph Ratzinger, Die große Gottesidee "Kirche" ist keine ideologische Schwärmerei, in: Frankfurter Allgemeine Zeitung 22 December 2000, 46.

[75] See W. Kasper, Zukunft aus der Kraft des Konzils. Die Außerordentliche Bischofssynode, 85. Die Dokumente mit einem Kommentar, Freiburg 1986.

[76] Huizing, Subsidiarität (Anm. 40), 487.

with the hierarchical structure of the Church?[77] The Bishops' synod did not yet go so far – but by 1985, sympathizers with strong decentralisation and a clear division of competences in the Church accompanied by a deepening of collegial elements in the governance of the Church were obviously on the defensive. They couldn't call upon Council texts, on the new law book, and not even on academic theology

It also did not help that briefly before, in 1984, the well-known German social ethicist, Walter Kerber, had, ex nihilo, given himself the role of the defender of the Subsidiarity principle in the Church in the journal "Stimmen der Zeit" [Voices of the Time].[78] "As a universal, which expresses something about the nature and idea of every social action, it does not countenance any exceptions. It is also valid for the Church, if and in as much as it is regarded as a visible, institutionally conceived community." While that sounds banal, yet it was revolutionary – at least in theory – for after Kerber unfolded the argument that even the division of competences in the church was subject to the requirements of subsidiarity[79] there occurs the parting proof: "But this would also lead us too far astray in this framework."[80]

Two years later Oswald von Nell-Breuning SJ, the highly esteemed scholar of Catholic social ethics doctrine, took up this issue – once again in the "Stimmen der Zeit," and with the same affirmative tendency.[81] "Because the Church is not exhausted by being a social structure, but rather is so while being at the same time essentially more than a social structure, it pays to carefully distinguish the Church as a social structure ('Ecclesia ut societas') and as a Church, in as much as it is more than simply a social structure ('Ecclesia ut mysterium') and to avoid the error, that what is valid for the 'Ecclesia ut societas' can be blindly extended or transposed to the 'Ecclesia ut mysterium'. By definition, the subsidiarity principle only has to do with the 'Ecclesia ut societas'…" So far, so good. Yet the sentence goes on: "…which clearly does not exclude the fact that implications of analogous aspects of it can also be appropriate to the 'Ecclesia ut mysterium'…" And the sentence goes farther: "…on this very interesting

---

[77] Ibid. Hamers "Discurs à la reunion plenière" was published in the extraordinary Synod. Celebration de Vatican II, Paris 1986, 598-604.

[78] Kerber, Geltung (Anm. 38).

[79] "The legal assumption lies firstly with the individual or with smaller sub-communities, for they possess the ability, to govern their affairs self-responsibly without interference from above. The necessity of prescribing a uniform regulation or to brandish a decision from a higher office requires a reason. If such a reason is not forthcoming, the legitimacy of the measures is cast, at least, in doubt." Ibid. 671.

[80] Ibid. *Oskar Köhler* was definitely not the first to want to go into this "framework" in Der Kirche eigene "Sichtbarkeit," Zur Frage nach dem Subsidiaritätsprinzip in der Kirche, in: StdZ 202 (1984), 858-601.

[81] Nell-Breuning, Subsidiarität (Anm. 8).

question, which lies outside our theme, we will not enter."[82] Lies outside of our theme?

Yet, even if Kerber and Nell-Breuning had been more concrete, their explications had come a little late. In any case, late for Vatican II, later for the Codex Reform. The Canonist Jean Beyer, like Bertrams a teacher at the Gregorian University, but of another kind, hit off the tone of the time when he tried to substitute the unlikely, ambiguous concept of "iusta autonomia" for the subsidiarity principle "within the Church."[83]

Or was it that Nell-Breuning and Kerber believed that they had to engage in the same old battles in order to guard against new dangers that were seeded by the polyvalent ecclesiology of the Council and in the new Church law code, and that became manifest in the first years after the Pontificate of John Paul II? This assumption cannot be discarded out of hand, even if Nell–Breuning conceived of his exposition of the subsidiarity principle in the Church as an amicable answer to the request of the 1985 Bishops' Synod, which wanted to re-think this theme fundamentally.[84] Because even Walter Kasper, at that time still a Professor at Tübingen, but attached by higher authorities as a special secretary of this Synod, had perceived what the hour had brought forth. In the Herder-Correspondence two years after the Special Synod there appeared a programmatic article under the title, "Mystery does not annul the Social."[85]

Two years later, recently named by Pope John Paul II Bishop of Rottenburg-Stuttgart, Kasper came back to this theme in the "International Catholic Journal Communio." Yet again he publicized for respecting the principle of subsidiarity as the "competence rule" per se for the Church.[86] More than this, Kaspar, in contrast to Kerber and Nell-Breuning broke the taboo by naming the Church as a "concrete field of applications" of the principle of subsidiarity. The connections that he drew reached impressively from the respect for the fundamental rights of individual Christians over to the rights of individual Charismatics of the orders and other spiritual

---

[82] Ibid. 148f.

[83] Jean Beyer, Principe de subsidiarité ou "juste autonomie" dans l'Eglise, in: NRTh 108 (1986), 801-822; ders., Das Subsidiaritätsprinzip – auch für das Recht der Kirche? In: Franz Furger, Josef Pfammatter (Hgg.), Die Kirche und ihr Recht, Zürich 1986, 113-137; ders., Le principe de subsidiarité. Son application dans l'Eglise, in: Gregorianum 69 (1988), 436-459. In the preceding contribution, Johannes Schasching, SJ showed himself to be very cautious with respect to the application of the subsidiarity principle: "It is not the sociologist's job (sic) to reflect over the theological and canonical presuppositions [as they effect its application – D.D.] Ibid. 413-433, here 431.

[84] Nell-Breuning, Subsidiarität (Anm. 8), 148.

[85] W. Kasper, Der Geheimnischarakter hebt den Sozialcharakter nicht auf. Zur Geltung des Subsidiaritätsprinzips in der Kirche, in: HerKorr 41 (1987), 232-236.

[86] Kasper, Kirche, (Anm. 38), 163.

communities, respect for the rights of the laity, the determination of relations between the local and the universal Church over the theme of inculturation up to the defense of the legitimate autonomy of theology. [87]

A delegate of the German Bishops' Conference, the Mainz Bishop Lehmann, now participated in the discussion, while still in the habitually discrete way.[88] And in the United States, the Church lawyer, John G. Johnson, reconstructed the Synod of Bishops dealings with the theme of subsidiarity.[89]

An astonishing fact: In the six years between 1984 and 1990 there appeared more articles expressly dealing with the theme of "subsidiarity" in the Church than in the twenty previous years. The theme and the concept seemed more contemporary than ever. Could it be that theologians, dogmatists, canonists and social ethicists all at once became conscious that the sorry state within the Church was somewhat due to the fact that the validity of the subsidiarity principle was all this time being openly disputed by some, by many others sovereignly ignored, and that many do so still today?[90]

---

[87] Ibid. 160ff. Kasper's reference is also noteworthy and heartening, that the demand for respect for the subsidiarity principle should not be confused with the demand for "democratisation and decentralisation." "These concepts are so problematic that it is best to leave them entirely aside in this discussion." Ibid.

[88] Karl Lehmann, Anmerkungen zu Sinn und Gebrauch des Subsidiaritätsprinzips, in: Caritas 91 (1990), 112-117. Reproduced is a "short paper" that Lehmann gave on November 10 1989 before an audience at the Catholic Office in Mainz, which circles around the somewhat sybilline idea: "It [the principle of subsidiarity] is not a glib phrase that makes superfluous the careful analysis of the real state of affairs to which we relate it and the different regulations that are necessary in the face of a complex reality." Ibid. 116.

[89] Johnson, Synod (Anm. 40).

[90] One can find numerous other works within systematic theology that implicitly relate to this problematic. Peter Hünermann, Peter Neuner and Hermann-Josef Pottmeyer are some of the key authors that have produced extensive studies. Franz König, Cardinal of Vienna, even gave his name as an editor to the book, "Zentralismus statt Kollegialität" (Düsseldorf 1990). Further publications arrived in the nineties. The trail blazing before all others is by Hermann-Josef Pottmeyer, Die Rolle des Papsttums im Dritten Jahrtausend, Freiburg i. Br. 1999 (QD 179) and John R. Quinn, Die Reform des Papsttums, Freiburg i. Br. 2001 (QD 188). In the domain of Church law one must name the sweeping work of Ad Leys, Ecclesiological Impacts of the Principle of Subsidiarity, Kampen 1995 as much as – more succinctly – handlicher – his Communion (Anm. 7.); Paul-Stefan Freiling, Das Subsidiaritätsprinzip im kirchlichen Recht, Essen 1995 (derived from a dissertation by the State Church lawyer Alexander Hollerbach (Freiburg i.Br.); among the (much fewer) social ethical publications we can name: Franz Josef Stegmann, Subsidiarität in der Kirche. Anmerkungen zu einem gravissimum princium in der katholischen

There were enough grounds for this concern. In Western Europe there had been a series of spectacular bishop appointments that nourished the suspicion that the Pope and the Curia wanted to fix their stamp on a few insubordinate Bishops' conferences. In 1979 the Netherlands Bishops Gijsen and Simonis, who had backed the Papal line since the sixties; in Austria, since 1986, Hans Hermann Groer and soon also his suffragen Bishop, Kurt Krenn; and in Germany the Cologne metropolitan capital, after many unsuccessful ballots, acceded to the demand of the Pope and changed its status to elect the Berlin Cardinal Joachim Meisner to the Archbishop's seat. Yet can we suppose these events really had as a consequence a new phase of theological reflection over the subsidiarity concept, superceding all that had gone before quantitatively as well as qualitatively? Or was it a premonition of what was to come?

COMMUNIO

Flash forward again to 1999, to the middle of Walter Kasper's exposition of the excessive power of centralism in the World church. The Bishop of Rottenberg did not conceal the fact that this development was instigated by the teachings of Vatican II. Even after Vatican II the Bishop of Rome "by the force of his office as the representative of Christ and the universal Church [has] full, supreme and universal power that he is always free to exercise," which meant looking to Peter's seat as the visible principle and foundation of the unity of the plurality of Bishops. But at the same time, according to Kasper, the Council affirmed that Bishops too as members of the College of Bishops were invested with care for the universal church. "But the question is," according to Kasper, "whether the authority and the initiative of the College is *practically* a fiction: which it becomes if the Pope can hamstring them every time, when conversely he can decide and act everytime also without the formal cooperation of the College – not as a *persona privata*, but rather as the head of the College."[91]

In 1999 the question was as easy to answer as it is in 2011. Not only has the authority and initiative of the College over the past decades become a sheer fiction; but also de jure, for according to the 1983 Codex, the Pope is not instructed to be in "communion" with the episcopacy. Thus, the call upon the subsidiarity principle is only a counterfactual cry for help, if even a de jure senseless one. Is the Pope supposed to feel his actions bound by this principle, where he is not even bound by the law that he himself institutes, and be it – as in the "Cologne affair" – a contract binding under

---

Kirche, in: Wilhelm Geerlings/Max Seckler (Hgg.), Kirche sein (FS Pottmeyer), Freiburg i.Br. 1994, 361-371, as well as Hans Halter, Widerspruch zwischen katholischer Soziallehre und kirchlicher Praxis? Diakonia 22 (1991), 151-159.

[91] Kasper, Theologie (Anm. 71), 42.

international law?[92] Classical political philosophy understood the idea that the monarch was not bound to the prevailing law and could act contrary to it as an unfailing mark of tyranny, thus of arbitrary rule. Pope John Paul II and some of his closest co-workers in the Curia were not very impressed by this circumstance.

For instance, the German Curial Cardinal Joseph Ratzinger, who Pope John Paul II called to the head of the Vatican Congregation on the Doctrine of Faith in 1981, and who was chosen as John Paul II's successor under the name Benedict XVI in April 2005. In 1993, as a Curial Cardinal this self-conscious, mission conscious dogmatist in one gesture put an end to the "abusive" interpretations of communio-ecclesiology. In a letter dated May 28 1992 he affirmed for the Congregation that the correct interpretation of communio is tied into the idea that the universal church has ontologically, by its very existence, as also chronologically, that is to say, in the historical process, priority before its ecclesiastical parts.[93] If one follows this interpretation, then one must not imagine the emergence of the church as an organic process, in which the default unity of the Church unfolded in the appearance of different churches and therewith in a mutual play of forces. The Church did not develop from "under" but instead from above. What the churches are and what they have is not out of their independent right, and from thence in community one with the other. What they are and what they have comes always only from above.

One can criticise this interpretation as historically fallacious and, more, be of the view that here we find a tendentious totalitarian form of theological thinking in power, namely the doctrine of ideas that goes back to Plato. One can even go further and affirm that Joseph Cardinal Ratzinger as well as Pope Benedict XVI is a singularly pure representative of this form of thinking and has, along with the writing of the Congregation of Faith, made his binding on the entire Church, to the point that thereafter other, competing forms of thinking no longer have any justification. And one can go still further and hold that the destruction of other forms of thought is not only in bad taste, but also a direct betrayal of theological tradition. In the history of theology there has scarcely ever been one "school," but, quite officially, many "schools" that feed partially from distinct philosophical traditions. That leads to strong disputes, but even more to a very fruitful discussion, stimulating belief as well as reason.

Yet this should obviously not be – which Kasper's thesis of a historically unique concentration of power in the Church and the thus thoroughly disrespectful attitude to the subsidiarity principle demonstrated unintentionally, but also unambiguously.

---

[92] Cf. Gerhard Hartmann, Der Bischof. Seine Wahl und Ernennung. Geschichte und Aktualität, Graz 1990

[93] Kongregation für die Glaubenslehre, Communionis notio. Schreiben an die Bischöfe der katholischen Kirche über einige Aspekte der Kirche als Communio (Verlautbarungen des Apostolischen Stuhls, 109).

CAUSA FINITA!

But it is not at all unintentionally that the concept of subsidiarity is found in one of the few doctrinal texts in which the question of the constitution of the Church is discussed: the "Post-Synodal Apostolic Exhortation Pastores Gregis" signed by Pope John Paul II on October 16 2003, on the symbolically loaded 25th anniversary of his election to the position of Pope.

There are many places in the text that refer to the debates that were conducted during the 10th ordinary General Assembly of the Bishops' Synod from September 30 to October 27 2001, dedicated to the theme, "The Bishop as the Servant of the Gospel of Jesus Christ for the Hope of the World." In Nr. 56, accordingly: "Vatican II taught," it reads unconditionally, "that the bishop, following the Apostle in the diocese for the care of which he has been entrusted, stands by his own, ordinary, independent and immediate authority, as is required for the practice of his pastoral office. The authority that is invested in the Pope by the power of his office, to be held by himself or in some cases by another authority, remains thereby forever and in all things undisturbed."[94] That there is a certain tension between both statements has, ever since, been hidden from nobody. And as well, that the task of the Extraordinary Bishops' Synod of 1985, to study the possible validity of the subsidiarity principle "even in the church," was not yet fulfilled.

This desidera could have stood in the background when "in the hall of the Synod...the question was raised...whether the relationship that exists between the Bishop and the supreme authority of the Church, not be treated in the light of the subsidiarity principle, in particular in light of the relations between the Bishop and the Roman Curia."[95] Was it Walter Kasper, who in the meanwhile had been raised to the presidency of the Papal Advisory Council on the Requirements for Christian Unity, who threw out this inflammatory word into the Session? We do not know, but the following sentence could indicate an intervention of Kasper's: "Therefore the wish exists to form these relations in the sense of a *Communio*-ecclesiology, respecting current competencies and thus under the realisation of a greater decentralisation. It has also been requested that we reflect on the possibility of applying this principle to the life of the Church, whereby in any case the fact must be born in mind that the constitutive principle for the practice of bishop's authority is the hierarchal community of individual bishops with the Pope and with the Bishops' Collegium."

So much for the starting point. The Pope's answer and the authors with whom the gravely ill Pontiff worked left nothing more to wish for, at least as regards clarity: "As we know, the subsidiarity principle was

---

[94] http://www.vatican.va/holy_father/john_paul_ii/apost_exhortations/documents/hf_jp-ii_exh_20031016_pastores-gregis_ge.html., Nr. 56

[95] Ibid.

formulated by one of my predecessors of blessed memory, Pius XI, for civil society." That Pius XI had also advised it for the Church was pretty rudely set aside. "The second Vatican Council never used the term 'subsidiarity'. Agreed. "Yet it has emboldened a sharing among the organs of the Church and thus set in motion a new reflection on the theology of the episcopacy, which has borne fruit in the concrete application of the principle of collegiality in the community of the Church." One could believe this – but one does not have to. "In regard to the practice of the authority of the bishops, the Synod fathers have opined that the concept of subsidiarity proves to be ambiguous. They have thereup insisted that the nature of the authority of the bishops must be theologically deepened in the light of the *Communio*-principle." Which means, in plain language: Causa finita.

PROFESSIO FIDEI

The doctrinal boundaries drawn around the communio-idea, the interpretation of which veils, under the multiple means and the false spiritualisation and harmony, the true relations of power,[96] is meanwhile a petitesse in comparison to what we now must bring into closer view. If Ratzinger's dogmatic intervention scorns the social principle of subsidiarity formally as well as substantially, then the so-called post-codical law should be seen as a direct effort to force the 'collegial' elements of Church law into the background, and to sharpen the primatial elements in leading the church back to the standards of Vatican I.

The up to now unresolved conflict within theology over the hierarchical place of the Bishops' conferences is characteristic of the repression of the collegial elements, as that place has been differentiated from the "supreme authority of the Church" as much as from the legal standing of the diocesan bishops. With clear words, Walter Kasper appealed to Pope John Paul II against the concepts in Motu proprio "Apostolos Suos" (21 May 1998), where the Bishops' conferences are represented as not partial realisation of the collegiality of the episcopate, but instead are basically useful forms of work and organisation.[97]

---

[96] Walter Kasper demonstrates correctly in this connection that the Council did well, "to not to ground the concept of societas on the divine-human natural structure, as the "progressives" at the time wished, but instead to preserve its particula veri (see "Lumen gentium", 8 [2. sentence]; "Dignitatis humanae", 13 [2 para.]), which in the framework of today's altered problem constellation once again gives many progressives with their construction of the sociological dimension of the Church a *relative* right." (Kasper, Geheimnischarakter [Anm. 85], 235).

[97] That this evaluation in ecclesiology has not been universally shared for some time can be traced in: Hubert Müller/Hermann Josef Pottmeyer (Hgg.), Die Bischofskonferenz. Theologischer und juridischer Status, Düsseldorf 1989.

The sharpening of the primatial elements of the leadership of the Catholic Church under John Paul II went far over the jurisdictional boundaries on the primate and on papal infallibility drawn by the First Vatican Council, not stopping, moreover, to minimize the role of the Bishops' conferences.[98] But even more, the greatest degree of the overextension of papal power was reached in the introduction of new formulas of the confession of faith ("Professio fidei") and the oath of fidelity (Iusiurandum fidelitatis) on January 8 1990. Both were prepared long before, and were personally blessed by Pope John Paul II on July 1 1988.

There is a good tradition in the church that assumption of office by certain officials is accompanied by the legal duty to declare the confession of faith (c. 380 CIC and c. 833 CIC). Since 1990, every official must not only declare the confession of faith, but all the three principles. According to this, they are firstly held to accept and preserve what the Church as its divinely revealed doctrine affirms. Secondly, all persons declaring the new professio fidei declares to hold and preserve all and every instance of what the Church "definitively" lays down in the domain of the doctrines of faith and morals. These doctrines are accordingly not published, but are defined by the Pope or the Bishops' Collegium in the practice of their infallible doctrinal office. The third pledge is conclusive religious obedience of the will and the understanding for all things demanded by the doctrinal office of the universal church according to Canon 752 CIC in those teachings that are not definite.

The Church lawyer Norbert Lüdecke has described the sense of this process as follows.[99] The formal act designated as a "confession of faith" includes the "declaration of adherence to doctrines...to which there is no adherence of faith in the authentic sense, which is true about the second and more certainly for the third clause," according to Lüdecke in addition to canonists Heribert Schmitz and Ladislaus Örsy.[100] This process – as well as the CIC itself – serves only one goal in the eyes of the Church lawyers: the authority of the Church's doctrinal office is thereby elevated. Obedience is

---

Therein is a very informative contribution by Franz-Xaver Kaufmann, Die Bischofskonferenz im Spannungsfeld von Zentralismus und Dezentralisierung.

[98] In regard to the Synod's modus operandi, see Johnson, Synod (Anm. 40), 488-491.

[99] See for a comprehensive treatment Lüdeckes's dissertation, "Die Grundnormen des katholischen Lehrrechts in den päpstlichen Gesetzbüchern und neueren päpstlichen Äußerungen in päpstlicher Autorität", Würzburg 1997 (FZKW 28) as well as the author's abridgment, Der Codex Iuris Canonici von 1983: "Krönung des II. Vatikanischen Konzils?," in: Hubert Wolf/Claus Arnold, Die deutschsprachigen Länder und das II. Vatikanum, Paderborn 2000, 209-237.

[100] Lüdecke, Grundnormen (Anm. 99), 443.

There still remains what Franz-Xaver Kaufmann has illuminatingly said before the cases of abuses shook the Catholic Church in the United States and in Europe to their foundations: "Excess of centralization is a characteristic defect of hierarchical organisations and often results in a substantial loss of efficiency. This is especially true of organizations which render personal services."[103]

Journalist/Theologian
Verantwortlicher Redakteur für "Die Gegenwart"
Frankfurter Allgemeine Zeitung
Frankfurt, Germany

---

[103] Franz-Xaver Kaufmann, The Principle of Subsidiarity viewed by the Sociology of Organizations, in: The Jurist 48 (1988), 275-291, here 290.

BIBLIOGRAPHY

Adams, Edward, 'The Coming of the Son of Man in Mark's Gospel', *Tyndale Bulletin*, 56 (2005).
——, *The Stars Will Fall from Heaven: Cosmic Catastrophe in the New Testament and Its World [LNTS 347]* (London and New York: T & T Clark/Continuum, 2007).
Adela Yarbro, Colin, *Mark* (Minneapolis: Fortress Press, 2007).
——, 'Mark's Interpretation of the Death of Jesus', *JBL*, 128 (2009).
Agamben, Giorgio, *State of Exception* (Chicago: University of Chicago Press, 2005).
——, *State of Exception*, trans. by Kevin Attell (Chicago and London: University of Chicago Press, 2005).
——, *The Church and the Kingdom* (Seagull Books, 2012).
——, *The Kingdom and the Glory: For a Theological Genealogy of Economy and Government* (Stanford: Stanford University Press, 2011).
Ahn, Yong-Sung, *The Reign of God and Rome in Luke's Passion Narrative: An East Asian Global Perspective* (Leiden: Brill, 2006).
Akveld, W. F., *De Romeinse Curie. De Geschiedenis van Het Bestuur van de Wereldkerk* (Nijmegen: Valkhof Pers, 1997).
Alberigo, Guiseppe, ed., *Conciliorum Oecumenicorum Generaliumque Decreta I: The Oecumenical Councils from Nicaea I to Nicaea II (325-787)* (Turnhout: Brepols, 2006).
Alison, James, *Broken Hearths and New Creations: Intimations of a Great Reversal* (London: Darton, Longman and Todd, 2010).
——, *Faith Beyond Resentment: Fragments Catholic and Gay* (London: Darton, Longman and Todd, 2001).
——, *Knowing Jesus* (London: SPCK, 1998).
——, *Living in the End Times: The Last Things Reimagined* (London: SPCK, 1997).
——, *On Being Liked* (London: Darton, Longman and Todd, 2003).
——, *Raising Abel: The Recovery of the Eschatological Imagination* (London: SPCK, 2010).
——, *The Joy of Being Wrong: Original Sin through Easter Eyes* (New York: Crossroad, 1998).
——, *Undergoing God: Dispatches from the Scene of a Break-In* (London: Darton, Longman and Todd, 2006).
Allen, Pauline, *Sophronius of Jerusalem and Seventh-Century Heresy* (Oxford: Oxford University Press, 2009).
Anderson, Douglas, 'Peirce's Common Sense Marriage of Religion and Science', in *The Cambridge Companion to Peirce*, ed. by Cheryl Misak (Cambridge: Cambridge University Press, 2004).

Aquino, Frederick D., *Communities of Informed Judgement: Newman's Illative Sense and Accounts of Rationality* (Washington DC: Catholic University of America Press, 2004).
Athanasius, *Acta Conciliorum Oecumenicorum*, II (ACO2) (Berlin, 1984).
———, *Acta Conciliorum Oecumenicorum*, II (ACO2) (Berlin, 1992), II.2.
Atkins, E. M., 'Cicero', in *The Cambridge History of Greek and Roman Political Thought* (Cambridge: Cambridge University Press, 2000).
Bacht, H., 'Vom Lehramt Der Kirche Und in Der Kirche', *Catholica*, 25 (1971).
Barth, Karl, *Church Dogmatics*, ed. by G. W. Bromley and T. E. Torrance, 4 vols. (Edinburgh: T & T Clark, 1956).
———, *Die Kirchliche Dogmatik 1*, 4 vols. (Zurich: Zollikon, 1936), I.
———, *Die Kirchliche Dogmatik 2*, 4 vols. (Zurich: Zollikon, 1936), II.
———, 'The Humanity of God', in *The Humanity of God* (London: Collins, 1961).
Baum, Gregory, 'My Vatican II', *The Tablet*, 2013.
Beaton, Richard, 'Isaiah in Matthew's Gospel', in *Isaiah in the New Testament*, ed. by Steve Moyise and Maarten J.J. Menken (London and New York: T & T Clark/Continuum, 2005).
———, *Isaiah's Christ in Matthew's Gospel [SNTSMS 123]* (Cambridge: Cambridge University Press, 2002).
———, 'Messiah and Justice: A Key to Matthew's Use of Isaiah 42:1-4?', *JSNT*, 75 (1999).
Begoglio, Jorge Maria, *La Mia Porta È Sempre Aperta: Una Conversazione Con Antonio Spadaro* (Milan: Rizzoli, 2013).
———, *Nell Cuore dell'Uomo: Utopia E Impegno* (Milan: Bompani, 2013).
Bellah, Robert, *Religion in Human Evolution: From the Paleolithic to the Axial Age* (Cambridge, MA: Belknap Press of Harvard University Press, 2011).
Bellah, Robert Neelly, and Hans Joas, *The Axial Age and Its Consequences* (Belknap Press of Harvard University Press, 2012).
Berger, Peter L., *Heretical Imperative*, 1st UK Paperback Edition (London: HarperCollins Distribution Services, 1980).
Biemer, Günter, 'Newman on Tradition as a Subjective Process', in *By Whose Authority? Newman, Manning & the Magisterium*, ed. by V. Alan McClelland (Bath: Downside Abbey, 1996).
Blackwell, Richard, 'Could There Be Another Galileo Case?', in *The Cambridge Companion to Galileo*, ed. by Peter Machamer (Cambridge: Cambridge University Press, 1998b).
———, *Science, Religion and Authority: Lessons from the Galileo Affair* (Milwaukee: Marquette University Press, 1998a).
Blastic, Michael, Jay Hammond, and J.A. Wayne Hellmann, eds., *Writings of Francis of Assisi: Letters and Prayers* (St Bonaventure, NY: Franciscan Institute Publications, 2010).

―――., eds., *Writings of Francis of Assisi: Rules, Testament and Admonitions* (St Bonaventure, NY: Franciscan Institute Publications, 2011).

Blenkinsopp, Joseph, 'Reading Isaiah in Early Christianity with Special Reference to Matthew's Gospel', in *Opening the Sealed Book: Interpretations of the Book of Isaiah in Late Antiquity*, by Joseph Blenkinsopp (Grand Rapids MI: Eerdmans, 2006).

Blondel, Maurice, 'Histoire et Dogme', in *Les Premiers écrits de Maurice Blondel* (Paris: PUF, 1956).

―――, *The Letter on Apologetics, and History and Dogma* (London: Harvill Press, 1964).

Boeve, Lieven, *God Interrupts History* (New York: Continuum, 2007).

Boff, Leonardo, *Ecclesiogenesis* (New York: Orbis Books, 1996).

―――, 'To Be Radically Poor so as to Be Fully a Brother' https://www.facebook.com/New Catholic Times/posts/5312247336 107657.

Bonaventure, *Breviloquium*, trans. by Jose de Vinck, The Works of St Bonaventure (Paterson, NJ: St Anthony Guild Press, 1963), II.

―――, 'Collations on the Gifts of the Holy Spirit', in *St Bonaventure's Collations on the Gifts of the Holy Spirit*, ed. by Robert Karris, trans. by Zachary Hayes, Works of St Bonaventure (New York: The Franciscan Institute, 2008), XIV.

―――, 'Collations on the Six Days', in *Works of St Bonaventure*, trans. by Jose de Vinck (Paterson, NJ: St Anthony Guild Press, 1970), V.

―――, 'Collations on the Ten Commandments', in *St Bonaventure's Collations on the Ten Commandments*, trans. by Paul Spaeth, Works of St Bonaventure (St Bonaventure, NY: Franciscan Institute, 1995).

―――, 'Defence of the Mendicants', in *Works of St Bonaventure*, trans. by Jose de Vinck and Robert Karris (St Bonaventure, NY: Franciscan Institute, 2010), XV.

―――, 'Disputed Questions on the Knowledge of Christ, Epilogue', in *St Bonaventure's Disputed Questions on the Knowledge of Christ*, trans. by Zachary Hayes, Works of St Bonaventure (St Bonaventure, NY: The Franciscan Institute, 1992), III.

―――, 'The Life of St Francis', in *Bonaventure. The Soul's Journey into God, The Tree of Life, The Life of St Francis*, trans. by Ewert Cousins, Classics of Western Spirituality (New York: Paulist Press, 1978).

―――, 'The Soul's Journey into God', in *Bonaventure. The Soul's Journey into God, The Tree of Life, The Life of St Francis*, trans. by Ewert Cousins, Classics of Western Spirituality (New York: Paulist Press, 1978).

Bougerol, Jacques, *Introduction to the Works of Bonaventure* (Paterson, NJ: St Anthony Guild Press, 1964).

Brandes, W., '"Juristische" Krisenbewältigung Im 7. Jahrhundert? Die Prozesse Gegen Papst Martin I. Und Maximos Homologetes', *Fontes Minores*, 10 (1998).
Braund, Susanna, ed., *Seneca: De Clementia* (Oxford: Oxford University Press, 2009).
Brown, Callum G., *The Death of Christian Britain: Understanding Secularisation 1800-2000* (London; New York: Routledge, 2000)
Brown, David, *Divine Humanity: Kenosis Defended and Explored* (London: SCM Press, 2011).
Brueggemann, Walter, *Deep Memory, Exuberant Hope: Contested Truth in a Post-Christian World* (Minneapolis: Augsburg Fortress, 2000).
Carroll, A. J., 'A Catholic Program for Advanced Modernity', in *Towards a New Catholic Church in Advanced Modernity*, ed. by S. Hellemans and J. Wissink (Vienna and Berlin: LIT Verlag, 2012).
Carroll, Anthony J, 'Faith, Reason and Modernity', *The Tablet*, 2006.
———, *Protestant Modernity: Weber, Secularisation and Protestantism* (London and Scranton: University of Scranton Press, 2007).
———, 'The Philosophical Foundations of Catholic Modernism', in *George Tyrrell and Catholic Modernism*, ed. by Oliver Rafferty (Dublin: Four Courts Press, 2010).
Carter, Warren, *Matthew and the Margins: A Socio-Political and Religious Reading*, JSNT Sup 204 (Sheffield: Sheffield Academic Press, 2000).
Casanova, Jose, 'The Church in the World: The Theological Responsibility of a Lay Sociologist; on the Contemporary Disjunction between Societal Morality' (unpublished Lecture on the occasion of the reception of the Theological Prize of the Salzburger Hochschulwochen, Salzburg, 2012).
Cavanaugh, William, *Torture and Eucharist* (Oxford and Malden MA: Blackwell Publishers, 1998).
De Certeau, Michel, *The Mystic Fable* (Chicago: University of Chicago Press, 1992).
Chadwick, Owen, *From Bossuet to Newman: The Idea of Doctrinal Development* (Cambridge: Cambridge University Press, 1957).
Cheney, Emily, 'The Mother of the Sons of Zebedee (Matthew 27:56)', *JSNT*, 68 (1997).
Clark, Kenneth Willis, 'The Meaning of [KATA]KYPIEYEIN', in *The Gentile Bias and Other Essays*, by Kenneth Willis Clark, NovTSup 54 (Leiden: Brill, 1980).
Coakley, Sarah, 'Kenōsis and Subversion', in *Powers and Submissions: Spirituality, Philosophy and Gender* (Oxford: Blackwell, 2002).
Cohoon, J. W., ed., *Dio Chrysostom/Discourses 1-11*, Loeb Classical Library (Cambridge MA: Harvard University Press, 1932).
Collins, H., and R. Evans, *Rethinking Expertise* (Chicago: Chicago University Press, 2007).

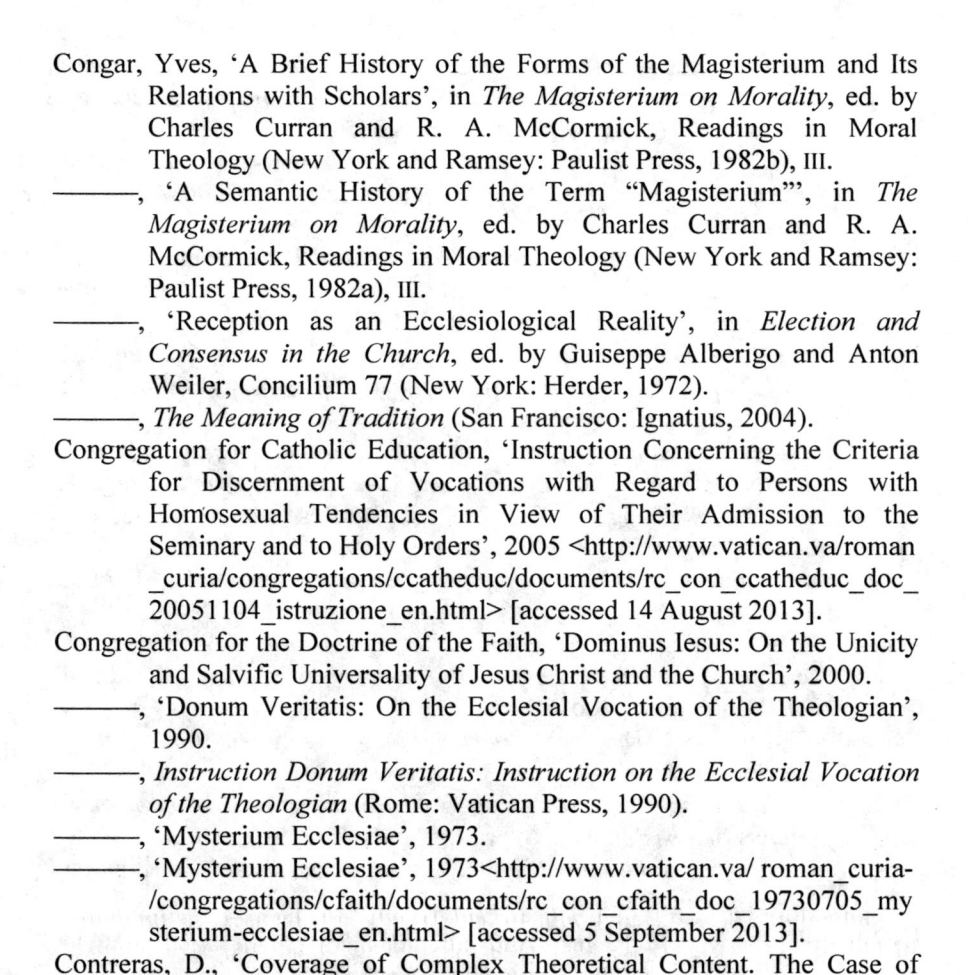

Congar, Yves, 'A Brief History of the Forms of the Magisterium and Its Relations with Scholars', in *The Magisterium on Morality*, ed. by Charles Curran and R. A. McCormick, Readings in Moral Theology (New York and Ramsey: Paulist Press, 1982b), III.

———, 'A Semantic History of the Term "Magisterium"', in *The Magisterium on Morality*, ed. by Charles Curran and R. A. McCormick, Readings in Moral Theology (New York and Ramsey: Paulist Press, 1982a), III.

———, 'Reception as an Ecclesiological Reality', in *Election and Consensus in the Church*, ed. by Guiseppe Alberigo and Anton Weiler, Concilium 77 (New York: Herder, 1972).

———, *The Meaning of Tradition* (San Francisco: Ignatius, 2004).

Congregation for Catholic Education, 'Instruction Concerning the Criteria for Discernment of Vocations with Regard to Persons with Homosexual Tendencies in View of Their Admission to the Seminary and to Holy Orders', 2005 <http://www.vatican.va/roman_curia/congregations/ccatheduc/documents/rc_con_ccatheduc_doc_20051104_istruzione_en.html> [accessed 14 August 2013].

Congregation for the Doctrine of the Faith, 'Dominus Iesus: On the Unicity and Salvific Universality of Jesus Christ and the Church', 2000.

———, 'Donum Veritatis: On the Ecclesial Vocation of the Theologian', 1990.

———, *Instruction Donum Veritatis: Instruction on the Ecclesial Vocation of the Theologian* (Rome: Vatican Press, 1990).

———, 'Mysterium Ecclesiae', 1973.

———, 'Mysterium Ecclesiae', 1973<http://www.vatican.va/ roman_curia-/congregations/cfaith/documents/rc_con_cfaith_doc_19730705_mysterium-ecclesiae_en.html> [accessed 5 September 2013].

Contreras, D., 'Coverage of Complex Theoretical Content. The Case of "Dominus Iesus"', *Westminster Papers in Communication and Culture*, 4 (2007).

Cope, O. Lamar, *Matthew, a Scribe Trained for the Kingdom of Heaven* (Washington DC: Catholic Biblical Association of America, 1976).

Cranfield, C. E. B., *The Gospel According to St Mark*, Cambridge Greek Testament Commentary (Cambridge: Cambridge University Press, 1966).

Crossan, John D., and Jonathan L. Reed, *In Search of Paul* (New York: Harper San Francisco, 2004).

Culpepper, R. Alan, *John: The Son of Zebedee. The Life of a Legend* (Edinburgh: T & T Clark, 2000).

Curran, Charles, *Faithful Dissent* (London: Sheed & Ward, 1986).

Danker, F. W., 'Graeco-Roman Cultural Accommodation in the Christology of Luke-Acts', in *Society of Biblical Literature 1983 Seminar Papers*, ed. by K. H. Richards (Chico CA: Scholar's Press, 1983).

Danove, Paul L., *The Rhetoric of the Characterization of God, Jesus and Jesus' Disciples in the Gospel of Mark*, JSNT Sup 290 (London and New York: T & T Clark/Continuum, 2005).
Darr, John, *Herod the Fox: Audience Criticism and Lukan Characterization*, JSNT Sup 163 (Sheffield: Sheffield Academic Press, 1998).
Davies, Mervyn, Crisp, Oliver, Gavin D'Costa, and Peter Hampson, eds., *Christianity and the Disciplines: The Transformation of the University* (London: T & T Clark, 2012).
Davies, W. D., and Dale C. Allison, *A Critical and Exegetical Commentary on the Gospel According to St Matthew*, ICC, 3 vols. (Edinburgh: T & T Clark, 1997).
Decker, Daniel, 'Subsidiarity', in *Church and People: Disjunctions in a Secular Age*, ed. by Charles Taylor, Jose Casanova, and George F. McLean (Washington: The Council for Research in Values and Philosophy, 2012).
Delio, Ilia, 'Bonaventure's Metaphysics of the Good', *Theological Studies*, 60 (1999).
Dhanis, E., 'Révélation Explicite et Implicite', *Gregorianum*, 34 (1953).
Dines, Jennifer, *Septuagint* (London and New York: T & T Clark/Continuum, 2004).
Dorandi, Tiziano, ed., *Diogenes Laertius/Lives of Eminent Philosophers* (Cambridge: Cambridge University Press, 2013).
Doyle, Eric, *The Disciple and the Master: St Bonaventure's Sermons on St Francis of Assisi* (Chicago: Franciscan Herald Press, 1983).
Doyle, Leonard J., *Saint Benedict's Rule for Monasteries* (Collegeville: Order of Saint Benedict, 1948).
Duling, Dennis C., 'The Matthean Brotherhood and Marginal Scribal Leadership', in *Modelling Early Christianity: Social-Scientific Studies of the New Testament in its Context*, ed. by Philip F. Esler (London and New York: Routledge, 1995).
Dulles, Avery, *Models of the Church*, Exp Rei edition (Image, 2002).
———, *The Survival of Dogma* (New York: Crossroad, 1971).
Dunn, James D. G., 'The Son of Man in Mark', in *Parables of Enoch: A Paradigm Shift*, ed. by Darrell L. Bock and James H. Charlesworth (London: Bloomsbury, 2013).
Dvomik, Francis, *Early Christian and Byzantine Political Philosophy: Origins and Background*, 2 vols. (Washington DC: Dumbarton Oaks Center for Byzantine Studies, 1966).
De Lubac, Henri, *Corpus Mysticum*, trans. by Gemma Simmonds (London: SCM Press, 2006).
———, *Corpus Mysticum: The Eucharist and the Church in the Middle Ages*, ed. by Laurence Paul Hemming and Susan Frank Parsons (London: SCM Press, 2006).
———, 'Le Problème Du Développement Du Dogme', *Recherches de Science Religieuse*, 35 (130AD), 1948.

De Mey, P., 'Authority in the Church: The Appeal to Lk 22:21-34 in Roman Catholic Magisterial Teaching and in the Ecumenical Dialogue', in *Luke and his Readers: Festschrift A. Denaux*, ed. by R. Bieringer, G. van Belle, and J. Verheyden (Leuven: Leuven University Press, 2005).

De Raeymaker, L., 'Les Origines de l'Institut Supérieur de Philosophie de Louvain', *Revue Philosophique de Louvain*, 1951.

———, *The Survival of Dogma* (New York: Crossroad, 1971).

Edwards, J. Christopher, 'Pre-Nicene Receptions of Mark 10:45 // Matt 20:28 with Phil 2:6-8', *JTS*, 61 (2010).

Evans, C. F., *Saint Luke* (Philadelphia and London: Trinity Press International/SCM Press, 1990).

Feldman, Richard, and Ted A. Warfield, eds., *Disagreement* (Oxford: Oxford University Press, 2010).

Figueiredo, Anthony J., *The Magisterium-Theology Relationship: Contemporary Theological Conceptions in the Light of Universal Church Teaching Since 1835 and the Pronouncements of the Bishops of the United States* (Rome: Pontificia Universita Gregoriana, 2001).

———, *The Magisterium-Theology Relationship: Contemporary Theological Conceptions in the Light of Universal Church Teaching since 1835 & the Pronouncements of the Bishops of the United States* (Rome: Editrice Pontificia Universita Gregoriana, 2011).

Fish, Jeffrey, 'Not All Politicians Are Sisyphus: What Roman Epicureans Were Taught about Politics', in *Epicurus and the Epicurean Tradition*, ed. by Jeffrey Fish and Kirk R. Sanders (Cambridge: Cambridge University Press, 2011).

Fix, B., and E. Fix, *Kirche Und Wohlfahrtsstaat. Soziale Arbeit Kirchlicher Wohlfahrtsorganisationen Im Westeuropäischen Vergleich* (Freiburg im Breisgau: Lambertus, 2005).

Fletcher, Paul, *Disciplining the Divine* (Farnham and Burlington: Ashgate, 2009).

France, R. T., *The Gospel of Mark: A Commentary on the Greek Text*, NIGTC (Grand Rapids MI: Eerdmans, 2002).

Gabriel, K., *Caritas Und Sozialstaat Unter Veränderungsdruck* (Berlin: LIT Verlag, 2007).

Gaillardetz, Richard R., *Teaching with Authority: A Theology of the Magisterium in the Church* (Collegeville: Liturgical Press, 1997).

———, *When the Magisterium Intervenes: The Magisterium and Theologians in Today's Church* (Collegeville: Liturgical Press, 2012).

———, *Witnesses to the Faith: Community, Infallibility and the Ordinary Magisterium of Bishops* (New York: Paulist Press, 1992).

Garcia Martinez, Florentino, and Eibert J. C. Tigchelaar, eds., *The Dead Sea Scrolls Study Edition* (Grand Rapids MI and Leiden: Eerdmans/Brill, 1997), I & II.
Gardner, Lucy, and David Moss, 'Something Like Time; Something like the Sexes - an Essay in Reception', in *Balthasar at the End of Modernity* (Edinburgh: T & T Clark, 1999).
Garlington, Don, 'Who Is the Greatest?', *JETS*, 53 (2010).
Geary, Brendan, and Joanne Marie Greer, eds., *The Dark Night of the Catholic Church: Gender, Power and Organisational Culture* (Oxford: Oxford University Press, 2011).
Giddens, Anthony, *Modernity and Self-Identity: Self and Society in the Late Modern Age* (Cambridge, U.K.: Polity Press, 1991).
Goldman, Alvin, *Knowledge in a Social World* (Oxford: Oxford University Press, 1999).
Gooch, Paul W., 'Paul, the Mind of Christ, and Philosophy', in *Jesus and Philosophy*, ed. by Paul K. Moser (Cambridge: Cambridge University Press, 2009).
Goodenough, E. R., 'The Political Philosophy of Hellenistic Kingship', *YCS*, 1 (1928).
Green, Joel B., 'The Death of Jesus, God's Servant', in *Reimaging the Death of the Lukan Jesus*, ed. by Dennis D. Sylva (Frankfurt: Anton Hain, 1990).
Gregorius XVI, 'Commissum Divinitus', 1835 <http://www.papalencyclicals.net/Greg16/g16commi.htm> [accessed 4 September 2013].
———, 'Mirari Vos', 1832 <http://www.papalencyclicals.net/Greg16/g16-mirar.htm> [accessed 4 September 2013].
Gres-Gayer, J., 'The Magisterium of the Faculty of Theology of Paris in the Seventeenth Century', *Theological Studies*, 1992.
Griffin, M. T., and E. M. Atkins, eds., *Cicero: On Duties* (Cambridge: Cambridge University Press, 1991).
Habermas, Jürgen, *Nachmetaphysisches Denken II: Aufsätze Und Repliken* (Berlin: Suhrkamp Verlag, 2012).
———, *Nachmetaphysisches Denken: Philosophische Aufsätze* (Frankfurt: Suhrkamp Verlag, 1988).
Hall, Pamela M., *Narrative and the Natural Law: An Interpretation of Thomistic Ethics* (Notre Dame: University of Notre Dame Press, 1994).
Hamerton-Kelly, Robert, 'A Girardian Interpretation of Paul: Rivalry, Mimesis and Victimage in the Corinthian Correspondence', *Semeia*, 1985.
———, *Sacred Violence: Paul's Hermeneutic of the Cross* (Minneapolis: Fortress Press, 1992).
———, *Sacred Violence: The Hermeneutic of the Cross in the Theology of Paul* (Minneapolis, MN: Fortress Press, 1992).
Hannah, Darrell D., 'Isaiah within Judaism of the Second Temple Period', in *Isaiah in the New Testament*, ed. by Steve Moyise and Maarten

J.J. Menken (London and New York: T & T Clark/Continuum, 2005).
Hanson, N. R., *Patterns of Discovery* (Cambridge: Cambridge University Press, 1958).
Hardt, Michael, and Antonio Negri, *Multitude* (New York: Penguin Books, 2004).
Harrison, James R., *Paul and the Imperial Authorities at Thessalonica and Rome*, WUNT 273 (Tübingen: Mohr Siebeck, 2011).
Hayes, Zachary, *Bonaventure: Mystical Writings* (New York: Crossroad, 1999).
Hellemans, S., and J. Wissink, eds., *A Catholic Program for Advanced Modernity* (Vienna and Berlin: LIT Verlag, 2012).
Hengel, Martin, and Daniel P. Bailey, 'The Effective History of Isaiah 53 in the Pre-Christian Period', in *The Suffering Servant: Isaiah 53 in Jewish and Christian Sources*, ed. by Bernd Janowski and Peter Stuhlmacher (Grand Rapids MI: Eerdmans, 2004).
Hill, David, 'Son and Servant: An Essay on Matthean Christology', *JSNT*, 6 (1980).
Honigman, Sylvie, 'The Narrative Function of the King and the Library in the "Letter of Aristeas"', in *Jewish Perspectives on Hellenistic Rulers*, ed. by Tessa Rajak, Sarah Pearce, James Aitken, and Jennifer Dines (Berkeley: University of California Press, 2007).
——, *The Septuagint and Homeric Scholarship in Alexandria: A Study in the Narrative of the 'Letter of Aristeas'* (London: Routledge, 2003).
Hooker, Morna D., 'Isaiah in Mark's Gospel', in *Isaiah in the New Testament*, ed. by Steve Moyise and Maarten J.J. Menken (London and New York: T & T Clark/Continuum, 2005).
——, *The Gospel According to Mark* (London: A & C Black, 1991).
Horkheimer, Max, and Theodor Adorno, *Dialectic of the Enlightenment* (London: Verso, 1979).
Horsley, Richard, *Jesus and Empire* (Minneapolis: Fortress Press, 2003).
Hubert, Jedin, 'Theologie Und Lehramt', in *Lehramt und Theologie im 16. Jahrhundert*, ed. by R. Bäumer (Münster: Ashendorff, 1976).
International Theological Commission, 'Theology Today: Perspectives, Principles and Criteria', 2012.
Irenaeus, St., 'Ad. Haereses' <http://www.earlychristianwritings.com/text/-irenaeus-book2.html> [accessed 17 April 2014].
Jankowiak, Marek, 'Essai D'histoire Politique Du Monothélisme' (unpublished Doctoral Thesis, 2009).
John Paul II, 'Ordinatio Sacerdotalis', 1984 <http://www.vatican.va/holy_father/john_paul_ii/apost_letters/documents/hf_jp-ii_apl_220519-94_ordinatio-sacerdotalis_en.html> [accessed 5 September 2013].
——, 'Veritatis Splendor',1993<http://www.vatican.va/holy_father/john-_paul_ii/encyclicals/documents/hf_jp-ii_enc_06081993_veritatis-splendor_en.html> [accessed 6 September 2013].

Joshel, Sandra R., *Slavery in the Roman World* (Cambridge: Cambridge University Press, 2010).
Joubert, Stephan, *Paul as Benefactor: Reciprocity, Strategy and Theological Reflection in Paul's Collection*, WUNT 124 (Tübingen: Mohr Siebeck, 2000).
Jüngel, E., *God as the Mystery of the World. On the Foundation of the Theology of the Crucified One in the Dispute Between Theism and Atheism* (Grand Rapids MI: Eerdmans, 2008).
Kasper, Walter, *Theology and Church* (London: SCM, 1989).
Keenan, Marie, *Child Sexual Abuse and the Catholic Church: Gender, Power and Organisational Culture* (Oxford: Oxford University Press, 2012).
Kelly, J. N. D., *The Oxford Dictionary of Popes* (Oxford: Oxford University Press, 1986).
Kenny, Nuala, 'The Clergy Sex Abuse Crisis: Dynamics and Diagnosis', *ET Studies: Journal of the European Society for Catholic Theology*, 4 (2013).
Kerkhofs, Jan, 'The Sensus Fidelium and Reception of Teaching', in *Readings in Church Authority: Gifts and Challenges for Contemporary Catholicism*, ed. by G. Mannion, Richard R. Gaillardetz, Kenneth Wilson, and Jan Kerkhofs (Aldershot: Ashgate, 2003).
Kerr, Fergus, *After Aquinas: Versions of Thomism* (London: Blackwell, 2002).
———, 'Foreword: Assessing This "Giddy Synthesis"', in *Balthasar at the End of Modernity* (Edinburgh: T & T Clark, 1999).
———, *Twentieth-Century Catholic Theologians* (Wiley-Blackwell, 100AD).
Kilmartin, Edward, 'Reception in History: An Ecclesiological Phenomenon & Its Significance', *Journal of Ecumenical Studies*, 21 (1984).
Kitschelt, H., *Latin American Party Systems*, Cambridge Studies in Comparative Politics (Cambridge; New York: Cambridge University Press, 2010).
———, 'Linkages between Citizens and Politicians in Democratic Polities', *Comparative Political Studies*, 33 (2000).
Komonchak, Joseph, 'The Epistemology of Reception', in *Reception and Communion Among Churches*, ed. by Hervé Legrand, Julio Manzanares, and Antonio García y García (Washington: Catholic University of America Press, 1997).
Kuhn, Thomas S, *The Structure of Scientific Revolutions* (Chicago; London: The University of Chicago Press, 1996).
Lacey, Michael J., and Francis Oakley, *The Crisis of Authority in Catholic Modernity* (Oxford: Oxford University Press, 2011).
Lakatos, Imre, *The Methodology of Scientific Research Programmes: Philosophical Papers* (Cambridge: Cambridge University Press, 1978), I.

Lash, Nicholas, *Theology for Pilgrims* (London: Darton, Longman and Todd, 2008).
Lawrence, D. H., *Apocalypse and the Writings on Revelation* (Cambridge: Cambridge University Press, 1980).
Leske, A. M., 'Isaiah and Matthew: The Prophetic Influence in the First Gospel: A Report on Current Research', in *Jesus and the Suffering Servant: Isaiah 53 and Christian Origins*, ed. by William H. Bellinger and William R. Farmer (Eugene OR: Wipf & Stock, 2009).
Lonergan, Bernard, *Method in Theology* (Toronto: University of Toronto Press, 1999).
Lull, David J., 'The Servant-Benefactor as a Model of Greatness (Luke 22:24-30)', *NovT*, 28 (1986).
Luz, Ulrich, *Matthew 1-7, 8-20, 21-28*, Hermeneia, 3 vols. (Minneapolis: Fortress Press, 2001).
Mannion, Gerard, 'A Teaching Church That Learns?', in *The Crisis of Authority in Catholic Modernity*, ed. by Michael J. Lacey and Francis Oakley, 1 edition (Oxford; New York: Oxford University Press, 2011).
Mannion, Gerard, and etc, *Readings in Church Authority: Gifts and Challenges for Contemporary Catholicism*, illustrated edition (Aldershot, Hants, England; Burlington, VT: Ashgate Publishing Limited, 2003).
Marcus, Joel, 'Crucifixion as Parodic Exaltation', *JBL*, 125 (2006).
———, *Mark 1-8: A New Translation with Introduction and Commentary* (New York: Doubleday, 2000).
———, *Mark 8-16: A New Translation with Introduction and Commentary* (New Haven and London: Yale University Press, 2009).
Marshall, Jonathan, *Jesus, Patrons and Benefactors: Roman Palestine and the Gospel of Luke*, WUNT 259 (Tübingen: Mohr Siebeck, 2009).
Martin, Dale B., *Slavery as Salvation: The Metaphor of Slavery in Pauline Christianity* (New Haven: Yale University Press, 1990).
Martin, David, *Pentecostalism: The World Their Parish* (Malden: Wiley-Blackwell, 2001).
Martini, Cardinal Carlo Maria, and Georg Sporschill, *Night Conversations with Cardinal Martini: The Relevance of the Church for Tomorrow* (New York: Paulist Press International, U.S., 2012).
Mayer, Annemarie C., 'Pope Francis: A Pastor according to the Heart of Christ', *International Journal for the Study of the Christian Churches*, 13 (2013).
Mayhew, Ray, 'Turning the Tables, Resurrection as Revolution. Review of N.T. Wright, The Resurrection of the Son of God', *Just Salvos*, 2008 http://justsalvosaus.blogspot.co.uk/2008/05/turning-tables-resurrection-as.html.
McAleese, Mary, *Quo Vadis?: Collegiality in the Code of Canon Law* (Dublin: Columba, 2012).

McCormack, Bruce, 'The Humility of the Eternal Son: A Reformed Version of Kenotic Christology', *International Journal of Systematic Theology*, 8 (2006).

McLean, George, Charles Taylor, and Jose Casanova, eds., *Church and People: Disjunctions in a Secular Age* (Washington, D.C: Council for Research in Values &, 2012).

McMahon, Christopher, *Reasonable Disagreement: A Theory of Political Morality* (Cambridge: Cambridge University Press, 2009).

Menken, Maarten J.J., *Matthew's Bible: The Old Testament Text of the Evangelist* (Leuven: Peeters, 2004).

Metz, Johannes Baptist, *Faith in History and Society: Towards a Practical Fundamental Theology* (New York: Crossroads, Seabury Press, 1980).

———, 'Karl Rahner's Struggle for the Theological Dignity of Humankind', in *A Passion for God* (New York: Paulist Press, 1998).

Metz, R., 'Pouvoir, Centralisation et Droit. La Codification Du Droit de l'Eglise Catholique Au Début Du XXe Siècle', *Archives des Sciences Sociales des Religions*, 26 (1978).

Milbank, John, 'Postmodern Critical Augustinianism', in *The Radical Orthodoxy Reader*, ed. by John Milbank and Simon Oliver (London and New York: Routledge, 2009).

———, *The Word Made Strange* (Oxford: Blackwell Publishers, 1997).

Miller, Vincent J., *Consuming Religion: Christian Faith and Practice in a Consumer Culture* (London: Continuum, 2003).

Miller, Walter, ed., *Xenophon, Cyropaedia, Vol II. Books 5-8*, Loeb Classical Library (Cambridge MA: Harvard University Press, 1914).

Mitchell, Roger H., *Church, Gospel and Empire: How the Politics of Sovereignty Impregnated the West* (Eugene OR: Wipf & Stock, 2011).

Monti, Dominic, 'The Experience of the Spirit in Our Franciscan Tradition', *The Cord*, 49 (1999).

Moore, Stephen D., *Empire and Apocalypse: Postcolonialism and the New Testament* (Sheffield: Sheffield Phoenix Press, 2006).

Moser, Paul K., *The Elusive God: Reorienting Religious Epistemology* (New York: Cambridge University Press, 2008).

Moxnes, Halvor, 'Patron-Client Relations and the New Community in Luke-Acts', in *The Social World of Luke-Acts: Models for Interpretation*, ed. by Jerome H. Neyrey (Peabody MA: Hendrickson, 1991).

Moyise, Steve, and Maarten J.J. Menken, eds., *Isaiah in the New Testament* (London and New York: T & T Clark/Continuum, 2005).

Of Assisi, Francis, 'A Letter to the Entire Order', in *Francis and Clare: The Complete Works*, trans. by Regis Armstrong and Ignatius Brady, Classics of Western Spirituality (New York: Paulist Press, 1982).

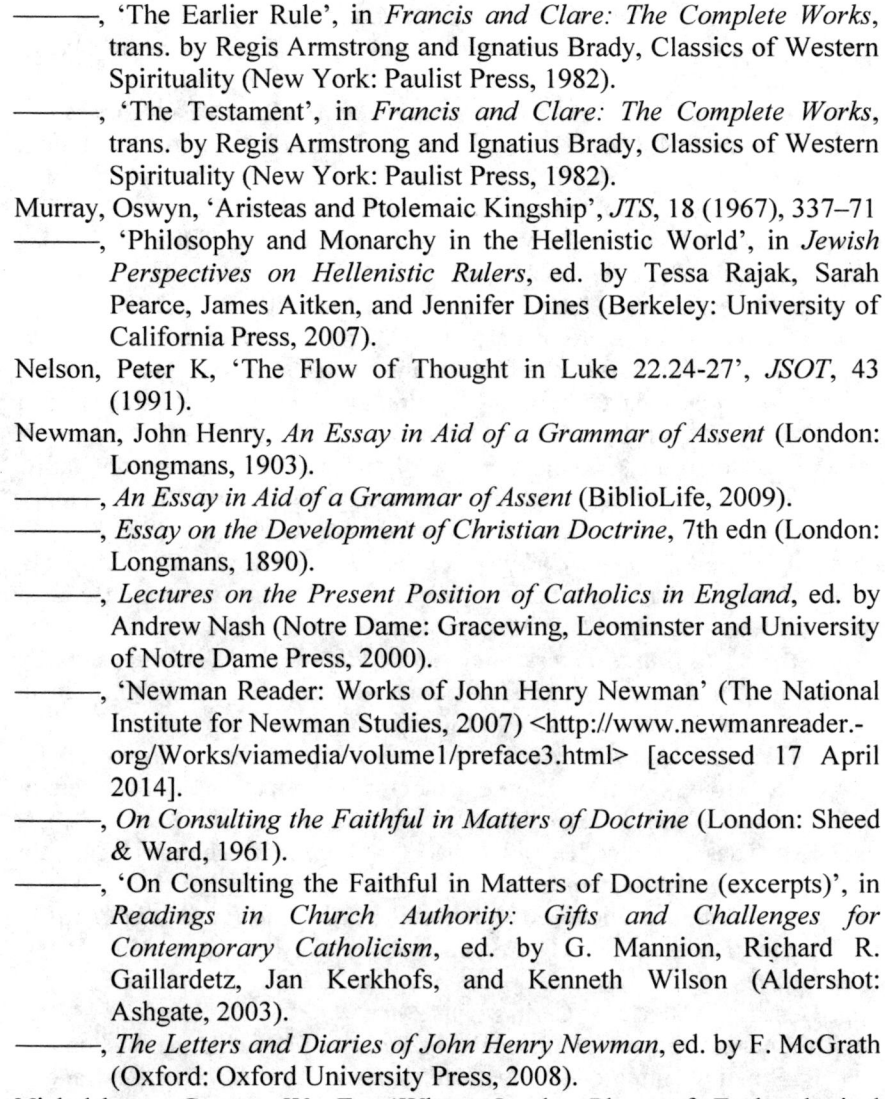

——, 'The Earlier Rule', in *Francis and Clare: The Complete Works*, trans. by Regis Armstrong and Ignatius Brady, Classics of Western Spirituality (New York: Paulist Press, 1982).

——, 'The Testament', in *Francis and Clare: The Complete Works*, trans. by Regis Armstrong and Ignatius Brady, Classics of Western Spirituality (New York: Paulist Press, 1982).

Murray, Oswyn, 'Aristeas and Ptolemaic Kingship', *JTS*, 18 (1967), 337–71

——, 'Philosophy and Monarchy in the Hellenistic World', in *Jewish Perspectives on Hellenistic Rulers*, ed. by Tessa Rajak, Sarah Pearce, James Aitken, and Jennifer Dines (Berkeley: University of California Press, 2007).

Nelson, Peter K, 'The Flow of Thought in Luke 22.24-27', *JSOT*, 43 (1991).

Newman, John Henry, *An Essay in Aid of a Grammar of Assent* (London: Longmans, 1903).

——, *An Essay in Aid of a Grammar of Assent* (BiblioLife, 2009).

——, *Essay on the Development of Christian Doctrine*, 7th edn (London: Longmans, 1890).

——, *Lectures on the Present Position of Catholics in England*, ed. by Andrew Nash (Notre Dame: Gracewing, Leominster and University of Notre Dame Press, 2000).

——, 'Newman Reader: Works of John Henry Newman' (The National Institute for Newman Studies, 2007) <http://www.newmanreader.org/Works/viamedia/volume1/preface3.html> [accessed 17 April 2014].

——, *On Consulting the Faithful in Matters of Doctrine* (London: Sheed & Ward, 1961).

——, 'On Consulting the Faithful in Matters of Doctrine (excerpts)', in *Readings in Church Authority: Gifts and Challenges for Contemporary Catholicism*, ed. by G. Mannion, Richard R. Gaillardetz, Jan Kerkhofs, and Kenneth Wilson (Aldershot: Ashgate, 2003).

——, *The Letters and Diaries of John Henry Newman*, ed. by F. McGrath (Oxford: Oxford University Press, 2008).

Nickelsburg, George W. E., 'Where Is the Place of Eschatological Blessing?', in *Things Revealed: Studies in Early Jewish and Christian Literature in Honor of Michael E. Stone*, ed. by Esther G. Chazon, David Satran, and Ruth A. Clements, JSJSup 89 (Leiden: Brill, 2004).

Nickelsburg, George W. E., and James C. VanderKam, *1 Enoch 2*, Hermeneia (Minneapolis: Fortress Press, 2012).

Nolland, John, *The Gospel of Matthew: A Commentary on the Greek Text*, NIGTC (Grand Rapids MI: Eerdmans, 2005).

Of Nyssa, Gregory, *The Life of Moses* (New Jersey: Paulist Press, 1978).

Oakley, Francis, *The Conciliarist Tradition: Constitutionalism in the Catholic Church 1300-1870* (Oxford: Oxford University Press, 2003).

O'Brien, Kelli S., *The Use of Scripture in the Markan Passion Narrative*, LNTS 384 (London and New York: T & T Clark/Continuum, 2010).

Orsi, L., 'Magisterium: Assent and Dissent', *Theological Studies*, 48 (1987).

Orsi, Robert A., 'A Crisis about the Theology of Children', *Harvard Divinity Bulletin*, 30 (2002).

Parsons, Mikeal C., *Acts*, Paideia (Grand Rapids MI: Eerdmans, 2008).

———, 'Luke and the Progymnasmata: A Preliminary Investigation in to the Preliminary Exercises', in *Contextualizing Acts: Lukan Narrative and Greco-Roman Discourse*, ed. by Todd Penner and Caroline van der Stichele (Atlanta GA: SBL, 2003).

Paul VI, 'Octogesimo Adveniens', 1971 <http://www.vatican.va/holy_father/paul_vi/apost_letters/documents/hf_p-vi_apl_19710514_octogesima-adveniens_en.html> [accessed 4 September 2013].

Peirce, Charles S, *Collected Papers of Charles Sanders Peirce*, ed. by P. Weiss, C. Hartshorne, and A. Burks, 8 vols. (London: Belknap Press of Harvard U.P, 1931).

———, *The Essential Peirce: Selected Philosophical Writings*, ed. by Nathan Houser and Christian J. W Kloesel (Bloomington: Indiana University Press, 1992), 1 (1867–1893).

Peirce, C. S., *The Essential Peirce: Selected Philosophical Writings*, ed. by N. Houser and C. Kloesel (Indianapolis, IN: Indiana University Press, 1992), 1 (1867–1893).

Pius IX, 'Tuas Libenter, D 1684', 1863 <http://denzinger.patristica.net/> [accessed 4 September 2013].

Plantinga, Alvin, and Nicholas Wolterstorff, *Faith and Rationality: Reason and Belief in God* (Notre Dame: University of Notre Dame Press, 1984).

Pope Benedict XVI, 'Deus Caritas Est', 2005.

Pope Francis, 'Address of the Holy Father Meeting with the Bishops of Brazil' http://en.radiovaticana.va/news/2013/07/27/pope_francis-_to_brazilian_bishops/.

———, 'Address to Brazil's Cardinals and Bishops, 27 July in Rio de Janeiro's St Sebastian Cathedral', *The Tablet*, 2013 <http://www.news.va./en/news/pope-to-clergy-religious-seminarians-respond-to-go>.

———, 'Address to the International Union of Superiors General 8 May 2013'. <http://www.vaticana.va/holy_father/francesco/speeches/-2013/may/documents/papa-francesco_20130508_visg_en.html>

———, 'Evangelii Gaudium', 2013.

———, 'Homily at Morning Mass in the Chapel of Saint Martha's House, 14 June 2013' http://www.catholicnewsagency.com/news/be-humble-from-head-to-toe-pope-francis-says/.

———, 'Homily in the Cathedral of Saint Sebastian, Rio de Janeiro, 27 July 2013' http://www.news.va./en/news/pope-to-clergy-religious-seminarians-respond-to-go.
Pope John Paul II, 'Ecclesia in Europa', 2003.
Pope John XXIII, 'Gaudet Mater Ecclesiae', 1962.
Pope Paul VI, 'Octogesima Adveniens', 1971.
Poulat, E., *Histoire, dogme et critique dans la crise moderniste* (Paris: Casterman, 1962).
Poulat, Emile, *L'Eglise, c'est un monde: l'ecclésiosphère* (Paris: Editions du Cerf, 1984).
Price, Richard, 'Aspects of the Composition of the Acts of the Lateran Synod of 649', *Annuarium Historiae Conciliorum*, 42 (2010).
———, 'Monotheletism: A Heresy or a Form of Words?', *Studia Patristica*, 48 (2010).
———, *The Acts of the Council of Constantinople of 553* (Liverpool: Liverpool University Press, 2007), I.
Pseudo-Dionysius, 'The Celestial Hierarchy', in *Pseudo-Dionysius: The Complete Works*, trans. by Colm Luibhéid and Paul Rorem, Classics of Western Spirituality (London: SPCK, 1987).
Quinn, John, 'Chronology of St Bonaventure (1217-1257)', *Greyfriars Review*, 32 (1972).
Rahner, K., 'Überlegungen Zur Dogmenentwicklung', *Schriften zur Theologie*, 4 (1960).
Rahner, Karl, *Confrontations* (Darton, Longman & Todd, 1974).
———, *Foundations of Christian Faith: An Introduction to the Idea of Christianity* (New York: Crossroad, 1982).
———, 'Towards a Fundamental Theological Interpretation of Vatican II', *Theological Studies*, 1979.
Ratzinger, J., *Das Problem Der Dogmengeschichte in Der Sicht Der Katholischen Theologie* (Cologne: Opladen, 1966).
Rawls, John, *A Brief Inquiry into the Meaning of Sin and Faith with 'on My Religion'*, ed. by Thomas Nagel (Cambridge MA: Harvard University Press, 2009).
Rawson, Elizabeth, 'Caesar's Heritage: Hellenistic Kings and Their Roman Equals', *JRS*, 65 (1975).
Reid, Thomas, *An Inquiry Into the Human Mind on the Principles of Common Sense*, 1810.
Ricoeur, Pau, 'Religion, Atheism, and Faith', in *The Conflict in Interpretations* (Evanston: Northwestern University Press, 1974).
Rogier, L. J., *De Kerk in Het Tijdperk van Verlichting En Revolutie*, Geschiedenis van de Kerk (Hilversum and Antwerp: Paul Brand, 1974), VII.
Rohr, Richard, 'The Franciscan Opinion', in *Stricken By God?*, ed. by Brad Jersak and Michael Hardin (Grand Rapids MI and Cambridge: Eerdmans, 2007).

Rotzetter, Anton, 'The Missionary Dimension of the Franciscan Charism', in *mission in the Franciscan Tradition*, ed. by Anselm Moons and Flavius Walsh (St Bonaventure, NY: Franciscan Institute, 1993).
Rout, Paul, *Francis and Bonaventure* (Liguori, Missouri: Triumph, 1997).
———, 'St Francis of Assisi and Islam: A Theological Perspective on a Christian-Muslim Encounter', *Al-Masaq: Islam and the Medieval Mediterranean*, 23 (2011).
Rush, Ormond, *The Eyes of Faith: The Sense of the Faithful and the Church's Reception of Revelation* (Washington: Catholic University of America Press, 2009).
Santos, Narry F., *Slave of All: The Paradox of Authority and Servanthood in the Gospel of Mark* (Sheffield: Sheffield Academic Press, 2003).
Schatz, K., *Papal Primacy* (Collegeville: Liturgical Press, 1996).
Schillebeeckx, E., 'Recent Views in the Development of Dogma', *Concilium*, 1967.
Schmitt, Carl, *Theory of the Partisan: Intermediate Commentary on the Concept of the Political* (New York: Telos Press, 2007).
Schreiter, Robert, *Constructing Local Theologies* (Orbis: Maryknoll, 1985).
Seeley, David, 'Rulership and Service in Mark 10:41-45', *NovT*, 35 (1993).
Shutt, R. J. H., 'Letter of Aristeas', in *The Old Testament Pseudepigrapha*, ed. by James H. Charlesworth (London, Darton: Longman & Todd, 1985), II.
Smith, Abraham, 'Tyranny Exposed: Mark's Typological Characterization of Herod Antipas', *Biblical Interpretation*, 14.
Smith, Dennis E., *From Symposium to Eucharist: The Banquet in the Early Christian World* (Minneapolis: Fortress Press, 2003).
Smith, Julien, *Christ the Ideal King: Cultural Context Rhetorical Strategy and the Power of Divine Monarchy in Ephesians*, WUNT 313 (T: Mohr Siebeck, 2011).
Stacey, Peter, *Roman Monarchy and the Renaissance Prince* (Cambridge: Cambridge University Press, 2007).
Struthers Malbon, Elizabeth, *In the Company of Jesus: Characters in Mark's Gospel* (Louisville KY: Westminster John Knox Press, 2000).
Sullivan, Francis, *Magisterium: Teaching Authority in the Catholic Church* (Mahwah: Paulist Press, 1983).
Sullivan, Francis A., *Creative Fidelity: Weighing and Interpreting Documents of the Magisterium* (Wipf and Stock Publishers, 2003).
Sullivan, John W., 'Critical Fidelity and Catholic School Leadership', in *International Handbook on Faith-Based Learning, Teaching & Leadership* (Springer, Forthcoming).
Sweeney, James, 'Catholicism in Britain: A Church in Search of Its Way', in *Towards a New Catholic Church in Advanced Modernity*, ed. by S. Hellemans and J. Wissink (Vienna and Berlin: LIT Verlag, 2012).

———, 'The Experience of Religious Orders', in *Authority in the Roman Catholic Church: Theory and Practice*, ed. by Bernard Hoose (Aldershot, Hants, England; Burlington, VT: Ashgate Publishing Limited, 2002).

———, 'Theology and Sociology', in *Christianity and the Disciplines: the Transformation of the University*, ed. by Mervyn, Crisp, Oliver Davies, Gavin D'Costa, and Peter Hampson (London: T & T Clark, 2012).

Von Balthasar, Hans Urs, *The Glory of the Lord: A Theological Aesthetics*, ed. by John Riches, trans. by Andrew Louth, 7 vols. (Edinburgh: T & T Clark, 1984).

'Instruction on the Ecclesial Vocation of the Theologian' (Congregation for the Doctrine of the Faith, 1990) <http://www.vatican.va/roman_curia/congregations/cfaith/documents/rc_con_cfaith_doc_19900524_theologian-vocation_en.html> [accessed 17 April 2014].

Van Meerbeeck, A., and A. Verlinden, 'De Juni-Storm. Een Sociologische Doorlichting van Enkele Reacties Na Het Verschijnen van Ordinatio Sacerdotalis', *Tijdschrift voor Sociologie*, 16 (1995).

Van der Stichele, Caroline, 'Herodias Goes Headhunting', in *From the Margins. Vol 2. Women of the New Testament and their Afterlives*, ed. by Christine E. Joynes and Christopher Rowland (Sheffield: Sheffield Phoenix Press, 2009).

Taylor, Charles, 'A Catholic Modernity', in *A Catholic Modernity? Charles Taylor's Marianist Award Lecture*, ed. by J. L. Heft (Oxford: Oxford University Press, 1999).

———, *A Secular Age* (Cambridge MA and London: Harvard University Press, 2007).

———, *Sources of the Self: Making of the Modern Identity* (Cambridge: Cambridge University Press, 1990).

Taylor, Charles, Jose Casanova, and George F. McLean, eds., *Church and People: Disjunctions in a Secular Age* (Washington: The Council for Research in Values and Philosophy, 2012).

Thomas, John Cristopher, *Footwashing in John 13 and the Johannine Community* (London and New York: T & T Clark/Continuum, 2004).

Thompson, Daniel Speed, *The Language of Dissent: Edward Schillebeeckx on the Crisis of Authority in the Catholic Church* (Notre Dame: University of Notre Dame Press, 2003).

Thomson, Alexander, *Tradition and Authority in Science and Theology with Reference to the Thought of Michael Polanyi* (Edinburgh: Scottish Academic Press, 1987).

Thümmel, H. G., 'Zur Phämenologie von Konzilien: Das 6. Ökumenische Konzil 680/1', *Annuarium Historiae Conciliorum*, 40 (2008).

Tolbert, Mary Ann, *Sowing the Gospel: Mark's World in Literary-Historical Perspective* (Minneapolis: Fortress Press, 1989).

Torrance, Thomas F., *Incarnation: The Person and Life of Christ*, ed. by Robert T. Walker (Downers Grove, IL: IVP Academic, 2008).
Turner, Seth, 'The Interim, Earthly Messianic Kingdom in Paul', *Journal for the Study of the New Testament*, 25 (2003).
Volkmann, Hans, 'Die Basileia Als ENDOXOS DOULEIA', in *ENDOXOS DOULEIA: Kleine Schriften zur Alten Geschichte*, by Hans Volkmann (Berlin and New York: De Gruyter, 1975).
Ward, Graham, *Christ and Culture* (Oxford: Blackwell, 2005).
———, 'Kenosis: Death, Discourse and Resurrection', in *Balthasar at the End of Modernity* (Edinburgh: T & T Clark, 1999).
Warner, Keith, 'Pilgrims and Strangers: The Evangelical Ministry of Itinerancy of the Early Franciscan Friars', *Spirit and Life: a journal of contemporary Franciscanism*, 10 (2000).
Warren, Kathleen, *Francis of Assisi Encounters Sultan Malik Al-Kamil* (St Bonaventure, NY: Franciscan Institute, 2003).
Watson, David F., 'The Life of Aesop and the Gospel of Mark: Two Ancient Approaches to Elite Values', *JBL*, 129 (2010).
Wayne Hellmann, J.A., *Divine and Created Order in Bonaventure's Theology*, ed. by Jay Hammond (St Bonaventure, NY: The Franciscan Institute, 2001).
Wolterstorff, Nicholas, *Practices of Belief: Volume 2, Selected Essays* (Cambridge University Press, 2010).
Wright, N. T., *Jesus and the Victory of God* (London: SPCK, 1996).
Wright, N. T., and Marcus Borg, *The Meaning of Jesus: Two Visions* (New York: Harper Collins, 1999).
Wuthnow, R., *Saving America? Faith-Based Services and the Future of Civil Society* (Princeton and Oxford: Princeton University Press, 2004).
Zagzebski, Linda Trinkaus, *Epistemic Authority: A Theory of Trust, Authority, and Autonomy in Belief* (Oxford; New York: Oxford University Press, 2012).

INDEX

A

Agamben, 47, 73, 163-167, 176-179
Alison, 163-164, 172-179
assent, 3, 11, 90, 103, 105, 128, 181-191
authoritarianism, 1, 5, 7, 112
authority, *pessim*

B

Barth, 44, 77, 78
belief, 1-2, 6, 12, 78, 84, 88, 91-96, 107, 114, 127, 145, 149-153, 161, 213, 226, 237
Benedict, 7, 58, 61-63, 67, 72, 110, 153, 159-160, 168-171, 208, 237
Bonaventure, 10

C

Carroll, 10, 69, 71, 75-76, 84
Caruana, 10, 76, 88-89
Christianity, 6, 40, 54, 57, 59, 66-69, 75, 124, 173, 178-179
church, *pessim*
Congregation for the Doctrine of the Faith, 75, 153, 157, 161, 170, 232
conjunctions, 10

D

Deckers, 12, 211, 229, 232
democratic, 5, 61, 75, 79, 80, 83, 87, 104, 220, 242
deposit of the faith, 3, 6, 72, 81, 87
disagreement, 7, 76, 84
disjunctions, 10, 65, 149, 179
doctrine, 6, 10, 55-63, 71, 75, 80, 86-87, 90-100, 105, 111, 120, 123, 125-128, 146, 149, 151, 153, 157-158, 161, 163, 171, 177, 197, 212-214, 221-222, 233, 237, 240-242

F

faith, 6-8, 11, 40-41, 46, 55-58, 67, 72, 74-78, 80-81, 83-89, 91, 94, 97, 99, 103-105, 107, 110-114, 119, 122-127, 145-149, 151-164, 173, 175, 181, 183-184, 187-190, 192-193, 200, 219, 240-242

G

God, 1-3, 5-8, 11-12, 18, 21-23, 27-29, 31-32, 35-37, 39-46, 48-49, 55, 64, 66, 68-69, 71-72, 74, 77-79, 81-89, 94, 97, 99, 106-107, 109, 118-120, 122-128, 145, 147-148, 150-151, 154, 158-160, 163-165, 175-179, 183-184, 187-188, 190, 194, 197, 209, 213-215, 221, 227, 241
Gospel, 15, 29, 31-33, 41, 68, 104, 107, 109, 111, 146, 150, 154, 157-158, 168, 174, 188, 191, 238

H

Habermas, 12, 79, 80, 84
Hellemans, 3, 10, 53

J

Jesus, 35-36, 56, 78, 112, 194-195, 238
John, 5-6, 8, 10-11, 21-23, 26, 36, 43-45, 57, 61-62, 67, 75, 79, 80, 90, 106, 110-111, 126, 147-148, 150, 152, 156-159, 169, 174, 184, 186, 197, 199, 213, 224, 230-235, 237-242

K

kenotic, 9-12, 41-45, 49, 76, 79, 84-87, 147-151, 153-163
Kerkwijk, 3
Kerr, 82, 188
Kilby, iv, 10, 181
king, 12, 15-23, 26-29, 34, 37-38, 160, 204
Kirwan, 10, 163

L

Luke, 5, 14, 33-37, 44-48, 157

M

magisterium, 1-10, 53-58, 60-63, 68-73, 82, 87, 89, 94, 99, 103-106, 110-113, 117, 125-128, 145-149, 151-152, 154-158, 161, 181-186, 188, 189, 191, 199, 204
Mark, 14, 22, 26, 29
Matthew, 3, 5, 14, 30-33, 47, 49, 87, 150, 203, 207
Mitchell, 9, 39
modernity, 6, 10, 40, 54-55, 58, 60-61, 64-69, 75, 78-79, 84, 106, 108, 114, 184

N

Newman, 10, 11, 57, 90-94, 98, 126, 145, 149, 152, 160, 186

O

Oakley, 4-5, 11, 71, 73, 81, 87, 110, 182, 188, 193, 195-198, 201, 207
Obedience, 71, 104, 182, 240
obligation, 105

P

Paul, 5-6, 8, 10, 40-41, 45, 48, 61, 63, 67, 75, 78, 83, 85-88, 103, 106, 110, 129, 147, 150-151, 154, 166, 169, 175, 179, 197, 205-209, 213, 215, 219, 221-222, 224, 226-227, 230-235, 237-242
Pierce, 10
Pius, 57-58, 60, 62, 67, 69, 76, 96, 103, 170, 173, 214-218, 220-223, 227, 232, 239, 241
Pope Francis, 3-8, 11, 81, 109, 111, 113-114, 146, 153, 155, 158
power, 5-6, 8-9, 14, 25, 29, 35, 37-44, 47-49, 54-56, 64, 67, 72-73, 82, 85, 96, 108, 112-113, 122, 146, 148-150, 153-154, 159, 167, 173, 182, 187, 193, 195, 197-206, 209, 212, 218, 220, 224-225, 229, 236-242
Price, 10, 117-118, 121

R

Rahner, 72, 94, 160, 178-179, 182-183, 224, 227
Ratzinger, 62, 72-73, 94, 160, 170, 208, 227, 230, 232, 237, 239
reason, 7, 19, 39, 47, 59, 74-75, 81, 84-86, 93, 96-97, 121-122, 124, 145, 147, 153, 159, 167, 169, 185, 213-214, 230, 233, 237
Roman Catholic, 1, 4-5, 11, 80, 106, 181-182, 202, 204, 208
Rout, 10, 129
Ryan, 9, 14

S

Schmitt, 46-47, 163
Second Vatican Council, 4-5, 9, 61, 70, 72, 99, 111, 126, 145, 164, 178-179, 183, 193, 196, 198, 207, 214, 218-220, 224
service, 5, 8-9, 12, 14, 19, 27, 29, 33, 37-38, 48, 113, 148, 153, 158, 159, 191, 204
Simmonds, 10, 145

sovereignty, 10, 19, 37, 39, 41-46, 49
St Francis of Assisi, 129
subject, 15, 55-56, 62, 64, 85, 106, 118, 120, 161, 172, 199, 207, 232-233
Sweeney, 10, 103, 106

T

Taylor, 53, 68-69, 71, 76-77, 149, 212
teaching, 7, 11-12, 22, 27, 31, 46, 53-58, 60-61, 64, 69, 71-76, 81-82, 84, 86, 92, 103-106, 108-110, 112, 118, 120-121, 124-127, 145-158, 161, 165, 170,176, 181-188, 190-191, 196, 199-200, 203, 207-208, 214, 217, 221
truth, 10, 40-42, 71, 73, 76, 84-88, 92, 97, 99, 103-105, 109-115, 122, 125, 145, 148-150, 152-155, 157-158, 161, 168, 184, 188, 208, 214, 218, 241

V

Vatican, 4-5, 9, 11, 57-58, 61, 70-72, 87, 98-99, 104-106, 110-111, 114, 126-127, 145, 147, 150, 154, 157-158, 160, 164-165, 173, 178-179, 183, 191, 193, 196-203, 207-209, 212, 214, 217-220, 224-227, 230, 232-234, 236-240

W

Weber, 66, 75
Wolterstorff, 184-187, 190
women, 2, 5-7, 10, 48, 73, 75, 82-83, 110, 154-155, 159, 164, 167, 171-172, 200, 241

THE COUNCIL FOR RESEARCH IN VALUES AND PHILOSOPHY

PURPOSE

Today there is urgent need to attend to the nature and dignity of the person, to the quality of human life, to the purpose and goal of the physical transformation of our environment, and to the relation of all this to the development of social and political life. This, in turn, requires philosophic clarification of the base upon which freedom is exercised, that is, of the values which provide stability and guidance to one's decisions.

Such studies must be able to reach deeply into one's culture and that of other parts of the world as mutually reinforcing and enriching in order to uncover the roots of the dignity of persons and of their societies. They must be able to identify the conceptual forms in terms of which modern industrial and technological developments are structured and how these impact upon human self-understanding. Above all, they must be able to bring these elements together in the creative understanding essential for setting our goals and determining our modes of interaction. In the present complex global circumstances this is a condition for growing together with trust and justice, honest dedication and mutual concern.

The Council for Studies in Values and Philosophy (RVP) unites scholars who share these concerns and are interested in the application thereto of existing capabilities in the field of philosophy and other disciplines. Its work is to identify areas in which study is needed, the intellectual resources which can be brought to bear thereupon, and the means for publication and interchange of the work from the various regions of the world. In bringing these together its goal is scientific discovery and publication which contributes to the present promotion of humankind.

In sum, our times present both the need and the opportunity for deeper and ever more progressive understanding of the person and of the foundations of social life. The development of such understanding is the goal of the RVP.

PROJECTS

A set of related research efforts is currently in process:

1. *Cultural Heritage and Contemporary Change: Philosophical Foundations for Social Life.* Focused, mutually coordinated research teams in university centers prepare volumes as part of an integrated philosophic search for self-understanding differentiated by culture and civilization. These evolve more adequate understandings of the person in society and look to the cultural heritage of each for the resources to respond to the challenges of its own specific contemporary transformation.

2. *Seminars on Culture and Contemporary Issues.* This series of 10 week crosscultural and interdisciplinary seminars is coordinated by the RVP in Washington.

3. *Joint-Colloquia* with Institutes of Philosophy of the National Academies of Science, university philosophy departments, and societies. Underway since 1976 in Eastern Europe and, since 1987, in China, these concern the person in contemporary society.

4. *Foundations of Moral Education and Character Development.* A study in values and education which unites philosophers, psychologists, social scientists and scholars in education in the elaboration of ways of enriching the moral content of education and character development. This work has been underway since 1980.

The personnel for these projects consists of established scholars willing to contribute their time and research as part of their professional commitment to life in contemporary society. For resources to implement this work the Council, as 501 C3 a non-profit organization incorporated in the District of Colombia, looks to various private foundations, public programs and enterprises.

PUBLICATIONS ON CULTURAL HERITAGE AND CONTEMPORARY CHANGE

Series I. Culture and Values
Series II. African Philosophical Studies
Series IIA. Islamic Philosophical Studies
Series III. Asian Philosophical Studies
Series IV. Western European Philosophical Studies
Series IVA. Central and Eastern European Philosophical Studies
Series V. Latin American Philosophical Studies
Series VI. Foundations of Moral Education
Series VII. Seminars: Culture and Values
Series VIII. Christian Philosophical Studies

****

CULTURAL HERITAGE AND CONTEMPORARY CHANGE

Series I. Culture and Values

I.1 *Research on Culture and Values: Intersection of Universities, Churches and Nations.* George F. McLean, ed. ISBN 0819173533 (paper); 081917352-5 (cloth).

I.2 *The Knowledge of Values: A Methodological Introduction to the Study of Values;* A. Lopez Quintas, ed. ISBN 081917419x (paper); 0819174181 (cloth).

I.3 *Reading Philosophy for the XXIst Century*. George F. McLean, ed. ISBN 0819174157 (paper); 0819174149 (cloth).
I.4 *Relations between Cultures*. John A. Kromkowski, ed. ISBN 1565180089 (paper); 1565180097 (cloth).
I.5 *Urbanization and Values*. John A. Kromkowski, ed. ISBN 1565180100 (paper); 1565180119 (cloth).
I.6 *The Place of the Person in Social Life*. Paul Peachey and John A. Kromkowski, eds. ISBN 1565180127 (paper); 156518013-5 (cloth).
I.7 *Abrahamic Faiths, Ethnicity and Ethnic Conflicts*. Paul Peachey, George F. McLean and John A. Kromkowski, eds. ISBN 1565181042 (paper).
I.8 *Ancient Western Philosophy: The Hellenic Emergence*. George F. McLean and Patrick J. Aspell, eds. ISBN 156518100X (paper).
I.9 *Medieval Western Philosophy: The European Emergence*. Patrick J. Aspell, ed. ISBN 1565180941 (paper).
I.10 *The Ethical Implications of Unity and the Divine in Nicholas of Cusa*. David L. De Leonardis. ISBN 1565181123 (paper).
I.11 *Ethics at the Crossroads: 1.Normative Ethics and Objective Reason*. George F. McLean, ed. ISBN 1565180224 (paper).
I.12 *Ethics at the Crossroads: 2. Personalist Ethics and Human Subjectivity*. George F. McLean, ed. ISBN 1565180240 (paper).
I.13 *The Emancipative Theory of Jürgen Habermas and Metaphysics*. Robert Badillo. ISBN 1565180429 (paper); 1565180437 (cloth).
I.14 *The Deficient Cause of Moral Evil According to Thomas Aquinas*. Edward Cook. ISBN 1565180704 (paper).
I.15 *Human Love: Its Meaning and Scope, a Phenomenology of Gift and Encounter*. Alfonso Lopez Quintas. ISBN 1565180747 (paper).
I.16 *Civil Society and Social Reconstruction*. George F. McLean, ed. ISBN 1565180860 (paper).
I.17 *Ways to God, Personal and Social at the Turn of Millennia: The Iqbal Lecture, Lahore*. George F. McLean. ISBN 1565181239 (paper).
I.18 *The Role of the Sublime in Kant's Moral Metaphysics*. John R. Goodreau. ISBN 1565181247 (paper).
I.19 *Philosophical Challenges and Opportunities of Globalization*. Oliva Blanchette, Tomonobu Imamichi and George F. McLean, eds. ISBN 1565181298 (paper).
I.20 *Faith, Reason and Philosophy: Lectures at The al-Azhar, Qom, Tehran, Lahore and Beijing; Appendix: The Encyclical Letter: Fides et Ratio*. George F. McLean. ISBN 156518130 (paper).
I.21 *Religion and the Relation between Civilizations: Lectures on Cooperation between Islamic and Christian Cultures in a Global Horizon*. George F. McLean. ISBN 1565181522 (paper).
I.22 *Freedom, Cultural Traditions and Progress: Philosophy in Civil Society and Nation Building, Tashkent Lectures, 1999*. George F. McLean. ISBN 1565181514 (paper).
I.23 *Ecology of Knowledge*. Jerzy A. Wojciechowski. ISBN 1565181581 (paper).

I.24 *God and the Challenge of Evil: A Critical Examination of Some Serious Objections to the Good and Omnipotent God*. John L. Yardan. ISBN 1565181603 (paper).
I.25 *Reason, Rationality and Reasonableness, Vietnamese Philosophical Studies, I*. Tran Van Doan. ISBN 1565181662 (paper).
I.26 *The Culture of Citizenship: Inventing Postmodern Civic Culture*. Thomas Bridges. ISBN 1565181689 (paper).
I.27 *The Historicity of Understanding and the Problem of Relativism in Gadamer's Philosophical Hermeneutics*. Osman Bilen. ISBN 1565181670 (paper).
I.28 *Speaking of God*. Carlo Huber. ISBN 1565181697 (paper).
I.29 *Persons, Peoples and Cultures in a Global Age: Metaphysical Bases for Peace between Civilizations*. George F. McLean. ISBN 1565181875 (paper).
I.30 *Hermeneutics, Tradition and Contemporary Change: Lectures in Chennai/Madras, India*. George F. McLean. ISBN 1565181883 (paper).
I.31 *Husserl and Stein*. Richard Feist and William Sweet, eds. ISBN 1565181948 (paper).
I.32 *Paul Hanly Furfey's Quest for a Good Society*. Bronislaw Misztal, Francesco Villa, and Eric Sean Williams, eds. ISBN 1565182278 (paper).
I.33 *Three Theories of Society*. Paul Hanly Furfey. ISBN 9781565182288 (paper).
I.34 *Building Peace in Civil Society: An Autobiographical Report from a Believers' Church*. Paul Peachey. ISBN 9781565182325 (paper).
I.35 *Karol Wojtyla's Philosophical Legacy*. Agnes B. Curry, Nancy Mardas and George F. McLean, eds. ISBN 9781565182479 (paper).
I.36 *Kantian Form and Phenomenological Force: Kant's Imperatives and the Directives of Contemporary Phenomenology*. Randolph C. Wheeler. ISBN 9781565182547 (paper).
I.37 *Beyond Modernity: The Recovery of Person and Community in Global Times: Lectures in China and Vietnam*. George F. McLean. ISBN 9781565182578 (paper)
I.38 *Religion and Culture*. George F. McLean. ISBN 9781565182561 (paper).
I.39 *The Dialogue of Cultural Traditions: Global Perspective*. William Sweet, George F. McLean, Tomonobu Imamichi, Safak Ural, O. Faruk Akyol, eds. ISBN 9781565182585 (paper).
I.40 *Unity and Harmony, Love and Compassion in Global Times*. George F. McLean. ISBN 9781565182592 (paper).
I.41 *Intercultural Dialogue and Human Rights*. Luigi Bonanate, Roberto Papini and William Sweet, eds. ISBN 9781565182714 (paper).
I.42 *Philosophy Emerging from Culture*. William Sweet, George F. McLean, Oliva Blanchette, Wonbin Park, eds. ISBN 9781565182851 (paper).

I.43 *Whence Intelligibility?* Louis Perron, ed. ISBN 9781565182905 (paper).
I.44 *What is Intercultural Philosophy?* William Sweet, ed. ISBN 9781565182912 (paper).

Series II. African Philosophical Studies

II.1 *Person and Community: Ghanaian Philosophical Studies: I.* Kwasi Wiredu and Kwame Gyekye, eds. ISBN 1565180046 (paper); 1565180054 (cloth).
II.2 *The Foundations of Social Life: Ugandan Philosophical Studies: I.* A.T. Dalfovo, ed. ISBN 1565180062 (paper); 156518007-0 (cloth).
II.3 *Identity and Change in Nigeria: Nigerian Philosophical Studies, I.* Theophilus Okere, ed. ISBN 1565180682 (paper).
II.4 *Social Reconstruction in Africa: Ugandan Philosophical studies, II.* E. Wamala, A.R. Byaruhanga, A.T. Dalfovo, J.K. Kigongo, S.A. Mwanahewa and G. Tusabe, eds. ISBN 1565181182 (paper).
II.5 *Ghana: Changing Values/Changing Technologies: Ghanaian Philosophical Studies, II.* Helen Lauer, ed. ISBN 1565181441 (paper).
II.6 *Sameness and Difference: Problems and Potentials in South African Civil Society: South African Philosophical Studies, I.* James R. Cochrane and Bastienne Klein, eds. ISBN 1565181557 (paper).
II.7 *Protest and Engagement: Philosophy after Apartheid at an Historically Black South African University: South African Philosophical Studies, II.* Patrick Giddy, ed. ISBN 1565181638 (paper).
II.8 *Ethics, Human Rights and Development in Africa: Ugandan Philosophical Studies, III.* A.T. Dalfovo, J.K. Kigongo, J. Kisekka, G. Tusabe, E. Wamala, R. Munyonyo, A.B. Rukooko, A.B.T. Byaruhanga-akiiki, and M. Mawa, eds. ISBN 1565181727 (paper).
II.9 *Beyond Cultures: Perceiving a Common Humanity: Ghanaian Philosophical Studies, III.* Kwame Gyekye. ISBN 156518193X (paper).
II.10 *Social and Religious Concerns of East African: A Wajibu Anthology: Kenyan Philosophical Studies, I.* Gerald J. Wanjohi and G. Wakuraya Wanjohi, eds. ISBN 1565182219 (paper).
II.11 *The Idea of an African University: The Nigerian Experience: Nigerian Philosophical Studies, II.* Joseph Kenny, ed. ISBN 9781565182301 (paper).
II.12 *The Struggles after the Struggle: Zimbabwean Philosophical Study, I.* David Kaulemu, ed. ISBN 9781565182318 (paper).
II.13 *Indigenous and Modern Environmental Ethics: A Study of the Indigenous Oromo Environmental Ethic and Modern Issues of Environment and Development: Ethiopian Philosophical Studies, I.* Workineh Kelbessa. ISBN 9781565182530 (paper).

II.14 *African Philosophy and the Future of Africa: South African Philosophical Studies, III.* Gerard Walmsley, ed. ISMB 9781565182707 (paper).
II.15 *Philosophy in Ethiopia: African Philosophy Today, I: Ethiopian Philosophical Studies, II.* Bekele Gutema and Charles C. Verharen, eds. ISBN 9781565182790 (paper).
II.16 *The Idea of a Nigerian University: A Revisited: Nigerian Philosophical Studies, III.* Olatunji Oyeshile and Joseph Kenny, eds. ISBN 9781565182776 (paper).
II.17 *Philosophy in African Traditions and Cultures, Zimbabwe Philosophical Studies, II.* Fainos Mangena, Tarisayi Andrea Chimuka, Francis Mabiri, eds. ISBN 9781565182998 (paper).

Series IIA. Islamic Philosophical Studies

IIA.1 *Islam and the Political Order.* Muhammad Saïd al-Ashmawy. ISBN ISBN 156518047X (paper); 156518046-1 (cloth).
IIA.2 *Al-Ghazali Deliverance from Error and Mystical Union with the Almighty: Al-munqidh Min al-Dadāl.* Critical Arabic edition and English translation by Muhammad Abulaylah and Nurshif Abdul-Rahim Rifat; Introduction and notes by George F. McLean. ISBN 1565181530 (Arabic-English edition, paper), ISBN 1565180828 (Arabic edition, paper), ISBN 156518081X (English edition, paper)
IIA.3 *Philosophy in Pakistan.* Naeem Ahmad, ed. ISBN 1565181085 (paper).
IIA.4 *The Authenticity of the Text in Hermeneutics.* Seyed Musa Dibadj. ISBN 1565181174 (paper).
IIA.5 *Interpretation and the Problem of the Intention of the Author: H.-G. Gadamer vs E.D. Hirsch.* Burhanettin Tatar. ISBN 156518121 (paper).
IIA.6 *Ways to God, Personal and Social at the Turn of Millennia: The Iqbal Lectures, Lahore.* George F. McLean. ISBN 1565181239 (paper).
IIA.7 *Faith, Reason and Philosophy: Lectures at Al-Azhar University, Qom, Tehran, Lahore and Beijing; Appendix: The Encyclical Letter: Fides et Ratio.* George F. McLean. ISBN 1565181301 (paper).
IIA.8 *Islamic and Christian Cultures: Conflict or Dialogue: Bulgarian Philosophical Studies, III.* Plament Makariev, ed. ISBN 156518162X (paper).
IIA.9 *Values of Islamic Culture and the Experience of History, Russian Philosophical Studies, I.* Nur Kirabaev, Yuriy Pochta, eds. ISBN 1565181336 (paper).
IIA.10 *Christian-Islamic Preambles of Faith.* Joseph Kenny. ISBN 1565181387 (paper).
IIA.11 *The Historicity of Understanding and the Problem of Relativism in Gadamer's Philosophical Hermeneutics.* Osman Bilen. ISBN 1565181670 (paper).

IIA.12 *Religion and the Relation between Civilizations: Lectures on Cooperation between Islamic and Christian Cultures in a Global Horizon.* George F. McLean. ISBN 1565181522 (paper).
IIA.13 *Modern Western Christian Theological Understandings of Muslims since the Second Vatican Council.* Mahmut Aydin. ISBN 1565181719 (paper).
IIA.14 *Philosophy of the Muslim World; Authors and Principal Themes.* Joseph Kenny. ISBN 1565181794 (paper).
IIA.15 *Islam and Its Quest for Peace: Jihad, Justice and Education.* Mustafa Köylü. ISBN 1565181808 (paper).
IIA.16 *Islamic Thought on the Existence of God: Contributions and Contrasts with Contemporary Western Philosophy of Religion.* Cafer S. Yaran. ISBN 1565181921 (paper).
IIA.17 *Hermeneutics, Faith, and Relations between Cultures: Lectures in Qom, Iran.* George F. McLean. ISBN 1565181913 (paper).
IIA.18 *Change and Essence: Dialectical Relations between Change and Continuity in the Turkish Intellectual Tradition.* Sinasi Gunduz and Cafer S. Yaran, eds. ISBN 1565182227 (paper).
IIA. 19 *Understanding Other Religions: Al-Biruni and Gadamer's "Fusion of Horizons".* Kemal Ataman. ISBN 9781565182523 (paper).

Series III. Asian Philosophical Studies

III.1 *Man and Nature: Chinese Philosophical Studies, I.* Tang Yi-jie and Li Zhen, eds. ISBN 0819174130 (paper); 0819174122 (cloth).
III.2 *Chinese Foundations for Moral Education and Character Development: Chinese Philosophical Studies, II.* Tran van Doan, ed. ISBN 1565180321 (paper); 156518033X (cloth).
III.3 *Confucianism, Buddhism, Taoism, Christianity and Chinese Culture: Chinese Philosophical Studies, III.* Tang Yijie. ISBN 1565180348 (paper); 156518035-6 (cloth).
III.4 *Morality, Metaphysics and Chinese Culture (Metaphysics, Culture and Morality, I).* Vincent Shen and Tran van Doan, eds. ISBN 1565180275 (paper); 156518026-7 (cloth).
III.5 *Tradition, Harmony and Transcendence.* George F. McLean. ISBN 1565180313 (paper); 156518030-5 (cloth).
III.6 *Psychology, Phenomenology and Chinese Philosophy: Chinese Philosophical Studies, VI.* Vincent Shen, Richard Knowles and Tran Van Doan, eds. ISBN 1565180453 (paper); 1565180445 (cloth).
III.7 *Values in Philippine Culture and Education: Philippine Philosophical Studies, I.* Manuel B. Dy, Jr., ed. ISBN 1565180412 (paper); 156518040-2 (cloth).
III.7A *The Human Person and Society: Chinese Philosophical Studies, VIIA.* Zhu Dasheng, Jin Xiping and George F. McLean, eds. ISBN 1565180887.

III.8 *The Filipino Mind: Philippine Philosophical Studies II*. Leonardo N. Mercado. ISBN 156518064X (paper); 156518063-1 (cloth).

III.9 *Philosophy of Science and Education: Chinese Philosophical Studies IX*. Vincent Shen and Tran Van Doan, eds. ISBN 1565180763 (paper); 156518075-5 (cloth).

III.10 *Chinese Cultural Traditions and Modernization: Chinese Philosophical Studies, X*. Wang Miaoyang, Yu Xuanmeng and George F. McLean, eds. ISBN 1565180682 (paper).

III.11 *The Humanization of Technology and Chinese Culture: Chinese Philosophical Studies XI*. Tomonobu Imamichi, Wang Miaoyang and Liu Fangtong, eds. ISBN 1565181166 (paper).

III.12 *Beyond Modernization: Chinese Roots of Global Awareness: Chinese Philosophical Studies, XII*. Wang Miaoyang, Yu Xuanmeng and George F. McLean, eds. ISBN 1565180909 (paper).

III.13 *Philosophy and Modernization in China: Chinese Philosophical Studies XIII*. Liu Fangtong, Huang Songjie and George F. McLean, eds. ISBN 1565180666 (paper).

III.14 *Economic Ethics and Chinese Culture: Chinese Philosophical Studies, XIV*. Yu Xuanmeng, Lu Xiaohe, Liu Fangtong, Zhang Rulun and Georges Enderle, eds. ISBN 1565180925 (paper).

III.15 *Civil Society in a Chinese Context: Chinese Philosophical Studies XV*. Wang Miaoyang, Yu Xuanmeng and Manuel B. Dy, eds. ISBN 1565180844 (paper).

III.16 *The Bases of Values in a Time of Change: Chinese and Western: Chinese Philosophical Studies, XVI*. Kirti Bunchua, Liu Fangtong, Yu Xuanmeng, Yu Wujin, eds. ISBN 156518114X (paper).

III.17 *Dialogue between Christian Philosophy and Chinese Culture: Philosophical Perspectives for the Third Millennium: Chinese Philosophical Studies, XVII*. Paschal Ting, Marian Kao and Bernard Li, eds. ISBN 1565181735 (paper).

III.18 *The Poverty of Ideological Education: Chinese Philosophical Studies, XVIII*. Tran Van Doan. ISBN 1565181646 (paper).

III.19 *God and the Discovery of Man: Classical and Contemporary Approaches: Lectures in Wuhan, China*. George F. McLean. ISBN 1565181891 (paper).

III.20 *Cultural Impact on International Relations: Chinese Philosophical Studies, XX*. Yu Xintian, ed. ISBN 156518176X (paper).

III.21 *Cultural Factors in International Relations: Chinese Philosophical Studies, XXI*. Yu Xintian, ed. ISBN 1565182049 (paper).

III.22 *Wisdom in China and the West: Chinese Philosophical Studies, XXII*. Vincent Shen and Willard Oxtoby. ISBN 1565182057 (paper)

III.23 *China's Contemporary Philosophical Journey: Western Philosophy and Marxism: Chinese Philosophical Studies, XXIII*. Liu Fangtong. ISBN 1565182065 (paper).

III.24 *Shanghai: Its Urbanization and Culture: Chinese Philosophical Studies, XXIV*. Yu Xuanmeng and He Xirong, eds. ISBN 1565182073 (paper).
III.25 *Dialogue of Philosophies, Religions and Civilizations in the Era of Globalization: Chinese Philosophical Studies, XXV*. Zhao Dunhua, ed. ISBN 9781565182431 (paper).
III.26 *Rethinking Marx: Chinese Philosophical Studies, XXVI*. Zou Shipeng and Yang Xuegong, eds. ISBN 9781565182448 (paper).
III.27 *Confucian Ethics in Retrospect and Prospect: Chinese Philosophical Studies XXVII*. Vincent Shen and Kwong-loi Shun, eds. ISBN 9781565182455 (paper).
III.28 *Cultural Tradition and Social Progress, Chinese Philosophical Studies, XXVIII*. He Xirong, Yu Xuanmeng, Yu Xintian, Yu Wujing, Yang Junyi, eds. ISBN 9781565182660 (paper).
III.29 *Spiritual Foundations and Chinese Culture: A Philosophical Approach: Chinese Philosophical Studies, XXIX*. Anthony J. Carroll and Katia Lenehan, eds. ISBN 9781565182974 (paper)
III.30 *Diversity in Unity: Harmony in a Global Age: Chinese Philosophical Studies, XXX*. He Xirong and Yu Xuanmeng, eds. ISBN 978156518 3070 (paper).
IIIB.1 *Authentic Human Destiny: The Paths of Shankara and Heidegger: Indian Philosophical Studies, I*. Vensus A. George. ISBN 1565181190 (paper).
IIIB.2 *The Experience of Being as Goal of Human Existence: The Heideggerian Approach: Indian Philosophical Studies, II*. Vensus A. George. ISBN 156518145X (paper).
IIIB.3 *Religious Dialogue as Hermeneutics: Bede Griffiths's Advaitic Approach: Indian Philosophical Studies, III*. Kuruvilla Pandikattu. ISBN 1565181395 (paper).
IIIB.4 *Self-Realization [Brahmaanubhava]: The Advaitic Perspective of Shankara: Indian Philosophical Studies, IV*. Vensus A. George. ISBN 1565181549 (paper).
IIIB.5 *Gandhi: The Meaning of Mahatma for the Millennium: Indian Philosophical Studies, V*. Kuruvilla Pandikattu, ed. ISBN 1565181565 (paper).
IIIB.6 *Civil Society in Indian Cultures: Indian Philosophical Studies, VI*. Asha Mukherjee, Sabujkali Sen (Mitra) and K. Bagchi, eds. ISBN 1565181573 (paper).
IIIB.7 *Hermeneutics, Tradition and Contemporary Change: Lectures in Chennai/Madras, India*. George F. McLean. ISBN 1565181883 (paper).
IIIB.8 *Plenitude and Participation: The Life of God in Man: Lectures in Chennai/Madras, India*. George F. McLean. ISBN 1565181999 (paper).
IIIB.9 *Sufism and Bhakti, a Comparative Study: Indian Philosophical Studies, VII*. Md. Sirajul Islam. ISBN 1565181980 (paper).

IIIB.10 *Reasons for Hope: Its Nature, Role and Future*: Indian Philosophical Studies, *VIII*. Kuruvilla Pandikattu, ed. ISBN 156518 2162 (paper).
IIIB.11 *Lifeworlds and Ethics: Studies in Several Keys*: Indian Philosophical Studies, *IX*. Margaret Chatterjee. ISBN 9781565182332 (paper).
IIIB.12 *Paths to the Divine: Ancient and Indian*: Indian Philosophical Studies, *X*. Vensus A. George. ISBN 9781565182486 (paper).
IIB.13 *Faith, Reason, Science: Philosophical Reflections with Special Reference to Fides et Ratio: Indian Philosophical Studies, XIII*. Varghese Manimala, ed. IBSN 9781565182554 (paper).
IIIB.14 *Identity, Creativity and Modernization: Perspectives on Indian Cultural Tradition: Indian Philosophical Studies, XIV*. Sebastian Velassery and Vensus A. George, eds. ISBN 9781565182783 (paper).
IIIB.15 *Elusive Transcendence: An Exploration of the Human Condition Based on Paul Ricoeur: Indian Philosophical Studies, XV*. Kuruvilla Pandikattu. ISBN 9781565182950 (paper).
IIIC.1 *Spiritual Values and Social Progress: Uzbekistan Philosophical Studies, I*. Said Shermukhamedov and Victoriya Levinskaya, eds. ISBN 1565181433 (paper).
IIIC.2 *Kazakhstan: Cultural Inheritance and Social Transformation: Kazakh Philosophical Studies, I*. Abdumalik Nysanbayev. ISBN 1565182022 (paper).
IIIC.3 *Social Memory and Contemporaneity: Kyrgyz Philosophical Studies, I*. Gulnara A. Bakieva. ISBN 9781565182349 (paper).
IIID.1 *Reason, Rationality and Reasonableness: Vietnamese Philosophical Studies, I*. Tran Van Doan. ISBN 1565181662 (paper).
IIID.2 *Hermeneutics for a Global Age: Lectures in Shanghai and Hanoi*. George F. McLean. ISBN 1565181905 (paper).
IIID.3 *Cultural Traditions and Contemporary Challenges in Southeast Asia*. Warayuth Sriwarakuel, Manuel B. Dy, J. Haryatmoko, Nguyen Trong Chuan, and Chhay Yiheang, eds. ISBN 1565182138 (paper).
IIID.4 *Filipino Cultural Traits: Claro R. Ceniza Lectures*. Rolando M. Gripaldo, ed. ISBN 1565182251 (paper).
IIID.5 *The History of Buddhism in Vietnam*. Chief editor: Nguyen Tai Thu; Authors: Dinh Minh Chi, Ly Kim Hoa, Ha thuc Minh, Ha Van Tan, Nguyen Tai Thu. ISBN 1565180984 (paper).
IIID.6 *Relations between Religions and Cultures in Southeast Asia*. Gadis Arivia and Donny Gahral Adian, eds. ISBN 9781565182509 (paper).

Series IV. Western European Philosophical Studies

IV.1 *Italy in Transition: The Long Road from the First to the Second Republic: The Edmund D. Pellegrino Lectures*. Paolo Janni, ed. ISBN 1565181204 (paper).

IV.2 *Italy and the European Monetary Union: The Edmund D. Pellegrino Lectures.* Paolo Janni, ed. ISBN 156518128X (paper).
IV.3 *Italy at the Millennium: Economy, Politics, Literature and Journalism: The Edmund D. Pellegrino Lectures.* Paolo Janni, ed. ISBN 1565181581 (paper).
IV.4 *Speaking of God.* Carlo Huber. ISBN 1565181697 (paper).
IV.5 *The Essence of Italian Culture and the Challenge of a Global Age.* Paulo Janni and George F. McLean, eds. ISBB 1565181778 (paper).
IV.6 *Italic Identity in Pluralistic Contexts: Toward the Development of Intercultural Competencies.* Piero Bassetti and Paolo Janni, eds. ISBN 1565181441 (paper).
IV.7 *Phenomenon of Affectivity: Phenomenological-Anthropological Perspectives.* Ghislaine Florival. ISBN 9781565182899 (paper).
IV.8 *Towards a Kenotic Vision of Authority in the Catholic Church.* Anthony J. Carroll, Marthe Kerkwijk, Michael Kirwan, James Sweeney, eds ISNB 9781565182936 (paper).
IV.9 *A Catholic Minority Church in a World of Seekers.* Staf Hellemans and Peter Jonkers, eds. ISBN 9781565183018 (paper).

Series IVA. Central and Eastern European Philosophical Studies

IVA.1 *The Philosophy of Person: Solidarity and Cultural Creativity: Polish Philosophical Studies, I.* A. Tischner, J.M. Zycinski, eds. ISBN 1565180496 (paper); 156518048-8 (cloth).
IVA.2 *Public and Private Social Inventions in Modern Societies: Polish Philosophical Studies, II.* L. Dyczewski, P. Peachey, J.A. Kromkowski, eds. ISBN. 1565180518 (paper); 156518050X (cloth).
IVA.3 *Traditions and Present Problems of Czech Political Culture: Czechoslovak Philosophical Studies, I.* M. Bednár and M. Vejraka, eds. ISBN 1565180577 (paper); 156518056-9 (cloth).
IVA.4 *Czech Philosophy in the XXth Century: Czech Philosophical Studies, II.* Lubomír Nový and Jirí Gabriel, eds. ISBN 1565180291 (paper); 156518028-3 (cloth).
IVA.5 *Language, Values and the Slovak Nation: Slovak Philosophical Studies, I.* Tibor Pichler and Jana Gašparí-ková, eds. ISBN 1565180372 (paper); 156518036-4 (cloth).
IVA.6 *Morality and Public Life in a Time of Change: Bulgarian Philosophical Studies, I.* V. Prodanov and A. Davidov, eds. ISBN 1565180550 (paper); 1565180542 (cloth).
IVA.7 *Knowledge and Morality: Georgian Philosophical Studies, 1.* N.V. Chavchavadze, G. Nodia and P. Peachey, eds. ISBN 1565180534 (paper); 1565180526 (cloth).
IVA.8 *Cultural Heritage and Social Change: Lithuanian Philosophical Studies, I.* Bronius Kuzmickas and Aleksandr Dobrynin, eds. ISBN 1565180399 (paper); 1565180380 (cloth).

IVA.9 *National, Cultural and Ethnic Identities: Harmony beyond Conflict: Czech Philosophical Studies, III.* Jaroslav Hroch, David Hollan, George F. McLean, eds. ISBN 1565181131 (paper).

IVA.10 *Models of Identities in Postcommunist Societies: Yugoslav Philosophical Studies, I.* Zagorka Golubovic and George F. McLean, eds. ISBN 1565181211 (paper).

IVA.11 *Interests and Values: The Spirit of Venture in a Time of Change: Slovak Philosophical Studies, II.* Tibor Pichler and Jana Gasparikova, eds. ISBN 1565181255 (paper).

IVA.12 *Creating Democratic Societies: Values and Norms: Bulgarian Philosophical Studies, II.* Plamen Makariev, Andrew M. Blasko and Asen Davidov, eds. ISBN 156518131X (paper).

IVA.13 *Values of Islamic Culture and the Experience of History: Russian Philosophical Studies, I.* Nur Kirabaev and Yuriy Pochta, eds. ISBN 1565181336 (paper).

IVA.14 *Values and Education in Romania Today: Romanian Philosophical Studies, I.* Marin Calin and Magdalena Dumitrana, eds. ISBN 1565181344 (paper).

IVA.15 *Between Words and Reality, Studies on the Politics of Recognition and the Changes of Regime in Contemporary Romania: Romanian Philosophical Studies, II.* Victor Neumann. ISBN 1565181611 (paper).

IVA.16 *Culture and Freedom: Romanian Philosophical Studies, III.* Marin Aiftinca, ed. ISBN 1565181360 (paper).

IVA.17 *Lithuanian Philosophy: Persons and Ideas: Lithuanian Philosophical Studies, II.* Jurate Baranova, ed. ISBN 1565181379 (paper).

IVA.18 *Human Dignity: Values and Justice: Czech Philosophical Studies, IV.* Miloslav Bednar, ed. ISBN 1565181409 (paper).

IVA.19 *Values in the Polish Cultural Tradition: Polish Philosophical Studies, III.* Leon Dyczewski, ed. ISBN 1565181425 (paper).

IVA.20 *Liberalization and Transformation of Morality in Post-communist Countries: Polish Philosophical Studies, IV.* Tadeusz Buksinski. ISBN 1565181786 (paper).

IVA.21 *Islamic and Christian Cultures: Conflict or Dialogue: Bulgarian Philosophical Studies, III.* Plament Makariev, ed. ISBN 156518162X (paper).

IVA.22 *Moral, Legal and Political Values in Romanian Culture: Romanian Philosophical Studies, IV.* Mihaela Czobor-Lupp and J. Stefan Lupp, eds. ISBN 1565181700 (paper).

IVA.23 *Social Philosophy: Paradigm of Contemporary Thinking: Lithuanian Philosophical Studies, III.* Jurate Morkuniene. ISBN 1565182030 (paper).

IVA.24 *Romania: Cultural Identity and Education for Civil Society: Romanian Philosophical Studies, V.* Magdalena Dumitrana, ed. ISBN 156518209X (paper).

IVA.25 *Polish Axiology: the 20th Century and Beyond: Polish Philosophical Studies, V.* Stanislaw Jedynak, ed. ISBN 1565181417 (paper).
IVA.26 *Contemporary Philosophical Discourse in Lithuania: Lithuanian Philosophical Studies, IV.* Jurate Baranova, ed. ISBN 156518-2154 (paper).
IVA.27 *Eastern Europe and the Challenges of Globalization: Polish Philosophical Studies, VI.* Tadeusz Buksinski and Dariusz Dobrzanski, ed. ISBN 1565182189 (paper).
IVA.28 *Church, State, and Society in Eastern Europe: Hungarian Philosophical Studies, I.* Miklós Tomka. ISBN 156518226X (paper).
IVA.29 *Politics, Ethics, and the Challenges to Democracy in 'New Independent States': Georgian Philosophical Studies, II.* Tinatin Bochorishvili, William Sweet, Daniel Ahern, eds. ISBN 9781565182240 (paper).
IVA.30 *Comparative Ethics in a Global Age: Russian Philosophical Studies II.* Marietta T. Stepanyants, eds. ISBN 9781565182356 (paper).
IVA.31 *Identity and Values of Lithuanians: Lithuanian Philosophical Studies, V.* Aida Savicka, eds. ISBN 9781565182367 (paper).
IVA.32 *The Challenge of Our Hope: Christian Faith in Dialogue: Polish Philosophical Studies, VII.* Waclaw Hryniewicz. ISBN 9781565182370 (paper).
IVA.33 *Diversity and Dialogue: Culture and Values in the Age of Globalization.* Andrew Blasko and Plamen Makariev, eds. ISBN 9781565182387 (paper).
IVA. 34 *Civil Society, Pluralism and Universalism: Polish Philosophical Studies, VIII.* Eugeniusz Gorski. ISBN 9781565182417 (paper).
IVA.35 *Romanian Philosophical Culture, Globalization, and Education: Romanian Philosophical Studies VI.* Stefan Popenici and Alin Tat and, eds. ISBN 9781565182424 (paper).
IVA.36 *Political Transformation and Changing Identities in Central and Eastern Europe: Lithuanian Philosophical Studies, VI.* Andrew Blasko and Diana Janušauskienė, eds. ISBN 9781565182462 (paper).
IVA.37 *Truth and Morality: The Role of Truth in Public Life: Romanian Philosophical Studies, VII.* Wilhelm Dancă, ed. ISBN 9781565182493 (paper).
IVA.38 *Globalization and Culture: Outlines of Contemporary Social Cognition: Lithuanian Philosophical Studies, VII.* Jurate Morkuniene, ed. ISBN 9781565182516 (paper).
IVA.39 *Knowledge and Belief in the Dialogue of Cultures, Russian Philosophical Studies, III.* Marietta Stepanyants, ed. ISBN 9781565182622 (paper).
IVA.40 *God and the Post-Modern Thought: Philosophical Issues in the Contemporary Critique of Modernity, Polish Philosophical Studies, IX.* Józef Życiński. ISBN 9781565182677 (paper).

IVA.41 *Dialogue among Civilizations, Russian Philosophical Studies, IV.* Nur Kirabaev and Yuriy Pochta, eds. ISBN 9781565182653 (paper).
IVA.42 *The Idea of Solidarity: Philosophical and Social Contexts, Polish Philosophical Studies, X.* Dariusz Dobrzanski, ed. ISBN 9781565182961 (paper).
IVA.43 *God's Spirit in the World: Ecumenical and Cultural Essays, Polish Philosophical Studies, XI.* Waclaw Hryniewicz. ISBN 9781565182738 (paper).
IVA.44 *Philosophical Theology and the Christian Traditions: Russian and Western Perspectives, Russian Philosophical Studies, V.* David Bradshaw, ed. ISBN 9781565182752 (paper).
IVA.45 *Ethics and the Challenge of Secularism: Russian Philosophical Studies, VI.* David Bradshaw, ed. ISBN 9781565182806 (paper).
IVA.46 *Philosophy and Spirituality across Cultures and Civilizations: Russian Philosophical Studies, VII.* Nur Kirabaev, Yuriy Pochta and Ruzana Pskhu, eds. ISBN 9781565182820 (paper).
IVA.47 *Values of the Human Person Contemporary Challenges: Romanian Philosophical Studies, VIII.* Mihaela Pop, ed. ISBN 9781565182844 (paper).
IVA.48 *Faith and Secularization: A Romanian Narrative: Romanian Philosophical Studies, IX.* Wilhelm Dancă, ed. ISBN 9781565182929 (paper).
IVA.49 *The Spirit: The Cry of the World: Polish Philosophical Studies, XII.* Waclaw Hryniewicz. ISBN 9781565182943 (paper).
IVA.50 *Philosophy and Science in Cultures: East and West: Russian Philosophical Studies, VIII.* Marietta T. Stepanyants, ed. ISBN 9781565182967 (paper).
IVA.51 *A Czech Perspective on Faith in a Secular Age: Czech Philosophical Studies V.* Tomáš Halík and Pavel Hošek, eds. ISBN 9781565183001 (paper).
IVA52 *Dilemmas of the Catholic Church in Poland: Polish Philosophical Studies, XIII.* Tadeusz Buksinski, ed. ISBN 9781565183025 (paper).
IVA53 *Secularization and Intensification of Religion in Modern Society: Polish Philosophical Studies, XIV.* Leon Dyczewski, ed. ISBN 9781565183032 (paper).
IVA54 *Seekers or Dweller: The Social Character of Religion in Hungary: Hungarian Philosophical Studies, II.* Zsuzsanna Bögre, ed. ISBN9781565183063 (paper).

Series V. Latin American Philosophical Studies

V.1 *The Social Context and Values: Perspectives of the Americas.* O. Pegoraro, ed. ISBN 081917355X (paper); 0819173541 (cloth).
V.2 *Culture, Human Rights and Peace in Central America.* Raul Molina and Timothy Ready, eds. ISBN 0819173576 (paper); 0819173568 (cloth).

V.3 *El Cristianismo Aymara: Inculturacion o Culturizacion?* Luis Jolicoeur. ISBN 1565181042 (paper).
V.4 *Love as the Foundation of Moral Education and Character Development.* Luis Ugalde, Nicolas Barros and George F. McLean, eds. ISBN 1565180801 (paper).
V.5 *Human Rights, Solidarity and Subsidiarity: Essays towards a Social Ontology.* Carlos E.A. Maldonado. ISBN 1565181107 (paper).
V.6 *A New World: A Perspective from Ibero America.* H. Daniel Dei, ed. ISBN 9781565182639 (paper).

Series VI. Foundations of Moral Education

VI.1 *Philosophical Foundations for Moral Education and Character Development: Act and Agent.* G. McLean and F. Ellrod, eds. ISBN 156518001-1 (paper); ISBN 1565180003 (cloth).
VI.2 *Psychological Foundations for Moral Education and Character Development: An Integrated Theory of Moral Development.* R. Knowles, ed. ISBN 156518002X (paper); 156518003-8 (cloth).
VI.3 *Character Development in Schools and Beyond.* Kevin Ryan and Thomas Lickona, eds. ISBN 1565180593 (paper); 156518058-5 (cloth).
VI.4 *The Social Context and Values: Perspectives of the Americas.* O. Pegoraro, ed. ISBN 081917355X (paper); 0819173541 (cloth).
VI.5 *Chinese Foundations for Moral Education and Character Development.* Tran van Doan, ed. ISBN 1565180321 (paper); 156518033 (cloth).
VI.6 *Love as the Foundation of Moral Education and Character Development.* Luis Ugalde, Nicolas Barros and George F. McLean, eds. ISBN 1565180801 (paper).

Series VII. Seminars on Culture and Values

VII.1 *The Social Context and Values: Perspectives of the Americas.* O. Pegoraro, ed. ISBN 081917355X (paper); 0819173541 (cloth).
VII.2 *Culture, Human Rights and Peace in Central America.* Raul Molina and Timothy Ready, eds. ISBN 0819173576 (paper); 0819173568 (cloth).
VII.3 *Relations between Cultures.* John A. Kromkowski, ed. ISBN 1565180089 (paper); 1565180097 (cloth).
VII.4 *Moral Imagination and Character Development: Volume I, The Imagination.* George F. McLean and John A. Kromkowski, eds. ISBN 1565181743 (paper).
VII.5 *Moral Imagination and Character Development: Volume II, Moral Imagination in Personal Formation and Character Development.* George F. McLean and Richard Knowles, eds. ISBN 1565181816 (paper).

VII.6 *Moral Imagination and Character Development: Volume III, Imagination in Religion and Social Life.* George F. McLean and John K. White, eds. ISBN 1565181824 (paper).
VII.7 *Hermeneutics and Inculturation.* George F. McLean, Antonio Gallo, Robert Magliola, eds. ISBN 1565181840 (paper).
VII.8 *Culture, Evangelization, and Dialogue.* Antonio Gallo and Robert Magliola, eds. ISBN 1565181832 (paper).
VII.9 *The Place of the Person in Social Life.* Paul Peachey and John A. Kromkowski, eds. ISBN 1565180127 (paper); 156518013-5 (cloth).
VII.10 *Urbanization and Values.* John A. Kromkowski, ed. ISBN 1565180100 (paper); 1565180119 (cloth).
VII.11 *Freedom and Choice in a Democracy, Volume I: Meanings of Freedom.* Robert Magliola and John Farrelly, eds. ISBN 1565181867 (paper).
VII.12 *Freedom and Choice in a Democracy, Volume II: The Difficult Passage to Freedom.* Robert Magliola and Richard Khuri, eds. ISBN 1565181859 (paper).
VII 13 *Cultural Identity, Pluralism and Globalization* (2 volumes). John P. Hogan, ed. ISBN 1565182170 (paper).
VII.14 *Democracy: In the Throes of Liberalism and Totalitarianism.* George F. McLean, Robert Magliola, William Fox, eds. ISBN 1565181956 (paper).
VII.15 *Democracy and Values in Global Times: With Nigeria as a Case Study.* George F. McLean, Robert Magliola, Joseph Abah, eds. ISBN 1565181956 (paper).
VII.16 *Civil Society and Social Reconstruction.* George F. McLean, ed. ISBN 1565180860 (paper).
VII.17 *Civil Society: Who Belongs?* William A. Barbieri, Robert Magliola, Rosemary Winslow, eds. ISBN 1565181972 (paper).
VII.18 *The Humanization of Social Life: Theory and Challenges.* Christopher Wheatley, Robert P. Badillo, Rose B. Calabretta, Robert Magliola, eds. ISBN 1565182006 (paper).
VII.19 *The Humanization of Social Life: Cultural Resources and Historical Responses.* Ronald S. Calinger, Robert P. Badillo, Rose B. Calabretta, Robert Magliola, eds. ISBN 1565182006 (paper).
VII.20 *Religious Inspiration for Public Life: Religion in Public Life, Volume I.* George F. McLean, John A. Kromkowski and Robert Magliola, eds. ISBN 1565182103 (paper).
VII.21 *Religion and Political Structures from Fundamentalism to Public Service: Religion in Public Life, Volume II.* John T. Ford, Robert A. Destro and Charles R. Dechert, eds. ISBN 1565182111 (paper).
VII.22 *Civil Society as Democratic Practice.* Antonio F. Perez, Semou Pathé Gueye, Yang Fenggang, eds. ISBN 1565182146 (paper).
VII.23 *Ecumenism and Nostra Aetate in the 21st Century.* George F. McLean and John P. Hogan, eds. ISBN 1565182197 (paper).

VII.24 *Multiple Paths to God: Nostra Aetate: 40 years Later.* John P. Hogan, George F. McLean & John A. Kromkowski, eds. ISBN 1565182200 (paper).
VII.25 *Globalization and Identity.* Andrew Blasko, Taras Dobko, Pham Van Duc and George Pattery, eds. ISBN 1565182200 (paper).
VII.26 *Communication across Cultures: The Hermeneutics of Cultures and Religions in a Global Age.* Chibueze C. Udeani, Veerachart Nimanong, Zou Shipeng, Mustafa Malik, eds. ISBN: 9781565182400 (paper).
VII.27 *Symbols, Cultures and Identities in a Time of Global Interaction.* Paata Chkheidze, Hoang Thi Tho and Yaroslav Pasko, eds. ISBN 9781565182608 (paper).
VII. 28 *Restorying the 'Polis':Civil Society as Narrative Reconstruction.* Yuriy Pochta, Rosemary Winslow, eds. ISNB 978156518 (paper).
VII.29 *History and Cultural Identity: Retrieving the Past, Shaping the Future.* John P. Hogan, ed. ISBN 9781565182684 (paper).
VII.30 *Human Nature: Stable and/or Changing?* John P. Hogan, ed. ISBN 9781565182431 (paper).
VII.31 *Reasoning in Faith: Cultural Foundations for Civil Society and Globalization.* Octave Kamwiziku Wozol, Sebastian Velassery and Jurate Baranova, eds. ISBN 9781565182868 (paper).
VII.32 *Building Community in a Mobile/Global Age: Migration and Hospitality.* John P. Hogan, Vensus A. George and Corazon T. Toralba, eds. ISBN 9781565182875 (paper).
VII.33 *The Role of Religions in the Public-Sphere: The Post-Secular Model of Jürgen Habermas and Beyond.* Plamen Makariev and Vensus A. George, eds. ISBN 9781565183049 (paper).
VII.34 *Diversity and Unity.* Joseph Donders, Kirti Bunchua and Godé Iwele, eds. ISBN 978156518... (paper).
VII.35 *Justice and Responsibility: Cultural and Philosophical Considerations.* João J. Vila-Chã, ed. ISBN 978156518... (paper).

Series VIII. Christian Philosophical Studies

VIII.1 *Church and People: Disjunctions in a Secular Age, Christian Philosophical Studies, I.* Charles Taylor, José Casanova and George F. McLean, eds. ISBN9781565182745 (paper).
VIII.2 *God's Spirit in the World: Ecumenical and Cultural Essays, Christian Philosophical Studies, II.* Waclaw Hryniewicz. ISBN 9781565182738 (paper).
VIII.3 *Philosophical Theology and the Christian Traditions: Russian and Western Perspectives, Christian Philosophical Studies, III.* David Bradshaw, ed. ISBN 9781565182752 (paper).
VIII.4 *Ethics and the Challenge of Secularism: Christian Philosophical Studies, IV.* David Bradshaw, ed. ISBN 9781565182806 (paper).

VIII.5 *Freedom for Faith: Theological Hermeneutics of Discovery based on George F. McLean's Philosophy of Culture: Christian Philosophical Studies, V.* John M. Staak. ISBN 9781565182837 (paper).
VIII.6 *Humanity on the Threshold: Religious Perspective on Transhumanism: Christian Philosophical Studies, VI.* John C. Haughey and Ilia Delio, eds. ISBN 9781565182882 (paper).
VIII.7 *Faith and Secularization: A Romanian Narrative: Christian Philosophical Studies, VII.* Wilhelm Dancă, ed. ISBN 9781565182929 (paper).
VIII.8 *Towards a Kenotic Vision of Authority in the Catholic Church: Christian Philosophical Studies, VIII.* Anthony J. Carroll, Marthe Kerkwijk, Michael Kirwan and James Sweeney, eds. ISBN 9781565182936 (paper).
VIII.9 *The Spirit: The Cry of the World: Christian Philosophical Studies, IX.* Waclaw Hryniewicz. ISBN 9781565182943 (paper).
VIII.10 *A Czech Perspective on Faith in a Secular Age: Christian Philosophical Studies, X.* Tomáš Halík and Pavel Hošek, eds. ISBN 9781565183001 (paper).
VIII.11 *A Catholic Minority Church in a World of Seekers: Christian Philosophical Studies, X.* Staf Hellemans and Peter Jonkers, eds. ISBN 9781565183018 (paper).
VIII.12 *Dilemmas of the Catholic Church in Poland: Christian Philosophical Studies, XII.* Tadeusz Buksinski, ed. ISBN 9781565183025 (paper).
VIII.13 *Secularization and Intensification of Religion in Modern Society: Christian Philosophical Studies, XIII.* Leon Dyczewski, ed. ISBN 9781565183032 (paper).
VIII.14 *Plural Spiritualities: North American Experience: Christian Philosophical Studies, XIV.* Robert J. Schreiter, ed. ISBN 9781565183056 (paper).
VIII.15 *Seekers or Dwellers: The Social Character of Religion in Hungary: Christian Philosophical Studies, XV.* Zsuzsanna Bögre, ed. ISBN 9781565183063 (paper).

The International Society for Metaphysics

ISM.1 *Person and Nature.* George F. McLean and Hugo Meynell, eds. ISBN 0819170267 (paper); 0819170259 (cloth).
ISM.2 *Person and Society.* George F. McLean and Hugo Meynell, eds. ISBN 0819169250 (paper); 0819169242 (cloth).
ISM.3 *Person and God.* George F. McLean and Hugo Meynell, eds. ISBN 0819169382 (paper); 0819169374 (cloth).
ISM.4 *The Nature of Metaphysical Knowledge.* George F. McLean and Hugo Meynell, eds. ISBN 0819169277 (paper); 0819169269 (cloth).

ISM.5 *Philosophhical Challenges and Opportunities of Globalization.* Oliva Blanchette, Tomonobu Imamichi and George F. McLean, eds. ISBN 1565181298 (paper).
ISM.6 *The Dialogue of Cultural Traditions: Global Perspective.* William Sweet, George F. McLean, Tomonobu Imamichi, Safak Ural, O. Faruk Akyol, eds. ISBN 9781565182585 (paper).
ISM. 7 *Philosophy Emerging from Culture.* William Sweet, George F. McLean, Oliva Blanchette, Wonbin Park, eds. ISBN 9781565182851 (paper).

The series is published by: The Council for Research in Values and Philosophy, Gibbons Hall B-20, 620 Michigan Avenue, NE, Washington, D.C. 20064; Telephone and Fax: 202/319-6089; e-mail: cua-rvp@cua.edu; website: http://www.crvp.org. All titles are available in paper except as noted.

The series is distributed by: The Council for Research on Values and Philosophy – OST, 285 Oblate Drive, San Antonio, T.X., 78216; Telephone: (210)341-1366 x205; Email: mmartin@ost.edu.